PRAISE FOR HUMANITY'S ENVIRONMENTAL FUTURE

"The Future of Humanity arrived a couple of days ago. After a bit of checking around, I found I really had to read the whole thing. I congratulate you—it's a great piece of work, and I hope it's a huge success."

> — Daniel Quinn, prize-winning author of *Ishmael*, *Providence*, *The Story of B*, and *Beyond Civilization*.

"I enjoyed reading your 'Future of Humanity' book very much. I think [it] is vital, and based effectively on the data you cite. Your comments are thorou   ook, of
immense   ure of Humanity'.   ze for human-
—   lbatross,
                                                les and

"I have re   t it down.
This is rea   leasure to read
on."
—   thor of *The*

Humanity's Environmental Future

Making Sense in a Troubled World

Humanity's Environmental Future

Making Sense in a Troubled World

William Ross McCluney

SunPine Press | Cape Canaveral, Florida

Humanity's Environmental Future

Making Sense in a Troubled World

William Ross McCluney

Published by:
  Sun Pine Press
  219 Johnson Avenue
  Cape Canaveral, FL 32920

ISBN: 0-9744461-0-6

LCCN 2003095484

Printed in the United States of America
by Jawbone Publishing.
Printed on acid free recycled paper

Dedication

Dedicated to my sons Alan and Kevin,
and to a viable future—
for them, and for all other sons and daughters,
of all species.

Preface

My elderly mother once asked me what I was writing about. I thought about it for a minute and then responded, "Everything."

"That would make a good title," she said.

I laughed and considered it for a moment. Of course, I cannot write about everything. That is too vast a topic. However, I do call on the reader to think vastly. Narrow thinking can no longer be afforded if we are to restructure into a sustainable society.

This book is about the big picture—or "whole systems" thinking, as Amory Lovins calls it. It is an attempt to describe an emerging new direction for society and to explain conceptually what necessitated the new direction and how it developed. My focus is on the future and humanity's participation in it.

I was motivated by this question: What does an educated person need to know about Earth, the place of the human on it, and what a prosperous and sustainable future might look like? My goal was to provide an introduction to the topic, offer some new concepts, and provide some specific suggestions.

The book's length and depth make it suitable for use in college classes, but the content and reading style should make it also appropriate for anyone interested in the subject.

Relating the story of human development and its impact on Earth is sometimes optimistic, and at other times pessimistic. A skeptical thinker might assume that humans will muddle through the next few generations, hopefully finding—whether by insight or by the force of natural consequences—a sustainable path into the long-term future. A premise of the book is that this probably won't work; a more concerted effort is necessary to achieve a sustainable society with hope for the future.

As the title makes clear, I root my concern directly with the human prospect. We all have an interest and stake in the viability of our own futures. But does this fail to address the needs of the rest of creation? Does it just continue the failed values of the past?

Chapter 12 addresses this human-centered philosophy, called *anthropocentrism*. Taken to its logical extreme, it must include a more holistic perspective. Humanity is so dependent upon the viability of the whole Earth and its ecosystems that human-centered arguments must necessarily embrace Earth-centered ones. We are part of the natural world, an imbedded component of the web of all life. Our extreme dependence on the natural world — our life-support system — allows me to begin with the anthropocentric motivation (probably the most appealing starting point for those new to this subject).

Speaking of *the* Earth as *our* life-support system acknowledges the modern tendency to consider humanity as somehow separate from it … from that Earth, out there, where we happen to reside. Images such as these must be subordinated by a more holistic understanding of the meaning of humanity. Whenever I appeal to human-centered arguments herein, I do so with the understanding that only when the whole is protected, valued, and revered will an optimistic future for humanity be possible.

Donella Meadows co-authored a complacency-shattering report on the limits to growth. Her group, studying alternate futures for humanity, concluded that there are limits to growth on a finite world and that various scenarios for human development are possible. Some lead to good consequences for humans and some to bad.

The media picked up only on the worst possible scenario, following the most pessimistic of her suggested alternatives.

Writing about this some years later (before her untimely death early in 2001), Donella cautioned environmentalists and other planners and policy makers. She warned us to take neither the most dire and pessimistic attitude nor the most optimistic one, but to push for conscious human action to limit the bad consequences while still leaving room, if possible, for human freedom to have children and to live a good life materially. (I think this is a rational response to the severe threats facing us. It is explored in some depth within this book.)

In Humanity's Environmental Future, you will find a variety of attitudes. Frustration over mankind's seemingly stupid attack of our life-support system leads to an attitude of despair and pessimism. However, people like Donella Meadows have been attempting to correct our worst practices by showing us a better way toward a life filled with peace and hope. Such an endeavor leads to an attitude of optimism.

I write, as a proud but concerned American, about my country's place in the world. As the only remaining superpower, we have a special responsibility not to force our views on others, nor to be pursuing (or even be perceived as pursuing) world domination. This is not the message heard from recent U.S. leaders. Much of what can be called "the American attitude"— our arrogance, even triumphalism, and our lifestyle excesses — is quite condescending to those living outside the U.S. I would prefer that we offer grace, strength, and humility, joining other nations and cultures in pursuit of a better future, rather than trying to force a possibly warped U.S. model of what the world should be like. A global consensus is needed to map out future directions, not unilateral enforcement of one nation's will. Though difficult, developing at least some semblance of such a consensus seems the only way to proceed—and have any hope that the needed changes can be made in time for them to be successful.

Though I attempt to report important issues factually and without any particular ideology, I cannot free myself completely from certain preconceived notions and philosophical beliefs. Furthermore, this book is not an attempt to report just the facts, but to interpret them, to explain how they came about, and to challenge the reader to have an open mind and consider the alternatives.

Suggestions for using this book as the textbook for a semester-long course are provided at www.futureofhumanity.org. Click on "For the Instructor."

An anthology of writings by prominent environmental thinkers is being simultaneously published as a companion to this volume: *Getting to the Source: Readings on Sustainable Values*, William Ross McCluney, ed. SunPine Press, Cape Canaveral, Florida, 2004.

This book is divided into four parts. "Part I. The Crisis" is about the nature of the threats facing us and the structural problems driving society toward great difficulty. "Part II. How it Happened," addresses what possibly in the makeup of the human — and in past history — led us to the brink of what could be self-annihilation. "Part III. Saving Humanity" discusses some of the ideas I believe critical to understanding where we are and what we must do to provide a viable future for humanity. "Part IV. Taking Action" provides suggestions for things we can do, as a species, to reverse the destructive trend and create a more viable future society.

Robert Frost once said, "Anyone with an active mind lives on tentatives rather than tenets." Surely there are some fundamental tenets of our environmental problems we can accept, such as the central importance of overpopulation and consumerism. The rest is here offered conjecturally, for your consideration. Accept only what you find convincing.

— Ross McCluney, November 2003, Cocoa, Florida

TABLE OF CONTENTS

Acknowledgments

Greatest appreciation goes to Paul Jindra, friend and colleague, for his many ideas and suggestions during the formative stages of this work. Our many penetrating discussions are warmly remembered. Grateful thanks and appreciation to my reviewers, all of whom offered excellent, constructive, and helpful suggestions. They include Virginia Abernethy, Albert Bartlett, Dianne Benjamin, Deena Blazejack, Jody Bryan, Colin Campbell, Frances James, Larry Kinney, Paul MacCready, Miriam MacGillis, Alan McCluney, Kevin McCluney, Lester Milbrath, Bill Nickle, Daniel Quinn, Joel Siegel, McGregor Smith, and Mathis Wackernagel. Al Bartlett, Colin Campbell, Deena Blazejack, Paul MacCready and Dianne Benjamin deserve special recognition for the quantity of work they put into their reviews. My heart was warmed by your dedication to the task. Special thanks to my wife, Jo Marilynn, for her love, support, and — above all — patience.

Part I

The Crisis

1
Earth in Transition

Humanity faces serious environmental threats.
What kind of future can we have?

*There is nothing more difficult to take in hand,
more perilous to conduct, or more uncertain
in its success, than to take the lead in the
introduction of a new order of things.*
– Niccolo Machiavelli, *The Prince*

Accelerated change is a defining characteristic of human life today. Because of human interception into nonhuman life processes, this change has become a defining moment for all life on Earth. Together we face serious challenges on many fronts. Overpopulation and the attendant assault on the natural environment provide the primary driving force for some very serious challenges. We see the beginnings of major social, economic, environmental, and spiritual upheavals, most stimulated by environmental losses. The "new order of things" which is likely to emerge, is by no means clear.

Optimism - Pessimism

"The sky is falling!" cried Chicken Little.

"The world is coming to an end," say a few radical environmentalists.

"Human beings are causing the extinction of species on the order of the mass extinctions that wiped out the dinosaurs 65 million years ago," says a group of botanists[1].

Serious additional warnings are offered by many of the world's most eminent scientists, including ecologists and paleontologists who study Earth matters closely.

"Things are just fine, going along well. The future looks bright," say most industrial economists, and political and business leaders. They argue that the cries of alarm coming from the "tree-huggers" are misplaced and destructive.

Who is right? What is the real future of humanity? And who cares, anyway?

Many reasons are offered *not* to care. "It's far into the future and I'll be dead anyway," is a common sentiment. Most people care most about what happens tomorrow, or next year, but not much about the next several decades. We work hard just to get through each day with a semblance of vocational satisfaction, personal contentment, and some pleasure. We don't have much time or interest in pondering the distant future. Is this a surface manifestation of our hectic industrialized lifestyle?

Deep within, nearly all of us *are* concerned about the future, but our worries and concerns are unfocused and indistinct. We deal with adversities as they come. We try to live for the moment—protecting ourselves from too many unpleasant thoughts or depressing possible future realities. To some, this is human nature. To others it is debilitating denial, avoiding the truth because it is unpleasant.

Few of us are in any position, nor do we have the motivation, to alter our behaviors radically (especially if the reasons for change are not considered strong, compelling, or immediately evident in our lives.) Hearing about some remotely perceived future threat—like the random collision of a giant asteroid—fails to stir us into serious action or personal change.

Industrialized Happiness?

Those of us living in the industrial world look at our lives as moderately comfortable. At least, most of us do. We see things as generally going well—with economic growth continuing in a usually positive manner, with our incomes rising (if slowly), and with our savings expanding, too. We believe we are well off, at least in comparison with poor people in less developed countries. (This is a fallacy, of course. Many of these "poor" people lead perfectly satisfying lives. And there are wealthy Americans who are living lives of psychological poverty and desperation.) Most of us don't feel much motivation to change, nor do we spend much time thinking about it.

On the other hand, we do know this picture comes with many caveats. Huge numbers of U.S. citizens live in poverty or close to it. Others suffer the many pressures resulting from living in a fast-paced society.

Joanna Macy described our hectic lifestyles: "The corporate mergers characterizing the advanced state of the Industrial Growth Society rob people of employment, make them scramble for jobs, and feel highly insecure in those they still manage to hang on to. Moonlighting, they rush from one job to another, to piece together a living wage. Most young families, in order to pay the bills, need both parents to work for pay, or try to. The pace accelerates, taking its toll on every spare moment, every relationship. As employment benefits are cut, and social health and welfare programs decimated, economic anxiety mounts. The world narrows down to one's own and one's family's immediate needs. There's little time to contemplate the fate of the world, or let it sink in. If a free hour is left at the end of the day, one prefers to zone out with a beer in front of the television–and the packaged fantasies of the Industrial Growth Society."[2, p. 33]

For most of us, the strongest motivation most of us have for protecting the future is the bond of love and responsibility we feel for our children and grandchildren. We want a healthy world in which they can grow up. And most of us *are* concerned. With all the reports of environmental, health, and economic problems we see regularly in the media, worry seems inevitable. Now we have domestic terrorism to worry about.

Though a terrible and demonstrably real threat, terrorism is unlikely to result in the extinction of the human species. Some of the environmental threats facing us could do just that. This amazing possibility could come from a rampant new viral strain infecting, and killing, all humans. It could come from extreme global warming coupled with human-induced extinction of critical species upon which humanity depends (or species on which those species depend).

The potential for annihilation following a large thermonuclear exchange between countries, the danger of massive global war, and the results of famine and disease are all real and serious threats. But they are not the focus here, except to the extent that they result from the pressures of overpopulation and environmental degradation.

Real Threats

Unlike the false alarm of Chicken Little, real environmental alarms are provided almost daily by knowledgeable scientists, scholars, educators, and religious leaders. The strength and directness of the relentless warnings from our most brilliant scientists are nothing short of astonishing. We would be foolish to ignore them. So, address them we must. Addressing them now, as a species, is a major purpose of this book.

Through the ages, many people have spoken out about the future of humanity. Fear of disaster is nothing new, of course. The Bible speaks of

Armageddon and apocalypse. The World Future Society publishes a magazine of articles by a variety of authors on many aspects of predicting the future. Though most are optimistic, some are not.

Michio Kaku has written a fascinating book, *Visions*, about the expected impacts of science and technology in the 21st century[3]. Many of the predicted developments seem sure to make our lives easier and more interesting. Some will make life more dangerous and precipitous. He warns that a degree of wisdom will be required to avoid the pitfalls of powerful technologies. Without that wisdom, humans may become just another extinct species. Sorting through the alternatives is one of the most important tasks to face us.

> Many people today, in many lands, have a gnawing feeling that something is profoundly wrong with modern society.... Could we not solve most of our problems by thoughtful reform? This question cannot be answered by merely taking a current assessment of how things are going in one's community or nation.... We must take a longer range view of the consequences of continuing our course.
>
> Most natural and social scientists who have examined the long-run prospects for modern society are not sanguine about our future. While they are not unanimous in their judgment about the viability of our society, the overwhelming weight of the evidence and analysis indicates that society, as presently constituted, cannot continue on its present trajectory. The kinds of changes required are so drastic that, when implemented, they will constitute a new society.
>
> —Lester W. Milbrath, *Envisioning a Sustainable Society*, 1989

Viewpoints

In reading the literature on this subject, three different points of view keep popping up.

The fatalists. These believe the future will just happen. There's not a lot we can do to alter it much, nor should we even try. The idea is that we have reached our current status by evolutionary processes. Whatever happens to us in the future is thought to be a natural consequence of that evolution.

Animals have become extinct naturally over Earth history. The fatalists believe there is no reason to expect humans to have any special immunity from extinction. (As far as we know, none of the previously endangered species were aware of the threat nor able or willing to take any action to prevent it. In this view, modern humans are considered to be in the same category. Even though we can *think* of the future and see dangers ahead, the fatalists say we are essentially unable as a species to alter the future, so we should just make the best of the present while we can.)

The Cornucopians. Another view is that we do have control, and we can and will anticipate the future and make it a better one for humans. In this view, there are no limits to growth (or they are far into the future) and resources are and always will remain abundant (or we can find, or make, substitutes forever). We have advanced technologies, and new ones on the horizon, which can solve every problem. We have and will create constantly improving democracies capable of watching over these developments, protecting the rights and needs of humans along the way. This thoroughly anthropocentric (human-centered) perspective generally claims that only humans really count and have rights. Another name for this viewpoint is *technological optimism*, the belief that technology can solve any problem.

The Holists. A third view claims that the anthropocentric argument is too narrow. Other creatures, here before us, have equal rights to (species if not individual) existence. It recognizes that the futures of all species of life on Earth are inextricably linked together. We must protect the whole to protect humanity.

There is a quasi-anthropocentric component to the holist belief. It follows from the fact that humans depend upon plants and animals for most of the essentials of life. Therefore their needs matter to us and have importance, if only for selfish reasons. The holist philosophy says that we should take actions today to insure a viable future for *all* living creatures on Earth tomorrow.

It is left to the reader to choose which of the above viewpoints is best able to protect our future. In my view, if you value the flora and fauna of this Earth, in the mountains, plains, brooks, streams, rivers, lakes, and oceans, if you care about what happens to them now and after you are gone, and if you care about having a viable world environment in which humans can prosper, then you should be concerned with the viability of the whole Earth. To a great extent, this book seeks to prove that protecting humanity's future means protecting Earth's future. (If you have difficulty accepting this conclusion, please consider it a premise, and determine if the remainder of this book adequately supports the conclusion.)

Spaceship Earth

The human population's massive growth on the planet and the powerful new technologies placed into mankind's hands have put the human species in charge of — and now responsible for — the operation of Spaceship

Earth. Our home is just that: a relatively tiny spaceship in the vastness of the universe, pursuing an elliptical course around our mother star, the Sun. The solar system is tiny compared to the huge galaxy in which it resides, and which itself is microscopic in the unimaginably vast extent of the universe.

When the term "Spaceship Earth" was coined by Buckminster Fuller, its usefulness was almost immediately apparent. Taken by the Apollo astronauts from space, photographs of a tiny Earth drove home the message of an immediate image of a self-contained system. With what we now know about our Earth, the analogy seems too mechanical, too manmade. Spaceships are technological inventions of humans. Earth is almost infinitely more complex and beautiful. It is bigger than humans. It is organic, not merely mechanical.

It is with no sense of denigration that I call Earth a spaceship. For those of us brought up in a largely materialistic and mechanistic culture, I think the analogy aids in understanding this one important dimension of a multi-dimensional Earth: it really is our life-support system.

That life support is provided by Earth's biosphere (the thin layer of air, water, topsoil, and below-ground aquifers covering the habitable regions of our planet). The organisms in the biosphere — and the chemical, physical, and geological systems on which they depend — provide us with, and replenish and purify, the air we breathe and the fresh water we drink. The plants and animals provide us with food, clothing, and shelter. Though it strains credulity, we might agree with Earth ethics guru Thomas Berry that Earth has come off "autopilot" and is now being "operated" "manually" by humans.

When we discovered the fossil remains of plants and animals beneath the surface of the planet — deposited as coal, oil, and natural gas over millions of years — we started a program of exploitation that seems bent on continuing to exhaustion. This is but one component of the operation of planet Earth which we have taken over and are trying to bend to our seemingly total control. We have supplemented our daily budget of energy from the sun (and the other renewable resources available to us) with a huge variety of products made from the fossil resources.

Our use of these non-renewable resources has grown to the point where we can clearly see their continuing decline in availability. At that point, we will have no choice but to return to sole reliance on the non-fossil, renewable sources, radical resource use efficiency, and vigorous population stabilization. It is doubtful that the current human population can survive without fossil fuels.

According to this reasoning, a major die-off of human population may accompany the exhaustion of our fossil energy resources. Increased public funding to continue extracting those resources at a faster rate can only hasten this depletion, and ultimately the human consequences. (Hopes of nuclear power and other technological innovations to make the die-off more gradual, or even non-existent, may be too illusory to count on. Do we want our very survival to depend on what *might* happen in the future?)

Failing Life-Support

The more we try to provide the material things humans consider essential for living, and the more human population grows, the more pressures we place on our life support system. Though most people are concerned about it and understand these threats, others do not, or feel the problems are over-blown or nonexistent.

We have learned that the industrialized societies, and the less developed ones which emulate them (also generally desiring industrialization), are together producing serious, growing, and lasting environmental consequences. The process can only be described as one whereby *modern civilization is systematically taking apart the life support system of Planet Earth.* According to population biologist Alan Thornhill of Rice University, we are systematically replacing non-human biomass with human mass, a process which clearly cannot continue indefinitely.

Daniel Quinn adds that we are, in essence, mining species; to feed a growing human population, we are killing off species left and right, at the approximate rate of 200 every *day*.[4]

These strong statements deserve elaboration. The "systematic taking apart of the life support system of Planet Earth" refers to habitat destruction from human expansion and land development, to the continued warming of our atmosphere (by so-called "greenhouse gases" and the resulting alteration of weather and climate), to the polluting of air, soil, and water, and to the resulting extinction of species and ill health of humans and animals. These consequences are growing worldwide, faster than our remediation efforts.

If we do not change the basic structuring of our society, the current course can lead to nothing other than growing environmental disasters and increased human suffering, and most probably a collapse of human population. Not all human life will quickly disappear from the planet, but we may be reaching a point where the natural restorative capabilities of the planet require more time than we have to avoid a major human population die-off. Though extinction of humanity is not a necessary consequence of such changes, it is a possible one.

How Did It Happen?

If you accept the truth of these strong statements, your next question may likely be, "How did we get to this place? How did humanity reach the point of destroying the very systems which make human life possible?"

Additional questions also come to mind: "Now that we have discovered the serious nature of the problem, why do we continue our destructive course?"

If humanity were as gifted, organized, and in control as believed by the Cornucopians, then wouldn't stronger measures be in place now for reversing the disastrous trend? If it is so obvious what we are doing to our Earth and ultimately to ourselves, then why isn't everyone talking about it? Why aren't we on a crash course to save the future and make our civilization sustainable?

Our lack of concern is not unlike the famous story of the Emperor's new clothes. It was obvious to the little boy that the emperor was naked (or at least was going around in his skivies). But everyone else was afraid to accept this obvious fact. So they continued the pretense of believing the Emperor to be fully clothed.

Breaking through deception and denial is an important beginning step. Along the way toward that goal, some common misconceptions should be avoided.

Clarifying Terms

Three terms are frequently confused in discussions of social reform.

1) *Material standard of living* is defined as the quantity of goods and services consumed by an individual, per unit time.

2) *Quality of life* is the degree of enjoyment, satisfaction, and fulfillment an individual achieves in the process of living.

3) *Lifestyle* is the general pattern of daily behaviors followed by an individual.

From these definitions we see that "material standard of living" is inherently materialistic, while "quality of life" is not. It is a mistake to confuse these two terms, as is so often done — especially in America, where life quality seems to be equated with affluence.

The word "standard" may seem a misnomer; it actually was intended to mean the average affluence level in a country. In other contexts, "standard" means the lowest one is permitted to go. A standard is seldom the ideal in such applications, only the lowest or least value allowed. But in the above context, and in generally materialistic America, high affluence has become the true "standard."

There is, of course, one way in which affluence level *does* equate to quality of life, and that is at the below-poverty level. If one's basic material needs are not satisfied, or if they are so low as to produce ill-health, it is clear that good life quality is not possible. Above some minimum level, however, I contend that quality of life and material standard of living become less and less coupled as the material standard of living increases.

The average standard of living for most industrialized nations is so high that these two concepts are completely decoupled, in spite of our protestations (and materialistic behaviors) to the contrary. We do not need to continue our consuming, Earth-depleting lifestyles to be happy — to have a high quality of life. We *do* need major shifts in our values and behavior patterns before we will be able to achieve a higher quality of life at a lower material standard of living — to live better with less. Paul MacCready calls it "Doing More with Less":

> A necessary, but not sufficient, strategy for achieving a desirable, sustainable world as growth impacts limits is to raise the priority on efficiency and restraint. This is not the principle on which the U.S. was founded, with the Declaration of Independence telling of our rights and to what we are entitled, instead of noting our responsibilities.[5]

It is tempting to think that lifestyle is also independent of the other two concepts — that your pattern of living does not inherently affect your quality of life or material standard of living. However, some affluent people choose lifestyles requiring high material standards of living, and others are able to live simply with less.

The difference lies in their value systems. Lifestyle is linked to standard of living and quality of life in other ways. Many would say that freedom to choose different lifestyles is an important prerequisite to quality of life.

Another term bandied about rather freely is *sustainability*. Al Bartlett, retired professor of physics at the University of Colorado explains that the term was drawn from the concept of "sustained yield" which is used to describe agriculture and forestry when these enterprises are conducted in such a way that they could be continued indefinitely, (i.e., their yield could be sustained.)

The introduction of the word "sustainable" provided comfort and reassurance to those who may momentarily have wondered if possibly there were limits. So the word was soon applied in many areas, and with less precise meaning, so that for example, with little visible change, "development" became "sustainable development," etc. One would see political leaders using the term "sustainable" to describe their goals as they worked hard to create more jobs, to increase population, and to increase rates of consumption of energy and resources.

In the manner of Alice in Wonderland, and without regard for accuracy or consistency, *sustainability* seems to have been redefined flexibly to suit a variety of wishes and conveniences.[6]

Sustainability can only be for a very long time, compared with a human lifetime — that is, for millennia. Bartlett's laws of sustainability follow from this definition and from straightforward arithmetic, and are hence not debatable, "unless one wants to debate arithmetic," he writes. Here is the first of his laws. (All can be found in the Appendix to Chapter 5 on growth.)

First Law. Population growth and/or growth in the rates of consumption of resources cannot be sustained. A population growth rate less than or equal to zero and declining rates of consumption of resources are necessary conditions for a sustainable society. Unsustainability will be the certain result of any program of "development," whether or not it is said to be "sustainable," which ignores the problem of population growth and that does not plan the achievement of zero or a period of negative growth of populations and of rates of consumption of resources. The term "sustainable growth" is an oxymoron.

The Good Life

That affluence equals happiness, or at least a degree of personal security and contentment, is a common misconception. Affluence does not assure a high quality of life, nor does a lack of affluence preclude leading a quality life. Since high material standards of living contribute strongly to the environmental crisis, defining "quality of life" is important. What is it that people need to live well, to live "the good life," so sought by everyone? If we can find non-material ways to achieve what we really need, then having them won't come at Earth's expense.

One can postulate a number of measures of "life goodness." To a great extent, the one each of us chooses is largely shaped by the culture and value system in which we live, by our families (which frequently tells us, directly or indirectly, what to want) and by our own personal experiences. Contentment, peace of mind, anonymity, laughter, personal and family security, the absence of psychological pathologies, and a rewarding vocation are some non-material measures of "life goodness."

For most of us, the non-material, non-tangible things matter most. For example, to be fully balanced and "happy" in their lives, most people want or need: 1) strong family closeness and support, 2) the companionship and love of a significant other person, 3) a rewarding vocation, 4) warm and supportive friends and acquaintances, and 5) some time for themselves in pursuit of creative, meaningful, and self-improvement activities. A life filled with humor and fun is a obviously beneficial, too. (None of these is inherently Earth-impacting. In some zen Buddhist cultures, it is the absence of cravings for money, power, prestige, and notoriety which are most prized [a].)

Colin Campbell says it is a great illusion that non-materialistic people are unhappy. "Has the affluent fraction of Americans been alone in finding happiness over recorded history?" he asks. "We are the victims of mass advertising and the baleful influence of television, which denies us the happiness of simple things, such as old men sitting on park benches." [b]

Restructuring Society

If you accept even part of the strong claims so far made, you must be astonished to contemplate what might be needed to reverse the trend. The problems are extensive.

The actions needed to overcome them are nearly overwhelming. Two major transformations will be needed. First will be a substantial reduction in population and second is a drastic restructuring of industrialized society, a rebuilding from the ground up. (The latter of these will be complicated, difficult, and problematic. The former is at least much simpler, if not easier.) Any strategy for reform that is realistic will include both simultaneously.

Before addressing the task of restructuring, more must be said about the nature of our problems, how we fell into them, and how we might start figuring out what must be done. Parts I and II of this book are devoted to that task.

The subject is difficult to approach for many reasons. One is the question of how to deal with people's preconceived views of what we are doing to

---

[a]Richard J. O'Halloran, Ph. D., private communication, 17 July 2002.

[b]Colin J. Campbell, private communication, e-mail, 12 January 2002.

our world. Most are concerned, but not that worried. They are encouraged that steps are being taken to at least partially ameliorate the adverse consequences of human action.

Others are not so optimistic, accepting that we are at a terribly important turning point. If we do not soon make drastic changes in our ways of living, we will become an endangered species — without intervention, headed for disaster.

With both viewpoints there is much confusion. How do we get out of the mess without compromising the great things humans have achieved through industrialization. I call this the *extrication question*. I would like to get right to the answer, devoting the remainder of this book to finding it. But I cannot.

First, many do not yet realize the seriousness of the problem and the short time we have to act. We must first make the case for the claim of imminent failure of Spaceship Earth's life-support system. Only then will the claim that the future of humanity is in doubt be taken seriously.

Second, we have difficulty understanding answers to the extrication question without fully understanding the problem leading us to it.

I hope you find this search for answers as challenging, stimulating, and exciting as I.

References

1. Peter Raven, "Botanists Warn of Mass Extinction," Reuters News Service, Tuesday August 3, 12:46 AM ET 1999.
2. Joanna Macy and Molly Brown Young. *Coming Back to Life*. New Society: Gabriola Island, BC, Canada,1998, 221 pp.
3. Michio Kaku. *Visions: How Science Will Revolutionize the 21st Century*. Anchor/Doubleday: New York,1997, 403 pp.
4. Daniel Quinn "A New Renaissance," (Speech), 2001, to Ross McCluney, 5 May 2001.
5. Paul B. MacCready, "Unleashing Creativity", in *Symposium on The Inventor and Society*, Jerome and Dorothy Lamelson Center for the Study of Invention and Innovation, Smithsonian National Museum of American History, 1995.
6. Albert A. Bartlett. "Democracy Cannot Survive Overpopulation." *Population and Environment: A Journal of Interdisciplinary Studies*. Vol. 22, no. 1 (2000): September 2000, 63-71.

2
The Great Puzzle

Cracking the enigma of our times

Have you ever tried to solve a difficult puzzle? It might have been an obscure riddle, or a mechanical puzzle, where you were supposed to separate two inextricably intertwined parts, or something like the famed "Rubik's cube." You try and try and can't find the answer. You give up in desperation, or perhaps take a break and then try again. Usually a friend who has either solved the puzzle or read the instructions finally shows you how it's done, or maybe you solve it yourself. Do you remember the excitement and wonderment when you finally have the solution? And the joy at seeing how it works, suddenly feeling your brilliance? A common response is to take the puzzle to someone else and watch smugly as *they* attempt it, usually unsuccessfully. Recall the joy on the person's face when the puzzle is finally solved. If it is not solved, after a time, they usually give up and say something like, "Show me, wise guy!"

But have you ever solved a difficult puzzle for someone who never saw it before, who never tried to solve it? If so, you are probably familiar with the lack of response, the "ho hum" attitude, and the disinterest which follows. If the person hasn't had a chance to work on the problem, to worry with it, to try and find the answer, and see its difficulty, seldom can they fully appreciate the joy you feel when, after a lot of struggle, you finally solve it.

Finding Meaning

For several decades now, a few ardent thinkers have been on a quest — pursuing a different kind of puzzle. For years they studied the terrible things humanity was doing to Earth's life-support system. This part was easy. Information abounds, in news reports, journal articles, and research reports. Then their quest became different and more difficult. It was for *meaning* — a search for an understanding of *why* we have been doing terrible things to the planet, and to the wonderful creatures of undisturbed nature. Initially the idea was that if only we could understand how or why things came to be this way, we could easily figure out how to change them, to stop the destruction that is happening wantonly around the globe.

Some of these thinkers have reached an amazing level of understanding, and a handful seems to have solved the puzzle, for all practical purposes. The wonderful discoveries of these great thinkers, these puzzle-solvers, the truth-seekers of our time, have been published in books, pamphlets, and audio and videotapes. Only a small fraction of the educated people of the world have read their materials or listened to their tapes. (One of the books achieved a modest amount of brief fame, through being on the Opra Winfrey book list and through having a movie inspired by it. The book was *Ishmael* by Daniel Quinn.[1])

The revelation available from these sources is amazing, penetrating, and enlightening. If you have struggled with this great puzzle yourself for some time, finding the answer will be just as thrilling and exciting as finding the solution to a Rubik's cube. The natural urge is to run out and tell everyone you know about it. That was one of the motivations that led to this book.

There is a big problem, however. It is the same one faced by the person who knows the answer to a riddle and tries to tell it to someone who has never attempted to solve it. Perhaps you have tried to crack the environmental riddle yourself and know what I'm writing about.

If you have *not* yet struggled for meaning and understanding in this area, have not seen how really intractable many of the environmental problems facing us seem to be, or if you aren't yet convinced that the threats are real and imminent, and as extensive as claimed by so many, then you might not feel the excitement available upon hearing the answer to the riddle. You're likely to respond with a yawn and the comment, "so what?"

Our Quest

To provide a glimpse of the enlightenment and joy in new understanding available when learning some of the secrets of our environmental history, we begin in Part I with a journey through some of the difficulties facing us.

There are some powerful forces at work making the problems worse and less likely to be solved in the foreseeable future. Part II, beginning with Chapter 10, addresses the question of how we reached the current predicament. Part III begins with Chapter 13 and offers a variety of skills and understandings to aid us as we seek to build a variety of sustainable societies worldwide. Part IV is devoted to recommending steps we can take, individually and collectively to reverse the destructive path on which we find ourselves. The information contained in Parts I and II should promote appreciation of the discoveries waiting in Parts III and IV.

If you will join me on this journey, I promise an answer to the great puzzle — and a totally new understanding of yourself, the world around you, and the things you see, hear, and read every day in the media.

The quest can be an exciting, though sometimes exasperating, one. The very survival of our children and grandchildren depends upon a successful solution, not only to the puzzle itself, but also to the still more difficult, and as yet unsolved dilemma of what we humans, as a species, should do about it. Our reward, beyond just avoiding disaster, is a chance to recover sense, meaning, and peace in a world gone mad with complexity, stressful living, and rage. Life can truly be better when living in a sustainable world.

We begin our pursuit with a little story, an allegory for our times.

Star Craft 6

Several undetected mistakes were made when the brains of a group of astronauts were altered to prepare them for a long deep-space voyage. The mistakes had a most unfortunate effect on crew behavior: every time any one of them carried out required spacecraft subsystem maintenance operations, an important electrical wire or hydraulic line leading to the ship's life support systems was disconnected. Because their brains inadvertently had been reprogrammed to perform these operations, nothing alerted them to the dangers of these errant behaviors. For safety sake, an amazing degree of redundancy had been built into the spaceship and the damages went undetected for a period of time.

Eventually, however, problems with onboard oxygen levels, contamination of drinking water, and odors from faulty waste treatment systems alerted the commanders to the growing problems on board the spaceship. Fault-detection procedures were initiated, tests of subsystem performance were made, and personal inspections of the damaged areas were performed. The problems were found, but not their causes, and try as they might, the terrible destruction of the spacecraft's life-support systems continued unabated.

All kinds of temporary, patch-up repairs were made to the damaged systems, by replacing or clamping off leaky pipes, by re-directing water and other fluid flow paths, and by sending more electrical energy to the waste processing systems. Even with the high degree of redundancy built into the craft, and intensive efforts to make repairs, the crew found themselves unable to keep up with the damage that seemed to get worse each day. The quality of life on board the ship continued to decline rapidly.

Then the captain called all personnel to a strategic meeting to assess the damage, the future prospects for the ship, and what else might be done to stop the frightening losses that were taking place. Many conflicting opinions were voiced as to the cause of the problem and what should be done about it. It became clear that the emergency patch-up operations had bought them a little time, but had not effected a permanent repair.

In discussing the problem, there were those who claimed that increasing the emergency repair operations would avert disaster for a very long time. However, an accurate estimate of the ultimate limits to the on-board consumables could not be made. In the end, continuation of the previous repair-and-replace policy was the selected course of action. A detailed document, called the "Agenda for Survival," was prepared which described the new responsibilities of all on board in tending to the subsystems needing protection and repair. Everyone followed the new procedures for a while, but eventually it was clear that a permanent solution had not yet been found.

A system of checks and counter-checks on the critical operations performed by crewmembers on the life-support system was instituted. After an extended period of scientific and behavioral observations, the real cause of their difficulties was finally discovered. The problem was in the minds of the human inhabitants of the spaceship. Errant human behavior was found to be the cause of the problem. This was traced to mistakes in the brain surgery performed on each crewmember prior to the mission. The surgery was intended to help them keep performing routine maintenance tasks without boredom for an indefinite period. The mistakes actually caused crew members to snip a wire or cut a pipe and then forget about it.

Fortunately, the medical bay on the ship was equipped with an extensive computerized database on brain operations. Robotic surgical procedures were located that could undo the damage that had been caused in all but a few crewmembers. The latter were confined to quarters and put under close observation for the duration of the voyage.[a]

The parallels between Star Craft 6 and Spaceship Earth should be clear, but they are neither identical nor complete. On the fictional space mission there was no equivalent of the large multinational corporation, or the other forces of unrestricted growth and environmental degradation.

But in many other ways the parallels *are* strong. The inhabitants and leaders on Star Craft 6 were not evil. None were intentionally bent on destroying the mission. Similarly, I cannot believe that the humans manning Spaceship Earth have malevolent intentions. We must conclude that our collective thinking has simply gone wrong and we, as a species, are insufficiently informed (or are misinformed) of the real dangers and terminal nature of the problem. On Star Craft 6, as well as on Spaceship Earth, it is our human brains that have gone wrong and we are suffering a lack of information about the problems and their true causes.

The Captain's meeting parallels the 1992 Rio Summit on the world environment. The spaceship's document "Agenda for Survival" parallels the "Agenda 21" publication that came out of the Rio meeting.

As the seriousness of the problem on Star Craft 6 finally became unmistakable, there was a nearly universal desire to get at the truth, to find the real cause of the ship's problems. Once discovered, the crew was willing to take great risk, allowing the robotic surgeon to enter their brains and perform that tricky and dangerous operation.

I believe that we humans, the "crew" of Spaceship Earth, can behave similarly, once given adequate information. We will readily submit to having our brains altered. Not by some tricky and invasive surgery. Instead, the mind-altering transformation will come from extensive global re-education, and the massive acquisition of a new literacy, an Earth literacy. This only can happen with extensive open, global discussion. Although true consensus on the nature of the problems and their solutions may be beyond our capabilities, at least the *discussion*, and a striving for commonly agreed upon directions, should be possible. From this might evolve a slow shift toward consensus, a new world view, and a new, more sustainable path to the future. Though true global consensus is probably beyond our reach, an attempt to achieve it could be the most important group undertaking ever to challenge humanity.

---

[a] This is a slightly modified version of a story which first appeared in "Sustainable Values," R. McCluney, *Ethics and Agenda 21: Moral Implications of a Global Consensus*, Noel J. Brown and Pierre Quiblier, ed., United Nations Environment Programme, 1994, New York, pp. 13-26.

Beginning the Transformation

Thomas Berry and other optimists say the transformation has already started, that it cannot now be stopped[2,3]. It is driven by the truth. We are fortunate in the great sweep of Earth history to stand here now, on the threshold of this new understanding. We can be thrilled at the prospect of embracing a new and truly better society. A unique opportunity has been presented to us, to witness and participate in the greatest transformation of human culture since the emergence of civilization and the development of agriculture!

At the beginning of this new millennium, however, it is not easy for many of us to accept this great optimism. The forces of degradation surrounding us are powerful and seem beyond our control. Corporate and government leaders are nearly unanimous in declaring, "Damn the torpedoes. Full speed ahead. Growth cannot be stopped." This great engine, a steamroller headed downhill, seems impossible to stop, difficult to divert, but redirect it we must.

Previous great human transformations required centuries to develop, mature, spread, and prosper. The coming transformation must take place much more quickly to be successful. Our scientists are telling us we have only a few years, and at most a couple of decades, to complete the core of the transformation. If we take too long, it may be too late, for critical components of our life support system may disappear or be altered in ways making human extinction unavoidable.

We have learned something else in the last several decades since the birth of organized environmentalism. It is not enough to be concerned about the environment. It is not enough to join an environmental organization, or even to be active in it. It is not enough to try and save habitats and species from destruction. It is not enough to recycle, to save energy, or to fight pollution, unless these are all components of a larger and more massive and comprehensive societal transformation.

This transformation must be based on an understanding of where humanity *is* at present — at a turning point in a long history of growth and development that has led to apparent prosperity but with massive exploitation of the planet and its resources along the way. The new understanding must include some knowledge of ancient human cultures, those that have lived at one with the Earth for millennia. (Many still do, if they are not yet contaminated by the exploitative development culture of the industrialized nations. Fortunately some have been studied and the studies are available to us.[4,5])

Where are the new enlightenments, the new understandings, and the discussion of these issues in the major media? From our local newspapers to the largest national ones, from our small-town radio and television stations to the huge national broadcast networks and the glut of cable channels — in none of these outlets is the true, awesome magnitude of the threat (and the decision that must be made) even mentioned, much less intelligently discussed.

There are a few exceptions, such as the June 2001 PBS documentary by Bill Moyers titled "Earth On Edge". Many elementary and secondary schools in the U.S. have courses involving access to some of the important information about how our world operates and what we humans are doing to it. There are a few excellent textbooks and curriculum guides available to guide educators on this subject.

But the voices of our most enlightened writers and scholars, such as Thomas Berry, Fritjof Capra, Paul Hawken, Joanna Macy, David Suzuki, E. O. Wilson, Peter Raven, and Daniel Quinn are not widely heard. Instead we hear only small minds and small voices, systematically chronicling each little, seemingly disconnected, example of our environmental demise.

A reason for this (apart from some theory of dark and sinister forces operating behind the scenes) is that we the people do not want to hear the real truth, or if we do, the forces of denial and disbelief are so strong that we can hear but are not willing to really listen and understand. So we continue our daily struggles, wrapped in and dominated by a system gone wrong. This leaves out meaningful action and makes us unable to access the critical information that, as on Star Craft 6, once heard, can lead to enlightenment, mental emancipation, and finally direct action.

The environmental optimists among us reassure us. "Be patient and hopeful," they say. "All is not yet lost. A glorious new life awaits. Not in the hereafter but in the here and now. Help us spread the word. The truth will set us free." Perhaps they are right. The number of books, videos, and public meetings telling the new truth is growing and starting to reach the occasional leader, the one or two lone and junior politician, a businessman here and an educator there. Though limited, this is encouraging.

Truth has a quiet power. It can slay even the largest of giants, sapping the strength they get from those untruths plaguing current society. Perhaps this truth, as it slowly spreads, will gather momentum and accelerate to become the more encompassing vision we seek.

Patience and hope are much needed. Plus excitement and thankfulness that we are so fortunate to be alive during the transition, to witness and participate in the greatest transformation of all human history. Let us begin exploring the dimensions of the coming paradigm shift, when we will begin to think differently about ourselves, this Earth which sustains us, and our connections—with each other and with the universe of which we are but a tiny part.

References

1. Daniel Quinn. *Ishmael*. 1st ed. Bantam/Turner: New York, 1992.
2. Thomas Berry. *The Dream of the Earth*. 1st ed. Sierra Club Books: San Francisco, 1988, 247 pp.
3. Thomas Berry. *The Great Work — Our Way Into the Future*. Bell Tower: New York, 1999, 241 pp.
4. Jean Liedloff. *The Continuum Concept: In Search of Happiness Lost*. Reprint, 1986 ed. Perseus Books: Cambridge, MA, 1985, 172 pp.
5. John E. Pfeiffer. *The Emergence of Society — A Prehistory of the Establishment*. McGraw-Hill: New York, 1977, 512 pp.

3
Houston, We Have a Problem

Spaceship Earth's life-support system is in trouble.
Can it be saved?

Like the crew of Apollo 13, facing life-support system failures on their way to the moon and back, we human operators of Spaceship Earth are faced with our own life-support problems. The threats to human survival on Planet Earth are many and varied, a considerable fraction of them environmental in origin.

Many deny there is a serious problem. Books have been written giving this view. Other people seem content with limited, patchwork reforms, many ignoring the critical core problem of over-population. Some offer information about the crisis on the Internet. Convincing arguments in support of the alarm can be found in most any library. (A few books on the subject are listed below.)

Considering the threats, what will be humanity's future? Are the threats serious enough to result in annihilation or extinction of humanity?

Some scientists who have studied these problems believe we might already have passed a point of no return ... that our species is already doomed and cannot recover. This pessimistic viewpoint is countered by others who claim that our ingenuity and ability to change in the face of clear and present dangers will not only rescue us from demise but will insure a healthy and fulfilled future.

It is not easy to choose between these extreme positions. Perhaps the most realistic choice lies somewhere between. An important presumption in most accounts is that humanity's future is in the hands (and minds) of humanity.

Connections

To understand the crisis, it is important to emphasize the depth of the connectedness of Nature: the intricate interrelationships existing between plant and animal species and the geologic, chemical, biologic, and hydrological systems which support the whole of life on Earth. Often called the "web of life," this interconnectedness has strength and flexibility. Losing some components may produce a minor disruption of the web—one that is temporary and not necessarily serious. Such a disruption is naturally accommodated and repaired by the remaining components.

Losing certain *other* components can produce a cascading effect and may lead to substantial damage to the whole system, with losses of major portions of it. These losses could prove catastrophic. Earth has seen such changes in the past. They are recorded in fossilized sediments and other geologic time markers of past climatic upheavals.

We can no longer ignore that ecosystem components throughout the web of life are being damaged by human action. The human is taking over ecosystems around the planet, replacing some species, dominating others.

Earth Organism/Earth Spirit

The Spaceship Earth analogy offered first in Chapter 1 seems logical to those steeped in a mechanistic understanding of Nature. However, holding this view is one of the factors contributing to the existence of our environmental crisis. Viewing the Earth system as an organic whole is closer to the truth and leads into whole systems thinking — valuing the Earth as more than just a mechanical vessel containing our life-support systems.

In reality, we humans are intimately connected with Earth, and have arisen out of it. We are like the parts of a larger organism, and not even the most important parts. Our destruction of life forms and the other devastations produced by humanity make us more like a malignancy.

Throughout this chapter, the Spaceship Earth imagery is continued as a useful tool for discussing and understanding some aspects of our symbiotic relationship with Earth. Such imagery must be set aside as we start thinking about what humanity must do to reverse the currently destructive path.

In the web of life, the human species is probably the most dependent component. We depend more on the nonhuman portions than they depend on us[1,2]. Earth could do just fine without us, but we cannot do fine without Earth. If the human became extinct, the world ecosystem would go on living. If critical species on which we *depend* becomes extinct, humanity will suffer — or in the worst case — even disappear.

I offer an example of a currently unthreatened group of species on which we are directly dependent. According to Tomotari Mitsuoka, "a large number of bacteria inhabit the human intestine soon after birth, and from then, there is not a single moment in man's life in which he is not associated with the intestinal bacteria. The relationship between humans and the bacteria can be said to be a pattern of existence acquired through the long biological history, in which symbiosis is a primary requirement. In the intestine of an individual, as many as a hundred trillion bacteria comprising 100 species are present.

"There are two kinds of bacteria in the intestine, beneficial and harmful. In healthy subjects, they are well balanced. Beneficial bacteria play useful roles in the aspects of nutrition and prevention of infections...." Some bacteria are potentially pathogenic and others produce substances harmful to the host. The beneficial species keep the toxic ones in check and provide other protective functions. [3, p. 110] If one or more of the beneficial species were to become extinct, massive worldwide disease would be a likely result. Or if a damaging new species were introduced, and became immune to our antibiotics and other tools for eliminating them, it would be equally disastrous for humanity.

We do not depend merely upon other living organisms. A prominent example of such a threat frequently appears in news reports. Certain heat-radiation-trapping gases are being emitted into the atmosphere in increasing quantities by a variety of processes. If these exceed a critical concentration, a cascade of disastrous effects can result. We are already seeing the ice caps at the poles recede, and changes in climate thought also due to this global warming. Ice is highly reflective, sending a major portion of the warming radiation incident on it from the sun back up through the atmosphere into outer space again.

The ice absorbs only a portion of the incoming solar radiation. Seawater and earth, however, are darker and more absorbing. If the ice recedes enough, exposing more dark soil and rock, and more deep blue ocean areas, solar radiation will be absorbed at a higher rate. This increased solar absorption will make the land and seas warmer; the ice will melt quicker, opening up new areas of low reflectance, adding to the warming effect. This cycle, coupled with a variety of additional global warming contributions (more carbon dioxide from burning fossil fuels and trees, the injection of additional global warming gases into the atmosphere) will proceed until huge volumes of the water trapped as ice above sea level melt, raising the level of the oceans. The reduced mass density of a warmer ocean will expand its volume. As a consequence, low-lying populated areas around the globe can be inundated. Some countries will nearly disappear.

The science supporting the human contribution to climate change is now strong. The evidence is described in a number of publications, including recent work of the National Academy of Sciences (NAS).[4] Following the issuance of the NAS report, at a news conference on 11 June 2001, President Bush admitted that global warming is real. He admitted that the U.S. "is the world's largest emitter of manmade greenhouse gases. We account for almost 20 percent of the world's man-made greenhouse emissions."

It is true that there have been strong fluctuations in climatic conditions through the geologic past; the current variations could be partially the result of astronomical or other naturally occurring changes not produced by humanity. On the other hand, the yearly atmospheric increase in carbon dioxide is real and has been documented for many years. (The CO_2 buildup is very evident in a variety of data, as are a number of additional changes in the atmosphere clearly produced by humanity. The latter are occurring at a much greater rate than the geological changes of the past — with the exception of changes induced by massive asteroid impacts.)

It is possible to build dams, dikes, and levees to hold back the encroaching sea, as Holland has successfully done. Such projects on a worldwide scale, however, would be very expensive — in money, in resources, and in time. Some countries could not afford such massive construction projects and would be forced to attempt a relocation of their citizenries. Or they might appeal to other countries for assistance. Financial assistance could tax the industrial world's ability to give. It is conceivable that some countries would refuse to give foreign aid on such a massive scale. Thus could begin a terrible cascade of effects spreading like dominoes around the world, producing significant ecological, societal, and economic disruption. Massive migrations of people from low-lying areas to higher ground can be expected to produce serious social disruption and terrible economic difficulties.

This scenario may seem extreme. However, scientists studying global warming list a large number of terrible effects that would face humanity. Perhaps the most serious one is the effect that cannot be predicted, the unexpected one that is more devastating than all the rest, but not identified until too late to prevent.

Threat Categories

Following this abbreviated introduction, I will categorize the types of threats facing us. They are what I will call functional, technological, perceptual, values-based, and spiritual.

Functional Threats. Functional threats are direct disruptions of important life-support systems. They include the depletion of natural resources, the destruction of global physical protection mechanisms, and loss of habitat for critical species of plants and animals. Also of concern are losses of minerals, energy, and biotic resources essential to the operation of critical world ecosystems and to the monetary economic system. Functional threats include damage to physical and biological systems providing the air we breathe, a stable and acceptable climate, drinking water, and insulation from the harmful ultraviolet radiation and the solar heat approaching Earth from the Sun. The driving forces for the functional threats are the continuous increase in human population, rising expectations for more per capita wealth and increased individual consumption.

Technological Threats. The industrialized and technologically advanced nations of the world produce additional threats. These include the many dangers of wayward or exploding nuclear materials. Radioactive waste from the nuclear weapons program, as well as that from nuclear power plants, is highly toxic; much of it is very long- lived, existing in toxic form for tens of thousands of years. Finding places to store this waste is one of the most difficult problems facing the governments that are responsible for finding solutions.

More obvious technological threats exist from toxic chemicals discarded during resource extraction processes, from manufacturing plants, in energy production and use, and from biological processing facilities. The latter category includes animal feed lots and intensive poultry production facilities. Many of these look more like animal factories than pasture and forest habitat. The wastes from these factories are troublesome and threatening to the water supply and the regional atmosphere where they are located (often close to residential areas).

Animals confined in unnatural cages with poor hygiene are more susceptible to disease, resulting in lost revenue and wasted investment. A response is to feed massive doses of antibiotic drugs to basically healthy animals — more than 24 million pounds per year in the U.S. alone. This practice "is threatening human health by undermining our arsenal of disease-fighting drugs, according to a January 2001 report by the Union of Concerned Scientists."[5]

Technology generally magnifies per capita impact. Redesigning all existing, and expected new, technology so that it *reduces* per capita impact is a lofty goal, but one unlikely to extend to all areas of consumption. If not coupled with population stabilization, whatever technological gains might be realized will be buried under the mass of new humans using that technology.

Numerous examples of technological threats to our life support system are found in newspaper, magazine, television, and radio reports. Public libraries, including those at high schools, colleges, and universities, are excellent resource centers. They are staffed with qualified people who can assist in finding information about technological threats to human health, safety, and even humanity's very existence.

Perceptual Threats. Many of us are aware of our severe environmental problems. But few know the full extent of them. A consequence is the belief that what we do each day has little or minimal long-term impact, since we don't see the impacts directly, daily, and personally. Earlier, more "primitive," societies were connected more closely to Earth and received obvious and direct signals when they did something harmful to Nature. Perhaps they became sick from water contaminated by fecal matter. Perhaps they depleted local forest areas of game and were forced to relocate.

Today we live in a complex technologically based society that has become exceptionally skillful at hiding from us the environmental consequences of our actions. These consequences are often displaced in both space and time. They are not evident to us until many years later (as with some toxin-induced cancers and other diseases) or until they loom so large that they invade our cocoons of luxury, giving us direct and immediate feedback in the forms of discomfort, disease, or even death.

> Industrialized countries sometimes offer "humanitarian" relief in the form of money, food, and medical services until the problem becomes less acute, or until we lose patience with it. Seldom do we examine the overpopulation and resource depletion issues underlying the problem. Seldom do we leave these countries with any substantive means of ameliorating the conditions that led to their misery. It seems that self-protection comes before charity. When charity begins to disturb our comfort, we abandon it, except for a few notable individuals. We justify these abandonments by saying we are merely being "realistic." Truly realistic would be efforts to address the ethical issues involved with foreign aid more directly, and get at the real causes of the problems necessitating aid in the first place.

In our industrialized societies, we are separated from the environmental consequences of our actions by complex and elaborate systems of manufacture, distribution, and waste disposal. "Out of sight — out of mind" seems to be the motto. Without direct feedback on the results of what we do, we cannot muster the necessary concern and outrage to motivate action to reverse damaging practices. It is ironic that we *pay* people to remove these unpleasant consequences from our immediate experiences. This lack of appropriate feedback is a serious perceptual threat, preventing us from getting public (and leadership) support for needed reforms.

Values-Based Threats. Human behaviors—including those resulting in environmental damage—in large measure follow from the underlying belief systems we rely on to provide meaning and direction in life. For example, because we believe in the nearly absolute prohibition of murder, most disputes are not settled in this manner. Because we believe in monogamy, most married people have only one spouse. Because we believe that prosperity is possible only with continued growth, we strive for continued economic expansion. We are not particularly worried about population growth, either, except when it reaches the point of dooming distant populations to famine, disease, misery, and premature death.

Values-based threats result when our beliefs lead to behaviors that are inappropriate for our situations. It is difficult to change dangerous behaviors without altering the misplaced belief systems underlying them. For example, a belief that fertility can remain above the replacement level indefinitely is dangerous and inappropriate for a finite planet filling with people.

Belief systems have a special place in all societies. When the behaviors associated with them lead to prosperity, material security, and abundant food, we cling to those values and are loath to change them. In some cases, we are able to set aside some values in favor of others that we think better fit the situation. Such "situational ethics" are often deplored. On the other hand, when they result from recognition that the previous beliefs were inappropriate, the ability to adopt more appropriate values is a healthy one. Unfortunately, changing to more appropriate values is infrequently practiced. This is a serious threat to humanity's future.

The WorldWatch Institute in late 2001 declared that "More people worldwide are now displaced by natural disasters than by conflict. But more and more of the devastation wrought by such natural disasters is 'unnatural' in origin, caused by ecologically destructive practices and an increasing number of people living in harm's way," Worldwatch Paper 158, "Unnatural Disasters" by Janet Abramovitz, explores the growing toll of these disasters, and shows what we need to do to reduce their impact.

The problem of competing values is common and can be a serious source of stress. This stress seems more acute these days because increasingly powerful technological arsenals amplify adverse environmental and social impacts.

Values-based strife sets up a powerful and important conflict. We are finally realizing that many of our behaviors are not appropriate to our environmental situations. These behaviors lead to terrible environmental problems, such as the increased extinction of plant and animal species due to human action. We are facing a mass extinction the likes of which Earth has not seen since the dinosaurs lost their battle with the asteroid.

The need to adopt new behaviors challenges many of our most basic beliefs, thus offering another threat — to our psyches. Values conflicts can lead to serious psychological disturbances, often called "cognitive dissonance"—saying and believing one thing while doing another. This malady can affect us both individually and collectively.

The obvious escape from a stressfully dissonant way of life — examining the appropriateness of our values — is too frightening for most to handle. So we do not. This leaves us with the exquisite torture of having one foot trying to follow a more environmentally benign path while the other tramples ecosystems right and left. Clearly, one of the first steps we humans must take to break out of this conflict is a systematic examination of our value systems, altering them as needed in more appropriate directions. Fortunately, the process has already started. We see it in many religious institutions, in some educational circles, and amongst the more radical environmental organizations.

This does not mean all our values are inappropriate and in need of change. Values encouraging people to care for each other, for other creatures, and for the Earth, need strengthening rather than altering. The value of education is good but must be extended to an Earth education—teaching children and adults how the nonhuman world works and what humans are doing to it. Many other traditional values most definitely are appropriate and consonant with a sustainable future for humanity.

Spiritual Threats. We are facing a crisis of more than just beliefs, values, and ethics. Our psyches have lost their former attunement to the natural world. A number of religious organizations are struggling to deal with the consequences. Some are not. Catholic Church opposition to birth control, for example, is a major inhibitor to lowering fertility levels around the world. Our disconnectedness from Nature has taken on a spiritual dimension, and most of the world's religions, struggling to meet the challenge, are trying to take a leadership role in addressing the values-basis in the threats facing us.

Additional Evidence

Information to provide positive action is offered in Part IV. The focus here is on providing evidence that environmental threats are real and serious.

The Worldwatch Institute, 1776 Massachusetts Ave., NW, Washington, DC 20036, is an excellent source of information on the environmental destruction of our life-support system. Though it attempts in its many publications to be positive, to describe the good things that are happening, and touts the successful actions we are taking toward environmental protection, most often its reports read as negative chronicles of the demise of various portions of the biosphere. The Institute publishes an annual *State of the World* report. Another annual publication, *Vital Signs*, offers "the environmental trends that are shaping our future." A series of numbered Worldwatch Papers is also available. The titles of a few are listed below.

Worldwatch Papers: 128 "Imperiled Waters, Impoverished Future: The Decline of Freshwater Ecosystems," 129 "Infecting Ourselves: How Environmental and Social Disruptions Trigger Disease," 131 "Shrinking Fields: Cropland Loss in a World of Eight Billion," 136 "The Agricultural Link: How Environmental Deterioration Could Disrupt Economic Progress," and 141 "Losing Strands in the Web of Life: Vertebrate Declines and the Conservation of Biological Diversity."

Several books speak to the problems and threats to humanity posed by environmental destruction. Here are a few.

Berry, Wendell, *The Unsettling of America*, 1977, Sierra Club Books, San Francisco

Brown, Lester R., *Tough Choices—Facing the Challenge of Food Scarcity*, 1996, W. W. Norton &. Company, New York.

Campbell, C.J., *The Coming Oil Crisis*, 1997, Multi-Science Publishing Company & Petroconsultants.

Carson, Rachel, *Silent Spring*, 1962, Fawcett Crest, Houghton Mifflin, New York.

Deffeyes, Kenneth S., *Hubbert's Peak*, 2001, Princeton University Press, Princeton, NJ.

Douthwaite, Richard, *The Growth Illusion*, 1999, New Society Publishers, Gabriola Island, BC, Canada.

Fagin, Dan & Lavelle, Marianne, *Toxic Deception*, 1999, Common Courage Press, Monroe, Maine.

Marine, Gene, *America the Raped*, 1969, Simon & Schuster, New York

Meadows, Donella, Dennis Meadows, Jorgen Rangers and William Behrens, The Limits to Growth, 1972, Earth Island, London.

Miller, G. Tyler, *Environmental Science*, 2nd ed., 1988, Wadsworth Publishing, Belmont, CA, and several more recent editions of this popular textbook.

Raven, Peter H., *The Global Ecosystem in Crisis – We're Killing Our World*, 1987, A MacArthur Foundation Paper. The John D. and Catherine T. MacArthur Foundation, Chicago.

Rees, Martin J., *Our Final Hour, A Scientist's Warning: How Terror, Error, and Environmental Disaster Threaten Humankind's Future In This Century—On Earth and Beyond*, Basic Books: New York, 2003.

Schneider, Stephen, *Laboratory Earth – The planetary gamble we can't afford to lose*, 1997, BasicBooks, New York.

Turner, M.J., *Extinction or Survival? – the Dilemmas of our Technological Existence*, 1996, Ardmore Publishing, Sidney, British Columbia.

Udall, Stewart L., *The Quiet Crisis*, (Intro by John F. Kennedy), 1963, Holt, Rinehart, & Winston, Inc.

Ward, Peter, *The End of Evolution*, 1994, Bantam Books, New York.

Rachel Carson's book, *Silent Spring*, is a classic, credited by many with starting the environmental movement, leading to significant governmental action to protect ecosystems. Gene Marine's *America the Raped* (now out of print but available from used booksellers) is a stinging critique of a number of terrible environmental practices of both governmental organizations and private corporations.

The Limits to Growth is worth special mention. The book, translated into 26 languages, sold more than 9 million copies. When it was published, the book evoked a firestorm of protest around the world. It seems that an important societal value was being trampled on, and the criticizers didn't like it one bit. That value was the belief that unlimited growth is both possible and the best mechanism for improving the human condition worldwide. The primary author, Donella Meadows, before her untimely death 20 February 2001, wrote about her book: "In the introduction to *The Limits to Growth*, we listed three main conclusions, one of danger, one of hope, and one of urgency. The press picked up only the first and the third. 1. If the present growth trends in world population, industrialization, pollution, food production, and resource depletion continue unchanged, the limits to growth on this planet will be reached sometime within the next 100 years. 2. It is possible to alter these growth trends and to establish a condition of ecological and economic stability that is sustainable far into the future. 3. If the world's people decide to strive for this second outcome rather than the first, the sooner they begin working to attain it, the greater will be their chances of success. You wouldn't think such simple conclusions would stir up much of a fuss, but the fuss was incredible. The storm went on for years. It inspired conferences, studies, books of denial, and books of affirmation and elaboration. Eventually, like all media-generated storms, this one settled back down."

With the benefit of some hindsight, Meadows concluded as follows:

> Since we wrote *Limits*, the human economy has more than doubled its physical presence, from vehicles to electric power plants to garbage. At the same time, there has been great erosion of the planetary resource base. Species, forests, wetlands, soils, and habitats have been lost, buffers and degrees of protection have decreased, and options have narrowed.

I have spent the past twenty years immersed in statistics that describe this decline. I've watched them unfold. I've presented them to classes and to audiences many times and in a calm tone of voice. I haven't cried over them. I haven't yelled in outrage.

That's because of psychic numbing, I'm sure. I haven't been hit all at once, as I was the first time I saw the birth rate graph. Watching the numbers slowly get worse is like watching a child grow up—or a better analogy would be watching someone die of a wasting disease.

Exponential growth of population and physical capital, exponential depletion of resources and degradation of the environment are not necessary to the human condition. But collectively we have been behaving as if they were. Growth is still the pattern of the human system. As yet no corrective processes have been strong enough to stop it. But there are signs of such processes. The good news is that some are coming from human ingenuity and restraint. The bad news is that some are coming from environmental breakdown.

I've grown impatient with the kind of debate we used to have about whether the optimists or the pessimists are right. Neither is right. There is too much bad news to justify complacency. There is too much good news to justify despair.

I am not afraid of the challenge of easing the throughput of human society back down within its limits— I think that can be done fairly easily and even with considerable benefit to the human quality of life.[6]

Web Sources

There is much evidence that humankind is in trouble. Numerous other books, and a variety of other sources can support this evidence. Finding this information on the Internet is both easy and relatively painless. The click of a mouse opens information about the strong, adverse human impacts on our Earth, from a variety of sources. Web search programs (called "search engines") are now powerful and fast, but be cautious of information obtained this way.

The Internet is freely available. Anyone can post information on it, including incorrect and deceptive propaganda. Care must be exercised to find accurate, truthful, and reliable information on the web. Develop your own criteria concerning what web information you accept and trust. (Information from university, government, and some individual web sites is somewhat more reliable.)

Putting web site addresses in books is tricky, since the addresses often change. To help avoid this problem, a number of useful web addresses has been placed at www.futureofhumanity.org.

Additional sources of information about human impacts on the biosphere are available beyond those listed above. U.S. government web sites offer a wealth of such information. Textbooks on environmental science generally offer comprehensive coverage of the subject. For additional assistance, the reference desk at your local library should be helpful.

I think reasonable people can only conclude that the situation is dangerous and the future of humanity in jeopardy. Once this is accepted, we can move on to learning about the causes and possible remedies.

Conclusion

The conclusion from the many sources available to us is unavoidable — we are systematically taking apart the life-support system of Planet Earth, posing a serious threat to humanity's future.

It is difficult for us to accept that we are poisoning the air, water, and ground to such a degree that humanity itself is threatened. But read reputable scientific journals, or accounts of their findings in environmental and other magazines, newsletters, and Internet "e-zines". You will learn of the level of injection of toxic chemicals, extinction of species, loss of critical habitat, systematic damage in many areas, and so on.

For example, someone makes a clean, clear, polycarbonate bottle for drinking water. Use of these bottles then spreads around the Earth. The water in them in many cases is claimed by suppliers to be ultra pure, or at least very clean and healthy. Then a 1998 study finds certain toxic chemicals leaching from the plastic into the water.[7] Perhaps not all bottles have this terrible problem, but even a few is too many. This is but a metaphor for all the other areas and ways in which we are, little by little, case by case, damaging our health and that of the Earth's ecosystems.

It is estimated, for example, that in the United States, "the country's 51 biggest, oldest, and dirtiest power plants kill 5,000 to 9,000 people and provoke 80,000 to 120,000 asthma attacks every year."[8] This is from a short note, in *Sierra* magazine, announcing that the U.S. Environmental Protection Agency issued a rule in August 2003. In the face of these statistics, the EPA allows industries in certain circumstances to modernize old power plants without installing pollution controls. Previously, state-of-the-art controls on emissions were required whenever upgrades increased emissions significantly. In this one case, government action seems to worsen the problem rather than improve it.

These are but two "small" examples of adverse environmental consequences of human activities. Thousands more are reported every year in newspapers, magazines, research journals, and radio and television news programs.

Do all of these insults to Mother Earth add up to a threat of human extinction? We cannot say for sure until it happens. But the trends are "as plain as the nose on your face," as my grandmother used to say. It is inescapable that human action is degrading, defiling, and damaging nearly every aspect of the human life-support system. So far laudable actions to reverse the trend have amounted to the proverbial drop in the bucket. Unless we can figure out how to make much more substantive reform, we may not be doomed, but we face seriously escalating problems with human health and environmental degradation.

The remaining chapters address the questions of how humanity has come to this position, what has gone wrong with "us," and what we might be able to do, if anything, to reform ourselves and reverse the trend, reaching, at some glorious time in the future, the grace of having achieved true sustainability.

References

1. Gretchen C. Daily, ed. *Nature's Services — Societal Dependence on Natural Ecosystems*. Island Press: Washington, D.C., 1997, 392 pp.
2. Yvonne Baskin. *The Work of Nature*. Island Press: Washington, DC, 1997, 263 pp.
3. Tomotari Mitsuoka. *Intestinal Bacteria and Health*. Harcourt Brace, Jovanovich Japan: Tokyo, 1978, 208 pp.
4. Committee on the Science of Climate Change. *Climate Change Science: An Analysis of Some Key Questions*. National Research Council, National Academies of Science: Washington, DC, 2001.
5. Danielle Nierenberg. "Antimicrobial resistance." *World Watch* Vol. 14, no. 3 (2001): May/June 2001, 8-9.
6. Donella Meadows, "Growth Me Out to the Max: The state of the planet is grim. Should we give up hope?," World wide web, Last update: 20 Apr 2001, http://www.gristmagazine.com/citizen/citizen042001.asp.
7. Frances Cerra Whittlesley. "Hazards of Hydration: Choose your plastic water bottles carefully." *Sierra* Vol. 88, no. 6 (2003): Nov./Dec. 2003, p. 16,18.
8. Reed McManus. "Fiddling With Lives." *Sierra* Vol. 88, no. 6 (2003): Nov./Dec. 2003, p. 17.

4
Scientists Speak

How science works.
New warnings from the world's scientists.

In making decisions about public policy, most industrial nations espouse rational thought and empiricism. This construct is built into our laws, our customs, and most of our public decisions. It is moderated by other moral and ethical beliefs, not attributable to empiricism, but rationality is supposed to lie at the core of our legal system, the way we decide issues in dispute.

This acceptance of logical, fact-based thought and analysis is a natural human development. Soon after birth we start exploring our surroundings. We soon learn the importance of cause-and-effect relationships — knowledge vital for protecting health and well-being. We learn that falling from high places can hurt and kill. We learn to keep our distance from poisonous snakes. We learn to take cover in a lightning storm, to hide from tornados, to prepare for hurricanes, and to protect our houses from fire.

We *could* have an irrational belief in the tornado's ability to provide us a wonderful adventure in the sky, as Dorothy experienced in *The Wizard of Oz*. Such a belief would be tragic if practiced.

Belief in rational thought —in cause-and-effect relationships and by extension science — is built into our culture, even our species.

Industrialized society places an especially high value on science and technology. These disciplines are seen as largely responsible for the affluence most of us experience. The teaching of science is required at all levels of public and private education. Science and the logical processes on which it is built are imbedded in our system of justice. Scientists are called upon to study reality and tell us the truth about it. When the truth is not very clear, due to lack of information, we ask them to give us a rational opinion. We act upon this knowledge, whether it be to put a man to death or set him free — or to fine a large corporation millions of dollars or let it off without penalty.

Belief in the value of rationality and science is nearly universal in the developed world. Concerning environmental dangers, however, we seem to think rationality can be suspended.

We'll explore this distrust of science in matters environmental, but first we begin with a description of how science works.

The Exceptions Rule

At its core, science is basically an informed opinion. Scientists begin investigations with observations of Nature and attempt to draw logical opinions about what is going on from the details of their careful observations. Often the opinions are couched in terms of mathematics. The opinions — at this point only hypotheses or theories — are then tested time and again, following rigorous rules of carefulness, thoroughness, evidence, logic, and honesty. As evidence builds that a given theory seems valid, the theory is considered more reliable; predictions made with it come true much more often than not.

The immense body of essentially irrefutable science we now have was developed this way — piece by piece, opinion by opinion, test by test — over the period of a couple of centuries. Many of the resulting theories have evolved into "laws of Nature." Every time they are tested, they prove to be true.

With laws of Nature, our confidence in their validity is so high that we are willing to stake our lives on them. We confidently drive across bridges, designed and built according to the laws of science. We fly in airplanes, and we send men to the moon and back. These acts all risk our lives for the laws of science.

It is the nature of science to promulgate only theories that are shown to be true, hopefully without exception — that is, with very high reliability. We like to think of the laws of physics, for example, as "Universal Truths." Universal truths cannot have exceptions. The existence of exceptions would mean they are not universal.

Of course, exceptions in physics have been discovered many times. But when they are, pain and anguish follow, along with study, debate, and renewed experimentation. Work proceeds until the exception is *eliminated,* either by more careful experimentation or by incorporation in a larger, more encompassing theory.

Occasionally scientists are able to surround an apparent exception with more theory, making the exception but an alternative embodiment of the larger theory. Either by discarding the theory or enhancing it to include the apparent exception, true exceptions are fastidiously eliminated.

This is how the exceptions rule in science. When discovered, much effort is exerted to eliminate them. The resulting body of established science is therefore very reliable, justifying its importance to us.

Settling Disputes

Science has been given a special place in our society. If some dispute arises about a matter of fact, scientists are summoned to set the record straight.

Not all disputes have simple, black and white answers. And some scientific theories offer probabilities rather than certainties. If the probability of some outcome is very, very high, then we are willing to trust the scientist's description of that outcome and accept it as real.

There are fuzzy areas, of course, where the evidence is insufficient for scientists all to agree about a matter. When this happens on something of great importance where a decision cannot be avoided, we choose a reputable group of scientists and ask for their best opinions. "Tell us what you think," we tell them. Then we weigh their opinion and make our decision, right or wrong. But extra weight is normally given to the scientific opinion.

For example, a hole appeared in the stratospheric ozone layer protecting us from excessive ultraviolet radiation from the sun. When the incidence of skin cancers increased under that hole, a group of scientists and other leaders around the world convened, under the auspices of the United Nations. They considered the problem and its causes — and offered recommendations for its amelioration. As a result of that process, we are phasing out the use of certain kinds of refrigerants thought to be one of the causes. Though a considerable time will elapse before the molecules attacking the ozone layer are cleansed from the stratosphere, scientists generally think that changing refrigerants has a beneficial effect.

This is a good example of how we turn to our scientists for guidance when faced with a serious threat.

Though we can find many more examples like this, to expect certainty from scientists offering opinions on uncertain matters is a mistake. Even in disputed areas like the ozone layer or the magnitude of the human input to global warming, however, we still turn to our scientists as expert witnesses for assistance in understanding and determining the truth.

This happens regularly, in the criminal justice system, in product safety, in the design of safe airplanes, and in assessing the severity of various aspects of our environmental crisis. We also listen to all manner of non-scientists, and rightfully so, except in areas where the science is really clear.

Earth Summit

Given this background, when a large number of our most reputable scientists speaks to humanity as a whole, we expect that the subject would be very important and that nearly everyone would pay attention. Humanity had a chance to do just that in the years following the United Nations Conference on the Environment and Development, the environmental summit held in Rio de Janeiro, in 1992.

That summit, and the *Agenda 21* document that it produced[1], marked an important milestone in the history of the human species. It even provided a detailed plan for the nations of the world to begin reversing the heretofore, relentless attack we humans have been making on our life-support system.

Agenda 21 is an important document. Its publication marks the beginning of the human species taking responsibility for the environmental consequences of its behaviors. It represents an important leap forward by the Earth's human inhabitants.

For the first time ever, a *global* consensus was reached that we must make some far-reaching and extensive changes in the way we go about the business of everyday life. Nonetheless, this great leap forward is but a small step toward protecting the planet for future generations and achieving the goals identified at the Rio meeting[2].

However important the *existence of Agenda 21*, its content is embarrassingly inadequate. It hardly mentions population, ignores overpopulation, and fills many pages with detailed steps whose usefulness is, at best, marginal without stopping population growth. It appears to have been written so as to offend no one. It is filled with double talk, unrealistic assertions that totally miss the most fundamental cause of our problems — population growth. Many believe this to be due, at least in part, to pressure from the Vatican. The implementation of its recommendations is mediocre, at best.

World Scientists' Warning

The response following Rio was underwhelming. A few years later, scant signs could be found that the event had taken place at all, at least according to the legislative bodies and power structures of most of the nations of the world, and in the world media.

This lack of response is astounding. In *The Sacred Balance*[3], Suzuki writes that in spite of over twenty years of knowledge of our growing environmental problems,

...since the beginning of the 1990's, the media have turned away from environmental issues as if avoiding an unpleasant sight. They have focused on debt, deficits and global competitiveness as our most pressing challenges — the "bottom line" — as we approach the next millennium, ignoring the voices of the planet's most eminent scientists. On November 18, 1992, only five months after the largest gathering of heads of state in history at the Earth Summit in Rio, a document titled "World Scientists' Warning to Humanity" was released. It was signed by more than sixteen hundred senior scientists from seventy-one countries, including over half of all living Nobel Prize winners. The document [a] began:

"Human beings and the natural world are on a collision course. Human activities inflict harsh and often irreversible damage on the environment and on critical resources. If not checked, many of our current practices put at serious risk the future that we wish for human society and the plant and animal kingdoms, and may so alter the living world that it will be unable to sustain life in the manner that we know. Fundamental changes are urgent if we are to avoid the collision our present course will bring about."

The warning went on to list crises in the atmosphere, water resources, the oceans, the soil, the forests, biodiversity, and human overpopulation. Then the words became stark:

"No more than one or a few decades remain before the chance to avert the threats we now confront will be lost and the prospects for humanity immeasurably diminished. We the undersigned, senior members of the world's scientific community, hereby warn all humanity of what lies ahead. A great change in our stewardship of the Earth and life on it is required, if vast human misery is to be avoided and our global home on this planet is not to be irretrievably mutilated."

Peter Raven, a noted scientist, 1985 MacArthur Foundation Fellow, and Director of the Missouri Botanical Garden, wrote in 1987[4]:

The world that provides our evolutionary and ecological context is in trouble — trouble serious enough to demand our urgent attention. The large-scale problems of overpopulation and overdevelopment are eradicating the lands and organisms that sustain life on this planet. If we can solve these problems, we can lay the foundation for peace and

---

[a] Union of Concerned Scientists, web page: http://www.ucsusa.org/resources/warning.html. It is instructive to note that this reference was found by the author after only a few seconds of searching for the key words "World Scientists Warning" using a widely available internet search engine. The search, which came back nearly instantly, listed many "hits" giving testimony to the power of the internet. A list of the signatories can be found at http://www.spiritone.com/~orsierra/rogue/popco/warn/warn02.htm.

prosperity in the future. By ignoring these issues, drifting passively while attending to what seem more urgent, personal priorities, we are courting disaster.

We live in a world where far more people are well fed, clothed, and housed than ever before. We also live in a world in which up to 100,000 people starve to death every day, in which we consume well over a third of total terrestrial photosynthetic productivity, and in which human activity threatens to eliminate nearly a quarter of those organisms we do not consume, yet upon which our civilization is almost completely dependent for survival. Their permanent loss limits the options available to our children and grandchildren.

Yet, there are those so desperate to avoid the need for governmental action of any kind that they attempt to lull us to sleep by pretending that there is no problem, that inaction is best, and that we should simply continue to indulge our selfishness. This is exceedingly dangerous counsel given at precisely the wrong time.

Noted Pulitzer Prize winning biologist E. O. Wilson, Pellegrino University Research Professor and Honorary Curator at Harvard University, offered the following assessment in a 1998 editorial in *Science* magazine[5]:

Arguably the foremost of global problems grounded in the idiosyncrasies of human nature is overpopulation and the destruction of the environment. The crisis is not long-term but here and now; it is upon us. Like it or not, we are entering the century of the environment, when science and politics will give the highest priority to settling humanity down before we wreck the planet.

Here in brief is the problem — or better, complex of interlocking problems — as researchers see it. In their consensus, "[t]he global population is precariously large, will grow another third by 2020, and climb still more before peaking sometime after 2050. Humanity is improving per capita production, health, and longevity. But it is doing so by eating up the planet's capital, including irreplaceable natural resources. Humankind is approaching the limit of its food and water supply. As many as a billion people, moreover, remain in absolute poverty, with inadequate food from one day to the next and little or no medical care. Unlike any species that lived before, *Homo sapiens* is also changing the world's atmosphere and climate, lowering and polluting water tables, shrinking forests, and spreading deserts. It is extinguishing large fractions of plant and animal species, an irreplaceable loss that will be viewed as catastrophic by future generations. Most of the stress originates directly or indirectly from a handful of industrialized countries. Their proven formulas are being eagerly adopted by the rest of the world. The emulation cannot be sustained, not with the same levels of consumption and waste. Even if the industrialization of developing countries is only partly successful, the environmental aftershock will dwarf the population explosion that preceded it."[8] Recent studies indicate that to raise the rest of the world to the level of the United States using present technology would require the natural resources of two more planet Earths.

The time has come to look at ourselves closely as a biological as well as cultural species, using all of the intellectual tools we can muster. We are brilliant catarrhine primates, whose success is eroding the environment to which a billion years of evolutionary history exquisitely adapted us. We are dangerously baffled by the meaning of this existence, remaining instinct-driven, reckless, and conflicted. Wisdom for the long-term eludes us. There is ample practical reason — should no other kind prove persuasive — to aim for an explanatory integration not just of the natural sciences but also of the social sciences and humanities, in order to cope with issues of urgency and complexity that may otherwise be too great to manage.

[8]E.O. Wilson, *Consilience: The Unity of Knowledge* (Knopf, New York, 1998), p.280.

Staking our Lives on Science

Why is it that in some areas we stake our lives on what our scientists tell us, taking their cautionary warnings seriously and acting upon them, while in others we ignore them, and refuse action to avoid the problems they warn about?

Perhaps the most important reason is a natural human tendency toward denial of unpleasant realities. The alcoholic is usually the last one to accept the seriousness of his or her condition. So, too, the drug addict.

As a group, humanity doesn't want to make the drastic changes apparently necessary to reverse our assault on the environment. So we say that global warming hasn't been proven, that scientists have mixed conclusions about the human responsibility for much of it, and that we don't have to take drastic action just yet.

Often when we find someone in denial, signs around them confirm that the problem is real. A spouse might find partially filled liquor bottles in unexpected places. Signs of freeze danger on a space shuttle might be apparent, but managers worried about slipping schedules launch it anyway. Or the increased frequency of unusual weather events, which scientists say accompany global warming, is ignored.

Laws of Nature

Daniel Quinn generalizes this discussion of science and offers new insight on our predicament. He says two kinds of laws exist: laws of humans, subject to vote, and laws of Nature, *not* subject to vote. According to Quinn, the problem is to find the ones not subject to vote and to get them right[6].

Consider the trial and error searches of the scientists and technologists for laws of Nature, such as how gravity works and so on... laws not subject to vote. These laws are real, independent of human existence or thought. Quinn offers a story of a person who, thinking he has the laws of gravity and aerodynamics mastered, jumps off a very high cliff with a completely flawed, human-powered aircraft. He sees everything working marvelously as he descends rapidly, more or less in control of the descent.

However, the law of gravity is catching up with him at an accelerating rate of 32 ft per second each second. The ground is rushing up to him at an accelerating rate.

"My craft has brought me *this* far in safety," he tells himself. "I just have to keep going." He starts pedaling with all his might, which does no good at all, because this craft simply isn't in accord with the laws of aerodynamics. And then, at the end, the inevitable crash happens.

"Here is the connection. Ten thousand years ago, the people of [our] culture embarked on a similar flight: a civilizational flight. Their craft wasn't designed according to any theory at all. Like our imaginary airman, they were totally unaware that there is a law that must be complied with in order to achieve civilizational flight. They didn't even wonder about it. They wanted the freedom of the air, and so they pushed off in the first contraption that came to hand...."

"At first all was well. In fact, all was terrific. [The people of our culture were] pedaling away and the wings of their craft were flapping beautifully. They felt wonderful, exhilarated ... Their flight could never end, it could only go on becoming more and more exciting. They couldn't know, couldn't even have guessed that, like our hapless airman, they were in the air but not in flight. They were in free fall, because their craft was simply not in compliance with the law that makes flight possible...like our airman, they see strange sights in the course of their fall. They see the remains of craft very like their own — not destroyed, merely abandoned...."

Pedaling away, having a wonderful time, they expect to enjoy the freedom of the air forever. But a law as unforgiving as the law of gravity, is catching up to them at an accelerating rate. A few thinkers along the way raise a couple of cries of alarm but go unheeded or misunderstood. And there are optimists who tell us to have faith in the craft; it's brought us *this* far in safety.

"But [our] craft isn't going to save [us]. Quite the contrary, it's [our] craft that's carrying [us] toward catastrophe. Five billion of [us] pedaling away — or ten billion or twenty billion — can't make it fly. It's been in free fall from the beginning and that fall is about to end."

I'm fond of a Brinkman cartoon showing two congressmen in front of the Capitol. One turns to the other and says, "Thinking is very upsetting, it tells you things you'd rather not know." It's much like an H. L. Mencken quote that people accept what is false but comforting and reject what is true but unpleasant.

Anti-Science

At one time in history science was in deep conflict with religion. With a few notable exceptions [b], this is, by and large, no longer true. Now science is in conflict with monetary economics, which acts as if it believes in human domination over Nature and the limitlessness of natural resources. This belief came about in the early days of the industrial revolution when the world was large, population small, and per capita environmental impact modest. A result today of that thought frame is continued denial of scientists' warnings.

Another more recent development has further blunted the scientists' warnings. It is a general drifting away from science as a profession — as something interesting and worth pursuing. In its place in popular culture, we see greater emphasis on fantasies, on bizarre stories clearly at odds with the known truth.

As a writing genre, science fiction is one of our most developed art forms. When science fiction and fantasy, however, begin to dominate television, the movies, and even the news, it can divert attention from the fantastic beauty, wonder, and astonishment available in real science and the important truths science has to offer.

This problem was considered so serious that the late Carl Sagan wrote a book about it. *The Demon Haunted World* resulted[7]. In it Sagan writes, "For centuries, science has been under a line of attack that, rather than pseudoscience can be called anti-science. Science and academic scholarship in general, the contention these days goes, is too subjective. Some even allege it's entirely subjective, as is, they say, history." He explains the truly

---

[b]Creationism, the extreme religious right, religious fundamentalists, and the Vatican's disregard for overpopulation. These remind us of Benjamin Franklin's statement in Poor Richard's Almanac that "The way to see by faith is to shut the eye of reason."

subjective nature of history as after-the-fact writings on events, the interpretation of which the author is free to bend to suit goals other than just getting at the truth. According to Sagan, often "Objectivity is sacrificed in the service of higher goals."

Scientists have biases, too, Sagan points out, and are fraught with "prejudices from our surroundings like everyone else ... Scientists are often reluctant to offend the rich and powerful. Occasionally a few of them cheat and steal." And scientists make mistakes.

There is something different about science, however, which distinguishes it from other, inherently subjective disciplines. It is the job of scientists "to recognize our weaknesses, to examine the widest range of opinions, to be ruthlessly self-critical. Science is a collective enterprise with the error-correction machinery often running smoothly. It has an overwhelming advantage over history, because in science we can do experiments."[7, pp. 252-254]

Scientists test and retest and test again every new hypothesis. Only those theories proving to be correct in every test are elevated to the level of truth and belief, called laws of science. Only these are allowed as building blocks in the intricate structure of established science. This makes science generally more reliable than subjective knowledge. The problem is that fewer and fewer people understand and accept this.

At the beginning of his book, Sagan describes an encounter with a gentleman filled with information about fantastic stories, most of them either untrue or not yet proven. His knowledge and interest in science fantasy, and in what Sagan calls pseudoscience, what we might call "junk science," was extensive. After describing how he debunked most of the young man's beliefs, Sagan wrote:

> I was dismissing not just some errant doctrine, but a precious facet of his inner life. And yet there's so much in real science that's equally exciting, more mysterious, a greater intellectual challenge — as well as being a lot closer to the truth. Did he know about the molecular building blocks of life sitting out there in the cold, tenuous gas between the stars? Had he heard of the footprints of our ancestors found in 4-million-year-old volcanic ash? What about the raising of the Himalayas when India went crashing into Asia? Or how viruses, built like hypodermic syringes, that slip their DNA past the host organism's defenses and subvert the reproductive machinery of cells; or the radio search for extraterrestrial intelligence; or the newly discovered ancient civilization of Ebla that advertised the virtues of Ebla beer? No, he hadn't heard. Nor did he know, even vaguely, about quantum indeterminacy, and he recognized DNA only as three frequently linked capital letters.

...well-spoken, intelligent, curious — [this man] had heard virtually nothing of modern science. He had a natural appetite for the wonders of the Universe. He wanted to know about science. It's just that all the science had gotten filtered out before it reached him. Our cultural motifs, our educational system, our communications media had failed this man. What the society permitted to trickle through was mainly pretense and confusion. It had never taught him how to distinguish real science from the cheap imitation. He knew nothing about how science works....

Spurious accounts that snare the gullible are readily available. Skeptical treatments are much harder to find. Skepticism does not sell well. A bright and curious person who relies entirely on popular culture to be informed ... is hundreds or thousands of times more likely to come upon a fable treated uncritically than a sober and balanced assessment.

Maybe [this gentleman] should know to be more skeptical about what's dished out to him by popular culture. But apart from that, it's hard to see how it's his fault. He simply accepted what the most widely available and accessible sources of information claimed was true. For his naivete, he was systematically misled and bamboozled.[7, pp. 4-5]

Perhaps bamboozlement is forgivable in a few individuals. But when a whole world is bamboozled into ignoring or downplaying the serious warnings of many eminent scientists and scholars, that is unwise and dangerous. The very extinction of the human species could be at stake. The future of humanity rests, in large part, on our ability and desire to listen to our scientists, take them seriously, and begin the monumental task of educating the populace about these matters.

The best way out of our difficulties is, apparently, to begin a massive search — to find and explore alternative structures for our society. The goal is to make it truly sustainable, so that the future of humanity will be one of hope and optimism again for the millions of years we expect Earth to remain a viable life-support system, powered by that giant flaming sphere, our Sun.

References

1. United Nations Conference on Environment and Development UNCED. *Agenda 21, the Rio Declaration on Environment and Development.* UNDSD, United Nations Division for Sustainable Development: 1992.
2. Ross McCluney. "Sustainable Values." In *Ethics and Agenda 21—Moral Implications of a Global Consensus,* edited by Noel J. Brown and Pierre Quiblier. United Nations Environment Programme, United Nations Publications, New York, NY 10017: New York, 1994.
3. David Suzuki. *The Sacred Balance — Rediscovering our Place in Nature.* Promethius Books: Amherst, NY, 1998, 259 pp.
4. Peter H. Raven. *The Global Ecosystem in Crisis – We're Killing Our World.* The John D. and Catherine T. MacArthur Foundation: Chicago, 1987.
5. Excerpted with permission from E. O. Wilson, SCIENCE Vol. 279:2048 (27 Mar 1998). Copyright 1998 American Association for the Advancement of Science.
6. Daniel Quinn. *Ishmael.* 1st ed. Bantam/Turner: New York, 1992.
7. Carl Sagan. *The Demon-Haunted World – Science as a Candle in the Dark.* Random House: New York,1995. Copyright © 1996 by Carl Sagan. Reprinted with permission from the Estate of Carl Sagan.

5
To Grow or Not to Grow

How growth works.
Good growth, bad growth, or no growth?

The road to the future leads us smack into the wall.
We simply ricochet off the alternatives that destiny offers:
a demographic explosion that triggers social chaos
and spreads death, nuclear delirium and the quasi-
annihilation of the species.... Our survival is no more
than a question of 25, 50 or perhaps 100 years.
— Jacques Cousteau 1910-1997

Key to the threats humanity faces is the phenomenon of continuing human population growth, coupled with the unsustainable consumption of resources. Both have strong impacts on Earth's life-support system. The combined impact of all humans on Earth is the product of both the size of the population and individual, or per capita, impacts of each human on the biosphere. These impacts are magnified by any technology that increases human impact. The relationship is expressed by a formula offered by Paul and Anne Ehrlich, in their 1991 book, *The Population Explosion*[1]:

$$I = PAT.$$

This formula signifies that total environmental impact I is the product of the population P, the affluence level A (material standard of living, per capita), and the technological level T (which magnifies the effects of affluence). High impact can result from huge populations with modest per capita impacts and technology or from modest populations with high per capita impacts and technology. When there is growth in population, in that population's per capita impact, and in the destructiveness of their technology, the resulting total impact on Earth will grow at an astonishingly high rate. Proposals to reduce just the technological impact will likely be offset by the increasing impacts from the other two growths.

The United States is a country with arguably the greatest material affluence on Earth, the largest per capita impact, and a growing population. According to the Ehrlichs, in the United States each child born, on average, has a per capita impact 35 times that of an Indian baby, and 280 times that of a Haitian child[1].

The United Nations Development Programme estimates[2] that the richest fifth of the world's population consumes 86 percent of all goods and services and produces 53 percent of all carbon dioxide emissions. That same wealthy fifth also consumes 80 percent of the world's natural resources and generates 80 percent of the pollution and waste. The U.S. alone, with only five percent of the world's population, uses up 30 percent of the natural resource base—including 20 percent of the planet's metals, 24 percent of its energy (the highest per capita consumption in the world) and 25 percent of its fossil fuels.

Carrying Capacity

Other regions have massive populations with lower per capita affluence and technology. In many of these areas, as well as in the U.S., population has exceeded what biologists call the "carrying capacity." Carrying capacity is that number of individuals of a species which can be supported and sustained indefinitely at their accustomed material standard of living by the naturally available assets of a region[3, p. 84].

Numerous cases, recorded in the literature on animals and humans, reveal where the carrying capacity of an area has been exceeded. The normal result is severe degradation of the environment, followed either by extinction of the species or a drastic reduction in its population, (Nature's way of correcting the imbalance). Miller puts it this way:

> Some populations (especially rapidly reproducing ones such as insects, bacteria, and algae) may surpass the carrying capacity and then undergo a rapid decrease in size, known as a population crash. Some population crashes involve sharp increases in the death rate; others involve combinations of a rise in the death rate coupled with emigration of large numbers of individuals to other areas. A population crash can also occur when a change in environmental conditions lowers the carrying capacity of an ecosystem.[3, p. 84]

Industrialized nations may no longer be considered susceptible to ecosystem changes as in the past. This may be true on a temporary basis, as long as our supplemental, non-solar, fossil fuel energy keeps flowing, and until irreplaceable natural services are severely or irreversibly degraded. In the long run, we are as dependent as the deer, antelope, and mountain lion on healthy ecosystems.

In nearly every region of the world, human impacts on Earth are high, whether from population pressures, high per capita impact, or both.

The local natural carrying capacity can be exceeded through:
- population growth beyond natural limits
- declines in the natural assets of a region, reducing carrying capacity below current population levels
- declines in the resource imports from outside a region

This latter option of supplementing natural resource inputs with those from outside a region, increasing the apparent carrying capacity of the second region, comes only at the expense of the first. Some countries that do not produce enough for themselves or enough to trade receive either a food supplement or food money donated from other areas. Such aid is often short-lived.

According to population growth expert Virginia Abernethy, the importation of resources to sustain a higher population can exist only where a nation has enough currency reserves to purchase resources from other countries willing to sell. In this way, some regions, countries, or cities can increase their own carrying capacity using inputs from outside their boundaries.

Carrying capacity can actually be increased, allowing higher population levels without crashing. This is done through technology that creates new uses for elements which were formerly useless. Natural gas, for example, is converted into fertilizer that adds immeasurably to crop production, increasing food output enough to support a larger population. Without developing technologies, the population in Western Europe, as well as the United States, Hong Kong, and Singapore, could not exist at anything approaching the current standard of living. Technology — coupled with supplemental inputs of energy, beyond the daily input of natural energy from the sun — has contributed to the wealth of the countries mentioned as well as that of many others.

No industrialized country in the world is operating sustainably—that is, in a manner that will continue indefinitely the standard of living expected by its current population. All industrialized countries depend upon energy from ancient deposits of coal, oil, and natural gas — the fossil fuels — that are not replaceable in human time frames. When these are withdrawn, depleted, or abandoned as too costly in economic or human health terms, the carrying capacity will be reduced. The artificially inflated population will also decrease. Any aid being sent to other countries would then likely be withdrawn, causing additional repercussions.

The human carrying capacity of a region may possibly be extended in a somewhat sustainable manner by making more efficient use of the available solar energy. However, according to Virginia Abernethy and other population experts, the populations of the industrialized countries have already exceeded the number that could be sustained by solar power alone. Moreover, the vast areas required for collectors limit solar power. This issue is discussed more fully in the next chapter on energy.

The need for energy is driven, as are most environmental impacts, by the $I = PAT$ formula. People desire extra energy. The more people, the greater the demand for that energy. The more affluent the people, the more energy each one consumes, magnifying the effect. The more industrialized they are, the more energy required to power their "labor-saving devices" and other accouterments of an affluent and materialistic lifestyle. Stop population growth, or reverse it in direct proportion to increases in per capita affluence and per capita technological impacts, and the overall impact would remain the same.

Food, Population, and Malthus

In the past, population was controlled (and still is in nonhuman nature) naturally by habitat and food limits. What is a reason for exponential human population growth? We have found mostly technological ways to avoid the habitat limits and to grow ever more food. Once that happened, our food production system supported not just settlement but growth, seemingly unlimited growth.

Thomas Malthus (1766-1834) explored the connection between food and population in a famous essay, published in 1798. In this essay he proposed the idea that without intervention, human population growth tends to exceed the growth of food production. "Population increases in a geometric ratio, while the means of subsistence increases in an arithmetic ratio." Malthus claimed that neither of humanity's hungers — for food and for sex — could ever be quelled or controlled. Since population is always increasing, humanity will eventually come up against a limit — the finite nature of the world's resources needed for life. The essence of the doctrine is that the population level cannot keep increasing without, at some point, pressing on the limits of the means of subsistence; a check of some kind or other must, sooner or later, be opposed to it.

Population is kept in line with food supply by the limiting influences of starvation, disease, and other factors increasing the death rate — and by "preventive checks" such as the postponement of marriage, intentionally reduced fertility, and other means intended to or involuntarily limiting the birthrate. "Malthusianism" is more generally described as a belief that population growth is a serious problem and at the core of most environmental problems.

The Social Contract devoted its entire Vol. 8, No. 3, spring 1998 issue to the celebration of the 200th anniversary of the publication of the famous Malthus essay. Albert Bartlett authored a particularly illuminating article for that issue, "The Massive Movement to Marginalize the Modern Malthusian Message,"[4] in which he wrote:

> Malthus showed that the use of numbers and simple analysis could yield an improved understanding of contemporary and future population problems, and that steady growth of populations would produce great and grave problems. Two hundred years of debate over the ideas of Malthus have left the debaters divided into two camps: the *believers*, who accept the idea that it is appropriate to use the quantitative analysis to gain an improved understanding of the growth of populations and of food supplies, and the *critics* who don't.

He characterizes the opposing views as follows:

> The world today faces enormous problems that the believers hold to be caused largely by population growth.
>
> The *non-believers* say that the world population is much larger today than Malthus could ever have imagined, and thus far starvation seems not to have been a major limiting factor in stopping the growth of world population. Hence, they assert, the Malthusian message of quantitative analysis is wrong. From this they sometimes extrapolate to say that the human population can go on growing "forever."

Quinn weighs into the debate by claiming that increasing food production to feed a growing population results in yet another increase in population:

> Malthus saw food production as tracking population growth (struggling to catch up), and this is the prevailing view today. Scientists are often quoted as saying that "We WILL be able to produce enough food to feed our growing population." My point is rather the obverse of [this]:

> Population tracks food availability—not just in humans but also in all
> species.... Like all other species, our population grows when more food
> becomes available (and declines when less food is available). Thus the
> correct statement should be something like this: "Our population WILL
> increase as long as we keep increasing food production."
>
> The food race (the race between food production and population
> growth) is like the arms race of the Cold War: every "win" on one side is
> answered by a "win" on the other side. Every time we improved our
> weapons status, the Soviets answered by improving THEIR weapons
> status. It was a race that could not be won, as, thankfully, Gorbachev
> finally realized. Similarly, every "win" on the side of food production is
> answered by a "win" on the side of population. There simply can't be a
> final win in the food race any more than there could be a final win in the
> arms race. [5]

Countering this view, many of the industrialized countries, having more than
sufficient food, have been able to stop and even reverse population growth.
In some cases, such as in the U.S. and portions of Europe, the influx of
immigrants from more rapidly growing areas often counteracts this trend
toward negative population growth.

Reversing Population Growth

In some respects, reducing human population might be the easiest
approach to making human life sustainable. At least it would keep
environmental impacts at approximately the present level, or buy us time
while we revolutionize the technology used to make it less impacting. If
people believe that they have a right to, and can continue, living a materialistic
and high energy lifestyle, then logically they must also be in favor of population
controls, stopping population growth completely, or even reducing world
population levels.

Bartlett has examined the issue of sustainability in some depth. His
several papers on the subject are illuminating and clarifying. Bartlett's Laws
of Sustainability are particularly cogent, and are reproduced in the Appendix
to this chapter.

Ecological Footprint

One use of technology is to remove the environmental and health impacts
of growth and development from view by displacing them in time and space.
The "ecological footprint" concept (defined in the previous section) offers a

way of looking at this phenomenon, aggregating the displaced components and relating the total impact to regional — or national or global — carrying capacity. William Rees of the University of British Columbia, originator of the eco-footprint concept, explains it this way:

> The ecological footprint is an accounting tool that estimates the human load on the Earth in terms of 'appropriated ecosystem area.' We can convert most categories of resource consumption by humans into the corresponding area of average productive land and water ecosystems required to produce the resources and to assimilate the wastes associated with their economic use and ultimate disposal. Ecological footprint analysis thus provides an effective way of assessing the sustainability of alternative life-styles.
>
> By the beginning of the 21st Century, the ecological footprint of the average Canadian had grown to about 8.8 hectares (22 acres). Americans had 9.7 ha (24 ac) eco-footprints. These numbers represent the total area of land and marine ecosystems required per person to produce food as well as the resources needed for housing, urban infrastructure, transportation, and consumer goods and services. Energy typically represents the largest component of the human eco-footprint: 5.8 ha (14 ac) of dedicated carbon sink forest per person would be necessary to assimilate the carbon dioxide emissions associated with the average North American's use of fossil fuels. (An even larger area would be necessary to grow a biofuel substitute for oil and natural gas.) Crop- and grazing land comprises the second largest component at about 1.9 ha (4.7 ac) per person. Each North American needs about 1.3 ha (3.2 ac) of working forest to provide his/her annual supply of wood-fibre for lumber, paper and other consumer goods, and about .3 ha (.7 ac) of marine habitat for seafood. The built environment takes up about 0.4 ha (1.0 ac) per person for housing, commercial structures and transportation systems (data from WWF 2002). Note that the global average eco-footprint is only about 2.3 hectares (5.7 ac) less than a quarter of the North American average.
>
> Could everybody on Earth live like the average North-American today?
>
> No. In fact, if everyone on Earth lived like the average North American, it would take four Earth-like planets to provide all the material and energy resources and biophysical life-support services that today's 6.2 billion people would use. Current estimates show that the aggregate ecological footprint of human consumption already exceeds long-term global carrying capacity by approximately 20 percent. This is problematic. The wealthiest quarter of humanity (1.5 billion people) consumes more than 80 percent of current global economic output. The remaining three-quarters of the population (4.7 billion people) live on only 20 percent of global output and our already over-stressed world is depending on sheer economic growth to relieve the political tensions generated by such gross economic disparity.

This approach spells ill for global ecological integrity and ultimately for geopolitical stability. Eco-footprint analysis thus raises serious questions about economic expansion as the remedy for poverty and highlights the ethical implications of the sustainability dilemma.[6,7]

Clearly, growths in population, material affluence, and technology are serious issues that must be addressed in assessing humanity's future. Before discussing policy issues and future projections, the general phenomenon of growth needs to be examined more closely.

Measuring Growth

Let's initially assume that for some period of time, the growth *rate* remains constant (the same). Exponential growth occurs when the same fixed fraction of a quantity is added to that quantity over a specific period of time, and the process is repeated for each subsequent period of time. Notice the word "fraction." For example, if 10 percent of 100 items are added each month, for the next several months, the total amount at the beginning of each month will be 100, 110, 121, 133, 146, 161, 177, 195, 214 ... taking just over seven months to double the original number. This is exponential growth.

If I said a fixed "amount" is added each time period, I'd be talking about *arithmetic* growth (also called linear growth). If we add the same number, 10 items, to 100 each month, the growth would look like this: 100, 110, 120, 130, 140...200 ... doubling the original quantity in ten months.. Exponential growth is different from this. For every time period, the amount added increases.

Exponential growth rates are normally quoted in terms of percentages, the percent increase in the size of a quantity — such as human population — in a year. For example we might hear or speak of a 1% growth rate, a 2% growth rate, or a 5% growth rate. The trouble is that rates like this look rather small. What is a mere 5% growth in a whole year? Surely that can't be much! But each increment of growth is added to the principal next year. The next 5% is 5% of a larger base, and so on.

Dr. Al Bartlett, Professor Emeritus at the University of Colorado, has explored the mathematics of exponential growth and their consequences. Bartlett points out that one dollar at 5% per year compounded continuously will grow in 500 years to 72 billion dollars!

Suppose you are a government official responsible for providing for the needs of an increasing population for such things as schools and streets.

You have the plan to add these services, you raise the money for them and do whatever impact studies are needed, and then carry out the construction and training tasks. The process of providing these *infrastructure* or support services can take quite a few years and demand a lot of financial resources.

Even if we ignore the environmental implications of development growth, when population doubling times are comparable to the times required to develop the needed services to support the added population, keeping up with growing demand is difficult. The consequences include significant losses of services, crowding of schools and highways, and overflowing of sewage treatment plants.

You have to raise money to pay for the additional services. New schools generally cost more than the old ones did, meaning that the cost of new growth is higher than old growth costs. In the end the people pay these higher costs (and usually suffer during construction). Often, by the time a new freeway is built it took so long to complete that the roadway is nearly full again. Since it generally takes a fair amount of time to build a new roadway, exponential growth nearly guarantees that the new roadway will be crowded by the time it is finished. (I saw this with a new freeway a number of years ago in Houston, Texas. When the freeway was completed, it was full of traffic. Also the original street, whose traffic the freeway was supposed to alleviate, was congested as well.)

Doubling Time

As shown above, growth rates alone can be deceiving. Another measure of growth is helpful in overcoming the apparent deception. It is the previously mentioned *doubling time*, the time required to double the original quantity. This is not the place to talk about the mathematical details of exponential growth, where the meaning of the term "exponential" becomes clear. For that you can search on "exponential growth" on the Internet.

It is only important to understand that with exponential growth at a constant rate of increase, the doubling time, too, is a constant. Every doubling time you have twice as much as before, and the next doubling time produces four times as much, and the next yields eight times as much.

The doubling time is related to the percent exponential growth rate as follows. If you know that I is the rate of *increase* in some quantity, on an annual percentage basis, then there is a simple trick you can use to convert this number I — like the interest rate in a savings account earning at a compound rate of $I\%$ — into the more useful *doubling time*.

The doubling time *T2* is the time in years it takes for whatever quantity you are talking about to grow to *twice* its size at the fixed annual rate I. Denoting the doubling time by the symbol *T2*, then the formula is

$$T2=70/I$$

Growth Rate in Percent	Doubling Time in Years
0.1	700
0.2	350
1	70
2	35
5	14

You divide the number 70 by the growth rate *I* in percent per year and you get the doubling time in years. The result of this arithmetic for several common growth rates is displayed in the Table. These numbers show the inverse relationship between percentage growth and doubling time.

The simple little formula shown above is probably more important than Einstein's famous equation, $E = mc^2$. The quantity *I* is much like the interest in a savings account. According to the doubling time formula, it takes only *T2* years for the original deposit to double in size. The equation assumes that the "interest" is plowed back into the principal on a continuous basis; whatever increase occurs over the course of a year is added to the principle continuously as the year progresses. This is the so-called "compound interest" we learn about in school. It is the same thing as exponential growth.

Why is the doubling time equation more important than Einstein's? It allows us quickly and easily to convert quotes of percentage growth rates into doubling times, which most people find easier to understand. And understanding growth rates — hopefully leading to curtailed growth — will be crucial for our survival as a species on planet Earth, a matter at least as important as knowing how much energy you can get from a quantity of mass.

The value of the little formula $T2 = 70/I$ is that you can use it to convert any percentage growth number heard or read in the media into its corresponding doubling time, thereby putting the implications of the growth rates quoted into better perspective. (Of course the growth rate must be constant during the doubling time period for the formula to remain valid. Most growths do not stay fixed, but fluctuate up and down a little from month to month or year to year. One should use the average growth rate to approximate doubling times. Even this is not perfect. But as long as the growth rate remains fairly close to the value you use in the formula, the doubling time predicted with it will not be far off the mark. We are more concerned here with the principles of exponential growth than with the details of any particular actual growth. For that we have census bureaus, demographers, and mathematicians.)

The above numbers indicate that even modest growth rates (such as 2 and 5 percent) lead to fairly short doubling times, and rapid increases over modest time periods. If we are talking about population growth, the meaning of the doubling time is clear. As the population doubles, so, too, does the need for food, clothing, shelter, schooling, hospitals, and prisons. If the need for sewage treatment plants doubles every 30 years, in that 30 years you need to have twice as many on line and operating. The next doubling time produces a need for four times as many, and in the next you need eight times as many.

Another way to illustrate exponential growth is to point out that steady growth at $n\%$ per year for 70 years will produce growth to an overall size of 2^n. Thus, when a city has one overloaded sewage treatment plant today, steady population growth at 5% means that in 70 years (5 doubling times) the city will need to have $2^5 = 32$, *thirty two* overloaded sewage treatment plants. The consequences for our children and for their children are an unrestrained population growth at even a modest rate of 5%.

Steady inflation in the prices of goods and services, at a fixed percentage rate, leads to exponential growth in those prices. A loaf of bread costing $1.50 today will increase by a factor of 64 in 70 years at a 6% rate (six doubling times). This loaf of bread for toddlers today will cost $1.50 x 64 = $96 when the toddlers are retired and living on their pensions. In 1979 the U. S. inflation rate was about 12% per year. If this had continued for 70 years the $.60 price of bread in that year would rise to $2,458 by 2049!

Grains of Wheat

Al Bartlett has a story to further help us understand the nature of exponential growth[8]:

> Legend has it that a mathematician who worked for an ancient king invented the game of chess. As a reward for the invention the mathematician asked for the amount of wheat that would be determined by the following process: He asked the king to place 1 grain of wheat on the first square of the chess board, double this and put 2 grains on the second square, and continue this way, putting on each square twice the number of grains that were on the preceding square. The filling of the chessboard is shown in [the table

below]. We see that on the last square one will place 2^{63} grains and the total number of grains on the board will then be one grain less than 2^{64}.

Al's table of grains of wheat on the square of a chessboard

Square number	Grains on square	Total grains thus far
1	1	1
2	2	3
3	4	7
4	8	15
5	16	31
6	32	63
7	64	127
64	2^{63}	$2^{64} - 1$

How much wheat is 2^{64} grains? Simple arithmetic shows that it is approximately 400 times the 1990 annual worldwide harvest of wheat! This amount is probably larger than all the wheat that has been harvested by humans in the history of the Earth. How did we get to this enormous number? It is simple; we started with 1 grain of wheat and we doubled it a mere 63 times.... Note that when 8 grains are placed on the fourth square, the 8 is greater than the total of 7 grains that were already on the board. The 32 grains placed on the 6th square are more than the total of 31 grains that were already on the board.

This final observation is true of all exponential growth at a constant rate of increase. Each doubling time *adds* more of the quantity than was produced in all of time before!

World population reached 6 billion in October 1999, according to the United Nations. At a growth rate of 2% per year, world population would reach 7 billion in seven years and eight months (in June, 2007) and would double to 12 billion in 35 years (in 2034). It took *several million* years of human history for world population to reach its first billion. Now it takes *less than a decade* to add the next billion. Small growth rates can yield incredible numbers in modest time periods.

Limits to Growth

Here's another helpful story told by Al Bartlett[8]. It introduces the important concept of *the limits to growth*. Bacteria grow by division so that one bacterium becomes two, the two divide to become four, the four divide to become eight, etc.

Suppose there is one strain which accomplishes its doubling every minute. (This is a growth rate of 1.16 % per second and a doubling time of 60 seconds–one minute.) One bacterium is put in a bottle at 11:00 AM; by noon the bottle is full of bacteria.

There are several important questions to ask about this situation: at what time was the bottle half full? Answer 11:59 AM. If you were a bacterium in the bottle ... at what time would you first realize you were running out of space? Perhaps a bit of worry seeps into your thoughts when the bottle is 3% full. This happens at 11:55 AM. The bottle at this time is 97% open space (as Al puts it, space "just yearning for development").

Suppose that at 11:58 AM, with 75% open space remaining, some farsighted bacteria realize they are running out of space. Consequently, with a great deal of trouble and effort (and money), they launch a campaign to expand their living quarters. They look for more bottles.

Al continues his story: "They look offshore on the outer continental shelf and in the Arctic, and at 11:59 AM they discover *three* new empty bottles. Great sighs of relief come from all the worried bacteria, because this magnificent discovery is four times the number of bottles that had hitherto been known." It expands their living space by an amazing 100 times the space available at 11:55 when they filled only 3% of one bottle. "The discovery quadruples the total space resource known to bacteria. The proponents of this bacterial 'Project Independence' rejoice because they are confident that the bacteria can now be 'self-sufficient' in space."

But now comes the really crucial question. How long can the bacterial growth continue as a result of the addition of these three new bottles? The answer is... just two more minutes, i.e. two more doubling times. All four bottles are full at 12:02.

This story is a metaphor for human population growth on a finite planet ... for the growth in human extraction of limited, non-renewable resources from the planet's surface layers, and for the growth in dumping of harmful wastes into a finite planet's air, water, and soil. Finding new resources only buys a little time, puts off the inevitable exhaustion of the resource, or the time when the waste dump is full. In no way can that extraction of the mineral and fossil fuel resources of Planet Earth continue indefinitely. Growth has limits, as pointed out in the famous report cited in Chapter 2, *The Limits to Growth*[9].

We cannot grow without limit. Growth must stop at some point, if not by conscious plan and design, then by default, as Nature solves the problem for us through famine, pestilence, disease, debilitating wars, and possibly nuclear explosions.

The story just told is fiction. Real growths may start out exponential with a relatively constant doubling time, but at some point negative pressures slow this growth. The pressures can come from adverse consequences or, in the case of humans, by conscious design. Fertility rates for the children of citizens of most of the developed world are nearing the replacement level. Many of these countries would approach population stability without immigration. However, there is a long time lag between the drop of fertility due to affluence or choice and when the population stabilizes, due to the large number of children "in the pipeline" toward reproductive age. This is called "population momentum."

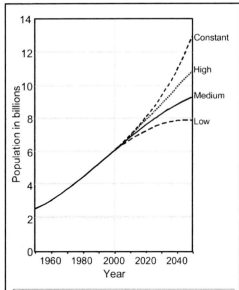

Though world population is currently growing rapidly, the combination of declines in the birth rate and increases in the death rate is expected to stabilize world population late in this century. A range of predictions is made by the United Nations Population Division at its web site http://www.un.org/esa/population/. World population is projected to range from about 8 billion to 13 billion in 2050, according to year 2000 projections shown in Figure 1. Growth continues past 2050 for all but the lowest of these projections.

Figure 1. United Nations Population Division world population projections, 2000. Future growths depend upon four different scenarios for future fertility rates, from constant (at the 2000 rate), to high, medium, and low.

As mentioned in Chapter 1, the term "sustainable" can only mean "continues indefinitely" for an unspecified long period of time. As illustrated above, it is a mathematical fact that steady growth at a fixed growth rate produces large numbers in modest periods of time. Thus the idea of "sustainable growth" means "increasing endlessly," a clear impossibility on a finite Earth. "Sustainable growth" is, indeed, an oxymoron, when applied to material things.

Confronting Accelerated Change

Paul MacCready led a team that successfully built a human powered aircraft, the Gossamer Condor, to win the prestigious Kremer Prize in 1977. This success, after a couple of decades of failures by many groups seeking the prize, resulted from remarkably creative insights. Over a period of years, MacCready was asked about and spent some time studying the origin and nature of those insights, and creative insights more generally, hoping to apply them to the larger problems of society. Years after winning the Kremer Prize, MacCready was asked to present the Keynote Address at a Symposium on The Inventor and the Innovative Society. In his remarks, he emphasized the radical nature of our current society, and the special problems this produces, referring to Figure 2.[10]

> Civilization is changing so rapidly that we can scarcely comprehend the
> rate, or realize that much of the wisdom of the past is irrelevant for the very
> different future. The change is so great that it represents a qualitative

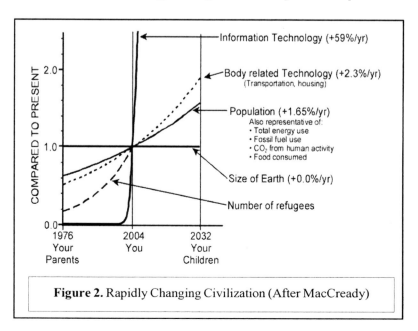

Figure 2. Rapidly Changing Civilization (After MacCready)

difference, not just a quantitative one.... Here [is an approach] to presenting the change in [a way] that help[s] us understand our present and near-future situation.[10]

Fig. [2] puts global change in your reference system. Various factors that define the present go through 1.0 in [2004]. They are followed back 28 years to represent the factors when your parents were your present age, and projected forward 28 years to when your children will be your present age. This is your tiny, two generation, half-century eye-blink slice of time in the 3.5 billion years history of life on Earth, about 1/2% of the 10,000 year history of civilization. The curves may not be exact, but are not misleading.

Information technology (capabilities, use, impact) has literally exploded—growing at the "Moore's Law" rate of doubling every 18 months. The next fastest growth "industry" is [the] number of refugees, up almost ten-fold in the past quarter century — but I don't know how to extrapolate this dreadful statistic into the future.

The upper limit of the capability and use of body-related technology (transportation, housing, and agriculture) is assumed to double every 30 years. More population has been added than existed at the start of this eye-blink of time (and the rate of consumption of total energy and fossil fuel energy, and the corresponding rate of CO_2 emissions, are approximately proportional to population). The Earth, incidentally, is not expanding. It is our own limited spaceship, and unlike the case of a conventional space capsule, we live only in the thin, exterior "skin".

Figure [2 is] focused on human accomplishments, growth, [and] consumption, and all the curves move up rapidly to the right, demonstrating opportunity for business. To complete the future, one could add environmental and limit factors, mostly moving down. The mass of fish in the oceans has been decreasing rapidly — some species being thoroughly fished out. With managed fishing the present harvest level might just barely be maintained. Without management, we will over-consume this natural capital — the conventional "tragedy of the commons" where short-term competition and greed assures longer-term disaster of renewable resources to which everyone has access. The amount of rain forest left, the number of natural species, and acres of arable land all are decreasing in absolute terms, and more so in per capita terms.

Taking a short-term view from a vantage point of affluence and privilege, we see little to concern us. But pretend you are a galactic explorer viewing the Earth from a broader perspective of distance and time, and your assessment changes. Pundits continually say Malthus was wrong; that experience shows civilizations can always grow, and, through science and technology, prosper. But 20 successive breaths into a balloon, each pressuring the balloon to look more beautiful, are no evidence that the balloon will not pop from some future breath. There are limits.

The sky is not the limit: the Earth is.

As Colin Campbell says, it is the false religion of economics that drives us down this suicidal path.

Good Growth–Bad Growth

Some kinds of growth *are* sustainable, at least in theory, perhaps not in practice. One can have sustainable growth in inflation, for example. Though the tone of previous sections has been decidedly negative toward growth, not all growths are bad; many are good and necessary. The growth of a child from birth to adulthood is generally accepted as good. There is a time to grow, however. It is not during maturity. The individual human growth process does not continue forever. Even this growth is unsustainable, and fortunately so, for soon there would be no room left for all the new babies.

Growths in human potential, artistic creativity, religious understanding, educational ability, knowledge, psychological health, peacefulness, and respect for each other and for the Earth are all good growths and perhaps know no limits. Any limits to these growths are not directly material. The limitations come mainly from the way humans are designed to operate, from the natural limitations of our current evolutionary status, not from some ultimate material limit.

If we wish to retain the concept that growth is good, we must clearly define growths as only the truly sustainable kind.

The Maximum Population

Joel Cohen wrote a book titled *How Many People Can the Earth Support?*[11] It is a scholarly work. Well researched, it considers its title's question from many viewpoints and perspectives. It even offers a timeline of all the estimates of the maximum possible human carrying capacity of the Earth. In his Appendix 3, Cohen tracks the historical answers to the primary question from the earliest one listed, in 1679, to the year 1994. Estimates range from the very small (500 million people, by Ehrlich) to the very large (a billion, obtained by assuming that heat removal is the only limitation — resulting in a population of around 500 people per square meter and an outer skin temperature of the structures containing those people of 2000 degrees Celsius). Over the years most estimate variation was due to the limited scientific knowledge available to earlier prognosticators, and to widely varying assumptions regarding what physical or biological factor forces the limitation.

How will people live at the maximum? Will they all live at similar standards of living, or will this vary widely, as is currently the case? What is the most important failure seen as ultimately limiting human populations? Is it loss of food, energy, or waste repositories? Or does the limit come from the spreading of killer diseases? Perhaps it comes from annihilation following global thermonuclear war resulting from the inability of too many people to live peacefully together on a planet of finite resources.

Assumptions are necessary whenever we predict the future. Many believe we don't have to look into the future to see that the problem is already out of hand. Only personal observation is needed for that. For future projections, however, we need to make the best possible educated guess concerning the future consequences of projected changes in policy, behavior, and/or environmental effects.

Ecologist and Agronomist David Pimentel of Cornell wrote a short article on the subject[12]. He made a fundamental assumption that all the people in the world had the 1999 average standard of living in the United States. His estimate called for a substantial *reduction* in the current human population, indicating that the Earth's carrying capacity is inadequate to support the current world population at the present U.S. affluence level. His numerical estimate for the Earth's carrying capacity came out to be from 1 to 2 billion people. This is similar to Wackernagle's conclusion that to support the current human population at North America affluence would require three Earths. (2 billion being a third of the 6 billion 1999 world population.)

Abernethy reaches a similar conclusion: "It is small wonder that numerous students of carrying capacity, working independently, conclude that the sustainable world population, one that uses much less energy per capita than is common in today's industrialized countries, is in the neighborhood of 2 to 3 billion persons. Note the congruence with Watt's projection of rapidly declining population size near the end of the Oil Interval. The absence of cheap, versatile, and easily used sources of energy, and other resources, seems likely to change the quality of human life and may even change, for many, the odds of survival."[13]

Since current world population is around 6.4 billion, the obvious question is how are we currently supporting such a larger population than Pimentel's estimate? The answer is that most of those 6.4 billion people have a much lower standard of living than the one assumed by Pimentel in his projection. In addition, temporary sources of energy are supporting populations, which cannot be supported within their borders once these energy sources are depleted. (Any estimate of long-term, maximum supportable human numbers must assume the absence of substantial quantities of fossil fuel resources.

(This topic is discussed in the next chapter on energy.)

A substantial increase in human population above the current 6 billion-plus mark, as the UN projects, might be possible, but only: (1) at the expense of other life-forms with which humans compete but on which humans also depend, (2) by lowering the overall material standard of living (and ecological impact) of the current human population, or (3) by finding a way to reduce human impact on other life forms while human population and affluence continue to grow. The last of these alternatives can only be considered wishful thinking, a radically non-conservative philosophy repeating what a few misguided economists have said: the human mind can *always* invent some technological solution to future problems; therefore we should not worry about them so much.

Even if this were true — even if we *could* find a way, for example, to rocket billions of people off the planet — the time lag needed to accomplish that monumental feat merely ensures that millions or billions will die prematurely and suffer before the "solution" is found.

As mentioned in Chapter 1, the first of these alternatives was put another way by Dr. Alan Thornhill when he said that we are systematically converting non-human biomass into human biomass.[14] The obvious conclusion is that at some point there will be insufficient non-human biomass to sustain human life. Many other life-support systems will break down, possibly irreversibly, before we reach this point. In certain regions, this turning point has already been reached and millions of people are starving for lack of food within their own local growing regions.

Affluence and Technology

Clearly the number of people the Earth can support has ultimate physical limits. Finding an exact value for the upper limit of human numbers on Earth is a very slippery slope. One thing is clear, though; the number depends very much on two variables, one easy to define, and the other illusory.

The first variable is the affluence level of the people "supported" by the Earth. We Americans know a lot about affluence Our environmental organizations spend a great deal of time *trying* to reduce the environmental impacts of the consequences of our per capita affluence, through better, less polluting technology (and more efficient energy consumption), as well as through some lifestyle changes, such as recycling and improved business practices. It is important to note, as my colleague Paul Jindra pointed out to me, that efficiency is just a multiplier. No matter how "efficient" our energy-consuming processes are, the Earth still gets consumed. With continued growth of population and affluence, and with overall consumption out-stripping energy conservation, "energy efficiency, by itself, is a false god," he says.

The second variable is more difficult to pin down. It has to do with the future of technology and new sources of energy to support an expanding population with expanding affluence. Those less concerned about population limits tend to believe that we can "technologize" our way out of *any* problem, no matter how large the scale. This is another way of saying, "The engineers will save us." So this second variable has to do with how benign and how rapid the "technologizing" process can be over the next several decades, in support of the increasing numbers of people with increased affluence. Opponents of this "salvation-through-science-and-technology" approach say that no human technology can replace a species that is lost through so-called "human advancement."

Added to this second variable, and to some extent part of it, is the question of human adaptability. Can we be relatively happy and content as a species with fewer other species in the "natural" world and with declines in green spaces? Can we be happy in a world without lions, tigers, gopher tortoises, elephants, whales, and all the other currently endangered species?

Perhaps parks can be set aside to ensure access to areas of seemingly unspoiled beauty, where at least the few remaining humans so inclined can have a relatively traditional outdoor camping experience. Consider the vision of some inventive Japanese who created an indoor ski slope not far from Tokyo, so skiers don't have to travel great distances to go snow skiing. They can do it year round, indoors. When the real ski slopes are gone, will humanity be satisfied with only artificial facsimiles? If Everglades National Park is gone, will we be satisfied with accounts of it in museums and old videos, or Disney World imitations?

When we try to make intelligent estimates of the maximum number of people who can live sustainably on Earth, we see how difficult it is to pin down an exact number. Perhaps we shouldn't even try. Bartlett issues the following challenge:[15,16]

> Can you think of any problem, on any scale, from microscopic to global?
> Whose *long-term* solution is in any *demonstrable* way,
> Aided, assisted, or advanced, by having larger populations
> At the local level, the state level, the national level, or globally?

How many People *Should* the Earth Support?

The human life-support system is very complex. A wide range of assumptions must be made to produce an estimated maximum population figure. Considering the options, it's not so much a matter of how many people the Earth can support as how many it *should* support.

Some of the larger estimates of carrying capacity ignore human rights, biodiversity, and aesthetic appreciations of natural beauty, considering humans only as mindless animals consuming food. Let's put these variables back into the equation and ask how many the Earth can support *then* at various levels of human affluence.

Pimentel estimated that the Earth could support from 1 to 2 billion people with an American standard of living, good health, nutrition, prosperity, personal dignity, and freedom. Using his two billion figure as the benchmark, several additional estimates of population limits can be offered.

Accurate numbers for each of these possible scenarios, or assumptions concerning living conditions, are very difficult to acquire. What follows results from no original research in exploring the topic. It is only offered as food for thought. For more detailed knowledge, consult Cohen's book[11].

Few rational people would claim that the Earth could support a population density of one person per square meter of land area, a population of some 140,000 billion people. Where would you grow the food? Short of that absurd limit, let us consider somewhat more reasonable estimates. These are crude estimates only, intended to provoke thought and illustrate the difficulties of determining good future predictions.

Each of these conjectures assumes that the current process of depleting fossil fuels has continued to near completion. No fossil fuels are left, except for a small stock, priced high, and used only for limited durable goods such as essential new plastic production. We begin with Pimentel's figure.[a]

1. Everyone at the current U.S. standard of living and with American health, nutrition, personal dignity and, including enforcement of current environmental protection laws — 2 billion[12]

---

[a]Though we are starting with Pimentel's figure it is important to note that other scientists, using similar assumptions get much smaller figures. For example, according to Dbholakia and Wackernagle the ecological footprint of the typical American lifestyle is 25 acres per capita. Robert Adams divided this number into the total available land area of Earth (excluding Greenland and Antarctica) to get "about 600 million as the number of humans that can inhabit the planet (sustainably and in comfort, living the typical American lifestyle). This calculation devotes 50 percent of the land area to other species, a figure considered reasonable by a consensus of wildlife biologists."

2. Everyone at the same affluence level as in 1, but with few restrictions on commerce, pollution, land use, personal behavior (within current law), etc. To accommodate the resultant increased environmental impact, the population must be reduced. It is basically a libertarian, laissez faire economy, with only limited environmental restrictions. This indicates a population price to pay for the current American way of commerce. — 0.5 billion

3. Everyone at the same affluence as indicated in 1, but with many and onerous restrictions on freedoms relative to behaviors leading to environmental degradation. In order to accommodate population levels greater than 2 billion, restrictions such as the following would have to be instituted: Massive recycling. Driving restrictions. Limitations on the transport of food (food transported no more than 100 miles for example to its point of retail sale). Prohibitions against cutting of trees on one's property. Prohibitions on the burning of fossil fuels, in order to save these complex molecules for more valuable or durable uses, such as in the manufacture of plastics and pharmaceuticals, and to avoid the emission of combustion products. Limitations on the areas of open spaces that can be converted to renewable energy power plants, such as solar thermal, solar photovoltaic, and wind energy systems. (This latter results from the need to preserve natural areas for atmospheric oxygen generation, wildlife habitat, and food growing.) Of course, many rooftops can accept solar energy systems and this scenario basically assumes a substantial coverage of rooftops for solar energy production. — 4 billion

4. Only people in the U.S. and Europe at current level of affluence. Everyone else at the current prosperity of Mexico. — 6 billion

5. Everyone in the world at Mexico's current prosperity level. — 10 billion

6. Everyone in the world at the current "prosperity" level of Northwest Africa.— 20-40 billion

The current world population is around 6.4 billion. Some say we have already exceeded the Earth's ability to sustain this many people when our coal, oil, and natural gas run out. They say that for nuclear energy to fill in the gap, humanity would have to accept the sizeable risks associated with massive construction of nuclear power plants and storage of radioactive wastes; to them, this risk is too great. Others say we still have a way to go before we reach our limits, pointing to solar energy and radical energy efficiency as our savior when fossil fuels all but run out.

What Kind of World?

When we try to answer the question of how many people the Earth can support, we come to an inescapable conclusion: the answer can only be the counter question, "What kind of world do we *want*?" If we want a world where citizens in the industrialized countries can continue living pretty much as they are, everyone else staying the same, then global human population is likely to be substantially less than it is now. If we wish to keep the current developed world standard of living where it is, while allowing the rest of the world to grow substantially in numbers, the consequence is to doom much of that "other world" to perpetual misery and lost expectations, while holding on to the industrialized way of life as desperately as possible. Such a scenario is likely to mean a sizable population crash, as limits are surpassed.

This is not a world most of us would care to see. One response would be to work at *reducing* the number of humans living on Earth. This can be done peacefully by conscious human action, or involuntarily, as is happening currently in Zimbabwe, with its 25% level of AIDS infection. (A quarter of the adult population is infected. Up to a fifth of the country's children have lost at least one parent to the disease.)

To a great extent, the arguments concerning maximum sustainable populations are beside the point. Do we really need to have a specific number to see that current world population is unsustainable in the long run?

Some say that we must start thinking less about how many people the Earth *can* support and focus more on how many it should support. Using a more ecocentric definition, what would be a desirable number of humans for the planet, rather than just how many we might be able to cram into it on a hopefully "sustainable" basis? With a substantially reduced and stable world human population, say ten *million* people or so, we could clearly expand a degree of material affluence to all nations. We would then worry less about technological fixes to our environmental problems — because the magnitude of those problems would be greatly reduced and, by and large, manageable by the huge biosphere.

Stopping Population Growth

Much can be said for a reduced human population. A major reduction would provide greater freedom. People liking high density could live in well-designed cities. Others could live in the new wildernesses that would return to Earth, in abundance, after a time. Non-toxic wastes could be discarded easily, or transported some distance from human contact. Recycling could be minimized. Pollution and habitat losses caused by humans could easily be absorbed by the Earth without great or permanent impact (except for a need to protect habitat for already endangered species until that habitat could spread sufficiently to make the species viable again).

If this scenario disgusts one's sense of respect for nature, we could employ present knowledge about reducing pollution, operating energy devices efficiently, and using solar energy as much as possible, saving fossil fuels for more durable, long term uses. This strategy might create a stable population of several hundred million humans for a few million years. Six *thousand* million people (6 billion), however, appears unsustainable.

Writing in 1991 the Ehrlichs began the Preface to their book *The Population Explosion*[1, p. 9] with these words [b]:

> In 1968, *The Population Bomb* warned of impending disaster if the population explosion was not brought under control. Then the fuse was burning; now the population bomb has detonated. Since 1968, at least 200 million people—mostly children—have perished needlessly of hunger and hunger-related diseases, despite "crash programs to 'stretch' the carrying capacity of Earth by increasing food production."

Thus the "die off" of human numbers has already started in some regions, just as we remain on the upslope in others. In a more personal perspective, the Ehrlichs start chapter 1 of their book with these paragraphs:[1, p. 13-14]

> In the early 1930s, when we were born, the world population was just 2 billion; now it is more than two and a half times as large and still growing rapidly. [They cite the 1989 World Population Data Sheet, issued by the

---

[b]Ehrlich, P., *The Population Bomb*. Explanation: "The mortality estimate is based primarily on information from UNICEF, WHO, and other sources on infant/child mortality and may be conservative. For example, it is now estimated that 40,000 children die daily (14.6 million a year) from hunger-related diseases, according to *International Health News*, September 1987. The number 'at least 200 million' is based on an average of 10 million deaths annually for 21 years."

Population Reference Bureau, 1875 Connecticut Ave. NW, Washington, D.C. 20009.] The population of the United States is increasing much more slowly than the world average, but it has more than doubled in only six decades from 120 million in 1928 to 250 million in 1990. Such a huge population expansion within two or three generations can by itself account for a great many changes in the social and economic institutions of a society. It is also very frightening to those of us who spend our lives trying to keep track of the implications of the population explosion.

One of the toughest things for a population biologist to reconcile is the contrast between his or her recognition that civilization is in imminent serious jeopardy and the modest level of concern that population issues generate among the public and even among elected officials.

Much of the reason for this discrepancy lies in the slow development of the problem. People aren't scared because they evolved biologically and culturally to respond to short-term "fires" and to tune out long-term "trends" over which they had no control. Only if we do what doesn't come naturally — if we determinedly focus on what seem to be gradual or nearly imperceptible changes — can the outlines of our predicament be perceived clearly enough to be frightening.

Unavoidably, we need to stop population growth worldwide (and in the developed countries, if only as examples for the rest of the world). Even if the overall fertility level were instantly reduced today to the replacement level of a little over two children per family, on the average, the large number of females below childbearing age would continue to increase world population for at least a couple more decades. Achieving instant replacement level fertility worldwide might be a nice idea, but it is an unrealistic one. The steamroller of population growth is moving down the slope. Only crash programs can bring it to a halt in our lifetimes.

Milbrath writes:[17, p. 327]

It is imperative for people to learn to limit the size of their families. This would reduce the demand for resources, reduce the need to displace other species from their habitats, reduce the waste load imposed on ecosystems, and reduce crowding, congestion, and competition in human settlements. A dense human population cannot live gently on the Earth.

Many informed scientists and scholars have written and spoken about the dangers of increasing human population. A glimpse into the kind of world that will result if we continue our current path and policies was provided by Jim Motavelli.[2]

Even though populations are declining in Europe, immigration levels are a source of conflict for some sectors of the population. Germany, for instance, had seven million foreign-born residents in 1997, and 4.7 million unemployed. The scapegoating of immigrants for high unemployment was axiomatic.

Despite the contractions in Europe, world population overall grows by 78 million a year, approximately the combined populations of France, Greece and Sweden combined, or a city the size of San Francisco every three days. This great growth, driven in particular by high fertility rates (above seven children per family) in parts of Africa, is accompanied by the annual loss of 27,000 species of animals and plants.

According to Peter Ward of Washington University, "Every forest, every valley, every bit of land surface capable of sustaining plant life, as well as much of the plankton in the sea, will have to be turned over to crops if our species is to avert unprecedented global famine." He adds, "In such a world, animals and plants not directly necessary for our existence will probably be a luxury not affordable."

Controlling world population growth is a generally desired goal, but one that seems always illusory. Ishmael says that[18, p.137] "Global population control is always something that's going to happen in the future. It was something that was *going* to happen in the future when you were three billion in 1960. Now, when you're five billion [in 1992], it's still something that's going to happen in the future ... Mother Culture talks out of both sides of her mouth on this issue. When you say to her *population explosion* she replies *increased food production*. But as it happens, increased food production is an annual event and global population control is an event that never happens at all.

"Within your culture as a whole, there is in fact no significant thrust toward global population control. The point to see is that there never will be such a thrust so long as you're enacting a story that says the gods made the world for man. For as long as you enact that story, Mother Culture will demand increased food production today—and promise population control tomorrow....

"At present there are five and a half billion of you here, and, though millions of you are starving, you're producing enough food to feed six billion. And *because* you're producing enough food to feed six billion, it's a biological certainty that in three or four years there will be six billion of you. By that time, however (even though millions of you will still be starving), you'll be producing enough food for six and a half billion — which means that in another three or four years there *will be* six and a half billion. But by that time you'll be producing enough food for seven billion (even though millions of you will be starving), which again means that in another three or four years there *will be* seven billion of you. In order to halt this process, you must face the fact that increasing food production doesn't feed your hungry, it only fuels your population explosion."[18, p. 139]

Immigration

Affluent nations, such as Germany, France, Norway, Finland, Great Britain, and the United States have experienced declining fertilities. On the other hand, many people in these nations are working harder than ever before, and growing numbers of women are entering the workforce. However, the population of some of these countries is rising anyway, due to immigration. The number of people entering the country from abroad exceeds the number leaving each year, in some cases by a wide margin.

In spite of tendencies toward declining fertility in the U.S., its population is actually increasing, at a rate slightly over 1%, a doubling time of less than 70 years. The causes of this population growth are both the high rate of immigration and increased fertility rates in the foreign-born population. The Center for Immigration Studies reports that immigration and U.S. births to immigrants accounted for seventy percent of U.S. population growth during the 1990s.[19] Others suggest a somewhat lower fraction is attributable to immigration.

In the year 1999, world population reached 6 billion and the U.S. found itself with 275 million people. Much of the growth in the U.S. over the last decade has been from direct immigration [c] and higher fertility rates for first generation immigrants[20]. This is partially the result of a change in U.S. immigration policy starting about 1966. Prior to this year, legal immigration was set at approximately 230,000 per year, near to the replacement level. In 1989 it was closer to half a million new citizens a year. Another change in

---

[c]U.S. population growth in the 90s was 25,572,000 of which 11,206,000 were 90s immigrants, or 44%. Adding to these the births to immigrants in the 1990s adds 1,663,000 more, for a total of 50%. Adding to these births to all foreign-born women during the 90s adds 6,398,000, for a total of 69%. Source: Steven A. Camarota, Center for Immigration Studies, Backgrounder, January 2001, Table 6. Each month the Census Bureau conducts the Current Population Survey (CPS), the primary purpose of which is to collect employment data. The March CPS includes an extra-large sample of Hispanics and is considered the best source for information on persons born outside of the United States — referred to as foreign-born by the

immigration law in 1990 increased immigration-related growth to around 1,000,000 per year. With this growth, the U.S. Census Bureau projects a population of a billion people in the U.S. by 2100. As of this writing, additional governmental action was being contemplated that would increase further the level of U.S. immigration, adding to U.S. population growth. The rate of population growth in the U.S. and other developed nations seems unlikely to decrease without legislation to halt mass immigration.

Since the U.S. has the highest per capita environmental impact of any nation on Earth, stopping U.S. population growth seems important. Most of this growth currently comes from a high immigration level. Reducing that level from the current approximately 1 million per year to the historic "replacement level" of around 230,000 per year would appear appropriate.

Such a proposal does not call for stopping all immigration, nor can it be considered "immigrant bashing," as some have suggested. It is merely a logical and appropriate response to the current high, adverse impact of the U.S. on the world environment and a desire to reduce that impact. Nothing in the proposal suggests anything is wrong with the current rich mixture of races and ethnic groups in the country, nor with the cultural diversity that have characterized America from its earliest beginnings.

Population Controversy

Though the arguments offered above are based on solid evidence, though most scientists agree to the need for stopping population growth (some call for making it negative for a while), and though most of us have painful experiences of the adverse consequences of unsustainable population growth, the subject has become controversial of late. This is astonishing to those who experienced and participated in the environmental reform movement of the 70s, guided in part by Paul Ehrlich's now classic *The Population Bomb*[21].

The source of the controversy seems two-fold. First is a concern for the rights of people to have children and a desire to keep governments out

Census Bureau, though for the purposes of this report, foreign-born and immigrant are used synonymously. Analysis of the March 2000 CPS done by the Center for Immigration Studies indicates that 28.4 million immigrants now live in the United States, the largest number ever recorded in the nation's history, and a 43 percent increase since 1990. As a percentage of the population, immigrants now account for more than one in 10 residents (10.4 percent), the highest percentage in 70 years. Immigration has become the determinate factor in population growth. The 11.2 million immigrants who indicated they arrived between 1990 and 2000 plus the 6.4

of the personal business of deciding how many children they want to have.

Second is an abhorrence by some to the notion of immigration restrictions. This seems motivated by the issue of human rights, by a desire to protect the rights of people to seek a better life, and to escape economically and politically difficult conditions. Those of us who see the truth and logic in this have no beef with the immigrants themselves, and we value their different points of view and the richness of their cultures. The problem is solely with the U.S. government policy on the numbers of permitted immigrants, not the immigrants themselves. Many recent immigrants share this view. Once they have been well assimilated into our society they see the adverse consequences of the high immigration levels permitted when they arrived in America. Some resent the competition from more recent immigrants, competing for the relatively low-wage jobs available to them. Allowing record high rates of immigration, adding more contributors to the most polluting country on Earth, seems to many an exercise in monumental bad judgment.

There is nothing inherently wrong with the immigrants' desire to have a better life, assuming there are no physical limits to population growth in a country or the world. But there *are* limits. To promote continued growth on a finite planet is like living in a never never world of dreams and idyll thoughts, unconnected to reality. In some respects the argument seems like the protestations of an immature child, throwing a tantrum to get what he cannot have. There are limits in life, and responsible people face them and deal with them.

The summer 2002 issue of *onearth*, published by the Natural Resources Defense Council contained an article "When Hate Goes Green" (by Michael Rivlin) that so incensed ardent environmentalist Bill Partington that he wrote NRDC to complain.[22] He cited Garrett Hardin's classic paper, "The Tragedy of the Commons," saying that "people acting reasonably in their own behalf will overwhelm resources that support them, resulting in tragedies for everyone." Partington lives in central Florida and particularizes his argument:

> In Florida we have among the most frightening examples of uncontrolled growth in the world and you'll have a hell of a time telling us that immigration isn't a major cause. Where do you think they're coming from, storks? They're immigrating not just from Latin America, Asia and every other land; they're also crowding in from North America. Those who can are moving to Central Florida from South Florida. They're mostly very nice people; like babies they're individually lovable but collectively terrifying....
>
> Newcomers don't know what's been lost; they never saw the original. Some say Florida's a lost cause. But it's like drowning — you try to do SOMETHING to the end.

Population Denial

The late Garrett Hardin, one of the leading thinkers and writers on the problems of human overpopulation became so distressed with widespread denial of the seriousness of the population crisis that he wrote a book about it, which he began as follows[23]:

> We know that the tale of the ostrich that buries its head in the sand is mythical, a myth that is both ancient and confusing. In the 1st century A.D., Pliny the Elder said that the stupid ostrich thrusts its head and neck into a bush, imagining "that the whole of the body is concealed."[d] Not until the 14th century was sand substituted for the bush: the altered version endured to the present (though only as a myth, not as natural history).... When a whole culture responds this way, it is said to be in the grip of a *taboo*, to use a term brought from the South Seas by Captain James Cook in 1777.... Adults who indulge in ostrichism can be said to be observing a taboo, which closes off the search for causes. The taboo now laid on the subject of human population growth is far from total, but it does inhibit the search for causes.

We cannot have unlimited population growth. Acting as if we could diverts the argument from the real issues into subsidiary ones — "red herrings." It is good to protect human rights. But not all "rights" can be protected. A responsible discussion of this issue must deal with the protection of the "rights" of the unborn — of future populations — to a viable and sustainable planet on which to live.

Of course, we should protect rights and freedoms as much as possible, but unlimited growth must stop, either sooner by design, or later by the force of Nature. We should focus on rights which are appropriate and which support sustainability. But by overpopulating the planet we are removing options, limiting our alternatives. If we are unsuccessful, some day we may even reach the point of seeing government-imposed fertility restrictions, as has been attempted with some success in China. The enforced "stop at one" China policy, started in 1979, has resulted in some unfortunate consequences[e]. In the long term, biologically irresponsible people ultimately must suffer the logical consequences of their irresponsibilities.

---

[d]See J. A Bierens de Haan, "On the Ostrich Which Puts its Head in the Sand in Case of Danger, or: the History of a Legend," *Ardea*, 32:11-24, 1943.

[e]China has little land left for new agriculture. In 1979 it decided it was necessary to constrain fertility. The resulting one-child policy resulted in a large number of coerced abortions. Parents have been known to abandon or kill girl babies because

Population and Freedom

Population growth creates a loss of the one thing pro-growth advocates seem to value most: freedom. As alluded to previously, increasing population density causes restrictions on behavior and freedom. Loss of freedom is an inevitable consequence of population growth[16,24]. Here's how it works.

As more and more people are crammed into any space, conflicts between them multiply. At some point rules of behavior must be imposed, by general consent, to minimize the adverse consequences of these conflicts. These losses of freedom are stimulated by Nature in some cases, and by forward-looking governments in others.

In Nature, when a species of animal exceeds the local food supply, the animals are weakened, more prone to diseases and predators; soon the population dies back, depriving the animals of the "freedoms" of health and a full life-expectancy. In the human world, overpopulation can have adverse psychological effects and ultimately also can produce die-offs, like those currently being experienced in Africa.

Government imposes many limitations on behavior and freedom. Nearly all result from population growth. This is easy to understand. For example, a sparsely populated region of Brazil can have very lax traffic laws and few traffic lights, but this is far from possible during rush hour in midtown Rio de Janeiro.

If few automobiles use sparsely populated roads, freedom of movement is nearly maximum. You are free to drive where you want, when you want, by whatever route you like, and at nearly any speed you want. You don't have to stop at intersections nor slow for school zones (because there are no cars approaching intersections and there are no schools needing school zones). But in a densely populated area with many vehicles and an abundance of people, laws have to be passed to protect the safety of everyone. No longer can you drive anywhere you want, at whatever time you want, or by just any route. You certainly cannot drive at very high speeds. Gates and fences and exclusion zones limit your destinations. Your routes are limited by bumper-to-bumper traffic, increasing your driving time considerably, and annoyingly. To reduce driving time, many people start their trip much earlier or later to avoid gridlock.

boy babies are favored. About a third of Chinese women are now sterile, owing to the ubiquitous, coerced implantation of ghastly steel-ring IUDs. Some peasant women were subjected, in government clinics, to lower-quality reproductive care than that which American livestock receives. Ref.: "TRB From Washington: Inconceivable" by Gregg Easterbrook, *The New Republic*, November 23, 1998.

Besides the natural or physical limitations imposed by crowded streets, governments intervene with traffic laws and stop lights, all intended to reduce our freedoms of movement.

Any rules of behavior represent, in principle, losses of freedom. If we want to maintain maximum freedom, we need to maintain minimum population. Of course, being social animals, humans don't wish to be isolated and reduced to tiny populations of individuals having nearly total freedom. We prefer a more reasonable compromise: having enough people to support viable community goals with the concomitant modest losses of freedom versus having too many people and the consequential too many rules and restrictions. For many of us, the most crowded regions of the world today have gone way past acceptable limits, and must be reduced, to restore freedom and liberty.

In 1989 Bill Moyers interviewed the amazing thinker and prolific author Isaac Asimov, asking him what happens to the dignity of the human species if population growth continues. The response:

> It will be completely destroyed. I like to use what I call my bathroom metaphor: If two people live in an apartment, and there are two bathrooms, then both have freedom of the bathroom. You can go to the bathroom anytime you want, stay as long as you want, for whatever you need, and everyone believes in Freedom of the Bathroom; It should be right there in the Constitution. But if you have twenty people in the apartment and two bathrooms, then no matter how much every person believes in Freedom of the Bathroom, there's no such thing. You have to set up times for each person; you have to bang on the door, "Aren't you through yet?" and so on.
>
> In the same way, democracy cannot survive overpopulation. Human dignity cannot survive. Convenience and decency cannot survive. As you put more and more people into the world, the value of life not only declines, it disappears. It doesn't matter if somebody dies, the more people there are, the less one individual matters[25].

That wonderful individuality so prized by most will be a thing of the past if we allow our population to continue growing. It is possible to use technology to partially ameliorate these losses of freedom, as when we use earphones to listen to loud music in order not to disturb the people in adjacent apartments. However, there is still a loss, since we no longer have the freedom to play the regular stereo as loud as we want at whatever time we want.

This loss of freedom is not something done by ideology or by people trying to make life difficult for us; it is much more fundamental than that. It results from the physical compression of people into smaller and smaller spaces, or, more accurately, the filling of limited spaces with more and more people.

Bartlett details more of the ways that overpopulation destroys freedom and individual liberty[16]. One is controversial:

> The actions of local public bodies to establish zoning and land-use regulations such as urban growth boundaries, are driven by population growth, yet these actions, which are made necessary by population growth, are clear infringements of individual freedoms. People, angered by these losses of freedoms, advocate passage of "Takings Laws" in an attempt to stem the loss of freedoms, but unfortunately neither the takings laws nor their advocates make any recognition of the fact that it is population growth which triggers the actions that take away treasured freedoms. Ironically, the persons who complain most loudly about these losses of freedom are often those who advocate continued population growth for the self-serving reason that they profit personally from it. People's eagerness to profit from population growth is beautifully explained in Garrett Hardin's essay, "The Tragedy of the Commons"[26].

The idea of government, acting on behalf of the people, determining what you can and cannot do with your land, incites many to rage. But government is merely doing what it must to protect the greater welfare of the people (except in rare cases of collusion for profit and other illegalities). You are not free to shoot firearms in a crowded subdivision, to start a fire in your woods during intense droughts, dump toxic chemicals into the stream flowing through your property, nor remove habitat of endangered species. These limitations of "property rights" imposed by governments are direct consequences of overpopulation.

If population growth continues unabated, then you can forget the Bill of Rights. This was pointed out by Boyd Wilcox in his article, "March 27, 1999: On the anniversary of the Rockefeller Report, Overpopulation Dilutes Democracy"[27]. Wilcox writes:

> One need not pander to Malthusian or apocalyptic thinking to ask in all seriousness whether the biosphere can survive another century like this one. Arguably, it is not biological survival of the human species that is in danger so much as it is the moral or spiritual survival of what it means to be human and to be part of a complex living community. We cannot count the ways in which human identity, imagination, and esthetic appreciation depend on the richly textured landscape of nonhuman nature. What but unbridled hubris could let us think that what we consider human nature will survive if we despoil all of nonhuman nature?

In Jonathon Porritt's penetrating book *Save the Earth*[28], he points out, "In the majority of large Third World cities, over 70 percent of all new housing is constructed 'illegally' on unofficial settlement areas. In some cities the figure can be as high as 95 percent." This exercise leads to Paul Jindra's conclusion[29] that "Ultimately, there is no such thing as the rule of law, only the rule of numbers." By this he means that as the population grows, freedoms of behavior and choice, and niceties such as human rights, take a back seat to more primordial struggles of humans to survive, by whatever means possible. Social niceties such as "legality" are washed away by the overwhelming rule of numbers.

Haves and Have Nots

The dichotomy between the "haves" and the "have-nots" is particularly acute when it is the haves most in favor of stopping population growth and the have nots who are either less concerned or less able to deal with the problem. The developed world is in the best position to initiate and carry out change, but the less developed world often resents "solutions" imposed from the outside.

The developed world has demonstrated its inability to care for the natural one. At least in the U.S., we still are growing, mostly as a result of government policy to permit higher levels of legal and illegal immigration than in the past. Many developed countries have taken the resources of undeveloped ones without adequate payment or other restitution. It is not surprising then if an underdeveloped country is suspicious of anything the developed world might offer to "help" it.

Fortunately, the United Nations, with most countries of the world as members (including haves and have-nots), has a fairly aggressive reproductive health program worldwide. Information, education, and materials are offered to help people limit family sizes and live well with the children they do have. Decreasing infant mortality alone goes a long way toward lowering fertility, in addition to the other factors described previously.

This is one way the developed world can provide assistance while shielding itself from accusations that it is telling the less developed ones what to do. Funneling aid through the United Nations, which represents all countries, in principle, allows all nations to be decision-makers. Even this may not be sufficient, however, if the underdeveloped world views the UN as dominated by the industrialized countries.

The UN Population Fund (UNFPA) and the UN Population Information Network have active programs to help countries control runaway population growth and to assess the causes of this growth. In releasing its "The State of World Population 2000" report, UNFPA Executive Director Dr. Nafis Sadik said, "Millions of women are denied reproductive choices and access to health care, contributing each year to 80 million unwanted or mistimed pregnancies and some 500,000 preventable pregnancy-related deaths. Nearly half of all deliveries in developing countries take place without a skilled birth attendant present." Such problems must be overcome if there is any hope of stopping world population growth.

Conclusions

The point of this chapter is to clarify that if we wish to grow the world population to the UN projection[30, Fig. 1, p. 6] of somewhere between 8 and 13 billion near the middle of this century (still larger by its end), such growth will come at the expense of much that we hold dear. The planned industrial development of underdeveloped countries — mostly toward the disastrous U.S. model — will inevitably lead to increased stress on critical biological, chemical, and physical systems important to human survival.

The choice of which path to take into the Brave New World is ours, as a species, to make. We can proceed blindly growing, as we now are, and allow diseases like AIDS, wars, pollution-related illnesses, and lowered fertility rates (due to the declining prospects of women) to reduce the most rapidly growing populations without affecting the developed nations. We have to acknowledge, however, that such a philosophy is not a compassionate one and says something we might not like to say about the kind of world we want for our fellow humans.

Due to transportation and communication technologies, such an isolationist position probably cannot really insulate us from the terrible consequences of this type of policy. Diseases spreading like wildfire over one continent are not likely to remain there.

Alternatively, we can take conscious steps now and become true to the special "gift" of intelligence that has come to us beyond all other species. We can use that intelligence to reduce our numbers, and provide a better future for all. The choice is ours to make. Education and dedication are required first steps.

References

1. Paul R. Ehrlich and Anne H. Ehrlich. *The Population Explosion*. 1st Touchstone, 1991 ed. Touchstone, Simon & Schuster: New York, 1991, 320 pp. Note: Touchstone Books, 1999, ISBN 0671732943.

2. Jim Motavelli. "Balancing Act." *E-Magazine*, (2000): November/December, 27-33.

3. G. Tyler Miller. From *Environmental Science: An Introduction*, 2nd edition by Miller. © 1988. Excerpted with permission of Brooks/Cole, a division of Thomson Learning: www.thomsonrights.com. Fax 800 730-2215.

4. Albert A. Bartlett. "The Massive Movement to Marginalize the Modern Malthusian Message." *The Social Contract*, 316.5 East Mitchell St., Petoskey, MI, 49770. Vol. 8, no. 3 (1998): Spring 1998, 239-251. soccon@freeway.net

5. Daniel Quinn. "Comments on food and population," (e-mail), 2001, to Ross McCluney, Thursday, December 20, 2001 8:57 AM.

6. William E. Rees "Eco Footprint analysis," (e-mail message), 2003, to Ross McCluney, 29 May 2003.

7. WWF. "Living Planet Report 2002." *World Wide Fund For Nature (and others)* Gland, Switzerland.

8. A. A. Bartlett. "Forgotten Fundamentals of the Energy Crisis." *Am. J. Phys.* Vol. 46, no. 9 (1978): November, 876-888. Note: *Jour. Geol. Ed.*, vol 28, 1980, pp. 4-35, Proceedings, Nat. Regulatory Conf. on Renewable Energy, Savannah, GA 3-6 Oct. 1993, NARUC, Room 1102, ICC Bldg., Washington, DC 20044. A later version of his writing on this subject "Reflections on Sustainability, Population Growth, and the Environment - Revisited" *Population & Environment*, Vol. 16, No. 1, September 1994, pp. 5-35. Revised version: *Renewable Resources Journal*, Vol. 15, No. 4, Winter 1997 - 98, Pgs. 6 - 23. Also in Focus, Vol. 9, No. 1, 1999, Pgs. 49 - 68, Carrying Capacity Network, 2000 P Street, NW, Washington D.C. 20036-5915.

9. Donella Meadows, Dennis Meadows, Jorgen Rangers, and William Behrens. *The Limits to Growth*. Earth Island: London,1972.

10. Paul B. MacCready. "Unleashing Creativity," in *Symposium on The Inventor and Society*, Jerome and Dorothy Lamelson Center for the Study of Invention and Innovation, Smithsonian National Museum of American History, 1995.

11. Joel E. Cohen. *How Many People Can The Earth Support?* W. W. Norton & Co.: New York,1995, 532 pp.

12. David Pimentel. "How many people can the Earth support?" *Population Press* Vol. 5, no. 3 (1999): March/April 1999. Note: Available at www.popco.org. Click on "Population Press" and "Newsletters & Publications" then look under the heading for the April 1999 issue.

13. Virginia Deane Abernethy. "Population and Environment: Assumptions, Interpretation, and Other Reasons for Confusion." In *Where Next: Reflections on the Human Future*, edited by Duncan Poore. Board of Trustees, Royal Botanical Garden, Kew: London, 2000.

14. Daniel Quinn and Alan Thornhill. "Food Production and Population Growth video tape." New Tribal Ventures: Houston, TX, Video tape, VHS, Performers: Daniel Quinn and Paul Thornhill.

15. Albert A. Bartlett. "Is there a population problem?" *Wild Earth* Vol. 7, no. 3 (1997), 88-90.

16. Albert A. Bartlett. "Democracy Cannot Survive Overpopulation." *Population and Environment: A Journal of Interdisciplinary Studies* Vol. 22, no. 1 (2000): September 2000, 63-71.

17. Lester W. Milbrath. *Envisioning a Sustainable Society*. State University of New York Press: Albany, NY, 1989, 403 pp.

18. Daniel Quinn. *Ishmael*. 1st ed. Bantam/Turner: New York, 1992.

19. Stephen A. Camarota, "Immigrants in the United States — 1998 A Snapshot of America's Foreign-born Population," 1999 Backgrounder, *Center for Immigration Studies*, January, Washington, DC.

20. Stephen A. Camarota, "Immigrants in the United States — 2000 A Snapshot of America's Foreign-Born Population Backgrounder Report 2001," *Center for Immigration Studies*, January 2001, Washington, D.C.

21. Paul R. Ehrlich. *The Population Bomb*. 1st ed., 8th printing Oct., 1969. Ballantine Books, Inc.: New York,1968, 223 pp.

22. William M. Partington. Letter concerning a Summer 2002 article "When Hate Goes Green" in *onearth* by Michael A. Rivlin, (Letter), 2002, to President Mr. John H. Adams, NRDC, 1 July 2002.

23. Garrett Hardin. *The Ostrich Factor: Our Population Myopia*. Oxford University Press: New York, 1998, 168 pp.

24. Ross McCluney, "Expanding Population and Loss of Freedom," Information Paper for Tropical Audubon Society, 1972. Revised 7 July 1997 as "A Fact of Nature — Population and Freedom".

25. Bill Moyers, Betty Sue Flowers, and Bill Moyer. *A World of Ideas: Conversations With Thoughtful Men and Women About American Life Today and the Ideas Shaping Our Future*. 26 May 1989 ed. Doubleday: New York, 1989, 513 pp.

26. Garrett Hardin. "The Tragedy of the Commons." *Science* Vol. 162, (1968), 1243-1248.

27. M. Boyd Wilcox. "March 27, 1999: On the anniversary of the Rockefeller Report, Overpopulation Dilutes Democracy." *Population Press*, (1999): March/April.

28. Jonathan Porritt. *Save the Earth*. Turner Publishing, Inc.: One CNN Center, Atlanta, GA 30348, distributed by Andrews & McMeel, 4900 Main Street, Kansas City, MO 64112,1991, 199 pp.

29. Paul. E. Jindra, 1999, to Ross McCluney.

30. United Nations Population Division UNPD. Volume III, "World Population Prospects: the 2000 Revision - Highlights," *United Nations Population Division* Report No. ST/ESA/P/WP.165, 28 Feb. 2001, New York, NY 10017.

Appendix: Bartlett's Laws of Sustainability

Bartlett, A., *Population & Environment,* Vol. 16, No. 1, September 1994, pp. 5-35.

Bartlett, A., *Renewable Resources Journal*, Vol. 15, No. 4, Winter 1997-98, Pgs. 6-23. *Reproduced by permission.*

First Law: Population growth and/or growth in the rates of consumption of resources cannot be sustained.

A) A population growth rate less than or equal to zero and declining rates of consumption of resources are a necessary, but not a sufficient, condition for a sustainable society.

B) Unsustainability will be the certain result of any program of "development," that does not plan the achievement of zero (or a period of negative) growth of populations and of rates of consumption of resources. This is true even if the program is said to be "sustainable."

C) The research and regulation programs of governmental agencies that are charged with protecting the environment and promoting "sustainability" are, in the long run, irrelevant, unless these programs address vigorously and quantitatively the concept of carrying capacities and unless the programs study in depth the demographic causes and consequences of environmental problems.

D) Societies, or sectors of a society, that depend on population growth or growth in their rates of consumption of resources, are unsustainable.

E) Persons who advocate population growth and / or growth in the rates of consumption of resources are advocating unsustainability.

F) Persons who suggest that sustainability can be achieved without stopping population growth are misleading themselves and others.

G) Persons whose actions directly or indirectly cause increases in population or in the rates of consumption of resources are moving society away from sustainability. (Advertising your city or state as an ideal site in which to locate new factories, indicates a desire to increase the population of your city or state.)

H) The term "Sustainable Growth" is an oxymoron.

Second Law: In a society with a growing population and/or growing rates of consumption of resources, the larger the population, and/or the larger the rates of consumption of resources, the more difficult it will be to transform the society to the condition of sustainability.

Third Law: The response time of populations to changes in the human fertility rate is the average length of a human life, or approximately 70 years. (Bartlett and Lytwak 1995)

A) A nation can achieve zero population growth if:

a) the fertility rate is maintained at the replacement level for 70 years, and

b) there is no net migration during the 70 years.

During the 70 years the population continues to grow, but at declining rates until the growth finally stops.

B) If we want to make changes in the total fertility rates so as to stabilize the population by the ... late 21st century, we must make the necessary changes [near the beginning] of the 21st century.

C) The time horizon of political leaders is of the order of two to eight years.

D) It will be difficult to convince political leaders to act now to change course, when the full results of the change may not become apparent in the lifetimes of those leaders.

Fourth Law: The size of population that can be sustained (the carrying capacity) and the sustainable average standard of living of the population are inversely related to one another. (This must be true even though Cohen asserts that the numerical size of the carrying capacity of the Earth cannot be determined [Cohen 1995]).

A) The higher the standard of living one wishes to sustain, the more urgent it is to stop population growth.

B) Reductions in the rates of consumption of resources and reductions in the rates of production of pollution can shift the carrying capacity in the direction of sustaining a larger population.

Fifth Law: Sustainability requires that the size of the population be less than or equal to the carrying capacity of the ecosystem for the desired standard of living.

A) Sustainability requires equilibrium between human society and dynamic but stable ecosystems.

B) Destruction of ecosystems tends to reduce the carrying capacity and / or the sustainable standard of living.

C) The rate of destruction of ecosystems increases as the rate of growth of the population increases.

D) Population growth rates less than or equal to zero are necessary, but are not sufficient, conditions for halting the destruction of the environment. This is true locally and globally.

Sixth Law: (The lesson of "The Tragedy of the Commons") (Hardin 1968): The benefits of population growth and of growth in the rates of consumption of resources accrue to a few; the costs of population growth and growth in the rates of consumption of resources are borne by all of society.

> A) Individuals who benefit from growth will continue to exert strong pressures supporting and encouraging both population growth and growth in rates of consumption of resources.
>
> B) The individuals who promote growth are motivated by the recognition that growth is good for them. In order to gain public support for their goals, they must convince people that population growth and growth in the rates of consumption of resources, are also good for society. [This is the Charles Wilson argument: if it is good for General Motors, it is good for the United States.] (Yates 1983)

Seventh Law: Growth in the rate of consumption of a non-renewable resource, such as a fossil fuel, causes a dramatic decrease in the life expectancy of the resource.

> A) In a world of growing rates of consumption of resources, it is seriously misleading to state the life expectancy of a non-renewable resource "at present rates of consumption," i.e., with no growth. More relevant than the life expectancy of a resource is the expected date of the peak production of the resource, i.e. the peak of the Hubbert curve. (Hubbert 1974)
>
> B) It is intellectually dishonest to advocate growth in the rate of consumption of non-renewable resources while, at the same time, reassuring people about how long the resources will last "at present rates of consumption." (zero growth)

Eighth Law: The time of expiration of non-renewable resources can be postponed, possibly for a very long time, by:

> i) technological improvements in the efficiency with which the resources are recovered and used
>
> ii) using the resources in accord with a program of "Sustained Availability," (Bartlett 1986)
>
> iii) recycling
>
> iv) the use of substitute resources.

Ninth Law: when large efforts are made to improve the efficiency with which resources are used, the added resources consumed as a consequence of modest increases in population easily and completely wipe out the resulting savings.

A) When the efficiency of resource use is increased, the consequence often is that the "saved" resources are not put aside for the use of future generations, but instead are used immediately to encourage and support larger populations.

B) Humans have an enormous compulsion to find an immediate use for all available resources.

Tenth Law: The benefits of large efforts to preserve the environment are easily canceled by the added demands on the environment that result from small increases in human population.

Eleventh Law: (Second Law of Thermodynamics) When rates of pollution exceed the natural cleansing capacity of the environment, it is easier to pollute than it is to clean up the environment.

Twelfth Law: (Eric Sevareid's Law) The chief cause of problems is solutions. (Sevareid 1970)

A) This law should be a central part of higher education, especially in engineering.

Thirteenth Law: Humans will always be dependent on agriculture.

A) Supermarkets alone are not sufficient.

B) The central task in sustainable agriculture is to preserve agricultural land.

The agricultural land must be protected from losses due to things such as:

        i) Urbanization and development

        ii) Erosion

        iii) Poisoning by chemicals

Fourteenth Law: If, for whatever reason, humans fail to stop population growth and growth in the rates of consumption of resources, Nature will stop these growths.

A) By contemporary western standards, Nature's method of stopping growth is cruel and inhumane.

B) Glimpses of Nature's method of dealing with populations that have exceeded the carrying capacity of their lands can be seen each night on the television news reports from places where large populations are experiencing starvation and misery.

Fifteenth Law: In every local situation, creating jobs increases the number of people locally who are out of work.

Sixteenth Law: Starving people don't care about sustainability.

       A) If sustainability is to be achieved, the necessary leadership and resources must be supplied by people who are not starving.

Seventeenth Law: The addition of the word "sustainable" to our vocabulary, to our reports, programs, and papers, to the names of our academic institutes and research programs, and to our community initiatives, is not sufficient to ensure that our society becomes sustainable.

Eighteenth Law: Extinction is forever.

Appendix References

Bartlett, A.A., Lytwak, E.P., (1995), Zero Growth of the Population of the United States. *Population & Environment,* Vol. 16, No. 5, May 1995, pp. 415-428.

Bartlett, A.A., (1986), Sustained Availability: A Management Program for Non-Renewable Resources, *American Journal of Physics,* Vol. 54, pp. 398-402. "Sustained Availability" involves having the rate of use of a finite non-renewable resource decline steadily in a way that guarantees that the resource will last forever.

Cohen, J.E., (1995), *How Many People Can the Earth Support?* W.W. Norton & Co., New York City, 1995.

Hardin, G., (1968), "The Tragedy of the Commons," *Science,* Vol. 162, pp. 1243-1248.

Hubbert, M.K., (1974) *U.S. Energy Resources: A Review as of 1972* A background paper prepared at the request of Henry M. Jackson, Chairman, Committee on Interior and Insular Affairs, United States Senate pursuant to Senate Resolution 45. *A National Fuels and Energy Policy Study,* Serial No. 93-40 (92-75), Part 1. U.S. Government Printing Office, Washington, 1974.

Sevareid, E., (1970), CBS News, December 29, 1970. Quoted in Martin, T.L., *Malice in Blunderland.* McGraw-Hill Book Co., New York City, 1973.

Yates, B., (1983) *The Decline and Fall of the American Automobile Industry.* Empire Books, New York City, 1983, p. 123. Charles E. Wilson was the president of General Motors who "would outrage many with his aphorism: 'What is good for the country is good for General Motors and vice versa.'"

6
Will We Have the Energy?

Energy drives nearly everything.
Human energy dependency is increasing.

Everything runs on energy. Our bodies do, of course, but everything else as well. When we feel "energetic," our bodies are fully fueled and ready to go. The fuel is the food we eat. Caloric content is a measure of the energy contained in food. When we go into the woods and pick an apple, its food energy comes from the sun. It is an astounding process.

Living Off the Sun

Continuous and extremely powerful nuclear reactions in our Sun release a full spectrum of energy, racing rapidly into the dark void of space. Planets circling the Sun intercept some of this energy and are warmed by it. A portion of the Earth-bound share of that solar radiation is taken in by living plants and used to create complex molecules bursting with biochemical energy. The energy of these molecules can be released in a variety of ways in the bodies of animals eating those plants. Biochemical reactions turn this stored solar energy into the energy needed to live and breathe and move about.

We run on solar energy. So do lots of other things. All plants, all animals run on solar energy, with a few peculiar exceptions. The process has proceeded for hundreds of millions of years and should continue for many millions more.

Planets close to the sun are hot, those far away much cooler. Earth is at the right distance to have a mild climate, just the right temperature, and also has the correct mixture of gases to support life — a profusion of life, the likes of which we have not found anywhere else in the universe. Solar energy powers our planet.

Some areas of Earth are heated more than others. Adding in the spin of the planet on its axis, the result is a vast movement of the fluids of our biosphere.

The atmosphere and ocean are constantly in motion. Ocean currents are driven by differential heating of their waters, waves are driven by the wind, and the wind itself is powered by solar energy. Hydroelectric energy comes from the sun, too, since the sun's energy lifts water from the ocean (as water vapor) and drops it (as rain and dew) high in the mountains and other elevated areas.

It is a miracle of the universe that we thrive on deadly powerful nuclear explosions constantly taking place 93 million miles from Earth. (We are protected from the deadly, high-energy particles streaming out of those nuclear explosions by the huge distance, and by our protective atmosphere shielding us from most of that radiation.) It is also a miracle that some of the more benign and beneficial energy from those explosions finds its way into our bodies and makes possible such delightful human activities as dancing, singing, running, painting, reading, hiking, sailing, loving, playing sports, and writing books! All of these activities are powered by solar nuclear reactions.

Before industrialized civilizations, even before agriculture, humans ran completely on the daily budget of energy from the sun. Sunlight arrived on Earth, energized our food, passed through us, and then moved on, working its way elsewhere through the biotic community. Some of this energy is stored temporarily and used intermittently.

The energy in our food comes from the lives of the plants and animals we consume. This is very convenient, for it permits short-term storage of food, enabling our survival through months of harsh winter when little fresh vegetation is available for consumption. The energy powering our rivers is also stored, as snow, ice, and groundwater, which later feed the rivers and make their motions possible.

Energy Basics

Radiation impacting the Earth resides here only temporarily. When it finishes its work, it moves as thermal radiation out into the far reaches of space. If this were not so, the Earth would get hotter and hotter until everything either melted or burned up. We survive by virtue of a delicate balance between the energy flows coming in and going out from the Earth, each minute of every day.

Our wonderful atmosphere traps some of this energy, thereby maintaining Earth temperature at a global and temporal average of about 15 degrees C

(59 F). The trapping works like this. The atmosphere passes the strongest solar radiation through it, relatively unattenuated. Some of this is visible to us as light. The rest is invisible *infrared* and a small amount of also invisible *ultraviolet* radiation.

The atmosphere impedes the transmission of the infrared radiation (also called "IR") from the sun, absorbing it and being warmed by the absorbed radiation. The Earth is much colder than the sun. But it still emits radiation. The outgoing radiation covers a broad range of the infrared spectrum, but at wavelengths longer than those of arriving solar radiation. The atmosphere also absorbs some of this long wavelength infrared radiation emitted by the warmed Earth, recaptures it and maintains the atmosphere's mild temperature. Through these processes, Earth retains heat before releasing it into space. Such heat retention maintains the thermal balance necessary for our lives to continue and flourish.

This process is called the *greenhouse effect*; the same physical mechanism is responsible for warming the interiors of glazed growing spaces, even when it is bitter cold outside. Solar radiation is transmitted freely by the greenhouse's glass and warms the interior of the building. Warmed interior surfaces emit long wavelength infrared radiation toward the glass, but it cannot escape, because most is trapped by absorption in the glazing. Our atmosphere acts like the glass in a greenhouse, transmitting incoming solar radiation and impeding long wavelength outgoing radiation.

The atmosphere's greenhouse effect is provided not by glass but by certain gases. These so-called "greenhouse gases" are in just the right concentration to permit the energy balance, and mild average temperature, we enjoy. If we lost those gases, Earth would cool, its ice caps would thicken and advance, sea levels would fall, and life would become very different. If their concentration were to increase, Earth would warm, the ice caps would melt, sea levels would rise, land areas would decrease, and life would also be very different. Remarkably, 95 percent of all the fresh water on Earth is bound up in the glacial ice of Antarctica and Greenland[1]. These ice caps constitute 2.5% of the volume of all the world's oceans[2, p. 325 & 532,3, p. 39]. Their melting would have serious consequences for coastal dwelling humans.

Our Energy History

All of Earth's biological processes are driven by energy. Energy is central and critical to any discussion of the future of humanity. We are now more dependent on energy than ever before. We still take energy from the sun — to operate our bodies, as well as the plants and animals around us. But at a certain point in our past, we decided that the daily budget of energy from the sun was not enough. We wanted more, and looked for ways to use energy faster.

The first way was burning wood. The discovery of fire had profound impacts on humanity's future prospects. The remainder of human history has been one of ever-increasing use of supplemental energy sources.

Our first ventures toward increased energy use were made possible by harvesting more plants and animals and consuming them at rates higher than before. We increased consumption for construction of dwellings, food, cooking heat, and space heating in winter. The development of agriculture was an important turning point in the process. Once we had agriculture, we could consume more food energy than we could find on the ground, in the trees, and in the bodies of animals during our hunting and gathering days. This permitted higher human populations.

We could plant large fields of crops, asking them to collect solar energy for us, store it temporarily in their leaves, seeds, and fruits, and then deliver that energy to us later. These crops were perishable — did not last for decades or centuries — but they were renewed each growing season. So we still lived in a sustainable manner, on average, within our daily budget of energy from the sun. It is just that we converted some areas of the land from the mixed species of plants and animals that had previously thrived there to only a few species raised for human consumption. And we increased the numbers of human consumers to match the larger quantity of food energy newly available.

Thus began our competition with the huge mass of plant and animal species — the Earth's diverse biomass — for food, clothing, and shelter. As our numbers grew, so too did our conversion of areas from great biodiversity to the few species deemed desirable by humans. As Earth's population continues to grow, the competition is becoming a rout, with human-induced species extinction a daily occurrence.

Our switch to agriculture was an important first step in expanding our use of solar energy, in making solar collectors. Now we could collect solar energy over larger areas, "concentrate" it in food stores, and then consume it at higher rates. We also domesticated animals, consumed their even higher concentrations of energy, and required even larger areas of land to grow the food for our animals, and thence for us. It takes approximately 20 times more land area to grow food for a modern meat-based diet than for a pure vegetarian one[4, p. 352,5, p. 69,6]. Our reliance on wood biomass as fuel for a variety of heating needs peaked about the time we discovered coal and expanded its use.

Energy Units

In talking about energy, we must quantify it. The basic definition comes from the combination of force and motion. The energy required to move an object with a force of one pound through a distance of one foot is called one "foot-pound" in the "Inch-Pound" or "IP" system of units used commonly in the U.S. In the metric system, the corresponding unit of energy is the "newton-meter." The international standard (metric system) unit of energy is the joule, equal to a newton-meter. The unit of energy in the IP system is the British thermal unit (or "Btu"), equal to 1054 joules.

The international system of units, the "metric system," formally named *Systeme International* (or just the "SI" system) is used almost exclusively around the world, especially in discussing the generation and sale of energy. Both systems are used in the U.S. — an unfortunate fact of life at the beginning of a new millennium.

In many cases, it is not the absolute quantity of energy that is discussed, but its *rate* of generation, flow, or delivery, in units of energy per unit time. Using the metric system, this is quantified by the watt, a joule per second of energy flow. A 100-watt light bulb, for example, consumes 100 joules of electrical energy every second it is employed. This is a consumption rate of 6,000 joules in a minute (100 joules per second for 60 seconds) and 360,000 in an hour (100 joules per second for 3,600 seconds). In the IP system a commonly used unit of power (energy flow) is the Btu/hr. A 100-watt light bulb consumes 341 Btu/hr.

How much energy is delivered in, say, an hour, if the rate of delivery is 100 watts? Since an hour consists of 3600 seconds, in one hour a 100 watt light bulb will consume 100 joules per second times 3600 seconds, a total of 360,000 joules. Because this number is fairly large, electric utility companies prefer to use a different unit of energy, a kind of hybrid unit, the "watt-hour" ... the energy consumed if one watt of power flows for one hour. Our 100-watt light bulb, therefore, consumes 100 watt-hours of energy in an hour.

A typical household in an industrialized country has many energy consuming devices. Adding them together and totaling their energy consumption, large numbers of watt-hours are consumed over the course of a month. To avoid the problem of dealing with large numbers, the "kilowatt-hour" unit is also used. "Kilo" means "1000," so a kilowatt-hour is equal to 1000 watt-hours. The electrical energy you consume is likely quantified on your monthly utility bill in units of kilowatt-hours (kwh or KWh).

Energy units commonly used in discussions of energy policy include the following, related to each other as indicated.

Energy
1 joule = 1 kg m^2 sec^{-2} = newton-meter
1 kilojoule = 1000 joules
1 Btu = 1054 joules = 252 calories = 0.000293 KWh
1 Quad = 10^{15} Btu = 1.054 x 10^{15} kilojoules
1 ft-lb = 1.36 joules
1 KWh = 3.6 x 10^6 joules = 3.6 x 10^3 kilojoules = 3410 Btu
1 KWh = 8.6 x 10^5 cal = 3.41 Kbtu

Power
1 horse power = 550 ft-lb/sec = 746 W = 2546 Btu/hr
1 W = 3.414 Btu/hr = 1 joule/sec
1 KW = 3414 Btu/hr

Fuels from Fossils

The processes of using wood energy and cultivating food energy worked for many centuries. Then we passed another turning point: the discovery of a new source of stored energy — the fossil fuels — an energy form we could consume at higher rates than before, much higher. It happened that the human population also increased, roughly in proportion to the increased fossil energy availability.

Two differences surfaced between the new stored fossil fuel energy and the energy we were already using. First, the new energy was amazingly concentrated; relatively easy to obtain, store, and transport; and easy to convert to other forms. Secondly, the storage time of this energy was unimaginably vast. Coal deposits date mainly from 250 to 350 million years ago. Arabian oil is about 145 million years old, Gulf of Mexico oil 90 million years old. Natural gas is generally found associated with oil, but sometimes with coal, and therefore shares the ages of these fossil resources. These fuels are derived from the remains of ancient living organisms, which themselves relied on energy from the Sun.

Energy expert Colin Campbell describes the origins of petroleum in some detail,[7, Chapter 15] offering the following summary:

Petroleum is derived from organic material under conditions that were met only rarely in the Earth's long history and then only in a few places. Oil comes primarily from algal material, and gas comes from vegetal remains. Such organic debris settled to the floor of the lake or sea in which it lived, and in most cases was oxidized by bottom dwelling organisms or currents, but in certain stagnant environments has been preserved and buried beneath other sediments. On deeper burial, it was heated by the Earth's heat flow, and chemical reactions converted it into petroleum. Oil on very deep burial is cracked [chemically] into gas.

Once formed, oil and gas migrate upwards through minute fractures and pores in the rocks, until they find a porous and permeable layer through which they can move. They then flow through this conduit until they are trapped in a fold, against a fault or where the conduit pinches out. Much is dissipated or held in the many constrictions encountered during its migration, so that only about one percent of what was formed is trapped in accumulations large enough to be exploited.

The fossil fuels are a form of stored solar energy. They are not renewable. Once gone, they are gone forever. (More precisely, the renewal rate is an extremely minuscule fraction of the current extraction rate.)

The substantive exploitation of fossil fuels constituted a banner day for technology. Easy and inexpensive generation and widespread distribution of electricity, the most versatile form of energy available to us, was employed. Steam engines and electric motors, immediately replacing hydropower for the milling of wheat and other grains, were introduced throughout the industrializing world. Steam and gasoline engines were much less trouble to operate and much cleaner to tend to than horses, oxen, and other beasts of burden. And they didn't consume a significant fraction of our crops.

Fossil fuels to power farm equipment made possible the cultivation of many more acres of land by the solitary farmer. Today most food for the western world is grown by large, technology-based industrial companies, as well as individual farmers, using this same technology to enhance the efficiency of their operations. As if fuel for tractors was not enough, farmers also use chemicals made from fossil fuels for fertilizers, herbicides, and pesticides. Modern industrial societies and their highly technological lifestyles use abundant and increasing extraction of fossil fuels to supplement the direct solar energy we already use.

Energy Transitions

In our recent past, we have seen several transitions from one predominant, supplementary energy source to another. Previously we burned wood and used it to make our shelters. We substituted coal for the wood formerly used for interior space heating and cooking stoves. (Coal was dirty to move around and use. But concentrated in its energy content and relatively easy to transport, it had certain economic advantages over wood.) When petroleum and natural gas were discovered, their fluid nature made them still easier to transport. They were cleaner than coal, both before and after burning. We also found ways of converting them into a variety of valuable products, such as plastics, chemicals, and paint constituents.

It is interesting to examine the nature of these previous transitions from one form of energy to the other (as illustrated in Figure 1) for the United States. This plot was drawn around 1975 so energy uses after that date are only conjectural and based on information available at that time. After 1975, nuclear energy grew slowly in the U.S. and then plateaued more than shown in the graph. Otherwise the essential features are correct for today. [a]

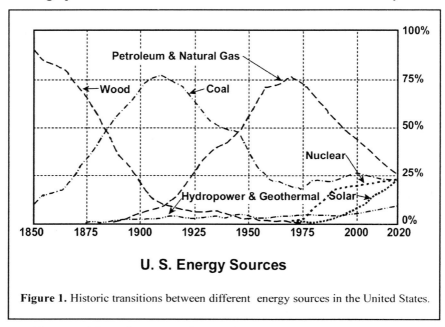

U. S. Energy Sources

Figure 1. Historic transitions between different energy sources in the United States.

The transitions from wood to coal and then to petroleum and natural gas were fairly rapid and singular. No other form of fuel competed successfully with the newly discovered one. Here are some reasons.

1. The new fuel was, in most respects, better than the former. It was a more concentrated form of energy, and easier to store and transport.
2. The alternatives were less economically viable.

---

[a]This graph was found a short time after 1975 but the reference to its source has been lost. If you know where it came from, please send the information to rmccluney@fsec.ucf.edu.

3. The economics were strongly favorable for the exploitation of the new fuel.

4. There was essentially universal agreement that the new fuel was better, so there was little dissension over the transition to it.

5. With the exception of coal, the new fuel was generally cleaner.

Hydropower and geothermal, although clean, obviously cannot be transported, except as the end-product electricity. Their availability for new energy generation is limited in the U.S. Thus the curve shows only modest increase in the use of these sources through 2020.

With the 1970s came an interest in accomplishing one more transition, to a new, even better, and more economically profitable source than oil and natural gas. In the 1950s and 1960s nuclear energy seemed our new source. However, it ran into serious cost and environmental limitations and never reached the anticipated widespread use in the U.S. that its early backers desired. Safety concerns arose after the terrible nuclear accident at Chernobyl in 1986, and the dilemma with what to do with radioactive waste products.

Is Solar Energy the Answer?

Solar energy, in all its forms, has been proposed as the great new replacement for fossil fuels. This resource, however, does not meet all the previously mentioned criteria for a good replacement source. Though relatively clean (except for some pollution during manufacture and disposal of the hardware), solar energy is a diffuse resource, less concentrated than petroleum. It is also not easily or cost-effectively stored. To store it requires conversion to some other energy form, such as heat, electricity, or chemical energy. This is difficult, expensive, and has inhibited the spread of the technology.

In a partially "solarized" society, we can envision using our few remaining non-renewable energy sources for "backup" — as a filler when solar is unavailable, thus avoiding the need for solar storage. In a more fully solarized economy, electricity generated with solar-derived stored energy could serve as a replacement. Biogas and methanol from (solar powered) crops are potential sources, since these energy forms are easy to store and transport.

We do receive a copious *quantity* of energy from the Sun each day. It falls all over the Earth, but locally it is rather dilute. To harvest it in sizeable quantities will require the alteration of vast areas of the land and water surfaces of the planet, changing biosphere systems even more in the process.

Solar energy is not the "be all and end all" energy solution for the world. As Baron described it in 1981, "A major solar energy cost component is the cost of nonrenewable resources of oil, natural gas, coal, and nuclear energy consumed in producing and constructing the systems for solar heating and solar electric plants."[8]

Proper assessment of a proposed solar technology should include a determination of the system's net energy production. In 1978 Peter Knudson described this as, "Net energy analysis, in its broadest sense, attempts to compare the amount of usable energy output from a system with the total energy that the system draws from society."[9] Another definition: *net energy is the magnitude of the solar-energy-derived output minus the non-renewable energy drawn from the Earth needed to make and operate a solar energy system.*

Calculations show that the net energy of solar collection and distribution systems in some cases is negative. Also, at the end of their useful lives they have to be dismantled and recycled (with additional expenditures of energy).[10]

If the net energy output of a solar technology is negative, logic leads to the question, "Why bother?" In such a case, wouldn't it be better to use the fossil energy directly rather than lock it up in an inadequately producing solar energy system?

This is a controversial topic. Perhaps the calculations are correct for some situations. Still, storing present-day (less expensive) fossil energy in solar collection devices can be used as a hedge against future depletion. Using this argument, we are going to deplete fossil fuels anyway. So why not invest that energy in the manufacture of renewable energy systems, so they can continue producing power when the fossil fuels are depleted? This way we will have some positive net energy systems left over when the fossil sources near depletion. Ultimately we would like to remove the nonrenewable energy inputs from the manufacture of solar energy systems altogether.

This is the basic idea of the solar "breeding" system — using solar energy in the mining and processing of ore and the manufacture of solar energy systems. For such a strategy to be successful, the solar-powered mining and manufacturing industry must be completed before the fossil fuel sources are gone (or become exorbitantly expensive). Such a system would enable the establishment of a society using solar energy alone to recycle worn-out solar systems. Ultimately we might even be able to develop a completely sustainable process that does not require the extraction of further minerals or fossil fuels from the Earth. Of course, a fundamental presumption of such a proposal is that Earth's human population is stabilized at a level that is entirely supported by totally renewable energy systems.

This argument is somewhat narrowly focused. As Knudson correctly points out, "Not every system, of course, needs to show a net energy gain to be desirable." Useful products, like aluminum, will require substantial energy input for mining, recycling, processing, and transport." The more of this energy provided by net solar energy, the better. But our society is still "capable of subsidizing some net energy losers, as long as the primary energy base can afford them. Still, it is absolutely critical to distinguish net energy losers from net energy gainers when comparing alternative primary energy systems."

For the short term, while we struggle toward a solarized economy, net energy losers can be useful intermediary energy sources, until the day when we stop or are unable to use fossil fuels.

Solar Pollution

The issue is not just one of the non-renewable energy subsidy required by solar energy systems. The degree of environmental destruction associated with an energy consuming or producing system of any kind is also critical. As Baron pointed out in 1981, "Even more serious would be the impact upon public health and occupational safety if solar energy generates its own pollution when mining large quantities of energy resources and mineral ores."[8] Some solar energy manufacturing processes, such as the manufacture of crystalline silicon solar cells, produce toxic or otherwise undesirable waste products that have to be either recycled or discarded.

Solar Limits

Physical limits exist to the production of solar energy. In the absurd limit, we clearly could not cover all available land area with solar collectors. A more reasonable limit would fill existing and future rooftops with solar collectors.

From data provided by the U.S. Energy Information Administration, I estimated the total combined commercial and residential building roof area in the United States in the year 2000 at 18 billion square meters. From a National Renewable Energy Laboratory web site, I found that the approximate annual average quantity of solar energy falling on a square meter of land area in the United States is about 4.5 kWh of energy per square meter of area per day. Multiplying this by 365 days in a year and by the 18 billion square meter roof area figure, yields the total energy received by rooftop solar systems in this scenario: 2.46×10^{13} kWh per year, or 84 Quads per year. This is just a bit below the 102 Quads per year U.S. primary energy consumption figure.

Not all roof area is usable, however. Roofs sloped away from the sun's strongest radiation, or shaded by trees and other buildings, or having interfering equipment, or insufficiently strong structurally, are not good for solar collectors.

The conversion from primary to end-use energy is not perfectly efficient in either the renewable or the nonrenewable cases. Both the 102 Quads and the 84 Quads must therefore be reduced in converting them to end-use energy. Determining accurate average conversion efficiencies for all technologies in both categories is difficult, but they are not likely to be wildly different. Thus the conclusion still remains valid that meeting total U.S. energy needs with 100% solar energy would require on the order of every square foot of roof area of every commercial and residential building in the country.

Since most of the current roofs were neither designed nor built to carry the loads of (and wind loading on) solar collectors filling them, achieving the goal of a 100% solar economy in this manner is unlikely. For every acre of existing roof-tops which cannot be filled with solar collectors, an equivalent acre must be found elsewhere. If U.S. population continues to grow, pressure will soar to expand developed areas into what are currently agricultural and wilderness areas. If the plan is to convert as much as possible of the U.S. energy economy to solar energy, solar collector farms will join in the competition for new lands to be opened up for this development.

In order to avoid converting agricultural or natural habitat areas to areas for engineered solar production, we must find other, already developed areas for these solar collectors, (such as street and highway corridors and parking lots.) While many of us in hot climates might like this proposal, it is probably economically unfeasible with current monetary conditions. In the U. S. A., a number of other objections to this possibility can be expected, leading to pressure to convert agricultural and wilderness areas to solar production fields. If this practice is limited to a modest portion of the total available area, the consequences should not be too serious. But if we attempt to obtain all of the existing and growing worldwide demand for energy from solar, significant and serious environmental impacts can be expected.

Ecosystem disruption can result from, for example, denuding a large forest area to make way for solar collectors. If the area involved is large enough, species extinction can be a serious consequence. Furthermore, the construction of many solar energy conversion systems involves toxic chemicals and the extraction of nonrenewable minerals from the Earth.

Thus there is an ultimate limit to the extent that solar can be used. We do not yet know the details of this limit. Though many consider technologically harvested solar energy as a nearly universal human good, excessive reliance on it could have additional unforeseen consequences that might prove very harmful in the long run. Solar energy is not a panacea for the problems of overpopulation.

What About the Deserts?

As already described, the diffuse Nature of solar energy means that significant increases in its use will require large land areas. We have learned from other experiences that there are adverse environmental and social impacts of growth and land development. Solar energy is unlikely to be exempt from these impacts.

We commonly react to the potential adverse impacts of solar energy collection systems in forests, on farms, or in developed areas by pointing out the vast "unused" desert areas in the U.S. and other places around the globe. Surely no one could object to covering such "wasteland" areas with solar collectors for the obvious benefits of humanity!

Visit your nearest desert, or read Edward Abbey's *Desert Solitaire*, to observe the indescribable beauty and magnificence of America's so-called wastelands. Deserts are not devoid of wildlife and they possess a remarkable variety of plant life, adapted over millions of years to the special conditions of desert living.

Do we really want every inch of "unused" desert landscape covered with solar collectors? Would it even be wise to do so, if we could? Consider the cost of transporting energy generated in remote deserts to areas of need, some distance away. This cost can be high, both in electrical line losses and in the funds needed to construct the energy transport system. Converting the energy generated to hydrogen could offset the line losses, but preventing hydrogen gas leaks is notoriously difficult. And the conversion to hydrogen and its use as fuel are not perfectly efficient processes, so there will still be energy losses.

Fortunately, a combination of actions can produce a copious but limited quantity of generally clean, renewable energy: limited use of desert sites, putting solar collectors on the rooftops where it makes good safety and technical sense (and is not too expensive), siting windmills on farmland in high average wind speed areas where such use is compatible with agriculture, installation of ocean wind, wave, and ocean current extraction systems at a few appropriate sites, and the use of additional solar technologies of a variety of kinds and at a variety of appropriate sites.

Do not think of solar as an unlimited source, however. Such thinking inhibits energy conservation, promotes continued population growth, and can lead to over-use and serious loss of valuable animal and plant wilderness habitat.

Conservation Limitations

Energy conservation is another important strategy, almost like having a new source of energy: energy freed up from one use is available for another use. This includes both changes in energy use patterns and the development of energy consuming technology that is radically more efficient than the technology it replaces.

Conservation is an important component of any plan for meeting future energy needs. Solar energy is a relatively dilute form of energy and the equipment needed to collect it and convert it to a more useful form is generally expensive. Reducing energy needs also reduces the size of the solar system needed, and hence its cost, making solar a more economically viable option. Stuart Gleman, has pointed out that "solar energy provides *just enough*," but not enough that we can be wantonly wasteful of it.[27]

If you try to provide the energy needs of a high-energy-consumption household, the cost of the solar energy equipment will be exorbitant. If you reduce that consumption considerably, with radical energy efficient design and construction, then the solar energy system can be smaller and more affordable.

The conclusion is obvious. Solar energy cannot be considered a panacea for all our energy problems as long as population growth continues and worldwide per capita demand keeps rising. There is a fallacy in relying on energy conservation and solar energy alone to save our energy futures.

With a stabilized population and fixed per capita demand, however, energy conservation and solar energy will be very important. They will be needed in order to conserve the valuable complex molecules of fossil resources for more durable and more important uses. They will be essential for reducing, hopefully eliminating, harmful emissions of greenhouse gases and toxic pollutants.

If world population and per capita use of energy continue growing, however, our demand for new energy could grow faster than our ability to supply it from renewable sources. As supplies of non-renewable sources dwindle, it will become increasingly expensive to supplement solar or back it up with these depletable sources. This reminds us of Bartlett's Second Law of Sustainability: "In a society with a growing population and/or growing rates of consumption of resources, the larger the population, and/or the larger the rates of consumption of resources, the more difficult it will be to transform the society to the condition of sustainability."

Petrochemicals as Feedstocks

The entire petrochemical industry is based upon the ready availability of fossil resources as feedstocks. The products produced include a wide range of plastics and synthetic fibers. Fertilizers, pesticides, lubricants and other polymer-based products are also made from fossil fuels. This prompted Kenneth Deffeyes to write: "In the long run, the eventual use for oil will be for manufacturing useful organic chemicals. I expect our grandchildren to ask, 'You burned it? All those lovely organic molecules, you just burned it?'"[11, p. 164]

Pressure is growing to reduce or even eliminate the combustion of fossil fuels worldwide, mainly through better mileage on cars and trucks, and by ultimately running them on other sources of energy.

In a completely "solarized" society without fossil feedstocks, we might be able to fabricate the needed complex molecules from baser materials. But the fabrication processes will require energy. If we had an unlimited supply, this might work (apart from concerns about thermal pollution and its contribution to global warming). But in an era of shrinking fossil fuel availability, obtaining large volumes of complex molecules by synthesis becomes more and more expensive.

This comes at a time when the huge populations of China, India, and South America, half the world's population, seek to increase their fossil-fuel-based transportation and manufacturing systems dramatically. (There is laudable effort to base the new systems on renewable, environmentally benign technologies, but the extent of this development is modest.)

Pressure is building for substantial increases in energy production worldwide. What is our current response?

Dig and Drill Mentality

As we approach the peak and subsequent decline of world oil production, the knee-jerk response we have been seeing is to drill more holes in the ground and pump oil faster. The hope is that this will keep prices in check and extend the time to oil depletion. This may work for a while, but only makes the longer-term situation worse. Consider the following story.

> You are sitting at a table in a fast food restaurant, enjoying your "Big Gulp." A friend comes in and, seeing the size of your drink, asks if he can join you. You say yes, of course, and hand him a straw.
>
> He begins drinking and enjoying this large cup of soda. Twice as many people are being satisfied as before he arrived.
>
> Then another friend enters and you offer her a straw. After she joins you, there is now three times the satisfaction at the table than when it was just you.
>
> A fourth friend joins you and the satisfaction rate reaches an all-time high. You are experiencing a four-fold increase in the extraction of soda from the cup.
>
> Then something terrible happens. You hit bottom, before any of you was satiated. Now no one is satisfied and the rate of extraction is zero. The termination of your enjoyment of your soda has happened much sooner than it otherwise would have, and your friends are peeved, especially the last one, who hardly got two sips before the bottom was reached.

The analogy with oil exploration, discovery, and extraction is clear. As human population increases, and as that population becomes more affluent, using more energy per capita, the demand for energy increases. The response has been to expand oil exploration and production, putting more "straws" into the finite resource, and increasing the pumping and refining speed.

Some say the analogy is flawed because we are continually finding new oil deposits. Also the story ignores the fact that your friends have plenty of money in their pockets and can simply purchase their own cups of soda, thereby not affecting you at all. If the restaurant were to temporarily run out of soda, it would be resupplied rather quickly. This is true, but what if there were no one to resupply the restaurant once the current batch is sold out? More people drinking more soda merely hastens the depletion.

While new oil is found from time to time, most of the new discoveries are in remote locations that are difficult to reach and where extracting is expensive. And they are not large enough to keep up with an exponentially growing demand. We cannot avoid the depletion of petroleum, at some time in the future. All we can legitimately debate is how much is left and when it will run out. These are matters of degree only, not of fact. Pretending the resource to be infinite is a very big mistake, one that our children will be forced to handle, and a terrible legacy for us to leave them.

Peak Oil – Peak Humanity

The need to escape petroleum based fuels was made clear by noted petroleum expert M. King Hubbert as far back as the 1950s[12]. A Shell Oil geophysicist, Hubbert (1903-1989) was well known as a world authority on the estimation of energy resources and on the prediction of their patterns of discovery and depletion. He was probably best known because of his startling prediction, first made public in 1949, that the fossil fuel era would be of very short duration. ("Energy from Fossil Fuels," *Science*, February 4, 1949.)

Hubbert's minor celebrity grew with his prediction in 1956 that U.S. oil production would peak in the early 1970s and decline thereafter. He was ridiculed then, but his analysis later proved to be remarkably accurate. He stuck to his guns, in spite of the ridicule and was vindicated in 1970 (or 1971, depending on the information source) when U.S. production passed its peak level. (This event went mostly unnoticed, thanks to imported oil from around the world, most notably from the Middle East.)

The 200 or so year period when most of the *world's* oil is being discovered, used, and depleted has come to be known as "Hubbert's Peak." The short period from the first major oil production in Titusville, PA, in 1859, through the peaking of world oil production about now and ending when it is largely depleted near the end of this century, stands in stark contrast to the hundreds of millions of years the oil deposits took to form.

Predicting the peak in world oil production is a difficult and controversial subject, but the peak is expected by several experts to occur in the first decade of the 21st century. As world production declines thereafter, and since world *demand* is expected to increase, prices can be expected to soar, stimulating major shifts in transportation systems and in locating residences and places of work. Countering this view, some prognosticators seem to think we can increase our fuel efficiency in all sectors rapidly, decreasing per capita demand for oil enough to postpone the peak of world production for several decades. Needless to say, the topic is very controversial.

If world oil production is peaking now, fated to decline slowly thereafter, we will experience many serious ramifications if demand is not made to decline at the same rate. As world population continues to grow, the pressure for world energy demand to also grow is expected to be relentless. If petrochemical fuel energy is central to providing food energy at current high rates, and if food is central to maintaining high human populations, then the logic seems unassailable that when petrochemical energy starts declining, population will fall as well, possibly rapidly and drastically.

Many claim there will be clean replacement energy sources. If so, where are they? Can we even tolerate massive production of energy from alternate sources? Who has thought this out carefully?

The link between energy production and human population is a strong one. The expected decline in energy production is a serious matter, not to be minimized.

Future Prospects

The Rocky Mountain Institute (RMI) explained the problem in its Spring, 1998 newsletter, responding to a prediction by Colin Campbell that the world would pass its peak of oil production near the year 2010[7]:

> Clearly we're gutted with oil right now, but just as clearly, we can expect to run out of it at some point—it's a finite resource, after all. The real question is, is the you-know-what really going to hit the fan as early as 2010, or indeed ever?
>
> Debate over such resource questions is all too often polarized by ideology. The prospect of an oil crunch fits environmentalists' sense of ecological limits, and bolsters their argument that humankind must change its ways to live within those limits.
>
> On the other side, "cornucopians" aren't worried about ever running out of oil. Human ingenuity, technology, and market forces, they say, will work together to produce more oil, make it last longer, and invent substitutes for it (or for the machines that use it) before it's depleted.
>
> We tend toward the cornucopians. There are many good reasons the world should be weaning itself away from oil, but scarcity isn't one of them. However, an oil crunch *is* what we'll get if we don't make a conscious effort to change our present course. The cornucopia isn't automatic: you have to turn the crank.[13]

The concept of growth and man's philosophical and scientific attitude toward growth are at the center of this controversy. The previously mentioned growth guru, Al Bartlett, has written extensively on the subject, as have a number of other authors, including Hubbert himself[14], J. Laherrere[15], Campbell, author of *The Coming Oil Crisis*[7], and, more recently, Kenneth Deffeyes, author of *Hubbert's Peak*.[11]

Campbell predicts, as did Hubbert before him, the beginning of the final

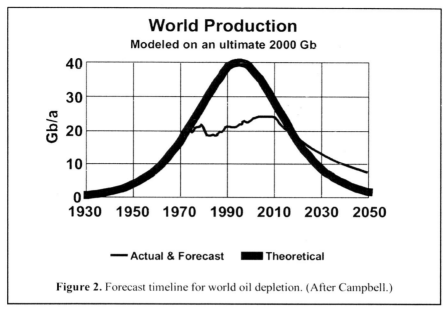

Figure 2. Forecast timeline for world oil depletion. (After Campbell.)

depletion of world oil reserves. Campbell places this important date before 2010[16]. The longer-range dimensions of this depletion are not difficult to grasp.

In using a resource of finite size, the rate of extraction starts slowly, rises somewhat exponentially, then the rate of increase slows, eventually peaking at some level—the peak extraction rate. Following this the extraction rate declines fairly fast at first and more slowly thereafter. A typical curve for world petroleum is shown as the thicker one in Figure 2, taken from Campbell.[17]

In the beginning actual world oil production followed this trend very closely in the beginning. But either anticipating the peak or as a result of political and economic forces, world extraction rates were capped at around 20 gigabarrels (billion barrels, or 10^9 barrels) per year, starting around 1972, thereby extending the time to depletion somewhat. The pressure on increasing production is strong, however, and can be seen in the slight predicted rise in oil production from 2000 to about 2008, when Campbell and others predict it will begin to decline.

Princeton professor and former Shell Oil researcher Kenneth Deffeyes in his 2001 book, *Hubbert's Peak: The Impending World Oil Shortage,* made a more recent projection. "Around 1995, several analysts began applying Hubbert's method to world oil production, and most of them estimate that the peak year for world oil will be between 2004 and 2008. These analyses were reported in some of the most widely circulated sources: *Nature, Science*, and *Scientific American*.[16,18,19]

The downturn in the forecasted rate of oil extraction (shown in Figure 2 to be around 2010) may not seem terribly dramatic, since the production rate seems fairly steady to that point and is not precipitous for a while afterward. However, if this happens, the beginning decline in oil production, coupled with any failure to make the technological fixes proposed by the Rocky Mountain Institute, will be accompanied by growing worldwide anguish and conflict. We understand the reason when we couple this information with world population growth, from around 6 billion now to 8 to 10 or even 12 billion sometime later this century, according to the United Nations projections cited in the previous chapter. This means that oil supplies will be declining just as the greatest increase in world population (and demand for energy) ever known is taking place.

The increasing demand for oil will come as underdeveloped countries learn to develop and flourish economically. The RMI claim that we can avoid serious difficulty after our passage through the energy peak seems based on a belief in reduced *per capita* demand for energy, as more people use more energy. This assumes that the new technology available to the billions of new people will be so efficient that it will offset the increased number of consumers. But will this really happen? And will known reserves still continue increasing as some suggest? Campbell offers the following assessment of oil reserves[17]:

> In rounded numbers, it appears that the total endowment is about 2000 Gb (billion barrels) of which about 1800 Gb have already been found and 850 Gb produced to date. Many claims are made that technology will extract more oil from known fields, but in fact the main impact of technology has been to hold production higher for longer, with little impact on the reserves themselves, as can be readily verified by examination of the production records of individual fields, such as Prudhoe Bay in Alaska.
>
> Most of this oil was formed during a few brief epochs of extreme global warming in the geological past, when prolific blooms of algae poisoned the seas and lakes, providing the organic material that was eventually converted to oil and gas under now well understood chemical and geological processes. Thus, most of the oil from the U.S. Gulf Coast to northern South America, including the vast degraded deposits of Venezuela, comes from one such event 90 million years ago, while the North Sea, much of the Middle East and Russia relies on another, 145 million years ago at the end of the Jurassic period. This underlines just how finite the resource is. Finding and producing oil is not just a matter of

investment and technology as the economists used to maintain, but is subject to now well understood natural limits....

In a country with a large population of fields, peak comes close to the midpoint of depletion, when half the total has been consumed. The world pattern is less straightforward, because production has been artificially constrained by the OPEC countries. The lower graph [in Fig. 2] shows world production to date superimposed on the theoretical curve based on the above estimates of the endowment, illustrating how the natural peak has been capped, delaying the onset of long term decline. Exactly when decline starts depends on many unpredictable factors, but we may be sure that we will have to face this historic turning point between 2005 and 2010.

This alarming prediction is either denied or ignored by every major politician and business leader in the world. Their apparent philosophy of life is to make money and prosper as much as possible for the next decade or so and let someone else deal with the difficulties.

A *Scientific American* report, "Preventing the Next Oil Crunch," and the article in that report titled "The End of Cheap Oil,"[16] warns of a permanent worldwide petroleum shortage beginning by 2010. The Rocky Mountain Institute (RMI) continues the argument set forth in the article previously cited:

Historically, resource depletion tends to follow a standard bell curve, whether for a single oil field, a group of fields, or a country. The *Scientific American* authors assume that global oil supplies will follow the same rise and inevitable fall.

The rub is that they predict the oil crunch will come long before we're on the downhill slide—it'll start, in fact, at the point of maximum output, when supply will stop keeping up with rising demand, so prices must rise to keep demand in check. The global economy will then have to adjust to a sudden reversal in century-long oil growth, and to the concentration of most of the remaining oil in the hands of a few Middle Eastern nations.

And that point will come sooner than we think, the authors predict, because they contend worldwide oil reserves have been inflated over the past decade or so for political reasons (the more reserves OPEC nations report, the more oil they can sell). The result, "and soon, is the end of the abundant and cheap oil on which all industrial nations depend."[13]

RMI claims this to be right in principle, but wrong and irrelevant in fact, claiming that reserves are increasing "and probably will continue to do so for the foreseeable future, according to Irvin 'Chip' Bupp, managing director of Cambridge Energy Research Associates and an RMI Board member." The reason, according to the RMI article, is that the definition of "reserves" is technical and economic, not geologic. "Improved technology or higher oil prices," they write, "boost reserves because more of the oil is worth finding and extracting. Alleged fiddling with reserve estimates is thus a red herring, Bupp says."

The RMI point is that a variety of alternatives to burning oil, including energy conservation, will be available. These will be driven by higher prices, which will greatly reduce the rate of use of oil. Coupled with new discoveries, these will extend the life of oil substantially beyond the turning point predicted by Campbell and Deffeyes. There is no doubt that these alternatives can become viable as the price of energy rises and that they can reduce energy use for the same level of output.

The article makes the powerful point that efficiency is a huge source of avoided oil use, which RMI calls "negabarrels," citing the RMI-researched "Hypercar®" [b] as an example—a new automobile design predicted to be four to eight times more efficient than comparable current vehicles. More generally, RMI argues, "Efficient use and substitution can restrain demand and prolong supplies, perhaps indefinitely."

RMI research director Amory Lovins has stated, "It's now plausible that oil—like uranium—will become uncompetitive even at low prices before it becomes unavailable even at high prices." He is also fond of telling audiences that "The stone age didn't end because the stone ran out, and the oil age will be just the same." The analogy is that oil will be abandoned before it "runs out" in favor of better alternatives, including conservation and renewables.

Perhaps this is true for highly industrialized countries with the knowledge, wealth, and infrastructure to take advantage of the negabarrel possibilities. But what of the billions of people, probably two-thirds current world population, without those resources? Even though efficient, new technology may be employed, continued population growth and rising per capita demand could far outstrip the developed and developing world's switch to renewables and energy conservation options (if ever that happens on a massive scale) not currently in the planning horizons of most government leaders.

The apparent conflict between Lovins and Campbell is not over the finiteness of oil supply (though they may differ on the total amount which will be discovered that can be extracted). It is more over the manner of the reversal of oil production, which is coming shortly. Campbell seems to feel that the coming oil shortages will drive up prices and reduce demand, causing a degree of societal upheaval. Lovins seems to argue that industry has

---

[b] Hypercar® is a registered trademark of Rocky Mountain Institute.

already started making the changes… before oil depletion forces strong price signals, and that this will stay ahead of any serious disruption in oil supplies likely to cause global anguish.

From the vantage point of the U.S. in late 2003, all we see are larger vehicles and a more energy-wasteful society, despite the relatively modest gains in energy efficiency often touted by the media and by energy research institutes.

Another problem is that energy efficiency must compete with fossil fuel energy purely on present-day economic terms, where only saved energy is counted as a benefit. This is then compared to the cost to install the energy conservation (or renewable energy) system. If the time-to-payback is greater than a few years, you can just forget it. Even when there are reasonably short payback times, inertia and reluctance to change inhibit the use of energy efficiency and renewables.

The current system of commerce is just not structured to consider the "intangible" values most energy-saving systems offer. These include improved human comfort, better energy security for the nation and the individual, saved petrochemicals for other uses, and a viable life-support system for our children and grandchildren. The problem appears to be not that we lack the technology—the technology is ready and available—but that we lack the political will.

Energy Policy

Al Bartlett was asked to testify before the Congress on this matter. After briefly mentioning several recent energy problems, Dr. Bartlett said that the only energy proposals we see are for short-term fixes, sometimes spread over a few years. Mentioning the decades-long history of scientist warnings that fossil fuels are finite and that long-range plans should be made, he suggests that we compare two recommended paths, the science and the non-science ones. Here is part of the transcript of that testimony, delivered to the House Subcommittee on Energy, 3 May 2001.

> The centerpiece of the scientific path is conservation; hence it is appropriate to call this path the "Conservative Path." On this path the federal government is called on to provide leadership plus strong and reliable long-term support toward the achievement of the following goals. The U.S. should:
>
> 1) Have an energy-planning horizon that addresses the problems of sustainability through many future decades.

2) Have programs for the continual and dramatic improvement of the efficiency with which we use energy in all parts of our society. Improved energy efficiency is the lowest cost energy resource we have.

3) Move toward the rapid development and deployment of all manner of renewable energies throughout our entire society.

4) Embark on a program of continual reduction of the annual total consumption of non-renewable energy in the U.S.

5) Recognize that moving quickly to consume the remaining U.S. fossil fuel resources will only speed and enlarge our present serious U.S. dependence on the fossil fuel resources of other nations. This will leave our children vitally vulnerable to supply disruptions that they won't be able to control.

6) Finally, and most important, we must recognize that population growth in the U.S. is a major factor in driving up demand for energy. This calls for recognizing the conclusion of President Nixon's Rockefeller Commission Report (Commission on Population Growth and the American Future, 1972)[21]. The Commission concluded that it could find no benefit to the U.S. from further U.S. population growth.

In contrast, the non-scientific path suggests that resources are effectively infinite, so we can be as liberal as we please in their use and consumption. Hence this path is properly called the "Liberal Path." The proponents of the Liberal Path recommend that the U.S. should:

1) Make plans only to meet immediate crises, because all crises are temporary;

2) Not have government promote improvements in energy efficiency because the marketplace will provide the needed improvements.

3) Not have government programs to develop renewable energies because, again, the marketplace can be counted on to take care of all of our needs.

4) Let fossil fuel rates continue to increase because to do otherwise might hurt the economy.

5) Dig and Drill. Consume our remaining fossil fuels as fast as possible because we "need them." Don't worry about our children. They can count on having the advanced technologies they will need to solve the problems that we are creating for them.

6) Claim that population growth is a benefit rather than a problem, because more people equals more brains.

....

For our U.S. energy policy, we must choose between the Conservative and the Liberal Paths. The paths are the exact opposites of each other. Academically credentialed experts advocate each. On what basis can we make an intelligent choice?

There is a rational way to choose. If the path we choose turns out to be the correct path, then there's no problem. The problems arise in case the path we choose turns out to be the wrong path. It follows then that we must choose the path that leaves us in the less precarious position in case the path we choose turns out to be the wrong one.

So there are two possible wrong choices that we must compare.

If we choose the Conservative Path that assumes finite resources, and our children later find that resources are really infinite, then no great long-term harm has been done.

If we choose the Liberal Path that assumes infinite resources, and our children later find that resources are really finite, then we will have left our descendants in deep trouble.

There can be no question. The Conservative Path is the prudent path to follow.[22]

This argument is polarized — an either/or description of future energy pathways. The polarization makes a forceful point. Though it is not realistic to suppose humanity will follow either of these extremes, their description is helpful on clarifying values.

In spite of Prof. Bartlett's relatively equal treatment of the two different approaches, and his willingness to accept a possibility that resources are infinite, the evidence (at least for the sake of argument), from scientists and technologists around the world is that the Earth's resources are *finite*, limited. Responding to every shortage with redoubled efforts to extract more resources more rapidly is folly of the worst kind.

Energy Proposals

A balanced energy policy would accept the limited nature of our fossil fuel resources and take steps to make our use of them much more efficient, prolonging them for future generations. It would reduce or eliminate their burning, conserving these resources for use as feedstock for more durable and lasting uses, such as in polymers and other solid and liquid products (like lubricants and certain critical chemicals, not cost-effectively available from any other source.) It would search for viable, environmentally benign, and cost-effective alternative fuels, such as biomass, solar-generated hydrogen, and other renewable fuels. And it would take action to stop population growth, possibly reversing it for a time. Reversing population growth would be the most important component of a viable energy policy. There are several proposals toward these ends.

Energy Tax. One way to stimulate energy conservation and renewables would be to institute escalating energy taxes. This approach was suggested during hearings of the Subcommittee on Energy and Power of the U.S. House of Representatives in 1976. Professor Jay Forrester of the Sloan School of Management at the Massachusetts Institute of Technology described it thus: "It would have to be a high tax to have any real effect. A tax on nonrenewable energy at its entry into the economy is fairly easy to administer. Such a tax produces revenue instead of incurring costs that have to be raised by other taxes.... A sufficiently high tax levied by the United States and other importers on all energy would, in all probability, force down the international price of oil because it would push down consumption enough to exert a very considerable amount of interpressure on oil exporters. [And] it would give incentives for private actions for efficient use of energy."[23]

When President Clinton proposed a "Btu tax" during his first term, a wise and far-sighted policy if ever there was one, he was practically removed from office. The Btu tax never passed, illustrating the constraints under which even forward-looking leaders work.

Maybe it's not enough just to ask our leaders to be honest with us. Perhaps we need to become more honest with ourselves. Then we might support courageous proposals to protect the future for our children and ourselves.

According to Al Bartlett, Rep. John Anderson proposed a 50¢ per gallon gas tax in 1980 and got nowhere. Jimmy Carter proposed a 10¢ per gallon tax, to escalate automatically by another 10¢ per gallon every time a year's consumption exceeded that of the previous year. It got nowhere. President Reagan proposed a 5¢ per gallon tax to repair the interstate highway system and Jesse Helms filibustered the proposal to death.

The news is not all bad, however. In July, 2002, Bernie Fischlowitz-Roberts pointed out that several countries have taxed environmentally destructive products and activities, while simultaneously reducing taxes on income:[24]

The market price for a gallon of gasoline, for example, reflects the cost of drilling, extracting, refining and transporting the oil. The market price does not account for the air pollution and acid rain produced by burning gasoline, nor its contribution to climate change as evidenced by rising temperatures, rising sea levels, and more destructive storms. Raising taxes on environmentally destructive products and activities is designed to more closely align the market prices with their actual costs.

He then summarized a number of examples where forward-thinking governments have increased taxes on environmentally destructive and energy-consuming products and processes:

Germany, a leader in tax shifting, has implemented environmental tax reform in several stages by lowering income taxes and raising energy taxes. In 1999, the country increased taxes on gasoline, heating oils, and natural gas, and adopted a new tax on electricity. This revenue was used to decrease employer and employee contributions to the pension fund. Energy tax rises for many energy-intensive industries were substantially lower, however, reflecting concerns about international competitiveness.

In 2000, Germany further reduced payroll taxes and increased those on motor fuels and electricity. As a result, motor fuel sales were 5 percent lower in the first half of 2001 than in the same period in 1999. Meanwhile, carpool agencies reported growth of 25 percent in the first half of 2000....

One part of the United Kingdom's environmental tax reform involved a steadily increasing fuel tax known as a fuel duty escalator, which was in effect from 1993 until 1999. As a result, fuel consumption in the road transport sector dropped, and the average fuel efficiency of trucks over 33 tons increased by 13 percent between 1993 and 1998....

The Netherlands has also shifted taxes to environmentally destructive activities. A general fuel tax, originally implemented in 1988 and modified in 1992, is now levied on fossil fuels; rates are based on both the carbon and the energy contents of the fuel. Between 1996 and 1998, a Regulatory Energy Tax (RET) was implemented, which taxed natural gas, electricity, fuel oil, and heating oil.... [T]he RET's goal was to change consumer behavior by creating incentives for energy efficiency....

Since sixty percent of the revenue from these Dutch taxes came from households, the taxes were offset by decreasing income taxes. The 40 percent of revenue derived from businesses was recycled through three mechanisms: a reduction in employer contributions to social security, a reduction in corporate income taxes, and an increased tax exemption for self-employed people. This tax shift has caused household energy costs to increase, which has resulted in a 15-percent reduction in consumer electricity use and a 5- to 10-percent decrease in fuel usage.

Finland implemented a carbon dioxide (CO_2) tax in 1990. By 1998, the country's CO_2 emissions had dropped by almost 7 percent. Finland's environmental taxes, like those in most countries, are far from uniform: the electricity tax is greater for households and the service sector than for industry.

Sweden's experiment with tax shifting began in 1991, when it raised taxes on carbon and sulfur emissions and reduced income taxes. Manufacturing industries received exemptions and rebates from many of the environmental taxes, putting their tax rates at half of those paid by households. In 2001, the government increased taxes on diesel fuel, heating oil, and electricity while lowering income taxes and social security contributions.... This has helped Sweden reduce greenhouse gas emissions more quickly than anticipated.

According to these examples, taxes can be used to encourage energy conservation. The U.S., however, has remained steadfastly opposed to this proven methodology.

Raising energy prices. A few years ago, I wrote an article claiming that energy prices are too low. Of course the proposal is counter to prevailing wisdom, or at least to what are called "political realities," meaning pressure from an uninformed electorate. The price of gasoline had risen sharply, toward the $2.00 per gallon level. Truckers complained that gas prices were too high. The Energy Secretary said the U.S. was caught napping. So how could I be so foolish to say energy prices should be forced to increase still further?

I began by sympathizing with the truckers. They had become accustomed to low gas prices. Then I wrote that:

The recent surge in gas costs is too large, precipitous, and disruptive. I think we can agree on that.

What we may not agree on is my suggestion that the price of fossil fuel energy sources should be made to rise slowly, steadily, incrementally, each year for a decade or more.

This should continue until gas costs around $5, $10, or even $15 per gallon. This same increase should be reflected in all other forms of petroleum-based energy.

Heretical you say?

I described how these resources contain complex molecules with high energy content and that the resource cannot last forever, I continued:

Punching more holes in the ground, pumping more oil and selling it at higher volumes, may flood the market and lower energy prices in the short run. But this just hastens the day when the oil flow peaks and heads downward, reaching bottom when we have sucked it all out.

Already we are approaching the time when the only oil remaining is what I call "remote oil," oil that is so deep, so far offshore, so hard to extract, and so diluted that the price of recovery soars.

The remaining petroleum should be preserved and conserved for more valuable and durable uses, like plastics and pharmaceuticals. Instead we burn it up smokestacks and send it out tail pipes, producing air pollution and contributing to global warming.

....

With these energy and their related environmental difficulties, wouldn't finding ways of encouraging *less* energy use be prudent? Offering energy at current low prices can't help.

A slow and steady increase in energy costs would encourage us to live better with less energy. We would have more efficient automobiles and more comfortable homes. We could take our time to find ways of living closer to work, or moving factories closer to our homes. More of us would work at home, and our houses and other buildings would be made more efficient while increasing comfort.

Instead, we have set policies over the decades that make us more dependent on cheap oil. Current policy makes us highly susceptible to what other countries do with an oil resource that belongs to them.

Our ire should not be directed toward these energy-producing countries but more rightfully toward our politicians, our energy secretaries, our congressional leaders, and at ourselves.

We need people who will tell us the truth about petroleum supplies, and their expected rate of depletion, as world population grows exponentially and per capita energy use expands.[25]

Depletion Protocol. Colin Campbell has proposed a "Depletion Protocol" which would require producers to limit production depletion rates. Importers would refrain from importing above their current world depletion rate, with some exemptions. He claims that the importers would have to allocate their entitlement in some manner by market auction or by more social means; such as through taxes or a world accord. World prices would be held to modest levels, prolong the life of the resource, and avoid the tensions and excessive flows of money to the Middle East.

Stopping subsidies for polluters. The previously cited report by Fischlowitz-Roberts noted that subsidies—both direct and hidden—to polluting industries and processes can blunt the effectiveness of government tax shifting efforts. Removing these incentives to pollute is now being instituted in some countries.

Eliminating subsidies to environmentally destructive industries will also help the market send the right signals. Worldwide, environmentally destructive subsidies exceed $500 billion annually. As long as government subsidies encourage activities that the taxes seek to discourage, the effectiveness of tax shifting will be limited.[24]

The Nuclear Option. As we seek ways of keeping our outrageously low energy prices, nuclear energy is often mentioned. This source deserves special consideration. The fissioning of energy-packed radioactive nuclei releases copious quantities of energy from what is the most concentrated "fuel" yet found. There are many safety and other problems associated with massive use of nuclear power; the costs are likely to remain high, at least without government subsidies that shift costs from the utilities to our taxes, sending incorrect price signals to the energy market.

With experience, and some serious and fatal accidents, we have found that the costs of nuclear energy can be high. Opposition rose quickly as the dangerous aspects and potential for disaster were discovered. The catastrophe at Chernobyl certainly didn't help. No orders for new nuclear plants in the U.S. have been issued since the Three Mile Island partial meltdown in 1979[26]. Radioactive waste has to be disposed of somewhere. To date there is no generally accepted method of waste disposal for long-lived radioisotopes.

Nuclear energy is a potential source of clean energy, if problems of waste disposal and safety can be solved. However, the mining, transportation, and "refining" of nuclear fuel are extremely energy intensive. If the government does not pay these costs, the price of electricity produced with this fuel will be higher.

The Population Solution. Hardly anyone in power has either proposed or even suggested this strategy. By reducing U.S. and world population, the demand for energy will rise more slowly or decline. Population reduction will be an essential component of any effective and viable long term energy policy.

A Sensible Energy Future?

Figure 1 clearly shows that what we face in the future will be a mix of different energy sources rather than dominant use of just one. A second conclusion is that the more fossil energy we use, the more waste products will be produced, no matter how well designed and built the waste management technologies. Were it not for continued population growth and rising expectations of less affluent people, the current mix of energy conservation and future less-polluting uses of numerous energy sources might be sufficient to sustain humanity at present affluence for an indefinite period. But the billions in poverty want more. This spotlights again the importance of population reduction.

Redesigning our resource extraction, conversion, and use processes, to make them less impacting on our life-support system, will be critical. As we approach the end of abundant oil and find that other fossil fuels are polluting and difficult and expensive to obtain, we realize that we need new energy and population policies.

Sensible energy policy proposals — most notably calls for energy taxes — have died rapid deaths, simply because masses of people did not want them. Most did not understand fully the principle on which they were based, or the other issues surrounding our energy policy.

Instead of a well-planned and sound policy, we have the Bush proposal to "dig and drill." This is but another example of the need for massive re-education, at the top of government and among the electorate — teaching people the facts of Nature, and all the operating principles of their life-support system. Perhaps then we can hope that well-informed logic will prevail.

Current U. S. national energy policy is biased in favor of fossil fuels such as coal and oil, at the expense of the environment and public health. Our modest conceptual commitment to energy efficiency and renewables is not supported by appropriate action.

Stung by complaints over the "dig and drill" philosophy espoused by its National Energy Policy, announced in 2001, the George W. Bush Administration had Energy Secretary Spencer Abraham speak in 2002 to the National Press Club in Washington, DC. According to a July 2002 article in the *ASHRAE Journal*, "The U.S. consumes almost 99 quads of energy annually. According to estimates from the Energy Information Association, in two decades the U.S. will require 175 quads of energy annually *as a result of population and economic growth*." [Emphasis added.]

"The Administration aims to close the gap between current energy supply and projected demand with 48 quads from conservation measures and 28 quads from new production sources, including drilling for oil in Alaska's Arctic National Wildlife Refuge." The article quotes Abraham as saying that "The critics who say that our plan depends on drilling our way out of future energy problems have it all wrong. The reality is that we are going to depend on conservation and energy efficiency, and we are going to look to our laboratories and to the genius of the private sector for the new technologies that will deliver on this promise."

Energy policy is not something to be taken lightly. Energy is what fuels all our societies. To a great extent the prized wealth of the industrialized nations is built on a foundation of abundant fossil fuel energy, most notably oil. Its depletion will have strong, adverse consequences.

References

1. James J. McCarthy and Malcolm C. McKenna. "How Earth's Ice is Changing." *Environment* Vol. 42, no. 10 (2000): December 2000, 11.
2. WorldBook. *World Book Encyclopedia.* Chicago, 1999.
3. Alyn Duxbury. *An Introduction to the World's Oceans.* Sixth ed. McGraw-Hill: New York, 2000.
4. John Robbins. *Diet for a New America.* Stillpoint Publishing: Walpole, NH, 1987, 423 pp.
5. Francis Moore Lappe. *Diet for a Small Planet.* Tenth Anniversary ed. Ballentine Books: New York, 1982.
6. Folke Doyring. "Soybeans." *Scientific American,* (1974): February 1974.
7. C. J. Campbell. THE COMING OIL CRISIS,. Multi-Science Publishing Company & Petroconsultants: 1997, 210 pp.
8. S. Baron. "Economics vs. Energetics." *Mechanical Engineering* Vol. 103, no. 5 (1981): May 1981, 35-41.
9. Peter Knudson. "Net Energy Analysis and Solar Technology, Part 1." *New Mexico Monthly Bulletin* Vol. 3, no. 2 (1978): February 1978, 16-17.
10. H. T. Odum, "Net Energy Analysis of Alternatives for the United States," Submitted with testimony before the Subcommittee on Energy and Power of the Committee on Interstate and Foreign Commerce, House of Representatives: Part 1, Middle- and Long-Term Energy Policies and Alternatives, *U.S. Gov. Printing Office* Report No. Serial No. 94-63, 25-26 March 1976, Washington.
11. Kenneth S. Deffeyes. *Hubbert's Peak: The Impending World Oil Shortage.* Princeton University Press: Princeton, NJ, 2001, 208 pp.
12. M. King Hubbert. "The Energy Resources of the Earth." *Scientific American* Vol. 225, no. 3 (1971): September 1971, 60-70.
13. David Reed and Amory Lovins. "Oil, Oil Everywhere... Are we Running Out of It or Aren't We?" *Rocky Mountain Institute Newsletter* XIV, no. 1 (1998): Spring 1998, 7. http://www.rmi.org Note: Editor: Dave Reed.
14. M. King Hubbert, Exponential Growth as a Transient Phenomenon in Human History, in *The Fragile Earth: Towards Strategies for Survival in San Francisco,* World Wildlife Fund, 1976. http://www.hubbertpeak.com/hubbert/wwf1976/.
15. J. Laherrere. "World oil supply - What goes up must come down: when will it peak?" Oil and Gas Journal, (1999): Feb.1 p 57-64 and in Letters of OGJ March 1, March 15 & March 29.
16. Colin J. Campbell and Jean H. Laherrère. "The End of Cheap Oil." *Scientific American* Special Report, "Preventing the Next Oil Crunch", (1998): March 1998, 78-83.
17. Colin J. Campbell. "The Oil Peak: A Turning Point." *Solar Today* Vol. 15, no. 4 (2001): July/August 2001, 41-43.
18. C. B. Hatfield. "Oil Back on the Global Agenda." *Nature* Vol. 387, (1997), 121.
19. R. A. Kerr. "The Next Oil Crisis Looms Large—And Perhaps Close." Science Vol. 281, (1998), 1128-1131.

20. Alex Kirby, "Alternatives to oil — Renewable energy could become more important," World Wide Web, Last update: Friday, 8 September, 2000, 15:00 GMT 16:00 UK, Access date: 10 NOV 01.

21. Chairman: John D. Rockefeller, "Population and the American Future: The report of the commission on population growth and the American future," Report to the President and the Congress, *Presidential Commission on Population Growth and the American Future*, 27 March 1972, Washington, DC. Note: Published 1972 as a Signet Special in New York by the New American Library.

22. Albert A. Bartlett, Subcommittee on Energy, Science Committee. Invited oral testimony, "Our national energy situation is a mess!" U.S. House of Representatives, 3 May 2001.

23. Anonymous, Subcommittee on Energy and Power of the Committee on Interstate and Foreign Commerce. *Middle- and Long-Term Energy Policies and Alternatives*, U. S. House of Representatives, Second Session of 94th Congress, 25 and 26 March 1976.

24. Bernie Fischlowitz-Roberts, "Restructuring taxes to protext the environment," Internet, Access date: 29 April 2003, http://www.earth-policy.org/Updates/Update14.htm.

25. Ross McCluney, "Time to raise, not reduce, energy prices for consumers," *Florida Today*, Sunday, July 9, 2000.

26. Martha M. Hamilton, "Live Discussion: Nuclear Power Since Three Mile Island," internet online discussion, Access date: Tuesday, March 30, 1999.

27. Ross McCluney, "Just Enough," *Solar Today,* Letters to the Editor, 8 July 1992, pp. 7-6.

7
Getting Down to Business

The system of commerce is pervasive.
Examining some proposals for reform.

Socialism collapsed because it did
not allow prices to tell the economic
truth. Capitalism may collapse because it
does not allow prices to tell the ecological truth.
— Øystein Dahle, VP Esso for Norway and the North Sea, retired

The king wanted a bridge so his subjects could cross the river easily. He asked the village carpenter to do the job. The carpenter said he had never built anything so large, and would need help both designing and constructing it. The bridge had to be secure and lasting. The teacher had seen plans for another bridge that might be used for the design, so she was brought before the king.

The plans were found, but they required special metal connecting pieces. Neither the teacher nor the carpenter knew how to make them. The village blacksmith was summoned. He agreed to do the job, but only if it did not interfere with his other work. Keeping horses shod and wagons running were essential to the farms and grinding mill, and these occupied most of his time.

The blacksmith said he would make the needed parts if he could do it in his spare time. The carpenter said he would need many workmen to excavate the sides of the river where the bridge would be implanted, and several helpers to help him fabricate and assemble the parts.

The king contracted with all the needed workmen and the job began. Conflict arose immediately, however, and managing it became a nightmare, well beyond the expertise of the King's assistants. They tried brute force, but a small uprising amongst the workers stopped the project cold.

Clearly a new management structure would be needed, something to help the disparate workers cooperate better on the project. The new entity was established with some difficulty, and rules of cooperation were written up and signed to by the participants.

A new "corporation" was established, on a temporary basis, solely for the purpose of building the bridge for the people. It would disband when the bridge was done.

Corporate Origins

This fictional story illustrates the origin of the modern corporation. Investors were paid small sums for the temporary use of their money, but their role was only ancillary. The main purpose of the project, and of the corporation, was to serve the public, providing a *public* return on the investment of money, time, and effort used to complete the project.

Ralph Estes explained it this way: "In the beginning corporations were chartered by monarchs to serve the interests of the state. These sovereigns may have harbored less-than-noble objectives, and they may have abused their powers, but in their time (and still today in monarchies) they embodied the political power and the interests of society. Democracies later adopted this tradition of chartering corporations to serve a public interest."[1, p. 22] This early public purpose of the corporation is still in effect today. [a]

According to Estes, early corporations were considered extensions of the government, chartered to perform public services the state found difficult itself to provide. The goal was to avoid a permanent increase in government bureaucracy. Some of this practice is still followed today, when governments hire private companies for work governments conduct directly in other jurisdictions. Examples include the provision of drinking water, the disposal of garbage, and the operation of transportation systems. The corporate charter was subject to revocation when government found itself able and desirous of taking over the functions of the corporation, when those services were no longer needed, or when the job was not being done properly.

Corporations still had that status through the middle of the 19th century. Then something happened to change things. As David Finn explained in *The Corporate Oligarch,* "...a profit-making commitment to stockholders was formulated as the major corporate goal. In the process, what was once management's obligation to contribute to the public good became a matter of personal taste."[2, p. 53]

It often happens that a good initial idea slowly drifts in a different direction

---

[a] See, for example, Senate Committee on Commerce, *Corporate Rights and Responsibilities: Hearing Before the Committee on Commerce,* 94th Cong., 2nd session, June 1976; James Ole Winjum, *The Role of Accounting in the Economic Development of England:1500 - 1750,* Urbana, Ill., Center for International Education and Research in Accounting, 1972; John P. Davis, *Corporations: A Study of the Origin and Development of Great Business Combinations and of Their Relation to the Authority of the State,* New York, Capricorn Books, 1961; James Willard Hurst, *The Legitimacy of the Business Corporation in the Law of the United States: 1780-1970,* Charlottesville, The University Press of Virginia, 1970; and Ronald E. Seavoy, *The Origins of the American Business Corporation: 1784 - 1855,* Westport, CT, Greenwood Press, 1982.

with different purposes. Such has been the case with the corporation, as charters were extended to other kinds of enterprises less concerned with public interest. Many initially considered this development dangerous and a number of legislatures placed strong limits on the corporations so chartered. Fearing this "nonhuman person, without conscience or soul, who could roam the world at will," said Finn, the new corporations were restricted by government. In the United States, according to Estes, "Limitations imposed on corporate charters by state legislatures included a time duration, usually twenty years or less, full liability of stockholders for corporate debts, a narrow interpretation of charters, and a reserve clause that allowed the legislature to amend any charter at any time for any reason.

"The people feared big corporations, but were sought by developing states to stimulate settlement and growth. Interstate competition quickly altered the climate; soon states prostrated themselves before corporations with inducements, benefits, and a general relaxation of restrictions. Populist concerns were swept aside; the corporation was king.... What states were doing in the 1800s, cities and communities continue today. Dowries are offered to corporations far out of proportion to possible community benefits. Citizens and other, usually smaller, businesses pick up the tab. Corporations are bribed, pampered, wooed, and worshiped. They are protected by the law, granted benefits through their charters, and courted by communities. No longer are they held to a standard of public service."[1, p. 25.3]

The Accountants

When sovereigns chartered corporations, they assigned or hired people to monitor operations to see if the corporations were adhering to their public purposes and to help decide if the charter should be revoked. Sovereigns had ultimate power over these enterprises, but the financial investors did not. Early investors sought to protect their investments and hired their own accountants to monitor how their money was being used.[1, p. 27]

But the accountants monitored little more than monetary flows, leaving it to the monarch to ensure the public good was being pursued adequately. As corporations grew in size and independence, they retained the services of financial accountants themselves. The independence of corporations, due to lack of interest by society following the Civil War in America, for example, set the stage for the later multinational corporate behemoths. "Rapacious, predatory tycoons, men like Cornelius Vanderbilt, Jay Gould, John D. Rockefeller, Daniel Drew, Andrew Carnegie, and J. Pierpoint Morgan—all celebrated in Matthew Josephson's *The Robber Barons*—

were building giant corporate empires as often as not through unscrupulous, violent, and criminal means. These robber barons were secretive and distrustful. They wanted to be accountable to no one." [1, p. 27.4]

This is a particularly poignant quote in 2004, considering that Enron and other prominent American businesses went into bankruptcy in 2003 over improper and misleading accounting practices. These businesses engaged in bad and possibly criminal management actions—as the Securities and Exchanges Commission considered only the mildest of reforms aimed at restoring public confidence in American business.

Large Multinational Corporations

The independence of large corporations reached epic proportions around the turn of the twentieth century. As corporations grew larger than one or a few people could monitor, bureaucracies grew within them, both to manage operations and to measure financial performance. By this time there was no one — and no ready mechanism or interest — for measuring overall performance against its chartered purpose. In America, charters were granted for indefinite periods by state governments. The purposes of the corporation continued to be more narrowly limited to financial goals.

This narrowing of the charter, coupled with the loss of public or even internal scrutiny regarding larger societal interests, made the corporation largely what it is today. The former system of accounting was retained, but this monitored only finances. Furthermore, the corporation itself now purchased accounting services. In a few exceptions, lip service to broader interests might have been cited, but accountants were not trained to perform comprehensive environmental or societal impact assessments, nor were they provided with funds to contract for these services. This is one reason the bottom line on the profit and loss statement came to be such a prominent driver in corporate operations, now at the heart and soul of the modern corporation.

Corporate Realities

The Western system of privately owned businesses, operating in a free-enterprise system with limited government intervention, has lead to an unprecedented and simply amazing growth in technological advancement, industrial productivity, and agricultural output. The envy of much of the world, these have resulted in a remarkable increase in the material standard of living of at least one half the populations of the countries involved. The

U.S., Germany, France, Italy, and the Scandinavian countries have all benefited in the process. If you watch television or read newspapers and magazines in the U.S., the triumphalism of American business blares out with the excesses of Madison Avenue, boasting of the materialistic glories which await if you spend more money now on the advertised products.

Not everyone agrees that these developments have been good. Along with these "advances" have come some equally unprecedented and really terrifying problems now evident in daily news reports. Corporate mergers, takeovers, and downsizing have taken their toll on employees, customers, and the public in general. An expanding human population — and the complex, corporate-dominated, technologically-based society it has developed — threatens severe damage to Earth and presents us with bleak prospects.

The long-range consequences of these developments on a global scale are now becoming evident. The human species, as a global civilization, is depleting stored solar energy (fossil fuels) and other resources faster than these are replaced by natural means. The waste products of our technologically based society are exceeding in quantity and toxicity the ability of the planet's natural physical, chemical, and ecological systems to assimilate them. The problem is, as Paul Hawken says, that the current industrial system is a "Take, Make Waste Society," which must be transformed to a more environmentally benign system.

Our expanding population is damaging or removing portions of the world's major ecosystems, threatening much of their regenerative capacities. The social consequences of our environmental, economic, and corporative failures make average adults doubt that their children will have as good a life as they have had. At the core of these successes, as well as the failures, is the basic philosophy under which businesses operate.

Success in Business: Corporate Profits

Life is exceedingly complex in the industrialized nations today. We have fast-paced lives; everyone works harder and harder to achieve their economic goals. The "overhead of life" takes increasing fractions of our time and effort. When stressed out and pulled in different directions, everyone welcomes any simple idea to help explain things and clear away the complexity.

Such a new idea entered the culture of industrial societies in the latter half of the 19th century. The idea is that there is but one universal measure of business success — *profit*, (income after all the costs have been subtracted away). This simple and powerful idea about financial success soon became the nearly universal measure of both corporate and personal success. Accumulation of wealth and influence became the primary goal of the educated citizen, and of the schools, colleges, and universities which trained them.

The greater the profit, the more successful the business, its leaders, and its workers—historically by accountant definition, now by personal philosophy as well. The lower the profit, the less successful the enterprise and the person — by definition, if not by charter.

This new measure of success meets the simplicity test perfectly. The dictum became: *Get your income up and your costs down.*

There are *legitimate,* Earth-sustaining and people-protecting ways of doing both. Like making better products that serve useful functions, so lots of people find them of value, thereby increasing income without greatly increasing costs. Or it may be through improving the efficiency of the enterprise, producing more output for the same cost, or automating repetitive tasks to reduce labor costs and increase job satisfaction.

There are also *illegitimate,* Earth-depleting and societal-harming ways of achieving the goal. One is to develop a monopoly and avoid government regulation of it. Another is to carry legitimate marketing to excess, offering inflated statements of product function and desirability — half-truths, and even outright lies. Then you can work more on the psychology of the thing to get people to buy products and services they really don't need, may even be harmful to them, and create new marketing opportunities where none existed before. The advertising industry has developed this to an art form. And at great cost to the environment — for along the way it has reinforced the mistaken notion that quality of life and material wealth are synonymous.

Externalizing Costs

Illegitimate ways of cutting costs are easily found. The most popular is to put as many of your costs as possible on somebody else's books. This way the other person pays those costs, not you. Shifting costs to some other economic entity (whether it be a local or state government agency, another business, or your neighbors) is relatively easy. Usually it is the cost of removal and/or clean-up of waste products which is displaced.

Managers may try not to break the law. But within the law a lot can be done to displace costs to the other guy.

This is the current way of life in American business. Wherever possible, avoid costs, even if it means letting the taxpayer pick up the tab you don't want to pay. Better this than to be forced to raise the price of your product and lose your competitive edge.

Who pays in the end? The people. And the environment on which they depend for survival — our life-support system.

Early industrialists probably did not think of external costs this way. In the beginning, when companies were small and dispersed, there were fewer and hardly noticeable impacts of dumping their wastes, at least away from major population centers. Operating this way probably seemed natural. And with costs down, profits could soar. Later, when the consequences became noticeable and difficult, managers could justify the process by saying that this is the way it had always been done. They could continue to secrete away their knowledge of adverse consequences or pay off critics to keep their mouths shut.

The problem has an even worse dimension. By displacing costs in time and space, natural price feedback mechanisms are lost. This defeats the proper functioning of the free market, and deceives customers into thinking the price they pay is proportional to the costs of production. The free market is disrupted and price signals corrupted when costs are externalized to the environment. They are not included in the prices of products and services.

If all the costs to recycle and make benign the waste products of industrial operations were *internalized* (passed on to the customers as increased prices), the proper feedback and restorative powers of the market system could act. People would stop purchasing products and services whose environmental and social costs were too high. The current system has not really completely removed the feedback mechanisms; they are merely displaced in space and time.

In a sense, the free market still prevails and self-corrects bad practices but this often comes only later, and is more severe. When life-support systems start breaking down enough to kill off a company's customers or reduce their health enough that they won't buy its products anymore, finally the company will get the message. Pollution kills — not only people but also profits. However, the appropriate feedback might not happen for a while. Or the feedback is broken by displacement of the adverse consequences to some remote village on another continent.

Thus, the profit motive — successful in accelerating corporate growth — has also led to many serious problems, both locally and globally. Perhaps chartered corporations should be held more accountable to the public, with charters actually being withdrawn when corporations violate the trust placed in their hands by the government. Their errors, excesses, and adverse environmental and social impacts can be exposed and widely publicized. This could be accomplished without excessive need for government regulation and bureaucracy. If successful, corporations might return to their original purpose — serving society and protecting its future.

Unfortunately, what we have now is far from this more desirable model. We can conclude that the very structure of global corporatism is contributing to the environmental declines, health care inadequacies, energy wastefulness, and economic downturns about which we read and hear daily.

Accounting Narrowly

When this view is described to businessmen, they generally reply that shifting environmental and health care costs to the public may be common in some businesses, but good businessmen don't do such things. They are moral people who work hard at being good neighbors. "But what if one of your suppliers raises his costs, a competitor lowers his prices, you do the same to compete, and your profit margin starts shrinking as a result? Isn't this a very strong incentive to find new ways of cutting costs, including taking them off of your books?" This simple question is seldom addressed by CEOs. But they do answer it with their actions.

The current system of *narrow monetary accounting* (placing profits at the center of corporate operations) does not account for injuries to workers, for reports of dangerous or defective products, or the quantities of various forms of pollution injected to the air, water, and soil of the surrounding community. The current balance sheet is quite simple: Benefits to stockholders and upper management with costs going to the public at large (and the occasional stockholder when the market plummets). It does not look as Estes suggests it might[1, p. 29]:

Benefits to employees	$xxx
Benefits to customers	$xxx
Benefits to stockholders	$xxx
Benefits to suppliers	$xxx
Benefits to lenders	$xxx
Benefits to neighboring communities	$xxx
Benefits to society	$xxx
Total benefits generated	$xxx

Costs to employees	$xxx
Costs to customers	$xxx
Costs to stockholders	$xxx
Costs to suppliers	$xxx
Costs to lenders	$xxx
Costs to neighboring communities	$xxx
Costs to society	<u>$xxx</u>
Total costs created	$xxx

Contributing to the problem is the technical difficulty of placing monetary values on external costs and benefits, which are not easily valued. In the current system, if it cannot be counted, it doesn't count. This is another example of the perversion of the original intent for which corporations were established. They not only operate to benefit the overall good of the public, they often expel dangerous, toxic, and otherwise harmful substances into the air, water, and soil. Thus they produce health problems, discomfort, pain, and death. Their operations contribute to the loss of habitats and the extinction of species.

Some of these costs have easy-to-determine dollar values. Most do not. Regardless of monetary value, the corporation seldom pays. Society pays. The environment suffers.

This is where we find ourselves today — with gigantic corporations reaching into nearly every corner of human society, but with inadequate controls on their behaviors, except for the few laws to which they are occasionally held accountable. The laws do have some control over corporate behavior, but the modern large corporation is very secretive and security conscious. Gathering the facts needed to bring violators into the justice system is difficult. Even lawbreakers within large corporations generally go uncharged and unpunished.

The scandals of 2001 and 2002, with Enron, WorldCom, and a number of additional corporations under investigation, and with televised images of Adelphi principals being led off to jail in handcuffs, seemed to indicate a crack-down by government against the excesses of corporate managers. It remains to be seen, however, if this will extend beyond true law breaking to other, less obviously criminal behavior.

Corporate Welfare

Another problem comes when government gives tax money to corporations. "In the United States, automobile companies and related industries have effectively been on welfare for most of the twentieth century. Hidden automobile costs total nearly $464 billion annually, from the expense of taxpayer-funded road construction to the cost of Persian Gulf forces earmarked to protect America's access to 'its' oil."[1] If our gasoline were not subsidized heavily by government, the price to the consumer would be higher. We would then have greater incentive to use less, to switch to alternatives, and to purchase more efficient vehicles, reducing overall environmental impact.

Commonly called *corporate welfare*, Hawken and Lovins call these hidden costs *perverse subsidies*. "They function as disinvestments, leaving the environment and the economy worse off than if the subsidy had never been granted. They inflate the costs of government, add to deficits that in turn raise taxes, and drive out scarce capital from markets where it is needed. They confuse investors by sending distorting signals to markets; they suppress innovation and technological change; they provide incentives for inefficiency and consumption rather than productivity and conservation. They are a powerful form of corporate welfare that benefits the rich and disadvantages the poor."[5, p. 160]

In their book *Natural Capitalism*, Hawken, Lovins, and Lovins describe, in page after page of vivid detail, the remarkable levels of corporate welfare being provided "under the table" by governments. This can only be termed *social engineering*, since these practices strongly bias markets and change the face of society. Social engineering, despite the connotation, is the use of government regulation to force markets in particular directions or to otherwise impose constraints on human behavior for the greater good of society. It can be an effective tool for promoting *desirable* change, but it can also be misused, as is currently the case with government largesse toward the corporate world.

Perhaps we need a new warning label, a new *Caveat Emptor* (Buyer Beware), something like:

> The true price of this product is not what it says on the carton. You pay an additional amount through your taxes. This product may be harmful to your health, either directly due to poor design and/or manufacture or indirectly due to the pollution and other environmental harm produced during manufacture.

If business leaders truly desire a libertarian system of commerce, a laissez faire approach to free-market enterprise, then at least they ought to be consistent and let businesses sink or swim without government interference, without corporate welfare, including tax subsidies in all their forms. Ironically, "Free markets for sound investment are advocated in the same breath as corporate socialism for unsound investments — if they benefit the advocates."[5, p. 163]

A prime example of this was America's savings and loan scandal of the 1980s. Rather than penalize the lending institutions involved, and their investors, letting them suffer the logical consequences of their bad decisions and improper management policies, taxpayer dollars were used to bail them out. Taxes directly subsidized the private corporations, at the expense of millions of people who never had anything to do with these lenders. This has happened time and again in the U.S., proving the rule that if you want to screw up, make sure you do so really big. That way not only can you get away with it, you will be rewarded for it by a government rescue. If you screw up really small, you're more likely to go to jail.

The Amoral Corporation

The U.S. Bill of Rights was designed to institutionalize and protect the rights of human beings. Under the U.S. Constitution, the people are the root of all power and authority for government.

In the late 1800s, American corporate lawyers established a new doctrine called *corporate personhood*. According to this new principle, corporations became a type of legal person. They were thereby given essentially the same legal status as individuals, enjoying that status and the legal protections created for individuals. But they are not individuals. They do not possess human attributes, public concerns, or the same sense of responsibility toward the greater good of society.

True, managers of large corporations have power to exercise considerable discretion and could, in principle, act responsibly. Some might — out of a sense of moral or ethical duty — report on the wider, more publicly-applicable performance, as Ray Anderson has been doing with his Interface Corporation.[6] In most cases, however, the managers are held hostage by the system. If performance is only measured by the bottom line, managers will only be measured by the bottom line. If they try to offer additional measures of performance — ones which do not contribute directly to earnings, especially any that might produce a modest reduction in profits — they are either reprimanded or fired. Corporations are inherently amoral. Asking them to behave morally is like asking a worm to sing or a river to flow uphill.

The Spoils of War

There are other pressures on corporate managers to consider only profits in directing their enterprises and to measure only profits in assessing performance. Besides the negative threats of lost employment, some fairly sizeable enticements are available to avoid diversion into areas of societal good (and away from the ever-present compulsion toward profits). The ballooning "executive compensation package" is but one of these.

Chief Executive Officers (CEOs) of large corporations receive large salaries, many times greater than that of the average employee of the company. They are given extensive fringe benefits and stock in the company. They often have company-provided chauffeured limousines, corporate jets, helicopter rides over snarled traffic jams, and a variety of other inducements. More importantly, they wield considerable power and influence, not only in the company but also in the halls of legislative bodies at all levels. Power and money are strong inducements to ignore public benefits and focus only on bottom lines.

On 28 July 2002, Pete Peterson, Chairman of The Blackstone Group, said on ABC television's *This Week* program that average CEO salaries 20 years ago were 40 times the salary of the average worker, while now the ratio is more like 500 to 1.

Estes reported that, "In 1992 the CEO of HCA-Hospital Corporation of America, Thomas F. Frist, Jr., topped the executive pay sweepstakes with a whopping $127 million. That one person's pay would cover the cost of employing over 4,000 workers at $30,000 per year. Imagine standing before 4,000 people and telling them, 'My work is worth as much as that of all of you put together.'"[1, p. 70-71]

Compensation packages can be thought of as bribe money, to keep CEOs from yielding to whatever moral sensibilities they might have, setting company policies accordingly, and to keep them from jumping to the competition. The money becomes an exorbitant way to compensate the individual for his or her abdication of moral responsibility, helping them feel good about themselves while they do bad things to other people. This gives a new meaning to the term, *executive compensation*.

Substantial stock options given as inducements to corporate managers, for example, have largely corrupted the managerial classes. Colin Campbell says they are depicted as incentives, yet they actually transform the role of their recipients from working for shareholders to working for themselves on a very short-term basis. Mergers often allow management to collect their options from failed enterprises.

This is another example of a misplaced feedback system — improperly directed price signals. Instead of rewarding the CEO and lower level managers for good policy, they are paid off for the bad — for downsizing and outsourcing and externalizing pollution costs. The misdirected feedback which large compensation packages provide is more disturbing than their mere magnitude. A television pundit deftly summarized the problem when he said that the goal of corporate management used to be to run a good company; now it is to make a lot of money.

Don't the Stockholders and Boards of Directors Rule?

We have difficulty believing that the modern large corporation operates toward just one narrow goal — putting all its considerable resources into the sole pursuit of profits, largely disregarding the public interest, and ignoring input from the public, all at the behest of the CEO. Aren't the stockholders in charge? Don't they have the ultimate say over corporate operations? After all, the stockholders own the company, don't they? What about the Boards of Directors? Don't they select the CEO and oversee that person's work? And don't they own stock in the company too?

According to a number of writers, the stockholders neither truly own the company nor have any real power over company operations. In principle they elect the Boards of Directors. In practice nearly every stockholder sends in a proxy, giving away his or her vote to the Board itself, or to the CEO, or to their minions. Also in practice, directors are usually in the hip pocket of the CEO, or are otherwise unable or unwilling to exert control over the operations of the corporation. In principle stockholders can attend the annual meeting and make their views heard. In practice few do, and company management has many ways both to ignore irate stockholders and silence their voices. There was even a book written about it: *Handling Protest at Annual Meetings.*[7]

This is well known to serious students of corporate operations. According to Estes, "large corporations are generally not controlled, except in rare circumstances, by their stockholders or by any other external entity. Powerful corporate enterprises are, in the main, unconstrained by any social, legal, or financial institution. They are accountable to no one for their substantial power."[1, p.38] He describes precisely how this is accomplished in his chapter, "Power Without Accountability."

No less an authority than *Business Week* weighs in with this account, by Nussbaum and Dobrzynski, speaking about corporate governance.

> The corporation, perhaps more than most institutions, is based on a series of myths. Managers serve owners... Shareholders elect representatives to the board of directors. The free market disciplines winners and losers. All the myths have a purpose: to make us believe the corporation is accountable and efficient.
>
> The truth of the matter is that the public corporation has generally been a benevolent autocracy for decades. Managers have run the show. Shareholder meetings have been elaborate ceremonies. Proxy votes have been foreordained rituals. People who have served as directors on boards have usually been friends of the boss.[8]

At least the boards of directors must be in control, you might think. This is a popular view. But in most cases in large companies, management, usually the CEO, selects the directors, a selection merely ratified by the stockholders, at least in principle. In practice the choice of directors is seldom opposed and when it is, proxies executed by or for management overcome the opposition. As if this were not enough, "Chief Executive Officers often set their own level of compensation, as well as that of the other executives. They even select their own replacement CEOs. Directors do not make policy, and those who ask too many questions or otherwise annoy are replaced." [1, p.63]

For more detailed information on the role and functions of directors in large corporations, see *Directors: Myth and Reality* by Professor Myles Mace of the Harvard Business School[9].

The Myth of Government Regulation

In the face of widespread corporate misbehavior and massive environmental destruction at the hands of some business managers, it is natural to turn to government as the right and proper entity to act on behalf of the people it represents and to impose limits on the so-called free enterprise of businesses. After all, government charters corporations.

There *are* laws governing corporate operations, including pollution regulations. Many corporations obey these. Some do not. Ways can be found to get around many of them.

Government does regulate businesses in the U. S. in many areas. We have environmental regulations, health and safety laws, "truth in advertising" provisions, and controls on health care costs.

One problem is that this system pits business *against* the people, represented by government regulatory agencies. The former seek to lower costs by whatever means available, and to avoid the limits imposed by regulatory agencies. This is often done with whatever means are available, including the use of hired scientists, lawyers, and expert witnesses. The regulators are often overworked, underpaid, and insufficiently staffed. Frequently the regulations, or the systems developed to administer them, are inadequate to the task, resulting in terrible environmental and health disasters, as well as other, less apparent abuses.

One response is to increase the number of regulations, and, unfortunately, the sizes of the regulatory agencies. The cost to business, the government, and the public of operating this regulatory system is large and growing. The businesses most restricted by the regulators, and the politicians to whom these businesses contribute regularly complain. In late 2003, the Securities and Exchange Commission and the Congress considered a number of new regulations and laws, in response to the Enron and WorldCom fiascos in mid 2002. Is more government regulation really the answer?

The adversarial nature of the current method of government regulation is a serious problem. Good behavior has to be *forced* by the threat of negative consequences from the outside, and other remedies government can require, often following long and costly litigation. It pits the corporation against the public, as represented by government agencies enforcing the laws, government lawyers litigating them, and the Congress in making them. Often the public itself is caught up in the conflict, having to push government to do its job against often powerful and influential corporations. When government enforcement is inadequate, volunteer public-spirited citizens take it upon themselves to try to limit corporate misbehavior themselves. Getting notices of dredge-and-fill projects from the Corps of Engineers web site, for example, and sending a reasoned, thought-out comment can be very effective. But asking unpaid volunteers lacking either the time or training to do the job on a routine basis is a failure in the design of the system.

Change the System

Do you believe in the importance of private-ownership and free market enterprise — as well as the need to protect public interests? Then you necessarily must also accept the logic of government intervention, on behalf of people individually incapable of policing all the business practices affecting them. Another alternative is to build into the basic structure and operation of business the controls needed to protect the greater interests of society and our life-supporting environment.

Very few proposals in current public debate support this second idea.

Fortunately, beginning steps are being taken by a few businesses to clean up their acts from within. One method being employed is to have the workers own and operate the business. They generally live in the community where the business operates. They can at least limit the local consequences of displacing costs from the accounts of the business to the public at large. These worker/owners can also provide for themselves adequate health care programs and other benefits, and generally ensure that the business is an ethical and caring member of the community in which it operates.

Large, multinational corporations are an extreme case. Converting the existing ones to labor ownership and operation is probably impossible. Furthermore, any labor-owned businesses would have to be protected from external hostile takeovers through the chartering mechanism or other creative regulation. Otherwise the giant corporations would just buy out their labor-owned competition. What laborer could resist selling his or her share in the company for the largest single sum ever received in one's lifetime?

If we eliminate the stockholders, the directors, the government, and the employees as controlling factors promoting the public interest in corporations, what is left? Perhaps it is the market that rules.

Will the Market Take Care of It?

Some, mostly libertarians, claim almost no regulation is needed, that regulation just costs everybody, slows the system down, and is unresponsive to changing markets. They argue for leaving the market to itself. The market rules. If the bottom line controls everything, then the customers really have the last word.

If this is true, it is so only in principle. Massive boycotts by consumers, sustained and effective, *can* nudge giant corporations somewhat (such as when public concern about Styrofoam cups and containers led McDonalds to switch to paper). But organizing and executing a massive boycott and sustaining it for long is very difficult.

How do you alert people to the planned action? The news media generally do not cover such stories unless they are massive, pre-publicized, or are already taking place. You can send the message out over the Internet. But where do you get e-mail addresses of large numbers of people? Even if you have them, your announcement is likely to be considered just part of the background of junk mail we all receive and which is discarded instantly.

Fortunately, if a product is defective or undesirable, few will purchase it. Giant corporations know this, and usually avoid marketing the real duds. The most effective control consumers have over corporations is normally related only to the price of the product and how it performs for them. Seldom do you see effective consumer action over such hidden issues as environmental destruction, exploitation and abuse of child labor, or price-fixing.

Estes says that customer discipline of corporate action can be successful only when three conditions are met: 1. The product is simple. 2. Buyers have complete information or can get it relatively easily. 3. Many sellers, alternate suppliers of the product, are not owned by one or a few corporations.

These conditions are seldom met in practice. I would add a fourth: 4. Effective communication channels must exist to spread the word of a planned action.

Of course, if the corporation's products kill off all its customers, the market will certainly dry up for that product, probably for any other product made by that company. But if killing and human suffering is not massive, or is spread over a large geographical range and over long time periods, it might not be that noticeable (such as with cigarettes). Another way to wriggle out of responsibility is for the company to rename itself, or restructure and merge with another company, slinking away from public scrutiny.

The absurdity of expecting the market alone to control corporations should be obvious. A parallel is less obvious. The argument is sometimes made that natural environmental limits will constrain corporate operations eventually, by loss of raw materials and other environmentally damaged resources, and by employee and customer disease and suffering directly attributable to corporate action. As this argument goes, we can just relax and let Nature take its proper control, exerting its own corrective action.

By the time this control is exercised, it may be too late to reverse the damage. Millions can be affected, possibly permanently, and Earth's ecosystems can be radically altered, permanently, in ways adverse to humanity. Such an approach denies human intelligence—our ability to gather information, draw inferences, and act on them.

Perhaps the free-market paradigm, of which corporate managers are so enamored, has become their philosophy of how the world works. They find parallels in the theory of evolution and proclaim that the principle of natural selection can apply to them. Thus, overpopulation is not a concern. When it gets too huge to be manageable, Mother Nature will take corrective action.

Campbell suggests that governments love "the notion of an open market as the supreme arbiter of good or evil. It allows them to ignore their basic responsibilities and blame all the many defects on all sides as a consequence of 'the market.'"

This provides a clue to what will later be described as one of the best proposals for reforming commerce. The key, as in so many other areas, is for humans to use their intelligence. Fundamental system reforms can be made aggressively, starting now, keeping just ahead of Nature's natural corrective mechanisms — depletion, destruction, and die-off.

Corporate Rule

I have made the argument that markets are largely controlled by the corporations and not the other way around. Though most of us don't think we are much affected, advertising is so pervasive we can hardly escape it.

Corporations control or even create artificial markets for their products in other ways. Powerful influences exist in educational systems and on radio and television. A movie star might be drinking a brand of soft drink or beer, or smoking a cigarette, the brand name of which is prominently displayed and visible on the package. Such "product placement" is an important tool of the advertising industry. It even extends into the classroom.

Schools are flooded with product logos and propaganda, and now even products too, as schools make cozy deals with vending machine companies to place these purveyors of junk food in prominent places on campuses.

It is possible that the case for corporate domination and badness is somewhat overstated here, mainly to make some important points. A few corporations are responsive to publicity and public pressure. Large corporations, especially, have a huge stake in their public images and take some pains to protect them. Occasionally this is done by sincere efforts to do the right thing; if not just for image purposes, then to avoid threats of large and costly law suits.

The fear of civil litigation and large settlements or fines may not be as powerful as one might expect, however. The cash reserves, held in a variety of liquid assets (or quickly obtainable from friendly lending institutions), are simply huge for many large corporations. Payment of a fine or civil settlement, however large, in most cases is but a minor perturbation on the corporate balance sheet.

Business and Growth

Suppose you have a modest-sized consumer-oriented business in a small town. More people move into the town and your business grows. If you are lucky, no competitors move in, at least for a while. As the town grows, your business grows. The money you receive personally from it each month grows as you expand operations to keep up with the growing market for your goods. What if you are not a particularly good business manager? The business will still grow, probably, unless you are really hard on your customers. What if the population growth of your community stops? Then you have difficulty keeping your income rising. You might even have to start running your company better.

In a nutshell, growth rewards bad management. You must exert much effort to keep a business operating, and even growing, when the population is stable. This fundamental process lies at the heart of the incessant desire for economic growth. With continued economic growth, you can get rich without working too hard for it. All you need is a little patience and modest management skills.

By changing our mindset, we can all live well without economic growth. Sustainable societies are non-growing societies. With exceptional management skills and good business practices, we can set aside economic growth as a society goal and replace it with more sustainable ones.

Corporate Beliefs

Though large corporations are devoted almost totally to the pursuit of profits, many who operate them, study them, and otherwise have interests in their financial success do have *belief systems* (sets of values used to justify judgments, decisions, and actions). Often these values are used to downplay environmental concerns and concerns that the future is otherwise not rosy for most humans. Many of their arguments are examined in the next chapter.

For this section I focus on corporate value systems, as expressed in business-oriented publications such as *The Wall Street Journal, the Economist* magazine, *Forbes*, and the writings emanating from conservative research organizations such as the Cato Institute.

Paul Hawken writes: "Many economists continue to insist that natural and manufactured capital are interchangeable, that one can replace the other. While they may acknowledge some loss of living systems, they contend that market forces will combine with human ingenuity to bring about the necessary technological adaptations to compensate for that loss."[5, p. 152]

One example is the belief that we can wait until ozone depletion and global warming problems become demonstrably bad before asking business to alter its practices, stopping its contributions to these terrible trends. The philosophy seems to be that once the abuses become bad enough they will naturally send price signals back to the corporations and the inappropriate business practices will change, or at least that government regulation, imposed on *all* businesses finally can be welcomed by them. This view suffers from the *too little, too late* effect described previously, and cannot be taken seriously in the light of current irrefutable scientific knowledge about the harmful effects of many business operations.

Misplaced and outmoded beliefs, such as this one, when they drive corporate decisions, can devastate the Earth. Examples include such statements as: "Growth is good, more growth is better" (referring to growth in sales, resources exploited, income generated, or material affluence rather than to spiritual, cultural, educational, or psychological growth) and "An unrestricted free-market economy is best for everyone."

An alternative view is that business *will* make changes, as needed, to protect critical natural systems, but only when scientifically recognized as necessary. This viewpoint does not extend to taking preventive action before problems become pronounced.

Hawken, Lovins, and Lovins speak of the commonly found economic fundamentalist value system as being like a "theology that treats living things as dead, Nature as a nuisance, several billion years' design experience as casually discardable, and the future as worthless. (At a 10 percent real discount rate, nothing is worth much for long, and nobody should have children.)"[5, p. 261]

Corporate Image

Most large corporations have become wealthy and powerful. Transcending national boundaries, they have generally lost their allegiances to any country or its people. With their wealth they finance elections, hire powerful lobbyists to make their cases to willing legislators (to whose campaigns they contribute, sometimes heavily), in all political parties. Influence in the executive branch of government is no less strong, due to "revolving door" practices and other connections.

Corporations have become enormously successful at doing what they direct themselves to do—make money. In the process they have built a huge, pervasive, and impersonal system to provide copious material goods, extensive services, and wealth for the few, the likes of which the world has not previously seen, save for a handful of monarchs and dictators.

With the success of corporations pursuing their narrowly focused widely lauded tasks, people tend to think the corporate model is more *generally* applicable — good for growth, good for economic prosperity, good for people, and good for society in general. With this mindset it is easy to accept the conventional wisdom that "what's good for General Motors is good for the country." The fallacy is becoming evident, as people question corporate dominance and start to wonder if corporate supremacy is really good for them.

The general belief, however, remains that economic growth is good and more growth is even better. If you have a problem in the world (whether it be medicine, bridge construction, broadcasting, use of public lands, education of children, or the operation of national parks and monuments), give it to a corporation. Wash your hands of any responsibility for it, except for the regular infusion of tax dollars to keep the operation going.

Unbridled belief in corporations was strongly tested in the wake of the Enron bankruptcy scandal of 2001 and 2002, and several others that followed.

Privatization

The previously growing acceptance that corporate success can be extended to nearly any enterprise even reaches to the running of government. The process of converting government operations to corporate operations, known as "privatization," or "privatizing," has spread through much of the industrialized world. The tenet is that a corporation can do it better and cheaper than government. So we are urged to turn our government operations over to corporations (with "proper controls," of course).

A legitimate point is noted here. Government operations are not for profit. But when bureaucracies become bloated, they can become distant from the political leaders elected and appointed to oversee them; and also distant from the people they serve who ultimately pay them. Government operations easily become wasteful and inefficient. Since the powerful driving motive of profit is not present, costs are allowed to drift upward. When the organization is large and complex, its efficiency is less directly tied to or observable by the public. Appropriations tend to drift upward, as well, to meet the bureaucracy's growing "demands".

We are enticed to think that the profound success of corporations at converting natural resources into consumer goods can be extended to the operation of government entities. In some cases when this has been tried, it has been very successful. The bloated bureaucracy has been thrown out, new people hired, and a more efficient management system put in its place. Hiring more qualified people and paying them well requires less micromanagement. When corporate profit is tied to operational efficiency and streamlined operations, a powerful incentive keeps costs down. However, the enterprise being so managed does not produce a profit for the government — only for the corporate operator. Its income depends only on the executive overseer's discretion and the willingness of legislative appropriators.

Normal business activities operate in the margin between income and costs. Income is tied to customer satisfaction, providing feedback for improving the product or service and thereby attracting customers. Business-in-government distances income from such "customer" satisfaction.

In between are political and governmental interlopers. They are the elected officials providing the funding and the executive branch overseers of the operations. If the public is unhappy with the way a corporate-operated government agency is run, feedback flows to the legislator, thence to the overseer, and then to the person in the corporation charged with keeping the "client" or "customer" happy. This indirect system is ripe for corruption and has built-in inefficiency.

Only alert, astute, careful, and ethical government and business overseers can keep the contractor doing the job well and efficiently. Often their roles are compromised by perquisites and other benefits provided them by the corporations they oversee. Or they can be bribed outrightly to look the other way as corporate profits soar and public service declines.

The solution to government waste and sluggishness is not to replace all of it with profit-making corporations, but to design the system well, hire good people, and adapt and use some of the excellent business management practices developed over the years to streamline government operations.

Fundamental Reforms — Redesigning commerce.

A far better approach than massive government regulation and citizen "watchdogery" would be to reform the corporation's structure, management, rules of operation, and very reason for being. Fundamental reform of the system of commerce has been proposed by a variety of writers. The most prominent suggestions are described here.

To keep private ownership and free enterprise, we *do* need to keep government regulation and intervention. The problem is how to do this fairly, equitably, effectively, and with least cost to society. How can we make this system more efficient and more effective, lowering the taxpayers' costs to support regulation while making sure businesses do not exceed important limits in their drive for increased income and higher profits?

These are difficult questions, deserving of creative, insightful responses. We must address them in all aspects of our economic lives. The fate of the industrial society, not to mention the fate of our children, could well be at stake. We need to make the system better, without letting narrow and outmoded values interfere and produce inappropriate responses.

The debate needs to be more clearly drawn. The underlying philosophy and values must be stated carefully and the consequences of those values on proposed public policy, government regulations, and re-structuring of tax collection must be detailed carefully. It seems best if protections can be built into the structure of the business enterprise, to take place as a natural part of daily business activities.

We will never eliminate commerce, nor should we even consider it. There will always be the exchange of goods and services, whatever we choose to call it. What we need is to change the paradigm under which the system works.

Business Reform Proposals

Corporate Accountability Reform. Ralph Estes offers a sensible proposal for business reform. He says corporations need a better scorecard, that corporate accountability must take place in the *mechanism* by which the corporation is operated, that the yardstick by which they are measured must be enlarged to include *all* stakeholders and interests.[1, p.202]

Corporate managers must be removed from the straightjacket of an ineffective performance evaluation system. They should be evaluated on the balance they achieve among several dimensions, including the overall societal goals, which the corporation was initially formed to pursue. The way to do it, Estes argues, is to "Make the [performance] information public, and stakeholders as well as the media will respond.... Put it out for the world to see, for stakeholders to act on, for the media to question, and executives are in a different ballgame." This avoids a government *command and control* approach with its inefficiencies and inequities. Already established is a system of financial disclosure which could be expanded to monitor business and publish corporate performance reports, the accuracy and comprehensiveness of which would be required.

Estes proposes a Corporate Accountability Act that would "call for the Securities and Exchange Commission to be redesignated as the Corporate Accountability Commission, charged with establishing requirements for an annual, comprehensive, public *Corporate* Report to stakeholders. The commission would also be charged with bringing order and greater usefulness to corporate regulatory reporting by consolidating such reports into the *Corporate Report*."[1, p. 209]

This report would tell such things as "how many people had died from workplace injuries last year, what that brown stuff is [that is] pouring out of a company's smokestacks, and how the company has settled with customers over product problems, and how much top executives were making while they were 'downsizing' your job."

One possible flaw in the Estes proposal is his narrow definition of stakeholder as "a person or other entity that has a significant interest in the performance, actions, and affairs of a corporation by virtue of an investment or potential investment (an investment being considered) in the corporation." If "or other entity" could be extended to all life forms on the planet, then perhaps this definition would be sufficiently inclusive. On the other hand, microbes cannot read corporate reports, so the report's utility would depend upon human surrogates to pursue their interests.

Appropriate Technology. An early idea for reforming the system of commerce came from E. F. Schumacher in his landmark book, *Small is Beautiful – Economics as if People Mattered.* Although Schumacher was most concerned with development in the third world, his book offered an early vision for a new system of commerce. Published in 1973, the book emphasized the importance of *people* in any system of commerce [10, p. 202]. He believed in handing people tools of manufacture appropriate to their cultures, economic situations, and environmental surroundings.

Rather than give a peasant farmer a diesel powered irrigation pump, and make him dependent on industrialized countries for fuel, spare parts, and the cash to purchase them, Schumacher advocated what was called *appropriate technology.* That is modest technology that does the job without putting people out of work. "The methods of production, the patterns of consumption, the systems of ideas and of values that suit relatively affluent and educated city people are unlikely to suit poor, semi-illiterate peasants. Poor peasants cannot suddenly acquire the outlook and habits of sophisticated city people. If the people cannot adapt themselves to the methods, then the methods must be adapted to the people... There are, moreover, many features of the rich man's economy which are so questionable in themselves and, in any case, so inappropriate for poor communities that the successful adaptation of people to these features would spell ruin."[10, p. 203]

Schumacher promoted the notion that the best foreign aid is useful knowledge, "infinitely preferable to a gift of material things." A gift that is not earned may be taken for granted, and one which is difficult to use (or in other ways totally unfamiliar to the recipient) is not much of a gift at all. "The gift of material goods makes people dependent, but the gift of knowledge makes them free — provided it is the right kind of knowledge, of course."[10, p. 209]

He reiterated the familiar saying, "Give a man a fish and he eats for a day. Teach a man to fish and he eats for a lifetime." (A current joke is that, in Georgia, if you give a man a fish he'll eat for a day. But if you teach him to fish, he'll sit in his boat and drink beer all day. The environmentalist version is, "Teach a man to fish, have the government subsidize his boat, or guarantee his loan on it, and refuse to set sensible fishing limits. Then he and his friends will deplete or destroy the world's fisheries." And we will end up like the guy who eats for just a day. Better to teach a man to grow grains, fruit, and vegetables, which can be produced more sustainably than fish or livestock, and he can eat for a lifetime, without destroying Nature in the process.)

Natural Capital. The concept of *natural capital* has become important in new, more encompassing, theories regarding the human endeavor. The idea is to expand the limits of economics to include the natural world.

Resources taken from Nature are the true capital of human enterprise. We need an expanded definition of "the economy" to include all parts of the biosphere involved in the process of taking materials and services from Nature and using them to support life, both human and nonhuman.

Every businessman bent on keeping his company in business for a long time knows that if you spend your capital (i.e. if you sell off your means of production), your output will drop and your business will fail. The same is true of the more encompassing economy. If you "spend the capital" of Nature, depleting resources, eventually the enterprise will fail for lack of input materials.

The concept of natural capital was described in some detail by Thomas Prugh in *Natural Capital and Human Economic Survival.*[11] Prugh writes that "a synthesis of ecological ideas and economic theory is necessary to correct the historical errors economics has made concerning humanity's relationship to the ecosphere." The central ideas of his proposals are:

1. The global ecosystem (the natural environment) provides a vast array of indispensable resources and services to human beings. Viewed this way, the environment is a form of capital, here called *natural capital*, which is necessary for human economic activity and survival. Natural capital can never be entirely replaced by any combination of human labor, wealth, and technology, although it is sometimes implied or assumed otherwise.

2. The Earth's natural capital endowment is under severe strains from rapidly increasing human economic activity and population. The available evidence of environmental problems strongly suggests that many forms of natural capital are, or are becoming, seriously degraded and scarce. If this continues, the remaining natural capital will be inadequate to allow human beings to continue living on the planet as we have in the past, much less to expand the global economy as nearly everyone demands. Accordingly, conserving and investing in natural capital should be among our most urgent priorities.

3. The view of natural capital offered by mainstream (neoclassical) economics suffers from a grave theoretical flaw that has critical policy implications. Mainstream economics views natural capital as only a single, rather unimportant, factor of economic production. In contrast, ecological economics views it as the very foundation of the economy. Without natural capital, human economic activity is impossible. Although neoclassical economics did not create the tendency to overexploit natural capital, it has aided and abetted that overexploitation and blinded citizens and policymakers to the need for a restructuring of the economic rules by which we play.

4. Revenue-neutral policy options could restructure the economic system to encourage conservation of, and investment in, natural capital. Such policies would help ensure our economic viability into the indefinite future. They would work, in part, by properly valuing natural capital resources and services, thus accounting for the indispensable contribution natural capital makes to economic production. By helping to *get the prices right*, they would promote true economic efficiency. This is the first and most important step toward sustainability.

The Natural Step. In the late 1980s, cancer researcher and physician Karl-Henrik Robèrt of Stockholm, was awakened to the destructive effects industrial society is having on our habitat, and confused about the seeming lack of interest on the part of the media and the public. He decided to do something about it. He used the metaphor of a funnel to visualize our declining life-sustaining resources and increasing demands, spelling disaster for humanity. "The converging walls of the funnel represent the globally declining productivity of renewable resources per capita. More and more resource input is required for each unit of production from forests, agricultural land, and fishing waters. At the same time, the declining vital life-sustaining resource base of Nature is exposed to climate change and increased concentrations of pollutants. Finally, the population of the world is increasing, projected to reach 10 billion people in the next generation, while the traditions that keep our cultures together are getting weaker and weaker."[12, p. xiii]

Robèrt knew that people largely blamed business for the problems, and in most cases with good reason. He sought a more restorative society, based on an intelligently designed economic engine, one transformed to serve Nature as well as humans. In his optimism, he figured that a number of simple solutions must be just waiting for discovery.

His response was to invite a number of knowledgeable scientists, business leaders, and other specialists in a variety of disciplines to study the problem and formulate some answers. He founded a non-profit organization called The Natural Step (TNS) in Sweden in 1989. They chose as a starting point "the first order principles of ecology, economy, and social sustainability for the whole ecosphere."

The Natural Step uses "a science-based framework to help individuals and organizations understand sustainability and build sound programs, tools and metrics. It is based on a well-developed planning methodology for assessment, visioning, and action."

The "Framework" has assisted many companies and organizations to develop *strategic sustainability initiatives*. These initiatives have helped them achieve greater effectiveness, competitive advantage, bottom line results, security, employee satisfaction and public acceptance.

The following four "system conditions" were defined as core principles of The Natural Step, with clarifications in brackets.

In the sustainable society, Nature is not subject to systematically increasing:

1. concentrations of substances extracted from the Earth's crust [sustainable businesses need to decrease their dependence upon heavy metals and fossil fuels, substituting renewable sources of materials and energy];

2. concentrations of substances produced by society [sustainable businesses need to avoid using persistent unnatural compounds such as brominated fire retardants, chlorinated plastics and solvents, and persistent pesticides.]; or

3. degradation by physical means
[We must live off the interest of what Nature provides and we must not use up Nature's capital. Sustainable businesses must not derive wood or food from ecologically maltreated land, and must not use materials that require long-distance transportation.]
And in that society...

4. human needs are met worldwide.
[We must be fair and efficient in meeting basic human needs and must stop wasting resources around the world.][12, p. 23]

TNS recognizes that the whole structure of industrial society is based on a faulty design, violating the conditions for sustainable human life on Earth. TNS calls for a natural systems approach.

TNS organizations have been created in the U.S., Canada, U.K., Australia, New Zealand, the Netherlands, Japan, and South Africa and the dialog has spread to other countries as well. It is a popular movement with active Internet communications with its members and other interested people.

The Ecology of Commerce. A more comprehensive proposal for the reform of commerce, an alteration of the very paradigm by which it operates, came from an unlikely place. Paul Hawken was attending a black tie banquet at the Waldorf-Astoria in New York City. The event celebrated the presentation of an environmental stewardship award, which his company had won. He describes what happened next:

I walked to the podium, looked out at the sea of pearls and black ties, and fell mute. Instead of thanking everyone, I stood there in silence, suddenly realizing two things: first, that my company did not deserve the award, and second, that no one else did, either. What we had done was scratch the surface of the problem, taken a few risks, put a fair amount of money where our mouths were, but, in the end, the impact on the environment was only marginally different than if we had done nothing at all.... All the recycling in the world will not change the fact that doing business in the latter part of the twentieth century is an energy intensive endeavor that gulps down resources.[13, p. xi-xii]

What Hawken realized in the months following this event was that the current system of commerce has been inadvertently designed for environmental failure. If we are to turn the system around, it will not be by adversarial processes designed almost entirely to force business to *do the right thing* but by a complete redesign of the system for success.

In his book *The Ecology of Commerce*, Hawken details what he learned.[13] He declares that business has just plain refused to face and to confront environmental issues. As a result there are tens of thousands of environmental groups around the world trying to abate or at least ameliorate the destruction of the world caused by human commerce. As important as the environmental gains have been, this battle cannot be won, because commerce and industry are growing faster than Nature and the environmental successes that seek to protect it.

Hawken points out that at the core of human life on Earth is the making and exchanging of goods and services — *commerce*. The present system of commerce may be killing the life-support system of Planet Earth, but we can't do away with it. We have no choice but to try to change it.

"To be successful we need a system of production and trade where each and every act is inherently sustainable and restorative of the Earth's life-support system."[13] How do we do this? If you think about it much, it's a very daunting proposition. As with many destructive and addictive behaviors, we must start with simple acknowledgement, however painful that might be. We must recognize that commerce lies at the core of our problems and then redesign the system to overcome them.

A Natural Model. Hawken came across a very important principle that can be used in redesigning commerce. When looking around for a template for our newly designed economic system, we can turn to Nature itself for models of sustainability.

In Nature the practice of poisoning your food with your wastes is self-correcting. There are *natural feedback mechanisms* available to restore the health of the system. If we put health and environmental costs back into the prices of products and services, then the resulting new price signals will lead to more appropriate buying decisions.

An interesting characteristic of the current system of commerce leads to disastrous environmental consequences: *linearity*. The system is based on a one-way flow of goods from the Earth, through the system, back to the Earth as useless — or even toxic — waste. This is the origin of Hawken's claim that the system is a "take, make waste" one. To counter this approach, Hawken appeals to another basic principle: *Nature cycles*.

The idea is that *waste equals food*. What is waste from one organism is food for another. It is not so much that Nature recycles, but that the whole system is designed to be cyclic from basic principles. We need to place cycling and recycling at the core of our new system of commerce.

Hawken offers three basic principles to guide the new system he envisions:

- Every manufacturing entity must be responsible for the materials it processes, even after they leave the plant.
- Nature runs off of solar income. We must learn to live within our daily budget of energy from the sun. Industry must learn to reduce drastically its energy use and to obtain the remainder from renewable sources.
- In Nature there is strength in diversity. Healthy systems are varied and specific. A strong and secure economy will be a diverse one. More than profit and loss must measure business success: Useful employment, quality products, and loyal and healthy customers.

These and other good models can be used in redesigning commerce. Some are already being tested with good success. Many businesses have discovered ways to work together for their common economic good as well as for a lessened impact on the environment. In some cases one industry finds that its declining or expensive raw material can be obtained from the by-products of some other industry's operations. (There are cases where multiple separate organizations have developed a symbiotic relationship producing significantly less toxic and other waste products while reducing the costs of doing business for all partners in the enterprise.)

Intelligent Products. An important new development is being pioneered in Germany. Called the "Intelligent Product System", this approach seeks to eliminate waste altogether. There are three categories of products in this system:[13, pp. 67-70]

Consumables. Consumables are products that are used and consumed, usually only once, and then become waste of one sort or another. In order for a product to qualify as a consumptive product, its waste must be wholly biodegradable, capable of transforming itself into food for another organism with *no toxic residue* that would cause harm or be accumulative. In essence, it would have to be capable of turning back into dirt, with no harmful intermediary process inherent in its decomposition. Most foods fall into this category, although food tainted with persistent pesticides does not.

Products of Service. Products of service are valuable only for the service they provide. They are generally durable goods, such as refrigerators, automobiles, and television sets, although they can include non-durables such as packaging.

Under the intelligent product system, these would not be sold. They would be licensed to the purchaser, with ownership (and responsibility) retained by the manufacturer. You could transfer the license to another person, but you could not throw away or dispose of the product. The final user must eventually return it to the manufacturer who maintains ownership.

Retailers of these licensed products would become "de-shopping" centers where we would drop off the products we no longer need and obtain newer ones. The old ones would become valuable sources of raw materials for new products to their owners, the manufacturers (because they could not be just trashed, discarded in a waste dump). This idea is being adopted by many industries now, but the development is only a meager beginning.

In an intelligent product system, products of service would be *designed* for easy disassembly into their component parts for ready re-use, remanufacture, or reclaiming. This would come about naturally and economically, because it would be just too expensive not to design this way.

Hawken points out that, "A television set contains some 4,000 chemicals, 10 to 20 grams of mercury, and an explosive vacuum tube. There is no safe place to dispose of a television set. If you transport 20 of them in a truck, you are technically required to be licensed by the EPA as a toxic waste hauler. The television sets are not toxic waste, however, if they are being returned to Sony to be assembled into another television."

Unsaleables. Unsaleable products are toxic chemicals, radioactive materials, PCB's, heavy metals, and the like. There is no "cycle" that will not cause harm from these products within the natural environment. The goal of the intelligent product system is to design these products out of the system. In the meantime, unsaleables would be gradually phased out and replaced, meaning that safe and effective storage methods must be found. These would be sites owned by the state or other public authorities and then rented to the manufacturer until the industry or some other agency devised a safe method of detoxification. The only type of waste communities would deal with in their landfills would be organic or biodegradable. Landfills would become compost piles and, once processed, turn back into fertile soil possibly to be sold again. As the costs of storage of unsaleable products rise, so too would the incentive to manufacturers not to include these chemicals in their products and to devise safe technologies for detoxification of what they have already made.

Conversion to some form of the intelligent product system has already started, as the following example illustrates. In the spring of 2001, Jim Motavelli wrote, "On October 18, the nation's most colorful governor, Jesse Ventura of Minnesota, took the podium at the Riverfront Radisson in St. Paul and announced a radical new program to reduce the state's waste stream. For the next five years, he said, Sony Electronics had agreed to fund a program that will take back for recycling any and all outdated Sony products currently in the hands of state consumers."

According to Motavelli, Sony's program was scheduled to spread to five other states in 2001. Calling the new program an example of Extended Producer Responsibility, he said that such programs are business-as-usual throughout Europe, "where the concept of legislatively mandating manufacturers to take responsibility for the waste they create has taken firm root." (The caption to this article is "No longer content to just recycle waste, environmentalists want us to reduce it to nothing."[14])

The goal of the intelligent product system is to move all products into the first two of these three categories. There are a number of ways to accomplish this. One of the tools available to government is green taxes, taxes imposed on business in direct proportion to the external costs generated by their products. The result is higher prices for environmentally damaging products and services, and lower prices for environmentally safe products and processes. Green taxes seek to send more appropriate price signals to the buying public and to better internalize environmental costs.

Natural Capitalism. In 1998 Hawken teamed with energy and societal transformation gurus Amory and Hunter Lovins, CEOs of the Rocky Mountain Institute, to extend the notions presented in the previous book. These authors focus on the concept of natural capital described previously. Familiar business terms are used to explain what has happened and to offer suggestions for reforming the system. It is accepted that the purpose of a corporation and the system of commerce of which it is a part is to serve the public. They designate four forms of capital needed for the total human/biosphere partnership to function sustainably:

  • human capital, in the form of labor and intelligence, culture, and organization
  • financial capital, consisting of cash, investments, and monetary instruments
  • manufactured capital, including infrastructure, machines, tools, and factories
  • natural capital, made up of resources, living systems, and ecosystem services[5, p. 4]

The focus is on ecosystem services: the provision of fresh air, clean water, functioning soil microbes, food, habitable temperatures, medicines, natural fibers, and all the other "inputs" to human activities. The traditional economic concept of capital is expanded to include the systematic production of these services.

By incorporating all four of the above types of capital in business planning, management, and operations, the total capital stock of the planet will be conserved and enhanced.

Four central strategies are suggested as a means for countries, companies, and communities to operate as if all forms of capital were valued:[5, pp. 10-11]

1. *Radical resource productivity.* Taking what we know and are doing with energy efficient technology and more efficient and less wasteful use of natural resources and pushing it to the extreme, reducing per capita and total resource needs and human impacts on the natural world. The process can be labor-intensive, thereby increasing worldwide employment in meaningful and rewarding jobs. "Nearly all environmental and social harm is an artifact of the uneconomically wasteful use of human and natural resources, but radical resource productivity strategies can nearly halt the degradation of the biosphere, make it more profitable to employ people, and thus safeguard against the loss of vital living systems and social cohesion."

2. *Biomimicry.* Redesigning industrial systems on biological lines, changing the nature of industrial processes and materials, enabling constant reuse in closed cycles and the nearly perfect elimination of toxicity.

3. *Service and flow economy.* Switching from a consumer economy (where durable goods are sold, used, and discarded) to a service economy (where goods are leased or rented, and upon failure are returned to the manufacturer/owner for repair or replacement). This will involve a shift from possessions as a measure of affluence to quality, utility, creativity, and comfort—the general promotion of well-being.

4. *Investing in natural capital.* Instead of extracting resources and destroying important planetary life-support systems, not only will these be protected, but they will be restored through investments. The return will be in the form of the secure ecosystem services that are essential for a sustainable and well-functioning society.

The authors discuss each of these in detail and explain how such a system can be put in place and maintained. Their approach has already started, through The Natural Step and with numerous additional examples of small versions working well and profitably. The conversion can take place incrementally, without great societal disruption, if we accelerate the processes already started and complete the transformation in a few decades.

Just Design the System Better. In his book, *Cradle to Cradle*, noted architect and system thinker William McDonough, along with Michael Braungart, claims that what's really wrong is that the whole system of human civilization is not designed well. They claim that waste is just a result of bad design. The fundamental principle of Nature offered by Paul Hawken, that "waste equals food" is accepted as central.

Everything is part of the overall system, which is inherently cyclic in Nature. A sustainable economy must mimic Nature's economy, so the argument goes. Regulations are enacted to control waste, but the message of government regulation currently is "be less bad." Good design, on the other hand, tells us to "be good."

Critique

Natural capitalism is not a panacea for all our environmental problems. It does not help stop population growth. Indeed, the system offers ways to eliminate shortages, which might otherwise serve to limit population growth.

The above approaches seem very good. Indeed, nothing is wrong with the basic principles involved, except avoiding any serious mention of the need to stop population growth. This leaves the impression that we can honor the tenets of these proposed reforms, ignoring population, and still save the world for humanity. This is a doubtful proposition.

The authors write of integrated design, whole system thinking, and seeing the connections, which exist between most problems. They recommend that "solutions" be attempted not in isolation, but only through an understanding of the whole system of which they are but a part. However, reversing overpopulation is not a strong component of the recommended reforms.

The suggestions are still good ones. But *the system* they speak of seems limited. Little is said about the role of values, ethics, and voluntary behavior changes, all necessary to accomplish the needed transition. The authors seem to believe that the changes they propose will be sufficient. They imply that adequate reform will occur without major changes in values, beliefs, and philosophical convictions, and without strong and vigorous action on the overpopulation front. The principle is that a reformed system of commerce will naturally "incentivise" societal transformation to sustainability. It remains to be seen whether this approach will be adequate.

Make the Whole System Better

The suggestions provided in this chapter for redesigning commerce have much merit. To be successful in the long run, however, they must be extended to include all the "system." Business reforms alone, of course, cannot be expected to solve the whole problem. The growth component of current business directions and business domination of the media are important contributors to the problem. Addressing these will be essential. Business lies at the heart of industrialized societies. Its reformation to a non-Earth-depleting model is critical.

References

1. Ralph Estes. *Tyranny of the Bottom Line: Why Corporations Make Good People Do Bad Things*. Berrett-Koehler: San Francisco,1996, 294 pp. Reprinted with permission of the publisher. From *Tyranny of the Bottom Line*, copyright © 1996 by Ralph Estes, Berrett-Koehler Publishers, Inc., San Francisco, CA. All rights reserved. www.bkconnection.com.
2. David Finn. *The Corporate Oligarch*. Simon & Schuster: New York,1969.
3. Ronald E. Seavoy. *The Origins of the American Business Corporation, 1784-1855*. March 1982 ed. Greenwood Publishing Group: 1982.
4. Matthew Josephson. *The Robber Barons*. Harvest Books, 1962.
5. Paul Hawken, Amory Lovins, and L. Hunter Lovins. *Natural Capitalism: Creating the Next Industrial Revolution*. Little, Brown and Company: Boston, 1999, 396 pp.
6. Ray C. Anderson. *Mid-Course Correction — Toward A Sustainable Enterprise: The Interface Model*. Chelsea Green: White River Junction, VT, 1998, 207 pp.
7. The Conference Board. *Handling Protest at Annual Meetings*. The Conference Board: New York, 1971. Note: I could not find this book searching on Amazon, but did find a number of publications by the Conference Board, most published by mainline publishing houses.
8. Bruce Nussbaum and Judith H. Dobrzynski. "The Battle for Corporate Control." *Business Week*, (1987): 18 May 1987, 76.
9. Myles L. Mace. *Directors: Myth and Reality*. revised ed. Harvard Business School Press: Boston,1986.
10. E. F. Schumacher. *Small Is Beautiful : Economics As If People Mattered*. 1989 ed. HarperCollins (paper): New York,1973, 352 pp.

11. Thomas Prugh. *Natural Capital and Human Economic Survival.* 2nd ed. Lewis Publishers: New York, Boca Raton, 1999, 180 pp. Note: Chapter 3: What Natural Capital is and Does.

12. Brian Nattrass and Mary Altomare. *The Natural Step for Business — Wealth, Ecology and the Evolutionary Corporation.* New Society Publishers: Gabriola Island, BC, Canada, 1999, 222 pp.

13. Paul Hawken. *The Ecology of Commerce — A Declaration of Sustainability.* HarperBusiness, div. HarperCollins: New York, 1993, 250 pp.

14. Jim Motavelli. "Balancing Act." *E-Magazine*, (2000): November/December, 27-33.

8
The Contrarians
The nay-sayers have their arguments.
We must listen.

"I do not believe that there is either a moral or any other claim upon me to postpone the use of what Nature has given me, so that the next generation or generations yet unborn may have an opportunity to get what I myself ought to get." – Senator Henry M. Keller, Colorado, 26 Feb. 1909[1].

"You chaps who are in favor of this conservation program are all wrong. You are hindering the development of the West. In my opinion, the proper course to take with regard to this [public lands] is to divide it up among the big corporations and the people who know how to make money out of it and let the people at large get the benefits of the circulation of the money." Secretary of Interior, Richard Ballinger, 1909[1, p. 63].

"Minerals are inexhaustible and will never be depleted. A stream of investment creates additions to proved reserves from a very large in-ground inventory. The reserves are constantly being renewed as they are extracted...... How much was in the ground at the start and how much will be left at the end are unknown and irrelevant." Economic Professor Emeritus, M. A. Adelman,, 1993[2,3, p. xi]

"We will mine more, drill more, cut more timber." Secretary of the Interior, James Watt, 1981[1, p. 63].

Most of the material presented so far has been devoted to ideas, values, and actions aimed at preserving and protecting Nature, or at least components of it critical to human life. Many inappropriate practices, values, and beliefs have been identified. The viewpoint expressed has tended toward the slight pessimism of the neo Malthusians (the tree-huggers) and away from cornucopian optimism. (This is not to say that the environmentalist view is devoid of optimism, nor is it Nature-centered to the exclusion of human values.) Most of us approach threats to "our" life-support system from the anthropocentric perspective. Not only do we wish to save Nature for other plants and animals, but we want it for ourselves.

Selfish? Well, yes — and most of us make no apology for that. As mentioned previously, both goals can serve the same purpose: to save Nature for itself and for *limited use* by people. The problem arises when defining appropriately limited use. This seems to lie at the heart of the disagreement of environmentalists with *The Contrarians* — those with views seemingly opposed to protection of the biosphere. Most profess support for saving Nature. Many claim to be environmentalists. But all generally oppose reducing population growth, stopping growth of any kind, or governing the behavior of corporations or their land use. Some Contrarian voices are presented in this chapter.

I might call some people *immoderates*, those at the far ends of the spectrum on environmental issues. A few are quoted here. More reasonable arguments, made by what I call the *moderates*, lie closer to the center of the scale.

We must hear varying ideas. For one thing, we must know the arguments presented to understand them. Secondly, these views must be considered and evaluated. One or more may be correct. We should be open to good information and arguments, regardless of their location on the belief scale. We should be ready to change our views when warranted.

Three themes run through most of the Contrarian literature:

- Growth is good and can and will continue indefinitely
- Technology can overcome any limits to growth we may confront.
- Property rights are sacrosanct. Land owners have an inalienable right to use their land any way they see fit, and the government has no business intruding and interfering

Focusing on the third theme, moderates admit that some government controls are necessary to prevent abuses. Others believe that the market will limit the excesses.

Some see even *public* lands as their private domains for profit. (There is still on the books an 1872 Mining Act, which allows mining companies to take title to public land for $2.50 per acre, thereby avoiding a need to pay fees for the minerals extracted. Former Secretary of the Interior Bruce

Babbitt said the law is "the biggest gold heist since the days of Butch Cassidy." Even when private interests pay for their uses of public lands, as in the case of cattle grazing, the price paid is generally below market value and amounts to a public subsidy, paid by the taxpayers.)

The Immoderates

To most reasonable people, extreme or radical views hold little charm. Their erroneous logic or misrepresentations of fact tend to be obvious and easily debunked. Consider these excerpts from an Opinion Editorial, which appeared in the 21 April 2001 edition of *Florida Today*, by Michael S. Berliner, former executive director of the Ayn Rand Institute in Marina del Rey, California. If the quotations included in Berliner's editorial accurately represent the real views of their authors, this excerpt shows that extremism is not restricted to one end of the linear value scale of environmental beliefs. Most environmentalists would protest that the environmentalist position is mis-characterized by Mr. Berliner. You be the judge.

> The approach of another Earth Day is the occasion for a lesson in cause and effect. It is no coincidence that an energy crisis is beleaguering California, where environmentalists have campaigned against the construction of much needed power plants and even now are continuing to sabotage new sources of energy. Also witness their current campaign against the drilling of oil in the Arctic National Wildlife Refuge, with one of its effects being higher prices at the gas pump.
>
> But the lesson goes further. It is a lesson in the real motives of the environmentalists: not clean air and clean water, but the demolition of technological/industrial civilization. Their goal is not the advancement of human health, happiness and life; rather it is a subhuman world where "Nature" is worshiped like the totem of some primitive religion.
>
> In a nation founded on the pioneer spirit, environmentalists have made "development" an evil word. They inhibit or prohibit the development of Alaskan oil, offshore drilling, nuclear power — and every other practical form of energy.
>
> No instance of the progress that brought man out of the cave is safe from the onslaught of those "protecting" the environment from man, whom they consider a rapist and despoiler by his very essence.
>
> Nature, they insist, has "intrinsic value," to be revered for its own sake, irrespective of any benefit to man. As a consequence, man is to be prohibited from using Nature for his own ends. Since nature supposedly has value and goodness in itself, any human action that changes the environment is necessarily immoral.

The ideal world of environmentalists is not 21st century Western civilization. It is the Garden of Eden, a world with no human intervention in Nature, a world without innovation or change, a world without effort, a world where survival is somehow guaranteed, a world where man has mystically merged with the "environment."

The expressed goal of environmentalism is to prevent man from changing his environment, from intruding on Nature. That is why environmentalism is the enemy of man, the enemy of human life. Intrusion is necessary for human survival. Only by intrusion can man avoid pestilence and famine. Only by intrusion can man control his life and project long-range goals. Intrusion improves the environment, if by "environment" one means the surroundings of man — the external material conditions of human life. For the environmentalists, the "natural" world is a world without man.

They don't mean it? Heed the words of the consistent environmentalists. "The ending of the human epoch on Earth," writes philosopher Paul Taylor in *Respect for Nature: A Theory of Environmental Ethics*, "would most likely be greeted with a hearty 'Good riddance!'" In a glowing review of Bill McKibben's *The End of Nature*, biologist David M. Graber writes (Los Angeles Times, Oct. 29, 1989): "Human happiness [is] not as important as a wild and healthy planet . . . Until such time as Homo sapiens should decide to rejoin Nature, some of us can only hope for the right virus to come along."

The guiding principle of environmentalism is self-sacrifice, the sacrifice of longer lives, healthier lives, more prosperous lives, more enjoyable lives; i.e., the sacrifice of human lives. But an individual is not born in servitude. He has a moral right to live his own life for his own sake. He has no duty to sacrifice it to the needs of others and certainly not to the "needs" of the non-human.

To save mankind from environmentalism, what's needed is not the appeasing, compromising approach of those who urge a "balance" between the needs of man and the "needs" of the environment. To save mankind requires the wholesale rejection of environmentalism as hatred of science, technology, progress and human life. To save mankind requires the return to a philosophy of reason and individualism, a philosophy that makes life on Earth possible.[4]

Another example is the following quote from *Prosperity: The Coming 20-Year Boom and What it Means to You*. This 324 page book, published in 1998 by two "Award-winning Wall Street Journal reporters," offers only scant mention of any environmental problem, difficulty, concern, or threat: "The Seeds of Prosperity are Sprouting. The next ten to twenty years will see the flowering of an era of broadly shared prosperity for the American middle class, a contrast to the economic disappointments of the past twenty years."[5]

The Moderates

Moderates are the contrarians who use not just polemic but at least partially correct (but often selective) facts to prove their arguments.

Ronald Bailey edited *The True State of the Planet* to "set the record straight" on what he claims are the errors of environmentalists.[6] In the beginning of this book, he writes almost like a pragmatic Earth-protector, offering good advice to his environmentalist compatriots: "Only if policymakers and citizens have access to sound scientific information and careful analyses of past policy successes and failures can they make the critical decisions about how best to preserve the world's natural heritage for future generations." He claims that his 1995 book "is dedicated to providing that information," by seeking "to close the widening gap between environmental activists and environmental science." He speaks of the "first wave" of the modern environmental movement, from approximately 1970 to the mid 90s, and the "second wave" is what he thinks should replace it.

Bailey's book includes chapters written by "eleven leading researchers" on "the latest facts about resource use and availability, environmental cleanliness, and other trends." These authors "puncture [environmentalist] illusions" and "refocus our priorities on the very real problems still to be faced. The key difference for the second wave is how to solve them: not by fiat but by freely available and accurate information; not by doomsaying but by developing new structures of responsibility that allow the vast human resources that we already enjoy to be employed for ensuring the safety and abundance of the natural resources we all desire."

This reasonable-sounding beginning is followed by some more clearly contrarian views. One of the chapters is titled, "Saving the Planet with Pesticides: Increasing Food Supplies While Preserving the Earth's Biodiversity," by Dennis Avery, Director for Global Food Issues at the Hudson Institute. Another is "Global Warming: Messy Models, Decent Data, and Pointless Policy," by Robert C. Balling, Jr., a geography professor at Arizona State University. "The Coming Age of Abundance," by Stephen Moore is a comprehensive 30-page account of the cornucopian argument. Additional chapters cover population, food, and income; cancer; forests; biodiversity; water options; ocean rescue; and global air quality.

At the beginning of Moore's contribution, the following "Highlights" of the chapter are listed:

• *The objective, scientific evidence available today shows that the prophets of doom were wrong in virtually every prediction they made in the 1960s and 1970s when they forecast increasing natural resource scarcity and rising commodity prices.*

• *Every measurable trend of the past century suggests that humanity will soon enter an age of increasing and unprecedented natural resources abundance.*

• *Technological improvements and advances in productivity have continually outpaced our consumption of natural resources and have led to the net creation of more resources available to future generations.*

• *Today, natural resources are about half as expensive relative to wages as they were in 1980, about three times less expensive than they were fifty years ago, and roughly eight times less costly than they were in 1900.*

• *In spite of Paul and Anne Ehrlich's projection that mineral supplies would be largely depleted by 1985, proven reserves of virtually all important minerals have skyrocketed since 1950.*

• *The continuing discovery of new mines, technological innovations in mining techniques, and introductions of less expensive or superior substitutes for the use of some minerals have caused most minerals to become less scarce rather than more scarce over the past 100 years.*

• *Although Paul Ehrlich refers to the 1980s as a "catastrophic decade" in terms of consumption, the period witnessed tremendous increases in the supply of almost all raw materials*

• *A well-publicized book, The Energy Crisis, projected in 1972 that the Earth held thirty years left of gas reserves and twenty years left of oil reserves. Since 1950, however, proven reserves for oil and gas have climbed by over 700 percent.*

• *The very concept of "finite natural resources" embraced by geologists is a flawed way of thinking about the Earth and Nature. "Natural resources" have value only when humanity invents a use for them.*

Below are excerpts from Bailey's Foreword to his book.

The first wave has scored some major successes in its twenty-five-year history: in the Western developed world, air and water are much cleaner; automobiles are far cleaner to operate; belching smokestacks are far fewer and generally more efficient than ever before. Clearly developed societies can come together to clean up much of the pollution produced by industries and cities.

But the first wave has also turned out to be spectacularly wrong about certain things. The good news is that many of the looming threats predicted in the early days of the environmental movement turned out to be exaggerated. For example, the global famines expected to occur in the 1970s never happened. Fears that the United States and Europe would cut down all of their forests have been belied by increases in forest area. Global warming, despite so many continuing reports, does not appear to be a major problem. And it turns out that the damage to human health and the natural world caused by pesticides is far less than Rachel Carson feared it would be when she wrote *Silent Spring* in 1962.

It is inevitable, perhaps, that the first wave would begin to run its course and give way to a new strategy. The problem with the past twenty-five years of environmentalism has been a simple one: a failure of theory. From Rachel Carson to the Club of Rome (The Limits to Growth) to Paul Ehrlich *(The Population Bomb)*, the leaders of the first wave all operated under a false assumption, Malthusianism....

Malthus's theory was wrong. This failure of theory has been compounded by failures of information gathering. Modern environmentalists have learned to question the efficacy of computer models to help set priorities and guide policies. The famous limits-to-growth computer model of the 1970s, for example, has been drastically wrong in its predictions. Atmospheric models designed to estimate the effects of the refrigerants called chlorofluorocarbons on stratospheric ozone completely failed to predict the development of the Antarctic "ozone hole." More recently, the original global climate models that predicted significant global warming as a result of higher levels of human-generated carbon dioxide in the atmosphere appear to have overestimated potential increases in global temperatures by as much as an order of magnitude. The Earth's atmosphere has actually *cooled* by 0.10 degrees Celsius since 1979, according to highly accurate satellite-based atmospheric temperature measurements. Taking into account the effects of volcanoes and El Niño, scientists calculate that global temperatures are rising at only 0.09 degrees centigrade per decade— Or less than 1 degree centigrade per century. This increase is far less than the earlier predictions that sparked so many apocalyptic pronouncements....

The greatest problem with the first wave has been its solutions, which involve the top-down imposition of laws and regulations, some of which, in turn, impair the capacity of people to change their behavior on their own. This seems paradoxical, but it is all too often true....

...[O]ur most serious instances of environmental degradation have proved hard to fix by law. The deplorable state of global fisheries is a case in point. Over fishing results from the all-too-familiar problem known as the "tragedy of the commons." The analogy to over fishing is overgrazing of lands held in common. When land is open to anyone who wants to use it, the tragedy of the commons is an almost inevitable result. In the case of commonly held grazing land, herdsmen have no incentives to restrain the number of cows grazing on the commons. In fact, the reverse is true. If a herdsman does not put a cow on the land, his neighbor will, and thus reap the benefits of raising an additional cow. This "logic" leads inexorably to overgrazing and the eventual destruction of the common pasture land. This is what has happened to many of the world's fisheries. First-wave environmentalists fail to realize that the problem lies in the commons, not in the herdsmen. They typically want to regulate the herdsmen instead of abolishing the commons. History shows that the better way to avoid the tragedy of the commons is through privatizing resource ownership. If individual herdsmen (or fishermen) can fence in portions of the commons and secure ownership rights and responsibilities, their incentives to protect the land (or sea) from overgrazing dramatically increase.

This is precisely why second-wave environmentalists propose that private owners, individual or group, commercial or non-commercial, offer the best defense against environmental degradation. Simply by protecting their property — trees, animals, fish, grazing areas, and rivers — they incidentally protect the Earth for the rest of us.

While governments and interest groups spend a lot of time fighting about every last drop of "toxic" waste, the ecological systems of ocean fisheries have deteriorated far more than any damage that landfills have caused. Creative thinking must be devoted to figuring out what arrangements and institutions can successfully restore these imperilled oceanic ecosystems. As another example, indoor air pollution in the form of smoke and carbon monoxide — the result of burning biofuels like wood and dung in houses in the developing world — is one of the chief global threats to human health. It is also one of the least discussed.

It is time for environmentalism's second wave. Second-wave environmentalists must recognize that people modify their activities to avert environmental crises and disasters. Humanity's growing store of knowledge about resources and Nature can help us identify more clearly the problems and the opportunities for environmental improvement. First-wave environmentalists' concerns about running out of nonrenewable resources or poisoning the environment by overusing pesticides may not have been unreasonable two and half decades ago. But twenty-five years of research has dispelled many of the first wave's earlier fears. There has been a growing gap between the mounting scientific evidence about the actual status of various environmental problems and the often bleaker views promoted by environmental activists. It is time to close that gap.

Many conventional environmentalists advocate the "precautionary principle," which says that humanity must not interfere with Nature until all the consequences of an action can be taken into account. But it is impossible to know all the consequences of even the most trivial action. The second wave of environmentalism must recognize that following the precautionary principle can lead to greater environmental degradation. It is better to move forward using intelligent trial and error to uncover new knowledge. Moving forward can increase resources and wealth. Greater knowledge and wealth give human communities resilience, enabling them to respond flexibly and effectively to the unexpected. In other words, if something does go wrong, our increased knowledge and greater economic resources can be mobilized to solve the problem. This is why impoverished people in Bangladesh die by the thousands when cyclones strike their villages, while only fourteen Americans died when Hurricane Andrew hit Florida and Louisiana in August 1992. Better roads, housing, medical facilities, and emergency response measures made possible by American wealth make it far easier to weather storms in Florida than in Bangladesh.

Modern smart environmentalism must avoid the "crisis of the month" media mentality, and it must beware the dangers of interest group politics. It must focus on sorting priorities and dealing with the biggest problems first. It must recognize that all problems are not equally bad and that not all can be solved at the same time. The new, smarter environmentalism must also understand that there is no perfect solution to any problem; trade-offs have to be made. The good cannot be held hostage to the perfect.

In the twenty-first century it will be clear that the preservation of natural resources and the expansion of human ones are tightly linked. This concept may be very hard for traditionalists to accept, but history has shown that environmental improvement depends directly on rapid economic progress. If poor countries do not adopt modern high-yield agriculture, for example, then their impoverished farmers will be forced by hunger to level millions of square miles of wildlands. Agricultural intensification is essential to forestall famine and the plowdown of massive amounts of wildlife habitat. Currently, more than 75 percent of the land on every continent except Europe is still available for wildlife. It is this "undeveloped" land in developing countries that is of greatest importance to conserving biodiversity over the long term.

Modern forestry also helps preserve wildlife habitat. Although nearly 75 percent of total industrial wood production comes from industrialized countries in the Northern Hemisphere, the temperate forestlands of this region are expanding. With modern technology, the world's current industrial wood consumption requirements could be produced on only 5 percent of the world's total current forestland. Technology and progress are not the problem; they are the solutions.

Some of Bailey's criticisms of the "first-wave" environmental movement are valid. Others are not. The reader is left to select which is which. (In the above passage Bailey describes his version of second wave environmentalism. Chapter 22 describes another.)

A particularly interesting example of the Contrarian literature is the 1998 book *The Skeptical Environmentalist* by Bjørn Lomborg, published in English by Cambridge University Press in 2001. (Lomborg was Associate Professor of Statistics in the Department of Political Science, University of Aarhus, Denmark when the book was written.) In his book, Lomborg claims a scientifically based refutation of most of the dire claims made by environmentalists about the state of the planet. After its publication, most environmental organizations hoped the book would command little media attention, thereby sparing them the time and effort of preparing a rebuttal. This was not to be, so formal complaints were lodged against the book. Since its publication in English in 2001, many environmental scientists have claimed the text is deeply flawed. Many experts said that environmental conditions, in most cases, are not nearly as good as Professor Lomborg portrays them, but also not nearly as bad as some environmental groups and scientists have said.

On January 8, 2003, The Danish Committees on Scientific Dishonesty (DCSD), operating under the auspices of the Danish Research Agency, denounced the scholarship in the book. The DCSD undertook its investigation in response to three formal complaints filed with the Committees, including one submitted by Drs. Stuart Pimm and Jeffrey Harvey. After reviewing the publication, the DCSD reached this ruling:

> Objectively speaking, the publication of the work under consideration is deemed to fall within the concept of scientific dishonesty. In view of the subjective requirements made in terms of intent or gross negligence, however, Bjørn Lomborg's publication cannot fall within the bounds of this characterization. Conversely, the publication is deemed clearly contrary to the standards of good scientific practice.

Immoderate Beliefs and Violence

Huge forests once covered much of North America. These contained trees of various ages and other vegetation in balanced ecosystems that existed for tens of thousands of years before industrial civilization harvested them. Most of the remaining timber areas are regrowth, and thus younger and devoid of both old trees and dead old trees which provide food and habitat for other organisms. Often new-growth forests are planted on regular geometric patterns, equal spacing between trees, and can be recognized easily by this feature. A few "old-growth" forests *do* remain, however, often on federal land, in national forests, and in national and state parks.

Such forests can also be called "climax" forests, because tree growth has reached a climax, a sustainable mixture of new and young trees and old and dead and decomposing ones, in a perpetually stable arrangement representing what this form of Nature "used to be like." Such areas have become sacrosanct to environmentalists. The reasons extend beyond a desire for simple environmental protection and preservation of species diversity to an aesthetic or philosophical motivation. This stimulates strong emotions over clear-cutting of old-growth forests.

Ardent environmentalists, frustrated over the difficulty and failure to protect these forests from logging, have turned to a strong preservation advocacy. In the past, some have turned to considerably immoderate means to stop development of the few remaining stands of these unique and valuable woodlands. This includes sitting in front of bulldozers to keep them from doing their job and chaining themselves to (or sitting in the tops of) trees to protect them.

Occasionally these efforts have enjoyed limited success. We have also seen a very few cases of more direct intervention. For example, trees have been spiked with metal to destroy saw blades in lumber mills, and even bulldozers have been dynamited (hopefully with no workers around). Environmentalists, by and large, espouse nonviolence, so these latter events have been rare exceptions.

The preservationist philosophy directly opposes the cornucopian belief that "our" natural resources have been provided for our wise use and enjoyment. Cornucopians claim the prevention of logging is essentially *unAmerican*, even in old growth forests. A so-called *wise use* movement has sprung up to counter the preservationists. The philosophy is that clear-cutting forests is a "wise use" of the land (as long as seedling trees are planted on the land later), and provides jobs for the lumbermen so employed.

According to Sharon Beder, in her 1997 book, *Global Spin*[7], "The Wise Use Movement began in 1988; two hundred and twenty-four groups and individuals from the US and Canada convened in Reno, Nevada. The conference was co-sponsored by groups such as the National Association of Manufacturers, the United 4-Wheel Drive Association, the Independent Petroleum Association of America, the National Forest Products Association, the American Sheep Industry, Exxon USA and the American Pulpwood Association. Participating Canadian groups included the Council of Forest Industries, MacMillan Bloedel, Carribou Lumber Manufacturers Association, and the Mining Association of British Columbia.

"Today the WUM is able to claim millions of members through the association of large organizations within its domain, such as the American Farm Bureau which represents four million farmers and the Blue Ribbon Coalition, backed by Yamaha and Kawasaki, which represents 500,000 off-road vehicle enthusiasts. However, whether all these members endorse the Wise Use Movement's agenda is questionable."[7, p. 47]

Beder writes that the WUM is *stage-managed* by Ron Arnold and Alan Gottlieb from their base at the Center for the Defense of Free Enterprise. This non-profit 'educational' foundation is "devoted to protecting the freedom of Americans to enter the marketplace of commerce and the marketplace of ideas without undue government regulation."

According to veteran journalist David Helvarg, in *The War Against the Greens*, "At its core Wise Use/Property Rights is a counterrevolutionary movement, defining itself in response to the environmental revolution of the past thirty years. It aims to create and mold disaffection over environmental regulations, big government, and the media into a cohesive social force that can win respectability for centrist arguments seeking to 'protect jobs, private property and the economy by finding a balance between human and environmental needs,' and the deregulation of industry. Despite their insistence that they are not fronting for industry, many anti-enviro groups with green-sounding names — such as the Alliance for Environment and Resources (AER), Environmental Conservation Organization (ECO), and National Wetlands Coalition — have the same relationship to timber, oil companies, and developers that the smokers rights movement has to the tobacco industry."[1, p. 9]

(Helvarg has produced over 30 television documentaries and written for many publications, including the Associated Press, *Smithsonian*, and The Nation. An updated 10th anniversary edition of *The War Against the Greens* was scheduled for release in 2004. Helvarg is also the author of *Blue Frontier - Saving America's Living Seas*.)

Citing overlap in leadership and membership among hundreds of anti-environmentalist groups around the U.S., Helvarg offers a couple of broad generalities. In the West, the *Wise Use* movement has supported "protecting industrial and agricultural access to public lands and waters at below-market costs. The core constituency is workers and middle-management in limited-resource industries such as timber and mining whose livelihoods are threatened by industry cutbacks and who are open to the argument that environmental protection means lost jobs." Ranchers, corporate farmers, and businesspeople whose margin of profit is directly threatened by any fee increases on grazing, water reclamation, and other public land use, support their efforts. Still, these people are more likely to express themselves through anti-green organizations such as the Farm Bureau and the Cattlemen's Association.

"East of the Mississippi the movement is more oriented toward property rights, appealing to a constituency of landowners, developers, and developer wanabes whose opportunities for subdividing land and building commercial equity is limited or restricted by regulations governing wetlands, endangered species, wild and scenic rivers, and other environmental protections broadly favored by the American public."[1, p.11]

In his stinging review of anti-environmentalist efforts nationwide, Helvarg describes its links to the militia movement (arch-conservative groups advocating often violent means to stop government intervention and usually critical of environmentalist positions). That anti-environmentalists such as these can pursue their ends through violence is documented in Helvargs' chilling chapter, "Casualties of War".

In his chapter on "Bomb Throwers," he describes the connection between these two movements.

> Although they don't agree on everything, militant members of the Wise Use/Property Rights movement and members of America's armed militia movement have increasingly staked out common territory.
>
> "We're seeing incredible crossover of people and materials between Wise Use and the militias from Washington to western Montana, eastern Oregon and northern Idaho," says Eric Ward of the Northwest Coalition Against Malicious Harassment, a Seattle-based human rights organization.
>
> "Sometimes I have a hard time telling where the militia starts and the land-use movement ends," agrees Bellingham, Washington, Police Chief Don Pierce. Pierce was involved in the July 27, 1996 arrest of several Snohomish County property rights advocates, part of a larger militia group charged with possession of pipe bombs, which, according to their indictment, they planned to use in a war against the federal government and the United Nations."[1, p. 416]

He details a large number of attempts to discredit environmentalists and their arguments, and to prevent them from being heard. At the end of his introduction, Helvarg concludes, "The anti-environmental backlash represents both a danger and a challenge — not only to conservationists and antipollution activists but to all citizens concerned about their right to speak out and protest without fear and intimidation. In the last nine years, the anti-enviro ranks have grown from resource users protecting their federal subsidies and property owners unhappy with land-use regulations to the fringes of America's expanding underbelly of violence, where social causes become excuses for sociopaths motivated by fear, greed, and hatred, or private security agents working on behalf of outlaw industries. As issues of sustainability and survival become more critical..., affecting the things people hold most dear, such as families, health, and property, the urges to heap blame and deny reality will inevitably increase."

Corporations and Conservatives

Sharon Beder spotlighted the corporate assault on environmentalism in *Global Spin*.[7] "Corporate activism, ignited in the 1970s and rejuvenated in the 1990s, has enabled a corporate agenda to dominate most debates about the state of the environment and what should be done about it. This situation poses grave dangers to the ability of democratic societies to respond to environmental threats." [7, p. 15] She reviews the recent history of environmental and corporate activism.

Beder quotes from Kirkpatrick Sale's 1993 book, *The Green Revolution*, describing the process as follows:

> Right-wing businessmen like Richard Mellon Scaife and Joseph Coors, and conservative treasuries like Mobil and Olin foundations, poured money into ad campaigns, lawsuits, elections, and books and articles protesting 'Big Government' and 'strangulation by regulation'. Blaming environmentalists for all the nation's ills from the energy crisis to the sexual revolution.[8, p. 18]

and from an article by Eric Alterman in *Mother Jones:*

> Funded by eccentric billionaires, conservative foundations, and politically motivated multinational corporations, right-wing policy entrepreneurs founded think-tanks, university centers, and political journals, and developed the social and political networks necessary to tie this nascent empire together. The end product was a tidal wave of money, ideas, and self-promotion that carried the Reaganites to power.[9]

The role of conservative, and well-funded, think-tanks in pushing the anti-environmental rhetoric into public consciousness is not well known. Beder describes their growing influence.[7, p. 24]

> Conservative think-tanks have played a central ... role in the corporate battle against environmental policies and reforms. Think-tanks are generally private, tax-exempt, research institutes which are sometimes referred to as 'universities without students'. Their tax-free status depends on their ability to maintain a superficial appearance of political independence, so they present themselves as providing impartial, disinterested expertise. However they are generally partisan, politically or ideologically motivated and practice the art of 'directed conclusions.'

These organizations generally tailor their studies to suit the interests of their clients or donors. The most prominent of these are the Cato Institute and the Heritage Foundation. With its annual budget in 1997 of $25 million, the latter was the wealthiest think tank in Washington.

Think tanks in other countries play central roles in environmental debates in their regions. These include the Frankfurt Institute and the Institute for Political Science in Germany, the *Institut l'Entreprise* in France, Britain's Institute of Economic Affairs and its Centre for Policy Studies, and Sydney's Centre for Independent Studies. Mostly funded by business interests, their activities are shaped by general beliefs in a libertarian/laissez-faire philosophy and the importance of free and competitive markets, individual liberties with maximal choice, and especially the right to private property.

> Using approaches similar to those of corporate front groups and the Wise Use Movement, think-tanks have sought to cast doubt on the seriousness of environmental problems, to oppose environmental regulations, and to promote free-market remedies to those problems — such as privatization, deregulation and the expanded use of property rights. Corporations that wish to portray themselves in public as being environmentally concerned often fund such think-tanks (with which they are not readily identified) to oppose environmental reforms, just as some corporations privately fund anti-environmental Wise Use groups whilst publicly funding environmental groups.[7, p. 91]

A Critical Balance

Sorting through the different beliefs, positions, hidden agendas, and political perspectives can be a challenging task. When we read or view the claims of a reputed "expert," skepticism can be a valuable tool. When we seek the truth, getting as many of the facts as possible is vital. The role of the scientist and scholar in providing these is critical in controversial areas.

Current American television news outlets have many failings. The conservative bias of some channels often leads them to under-report environmental news, fail to ask the right questions of their experts, and default on the journalist's responsibility to analyze, explain, and interpret the news in an unbiased manner. Some channels try to provide a "balanced" view by inviting experts on *both* sides of an issue to debate on air. This gives roughly equal weight to the two sides. (Sometimes more than two sides to an issue are needed, but only two — or even just one — are represented.) Often one of the sides (usually the side favoring environmental protection) has many more true international experts recommending that position than the other. Yet both perspectives are presented equally.

Another problem comes when the two opposing spokespersons themselves are too narrowly focused and the on-screen moderator is not well versed in the issues. What results is "apparent news," a dialog essentially devoid of the relevant information but seemingly comprehensive and on-target.

All sides of the issues affecting the future of humanity must be heard. Some conservative ideas have merit and must be considered. Many liberal opinions do, too. Immoderate and ill-advised rhetoric come from both camps.

What we need between the conflicting views is a *critical balance*, a basing of these views on the facts of science and accurate human observation, and on the best opinions of reputable scientists (where opinions are needed). The current "debate" over the critical issues affecting humanity's future is a muted one, largely due to the domination of the means of debating by large corporations having their own agendas. Until this logjam is broken, the citizenry will find it very challenging to form reasonable, and hopefully correct, conclusions about our problems, the best ways of overcoming them, and good insights concerning future directions.

At the core of each of the conflicts described in this chapter is a war of values and beliefs. The combatants often exhibit a closed-mindedness that prevents even listening to factual and scientific evidence from both camps. Most conflict should disappear if those involved listen to and study basic information about human and natural history and see what humanity is and has been doing to the Earth. If they can agree to certain core truths, most of the controversy should subside, leaving the opponents to argue over matters more open for discussion: how best to protect our future and make sure industrial societies become sustainable into the distant future. Each of us has a part to play in this basic educational process.

References

1. David Helvarg. *The War Against the Greens*. Sierra Club Books: San Francisco, 1997, 502 pp.
2. Colin J. Campbell, "Submission to H. M. Government Consultation on Energy Policy," *The Association for the Study of Peak Oil*, 5 August 2002.
3. M.A. Adelman. *The Economics of Petroleum Supply*, 1993.
4. Michael S. Berliner, "Opinion Editorial," *Florida Today*, 21 April 2001.
5. Bob Davis and David Wessel. *Prosperity: The Coming 20-year Boom and What it Means to You*. Times Business/Random House: New York, 1998, 324 pp.
6. Ronald Bailey. *The True State of the Planet*. The Free Press: New York, 1995, 471 pp.
7. Sharon Beder. *Global Spin: The Corporate Assault on Environmentalism*. Chelsea Green Publishing: White River Junction, VT, 1998, 288 pp.
8. Kirkpatrick Sale. *The Green Revolution: The American Environmental Movement 1962-1992*. 1st ed. Farrar, Straus and Giroux/Hill and Wang: New York, 1993, 124 pp.
9. Eric Alterman. "Fighting Smart." *Mother Jones* Vol. 19, no. 4 (1994), 59-61.

9
Leadership

What it is.
Leadership failures.
True leadership.

Profiles in Courage, written by John F. Kennedy[1] while he was a Senator, presents stories of eight U.S. senators who held to their principles, at substantial political risk and against opposition within their own parties.

Writing in the *Los Angeles Times* in 1998, Rodger Schlickeisen recalled reading the book as a boy. "To me this was real leadership, senators willing to endanger their standing in 'the world's most exclusive club' by being true to what their consciences said best served the public interest."[2]

Leaders are people we have selected — or were selected for us — to look at the big picture, to see the forest *and* the trees. They direct enterprises through efficient operations toward worthwhile goals. They serve an important function in our society and have special responsibilities. We look to our leaders for guidance and direction — and for help in finding the means for pursuing goals.

Non-leaders who try to make changes in society are often frustrated. Most of us have some control over our own lives, but few of us have the power to educate, initiate change in others, and see the effort through to completion. Leaders in powerful positions have this power.

We look to our leaders for direction, to tell us what is most important, and to make important policy decisions on our behalf. It can be frustrating when national leaders, having access to the best informed experts in every field, seem to ignore the severity of the environmental crisis and fail to work toward systemic changes.

Political Leadership

Political leaders clearly have their limitations, many not of their own making. Politicians have to get elected. They must have moral courage and determination to do things not supported by the electorate. They must be willing to lose a re-election or even their initial campaign, if necessary. Few have that willingness.

Increasingly, politicians are required to spend huge sums of money on election campaigns. To raise the needed funds, they find themselves having to accept or even solicit funds from businesses and wealthy individuals, each of which generally has a non-altruistic motivation for making the contribution. So, in addition to not offending the electorate, politicians have to deliver the goods to their corporate sponsors, the new "kleptocracy." Their hands are tied by these often-conflicting masters of their political destinies.

These are all excuses, and should be seen as such. Of course, there is a time and place for a certain degree of pragmatism and realism. However, following rather than leading can become a habit.

Corporate Leadership

The CEO of a large corporation has enormous amounts of money and power at his or her disposal. The financial resources of many companies are in the billions. The CEO can direct employees to do important things and in different ways. In many respects, these individuals are in the best position to initiate and sustain change.

The new power of the CEO to rule with relative impunity, independent of shareholders, government intervention, and their boards of directors should be a blessing. This frees them to initiate radical changes in corporate procedures for the betterment of society. Unfortunately, the mindset of such leaders prevents vigorous altruistic action except in the rarest of cases.

In spite of what was said in Chapter 7 concerning the independence of the CEO, in some situations CEO power *is* limited. He or she may have to satisfy the Board of Directors. Both may be required to satisfy the shareholders. In this conventional view of corporate power, let us suppose that a corporate leader orders major beneficial changes in the company's operations or that substantial money from the company's reserves go toward environmental goals. Suppose that these changes adversely affect the profit margin. The CEO and directors will face considerable pressure to avoid taking these actions, even if they would like to personally. If they persist and profits fall as a result, these leaders could even lose their jobs, along with their valuable compensation packages.

When faced with the threat of demotion or dismissal, only a truly courageous leader defies conventional wisdom, goes against the grain, and does the right thing.

An Exception

An example of this (an exception to the general rule) is the case of Ray Anderson, CEO of the Interface Corporation, the world's leading commercial carpet and interior fabrics manufacturer. Ray met Paul Hawkin, author of *The Ecology of Commerce²* and read his book, and he read *Ishmael*. Then he started taking steps within his own company to reduce and ultimately eliminate the impacts of its operations on the environment. In order to keep his job, of course, he had to do a lot of talking and convincing. What resulted was one of the most aggressive programs of environmental reform undertaken by a large company anywhere in the world.

Leadership Literature

A search for literature on the nature and practice of leadership, including textbooks and chapters of books in several public and university libraries on dealing with the subject, produced none addressing what might be called *encompassing leadership*. Most accounts looked at leadership restrictively, offering suggestions for improving business operations, directing organizations and making enterprises successful, however that success is defined. Leadership, as it appears to be taught in business schools, seems confined to maximizing the efficiency and effectiveness of running organizations; it rarely deals with the larger issues of societal leadership and responsibility.

Few business leaders recognize the enormity of our environmental problems; fewer still are able to study the contributions of their companies to these problems and implement plans for their amelioration. Many work actively to get environmental restrictions removed or weakened.

If the leaders of powerful corporations ignore the obvious, because they don't like the implications or feel powerless to do anything about it, they do not act. And if government leaders aren't willing or able to get the job done, then who is left to lead us in the difficult task of preserving humanity's future?

Power to the People

It is often said that the real power is in the hands of the people. But this is true only when large numbers are informed, work together toward a goal, and reach a modest degree of consensus on the subject. While it is true that leaders in industry and the national government have power more vast than the ordinary citizen, with the citizenry also there is power — ultimate power.

Our superior strength comes with our numbers. Even powerful dictatorships can fall if a sufficient number of people rebel.

Effective leadership doesn't have to be confined to board rooms, legislative chambers, or executive offices. Leadership can come from below, from the ordinary citizen, the individual in a group. With an idea large enough to sustain many people, a real and ultimately powerful political movement can be started. For the movement to be effective, good leadership is essential.

Fortunately many skilled and knowledgeable leaders in the environmental movement are ready and able to mobilize us into action. However, the actions they have suggested in the past, while important, correct, and necessary, have been insufficient. More is needed than fighting a few battles to protect portions of the life-support system, however important that may be.

The inappropriate values and beliefs guiding many leaders in government, business, and education must be addressed and corrected. The public must be educated more fully about the nature and extent of these problems. It may even be necessary to adopt a completely new worldview, one more compatible with humanity's survival. To do these things will require massive education, discussion, debate, and ultimately action. For this we must join together in the common cause of protecting our futures. Good leadership will be essential.

Unfortunately, most of us are so busy and distracted by the mundane, we don't have time to gather the relevant information needed. We need help in making intelligent decisions on large-scale matters, such as the future of our species. Only mass public education can be effective in this pursuit. But current educational institutions are inadequate for the task, and the media are captives to their corporate owners' agendas. Good environmental leadership will be critical to mobilize public support for education and media reform.

"UnStifling" Leadership

In this era of what might be called over-specialization, many of us are workers in a large organization...in some cases, a very large one. Even when our employer is only modest in size, we generally focus on the tasks assigned to us. We do our best to perform well on those tasks in order to receive approval of our supervisors, some personal satisfaction of a job well done, and, of course, the financial rewards which are their reasons for working in the first place. The vast majority of us have little influence over the direction of the enterprise in which we work. Therefore, we do not think much about its larger policy issues.

We live within our vocational cocoons, going through daily tasks, working hard, making money, and enjoying life as best we can. Larger, long-range societal issues, while they may be mentioned in our religious organizations or in some other avocational or civic activity, are seldom brought to the attention of workers, supervisors, or higher management. Only occasionally does an employee take any interest in the larger issues surrounding the company's operation. Once finding a job that pays adequately, offers acceptable benefits, and is not too unpleasant, we generally leave issues of policy to our higher-paid bosses. In short, we are absorbed into Mother Culture and adopt its values.

Good leadership within an organization will solicit opinions, open discussions, and stimulate ideas, debate, and action. To take the risks inherent in such work requires courage and a degree of vision and determination. Before the communication channels can be opened, the leader must believe in the value of the process and the anticipated outcome. (Normally this is done from the top down, but occasionally it can rise from the bottom. Actions employees can take in opening a dialog with management are suggested in Chapter 23.)

Leader Values

One of the things making the task set forth in this book difficult is that high-level influential leaders are strongly pressured to narrow their thinking. Their values, beliefs, and even their ethics also tend toward more narrowly focused goals. In nearly every corporation, the emphasis is on making money, on the bottom line, or the next quarterly business report. The framework of such organizations does not include truly long-range planning or consideration for the long-range effects of their policies and actions, if these are not directly connected to the balance sheet. When push comes to shove, a little pollution here and some environmental degradation there are hardly noticed if the profit margin is high and the returns on investment substantial, since business leaders are paid and rewarded for achieving these.

A very unfortunate situation has arisen. The massive vehicle of industry is moving toward a cliff of environmental destruction, and there's no one at the wheel with the knowledge or ability to change its direction. An important role of government is to meet the overall needs of the people it represents, to see the really big picture, to regulate the practices of large corporations, and to assure the entire enterprise is headed in the proper direction. We are not now seeing the needed leadership in either business or government.

They have united in the race to the cliff, and hardly anyone is around to sound the alarm.

Education Leadership

Presentation of relevant informational material about Earth's history, present status, and likely future scenarios in the elementary and secondary schools can go a long way toward informing a populace. However, much of the information may be deemed inappropriate or politically unacceptable for young minds, and thus withheld from them. Furthermore, there is a time-delay involved; as youngsters need validation and support from their elders if they are to hold to important but revolutionary ideas gained in their youth. Improved environmental education is a very important goal, but, like most of our present "solutions," an insufficient one.

The real need is for mass public education, reaching all age groups. This is best provided by the mass media, the most powerful and extensive means of public education available. The spoken and written word enters our households, and our brains, numerous times each day. The mass media offer the one mechanism most likely to reach the public, to inform, educate, and mobilize for change. If the message fails to reach media outlets, however, their power to promote constructive change is obliterated. Such is the case today. The issues addressed so far in this book have barely caught major media attention.

The media do not *totally* ignore environmental concerns, and thank goodness for that. Stories of environmental atrocities and difficult environmental problems are difficult to avoid. They appear almost daily on the major news channels, whether print or broadcast. What do they miss? The interpretation, the discussion of what it means for humanity, and the debate needed to structure a global consensus on changes needed to protect us. This is another area of leadership vacuum. Time after time TV, newspapers, and magazines report on events or developments of strong environmental significance. Often they are very one-sided or in error. Even when fairly truthful, the lack of emphasis, interpretation, and connection to larger issues is pronounced. We can only conclude that the writers and producers of the piece have been warned to ignore relevant material.

Why is humanity's future not discussed more widely? Can it be those in control think the subject insufficiently important? That can hardly be the case. Perhaps these leaders lack essential information to fully appreciate the magnitude of the threat. Perhaps, on the other hand, they are themselves dominated by corporate influences. Such control does not have to be overt to be successful.

Suffice it to say that the message of concern about humanity's future must reach the corporate sponsors and owners of the mass media. Until then, controversial, difficult, and possibly unpleasant subjects will rarely be presented or will not be presented in a comprehensive manner.

Without the presentation of such material, support for local leadership on environmental issues will be difficult. Without grass roots support for change, corporate owners and sponsors will not push for that change, or will stifle it; the message will not go out, the people will not be informed, and we could all rush headlong, mindlessly and needlessly, toward ecosystem collapse and the resulting economic depression and turmoil.

The Power of Leadership

The power of a highly placed government official, politician, or businessman for gathering good information and making it widely available is significant. Information dissemination is one of the least expensive components of change. A second power is to execute — to initiate and sustain change.

Powerful leaders can easily explore (or task a group to explore) issues of relevance to humanity's survival. They can then direct action to promote that survival both inside and outside the leader's organization. Leaders have a moral responsibility to do this. Few are meeting that responsibility.

True leadership is effective leadership. Effective leadership stands on well-informed, carefully considered conviction, and is incorruptible. This is what we need. True leaders must step forward, tell the truth on important environmental issues, and follow with action.

References

1. John F. Kennedy. *Profiles in Courage.* Special Commemorative Edition. Harper Perennial: New York, 1956.
2. Rodger Schlickeisen, "Putting Public Interest Before Party's Interest; More Republicans must oppose the GOP's stealth attack on the environment." *The Los Angeles Times.* (Record edition). Los Angeles, Calif.: Sep 17, 1998. pg. 9. Metro; PART-B; Op Ed Desk.
3. Paul Hawken. *The Ecology of Commerce — A Declaration of Sustainability.* HarperBusiness, div. HarperCollins: New York, 1993, 250 pp.

Part II

How It All Happened

10
World Views and Human Nature

How did we come to this point?
Are we being true to our species?

How did humanity arrive at the point of becoming a species that systematically takes apart its own life-support system? Assuming that you accept this premise, it is clear that not all members of our species have been responsible. Small groups of aboriginal or indigenous humans still live in a manner hardly noticed by Mother Nature. At least their lives do not threaten the ecosystems within which they live. What impacts they do produce are fairly localized, and are certainly not felt thousands of miles away.

Most of us, on the other hand, lead high-impact lifestyles. Through our numbers and our high per capita consumption, we are leading an assault on our own life support system. We ask how the glorious developments of the industrial society brought us here, wondering if some human flaw led to this unfortunate situation.

Paul MacCready nicely encapsulated the answer and the grand problem facing us. In his keynote presentation to a symposium on inventors and an innovative society he said:

> Rather than finding some acceptable balance between technology and Nature (of which we humans used to be part), the past several centuries have seen an accelerating demise of the natural world because of the supremacy of humans, with their numbers, organization, culture, technologies, and minds. Humans, with their versatility and brains, are the only species immune to the checks and balances to which all other species are subject. The trend to human supremacy cannot be reversed, or even slowed, because of the characteristics inherent in human minds: humans (in our perhaps biased view) are the most important things on Earth (the value of other species being a function only of their value to humans); whatever can be developed and sold and used will be; only the short term has high priority; and narrow perspectives, irrationality, and competitiveness are self-organizing positive feedback features of the way human minds, through evolutionary selection pressures, have developed.[1]

Daniel Quinn has provided a rather entertaining account of how we came to this place.[2] *Ishmael* narrates the transformation of some members of the human species from a low-impact lifestyle (successful for hundreds of thousands of years and still successful today) to the high-impact lifestyle that has become the norm in industrialized countries around the world. The high-impact culture causes the greatest stress on our life-support system and threatens the future of humanity. The low-impact lifestyle is small and diminishing, being consumed by the larger and more aggressive high-impact society. (Thomas Berry also deals with this subject in his major books *The Dream of the Earth*[3] and *The Great Work*[4], and, with Brian Swimme, in *The Universe Story*.[5])

How it All Came to Be

First there was the universe. Fifteen billion years ago. That's 150 million centuries. A long span of time. Then came Earth. Four to four and a half billion years ago. Modern humans appeared more recently. A million or so years ago, depending on how you define a human.

For about a million years, 10,000 centuries, humans lived in balance with the environment, part of the fabric of Nature, the web of life. Think of the number of generations involved. Two to four per century and ten thousand times four or 40,000 in a million years. That's a lot of living with slow and relatively modest change.

For all the history of Earth and the early stages of human evolution, living creatures were integrated into the reality of Earth and its operating systems. One could say that all creatures were *hard-wired* into Nature, functionally indistinguishable from the core essence of Earth. Somehow Earth learned to collect solar energy, process it, and distribute it to both the energy-consuming plants and animals and to physical, non-biological systems. A guiding principle was the continual increase in diversity and complexity. From simple single-celled organisms life evolved to the most complex, and beautifully diverse, plants and animals we find on Earth today.

As humans developed consciousness and complex thought processes — such as the ability to be self-aware and plan for the future, they developed the ability to ponder big questions: "Why am I here?" "What is the purpose of all this?" "How did things come to be this way?"

Without answers from modern science and technology, these early humans devised origin- and world-explaining stories, *cosmologies*, handed down and modified, region-to-region, generation-to-generation.

Social anthropologists tell us humans used these origin stories not only to understand their positions in the greater scheme of things, but also to guide them in thought and action. These early origin stories were cosmos-centered, *without even the* **idea** *of questioning* that everything was part of and inseparable from Nature. Their understandings of the sun, moon, and stars may have been primitive by today's standards, but the appearance and movements of celestial bodies were very much a part of their lives. Their knowledge of biology and animal behavior might be considered primitive by modern scientific standards. Yet they developed what industrial humans would see as extreme sensitivity to, and understanding of, the physical and biological systems they needed for existence.

Nonhuman animals in the wild operate primarily on instinct with no concept of right and wrong behavior. They do what evolution programmed them to do and they live in balance with the rest of Nature. If local populations grow too large, the local carrying capacity of the land is exceeded and the population is reduced naturally, but sometimes brutally, to a sustainable level. These animals are *true to their species* and the way the planet functions.

The basic rule of Nature states that what works ecologically is successful and continues. What doesn't work disappears ... from lack of food, an inability to reproduce, or a failure to compete successfully, in an ecological sense, against other plants and animals for needed sustenance. "What works" means what is sustainable, fits well into the overall web of life, and can be expected to continue indefinitely.

There was no depletion of resources because everything was completely cyclic. There was no such thing as waste. "Waste equals food," Paul Hawken wrote in *The Ecology of Commerce.*[6] In spite of this, changes did take place, as seen in the current complexity of living systems. But they took place incredibly slowly, with millennia needed for even small changes. The lives of all species were nearly the same as those of their parents and grandparents.

Then human intelligence advanced and rudimentary scientific methods of investigation were developed. An explosion of knowledge ensued — about the world, our universe, and our places in the great scheme of things. Along with it came some early changes in our cosmologies, our origin stories, our *world views*.

With the advent of agriculture, people felt they had some limited control over the world around them. They planted some seeds and food would grow, at least most of the time. Though planting and cultivating required work, it seemed more reliable than the random method of finding game or edible plants or fruit "in the wild." (One can imagine an argument between an ancient hunter-gatherer and a farmer, each claiming to have a better way of life. When food is abundant in Nature, the hunter-gatherer clearly has the advantage ... at least in terms of time and work required to feed one's family. When such food is in short supply, it is time for the hunter-gatherer to move on, but the farmer must stay on his farm and suffer through the period of scarcity.) Agriculturalist thinking, coupled with increasingly powerful technology, drove the hunters and gatherers into decline, the farmers into ascendancy.

Separatist Cosmology

A scant several thousand years ago, agriculture's emergence was accompanied by a change of thinking, the likes of which the world had not seen before, and which has not since been rivaled. A few groups of Earth people, mainly in and east of the Mediterranean region, believed they could control even more of the world around them. Linked to this early concept — or developing naturally from what followed — was the idea that humans were now somehow separate from the rest of Nature. Nature was no longer the over-arching, infinite web of life in which humans were but one creature, one species. Instead, Nature became an "it," a thing, distinct and separate from humans, provided primarily for their use and benefit. It probably took many generations for this view to develop and flourish, but flourish it did.

This change of thinking was the most incredible, cataclysmic, conceptual shift in all of human history. It became imbedded in the new origin stories and cosmologies of the human groups involved. Stories of who we are, where we are, how we got here, and how the world works were dramatically altered. Eventually, in many societies and religious tendencies, the human was now seen as the sole purpose of creation, the single organism for which the Earth was provided.

Earth became a resource, something for the human to use. The cyclic flow of resources was broken. The process changed: extract resources, process and use them, then discard them as waste. Waste now equaled toxicity and not just food for other organisms. (Some substances buried within the Earth were toxic when brought up and released into the biosphere. Some say it would be better if they had stayed buried forever.)

Once this conceptual shift to separateness took hold, Earth was commonly considered an external entity for humans to use and consume. I call this separatist cosmology. This tangential new belief — this conceptual breaking away from the web of life, away from letting Nature tell us what works, to an arrogant, self-centered, anthropocentric belief that now humans were in charge of everything, has had enormous implications. It led to humanity's control and domination of nearly everything on Earth. The potential for harm became exceedingly great. But it also led to the flowering of civilization, a social and economic structure sufficiently advanced to create and nurture the likes of Plato, Michelangelo, Beethoven, Madame Curie, Sojourner Truth, Albert Einstein, W.E. B. Dubois, Eleanor Roosevelt, Martin Luther King, and Yo Yo Ma.

Takers and Leavers

After the agricultural turning point, humanity divided into two groups, called the "Takers" and the "Leavers" by Daniel Quinn.[2] The Takers structured their societies around taking from Nature and *conceptually* breaking the web of life. A by-product is that the web itself is *actually* being physically broken in many places.

Not everyone participated in this shift. Those groups of humans living integrated into the natural environment still have an essentially benign impact on the Earth and its functioning. Quinn calls these people the Leavers. Unfortunately, the number of Leavers and the viabilities of their tribes are diminishing yearly.

In community after community of indigenous people, the elders weep over the loss of their traditions and stories — as their children move away, forgetting the old stories and customs. They can only watch sadly as their way of life is systematically destroyed by the Separatist, or Taker, cosmology of the "outside world." This process of destroying indigenous human tribes by moving them into the developed world, physically and mentally, fits the definition of genocide. It is happening, regularly, all over the globe.

In the last several thousand years the new splinter groups of "separatists" — the agriculturalists, the technologists — became dominant, in their numbers and in their means for altering the Earth and its billions-of-years-old life-sustaining systems. Their technology has given us many apparently good things. It has also presented an enormous sense of control, and confidence that we can operate Spaceship Earth and its life-support systems better than Earth did on its own for billions of years.

From Leavers to Takers and Breakers

It is ironic that most early hunting and gathering societies needed only a few hours per day to collect all the food they needed and to build and maintain their shelters and make whatever clothing was needed.[7, p. 58-59]

Of course it varied with region, climate, and time, but, as Pfeiffer puts it, "Life was relatively simple before the change. It was a good life, better in many respects than anything that has evolved since. There were fewer people in the whole world than there are now in New York City, and they were all hunter-gatherers ... This strange new breed of primate seemed to have found its place in the scheme of things, living on what Nature offered, as small-band, small-time nomads in balance with other wild species."[7, p. 29] They had a lot of free time. They developed a variety of art forms; they loved to play and relax, and tell the old stories. Modern humans, especially those of us living in the U.S., work eight to ten hours per day and many

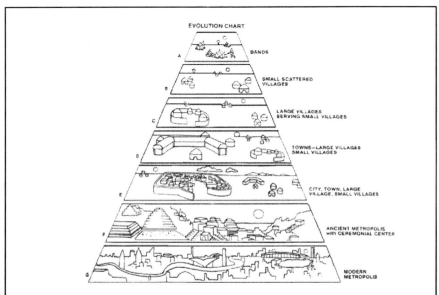

Figure 1. The emergence of society is an organic process, symbolically represented as a progression from band to village to metropolis, A through G. (After Pfeiffer)

work a couple more at night at home, just to keep the children and spouse fed, clothes on their backs, and to buy expensive toys. The monumental movement from a Leaver culture to a Taker one, occurring in the blink of an eye compared to Earth's total history, actually happened gradually in human terms, as illustrated in Figure 1.

As Pfeiffer says, "The people who changed the world beyond all recall were struggling not to change. First it was a matter of doing more hunting-gathering, settling down and exploiting wild species more intensively; then the use of cultivated plants as supplementary items in the diet; and finally complete dependence on domestication and widespread irrigation systems.

It is all recorded in the living sites of prehistory, in the patterns of artifacts. People concentrated in larger groups, and one of the chief reasons was that population kept increasing."[7, p. 41] (For an intriguing look into the lives of indigenous cultures see Jean Liedlof's book *The Continuum Concept*[8] and for a fuller understanding of the movement from hunting and gathering to farming, Pfeiffer's *The Emergence of Society* is an excellent source.[7])

A growing number of people, including those in both Taker and Leaver cultures, believe that the logic of our new, more highly "developed" way of life is flawed, as is the underlying separatist cosmology. It is flawed because it has allowed, even encouraged, human numbers to grow rapidly, alarmingly, and unsustainably. It is flawed because it does not adhere to the natural law that waste equals food. It spits out wastes that not only don't sustain other organisms but also kill them. These organisms are part of the web of life and the systems that sustain our air, water, and soil. Kill them and we kill the basic life-support systems of the planet. Ultimately we kill ourselves.

Displaced in Space and Time

If this were obvious to all, and if the adverse consequences were known and experienced immediately, personally, and dramatically, our advanced brains might get the needed feedback to alter the damaging practices. We would even question their cosmological underpinnings. Instead, we use our advanced technology to displace the bad consequences of our actions — of our wrong cosmology — in space and in time, away from our immediate experience, "Out of sight – out of mind."

The consequences are so delayed that we cannot immediately attribute the disease — the ecological destruction, the global warming, the cancer, and the mad cow disease — to the earlier action that precipitated it. Wastes are disposed of away from where we live, so we don't see or feel the consequences immediately and directly.

Quinn explains the problem in terms of our faulty cosmology. "There's nothing fundamentally wrong with people. Given a story to enact that puts them in accord with the world, they will live in accord with the world. But given a story to enact that puts them at odds with the world, as yours does, they will live at odds with the world. Given a story to enact in which they are the lords of the world, they will *act* like lords of the world. And, given a story to enact in which the world is a foe to be conquered, they will conquer it like a foe, and one day, inevitably, their foe will lie bleeding to death at their feet, as the world is now."[2, p. 84]

The New Religion

In the last few decades our separatist cosmology has entered a dangerous new era. This new development goes beyond mere separatist thinking. Ominous in its simplicity and terrible in its destructive power, it has taken over the developed world and is spreading rapidly and extensively to the less developed one. If people do not appear interested in adopting it, whatever connections they have to the developed world are used as tools to bring them to the new cosmology, along with the minds and hearts of their children. The Takers do not conduct this insidious movement consciously, but it still exerts pressure on the remaining Leavers to convert to the new belief system.

The new world view is *rampant consumerism* and a nearly religious belief in the central importance of a growing monetary economy, ultimately substituting material goals for spiritual and vocational ones.

The new belief system driving these changes is now based on one, single, all-powerful guiding principle, manifest in our schools, businesses, and governments. It is easy to state:

Whatever advances business — providing a good return on investment dollars, expanding the monetary economy, and making business leaders wealthier — is good and should be continued. Whatever harms business activity, slows the economy, or inhibits free trade is bad and should be stopped.

This is a very powerful force, pushing big and small business into every corner of the globe. What grows the economy is good. What does not is bad. A result of the new thinking is a tendency to cut off government and other public services that are not perceived as directly contributing to the goal.

Paul Tillich said that religion is whatever we take as the object of our ultimate concern.[9] Using this definition, we can say that pursuit of profits has become the new global religion. Colin Campbell adds that commercial (and more recently, public) television is the high priest of the new religion, distorting both observation and attitude with the warped new world view, the religion of profit.

With this narrow focusing of human enterprise toward profits and economic growth, public supported symphonies and ballet companies fail or become dependent on handouts from the very rich. Public radio and television stations struggle to make ends meet, having to survive mostly on private gifts and commercials for local corporations, and arts funding organizations suffer financial crises. School systems, from the elementary grades through graduate school, turn to business for guidance on what should be taught and how the operation should be administered. Whatever contributes to the growth of the profit machine is right. True education often suffers, being replaced by mere job training.

The business section of *Florida Today* contained a story on January 29, 2000, headlined, "Home builders have busiest year since '90." The story quotes Anita Cragg of Signature Quality Homes as saying, "It's fun and exciting to be involved in the business right now, but we're all just so busy trying to keep up with the demand."

With such "busy-ness," who has time or inclination to pause and rest, to reflect on the meaning of the enterprise, to seek wisdom? Cleverness is not the same as wisdom; the latter is needed to escape the current aberrant cosmology and find a new way, a new path to a sustainable future for humankind.

In spite of the warning signs, denial reigns supreme. We continue trying to patch up seemingly isolated environmental problems through pollution laws, personal recycling, and selective purchases of less impacting products. Some of these are successful, in a limited way, but run the risk of deceiving us into thinking they are effective in the long run. They delude us into thinking that we are properly dealing with the problems. I call this *incremental patchwork environmental do-goodism*.

By failing to address the root cause of our Earth destruction, our failed cosmology, we are at most prolonging the agony of our demise.

Guilt and Blame

How frightening to realize that with nearly every step and every breath we take, our Western way of life is systematically taking apart the life-support system of Planet Earth! Though we might argue that only some, or most, of us are doing it, everyone will suffer from it.

No one is to blame and none should feel guilt. It is just a place we have come to, with generally good intentions. My words may sometimes sound accusing and critical. The emotion with which I write them results from a frustration and exasperation in knowing how thoroughly we all participate in the delusion, the stupidity of our past and present actions. I prefer not to be critical, but find it unavoidable in this case. Hopefully it is constructive. The consequent anger can sometimes provide the energy needed to break us from our lethargy.

Perhaps self-loathing is a natural consequence of these ideas — at this juncture, where past and future are colliding in the greatest event of all human history: the coming transition from an unsustainable human culture to either a dying one or a sustaining one. The latter will come only with drastic shifts of attitude and understanding. We are on the threshold of a gigantic transformation, toward either annihilation or realization. Our negative thoughts about ourselves and what we've done to Earth are not constructive, accomplish nothing, and aren't deserved... unless we use them to energize us, providing self-affirming motivation for change.

Our crisis is no less serious than if a giant asteroid, large enough to wipe out fifty to seventy percent of the world's people and doom the remaining to lives of misery and fear, were hurtling toward Earth. When I wrote this, a NASA space probe, for the first time, had gone into orbit around an asteroid. It was analyzing the asteroid for possible ways to divert similar masses that might be headed for collision with the Earth. Structuring a multinational effort to determine a course of action and then carry it out could be one of our greatest challenges.

Similarly, the way to deal with the environmental threat is through rational discussion of the relevant issues, by the entire populace and by government officials — and by using the time available to select and execute a possible plan of action. Structuring a multinational effort to understand the environmental threat and take action on it is no less urgent than one to avoid an asteroid.

More Consumers for the Fatherland

The ecological crisis is subtler than an asteroid impact, and the threatened disaster will spread over a number of decades. If we take tentative steps at first to deal with the threat, as we are trying to do already, and allow ourselves to be deceived that they are sufficient, then surely we are doomed.

It is ironic that I wrote those words within one of the great symbols of Western decadence, the modern, many-story, downtown luxury hotel. Its impacts extend far and wide over the Earth, while deceiving us into thinking that life really is as grand as it seems right there. I was out of town on a business trip, using a few moments for reflection. If we must participate in the decadence that surrounds us, let us at least use it to find ways of breaking out of the conceptual cocoon in which we are imbedded.

I was in a place where parking lots have $70,000 automobiles, where many more energy-consuming devices and systems dwarf paltry attempts at energy conservation. The meager savings provided by the proud hotel's compact fluorescent lamps are blown away by so many more, and growing, energy-intensive activities. The very light in my room was electrically powered, when free natural daylight was but a few feet away, on the other side of the wall beside me.

We build ourselves into wasteful, Earth-depleting structures and then feel good about it by installing slightly more efficient equipment. We use Earth's old black blood in depleting quantities, and convert it to the city's invisible new blood, wired electricity. We use these bloodstreams to run unnecessary lights, to power always-on air heating and cooling systems, to homogenize and sanitize our air, and separate us further from the true source of all life, the Earth on which the building stands. Julia Allen Field once said, "We are using the Earth as if we were the last generation."[10, p. x]

Even as we improve the efficiency of our energy-consuming devices, we add more consumers to *demand* that efficient energy. New people are added to the world at an unsustainable rate, and we increase the demand for energy by the billions already here and previously living modest lives of low consumption. We spread our polluted and polluting Western "Taker" culture and its consumerism to the low-impact populations, coaxing them to use more energy and other resources, to a magnitude that dwarfs our meager attempts at material and energy reform.

In our relative luxury, we think we're doing well. Some of us give generously to those attempting — and succeeding — to make some of our consumptive ways a little less Earth-impacting. But most of these efforts are without attempts to change the misplaced Separatist values, the cosmology gone wrong, the Western paradigm being spread around the world. It is like giving food to starving masses in Africa, without also dealing with the underlying causes of the starvation. (The result, in that case, is to doom even more people to perpetual starvation. In the larger context, it is to doom even more people to greater suffering as part of the future environmental collapse.)

The "philosophy" professed herein suggests that we need fairly radical shifts in how we think about our place on Earth, how we go about our affairs, stopping population growth, and even reversing it, and substantially reducing our per capita use of energy and other resources. This seems heretical to some, merely unrealizable to others. The political reality, even our staunchest supporters point out, is such that no politician could or would recommend even a fraction of the measures suggested here. They are just too radical. Furthermore, the current ambient cultural materialism is just too strong a force to counter, given current apathy and other "realities".

The longer we wait for Nature to give us even stronger signals that current patchwork attempts at correction are inadequate, the greater the difficulty of turning the trend around, trying to avoid massive global system collapse as Nature corrects the imbalance. Coupled with the direct calamities will be massive, unplanned changes in lifestyle and behavior. Being unplanned for, they will be onerous. This will result in direct reductions in human quality of life, as the quantity of nonhuman life is forced to diminish, along with reduced habitat area and viability for all the other creatures with which we share the planet.

At the bottom of this issue lies a clear reality. The one attribute that makes us human — different from the other animals — is our highly developed intelligence. Our intelligence is responsible for our current course, headed for a distant but barely visible cliff, seemingly mindless of the danger that awaits us.

If we become extinct, it will be the result of our intelligence. But if we survive it will be because of it.

Genes or Jeans?

A very important question to consider is this: what is it in human makeup that has brought us to the point of initiating the last great mass extinction event in Earth history? That subject is examined somewhat by Leakey[11] and Morrison.[12] The former presents compelling evidence that the current extinction event is not the first in human history. The migrations of early human hunters, into lands previously devoid of humanoids, were devastating to some of the local species, precipitating "one of the swiftest and most profound biological catastrophes in the history of the Earth."[13, p. 52] Recent new archeological evidence adds to this view. These were not recent events, in human terms, but were the result of natural quests for food by early hunter-gatherers. People "struggled to survive by exploiting the only resources available to them — namely, the natural world around them."[13, p. 254]

Leakey adds, "We now inhabit a modern world, with this history behind us.... Some disagree, but I believe that what we face is profoundly disturbing, both in the loss of magnificent individual species, such as elephants, and in the global effect. I have talked...about human impacts in the past, not as an excuse for what is being visited now. We are aware of what we are doing and its consequences; earlier societies were not."[11, p. 194]

Morrison's view is somewhat different. In *The Spirit in the Gene*, he lays the blame not on a natural quest for survival but upon a dogged belief in human invincibility. This leads us to overpopulate the Earth, "resulting in wanton habitat destruction throughout the glorious nonhuman world," according to Lynn Margulis in the Foreword to his book.[14, p. vii]

Morrison describes our agrarian transition as a "relatively minor behavioral shift" that "had ramifications of monumental consequence: the primate *Homo sapiens* was transforming itself into a new kind of animal, an omnivore that no longer gained its food opportunistically but "grazed" at will on homegrown flesh, seed, or foliage; a genetically nomadic species that no longer had to keep moving to survive but could settle in one place and accumulate possessions." From a Darwinian point of view, without an underlying biological change this sudden behavioral mutation "radically departed from evolutionary precedent.... Within the space of just a few thousand years, a new kind of animal had conceived and given birth to itself."[14, p. 93-94]

Biologically, we are little different from the other animals. Not a scrap of hard evidence exists to prove otherwise. Morrison argues that "our peculiar genetic heritage purposefully blinds us to reality to make us malleable and compliant to its demands, and that our habit of assigning ourselves an imaginary uniqueness is the mechanism that delivers us willingly into genetic servitude." Instead, humanity's belief in its uniqueness was necessary for survival, he argues, but led to its domination and subjugation of the Earth. It is a case of a good thing gone wrong.

In the beginning, with human numbers still quite small and without possession of powerful tools of technology, the consequences were modest. Now, however, exponential growth and our newfound technological prowess have led us to the brink of self-annihilation. If the problem is not with our genes, perhaps it is in our designer *jeans*, symbols of rampant consumerism. This new world view is on the verge of destroying us. Will we be smart enough to halt the destruction?

Can Humans Save Humanity?

The forces of destruction have a certain momentum to them. This current push toward global corporatism and consumerism has had some time to build. By its own measure, it has been wildly successful. It will not easily be stopped, or redirected.

Before dealing with the growing movement to change our perspective, let us pause a moment and ask if the human species has the fundamental *ability* to make the needed changes. We have adapted in the past to a variety of stimuli and new environments. Some say humans are the most adaptable creatures on Earth. The question is whether we can gather the wherewithal to alter our story, to change our perspective on the world and how it operates, and to make the fundamental changes in our thinking and our ways of life to save the species before it is too late.

This question is a complex one. Humanity is being tested. To meet the challenge successfully, to make the necessary changes, we will need great talent, education, and ability. We will also need to alter our value systems, where appropriate. And we must transform our social and economic systems radically. Current governmental structures may need to be altered (in some cases, abandoned and rebuilt). The United States Constitution, for example, may need to be amended — or even be rewritten!

Do we have the talent to make the needed changes? Do we have it in us to see the light and take a new path toward a sustainable future?

Being True to Our Species

Nonhuman animals, those still living in the wild, operate on instinct and are true to their species. They do what evolution has programmed them to do, and the basic system is stable and lasting. What does it mean for humans to be true to *their* species?

Humanity is a part of the animal kingdom and a part of the natural order. Genetically we are 99 percent identical to chimpanzees. Jared Diamond argues "a visitor from outer space would classify humans as a third species of chimpanzee, not with the separate classification that we award ourselves."

In spite of this similarity, we are very special creatures. What makes us so special, what sets us apart from other species, Diamond says, is human inventiveness. A professor of biology at UCLA, he claims this talent developed as a consequence of the acquisition of language. "The first signs of inventiveness appeared around 50,000 years ago, judging from the evidence of elaborate tools, art, and burial of the dead." John Maynard Smith of the University of Sussex pointed to grammar, the awareness of the importance of word order that sets humans apart.[15]

However it evolved, we have developed a special intelligence, giving us the unique power to see ourselves as different from the other animals. We are losing our direct and personal connections with the natural environment that sustains us. It is as if we were trying to break from the ecological "hard-wiring" that connects us with Nature. As a result, we are in the process of destroying ourselves and the life-support system with us. Most people are unaware of the larger features of this process and feel no personal responsibility to do anything significant about it.

This is *not* being true to our species, using our special intelligence to assess our unique position and the destructive trend of things, and to change our ways of thinking to ensure a viable future for ourselves and all the other organisms upon which we depend.

Intelligence is what brought us to this place. It is the only thing that can save us—but only if we use it wisely and correctly, and start the process right now.

Can we do it?

Human Capability Index

Let me propose a measure of our ability to make the needed changes. I define the Human Capability Index (HCI) to be the capacity of a human individual to:

1. Grow to maturity and develop the skills to look after one's self.
2. Exhibit skills at providing food, clothing, and shelter for self and family.
3. Contribute to the betterment of society through occupation, avocation, and group sharing.
4. Look to the future, anticipate possible and real dangers and problems, and take appropriate action to protect self, family, friends, and the larger society from these dangers, whether the dangers are a year, decade or century away.
5. Alter one's behavior as needed to meet the above goals, and the perceived greater good of the community.

To my knowledge, the subject has not been studied scientifically. We can suppose that having a high HCI requires prerequisites: a reasonably stable, protected, and supportive childhood, good psychological health, and a feeling of being connected to other humans and to all other living creatures. It includes a good understanding of Earth and human history and some knowledge of other societies, including aboriginal ones. It includes knowledge of the basic physical, chemical, and biological processes that support life on Earth.

Though high intelligence is not essential, it is helpful. Maintaining good health is important, preventing a burden on family or society until one's later years. A degree of wisdom is an important contributing asset, and an ability to learn from life experiences. Though formal education is not essential it is also helpful. Education is here considered broadly, not just training for a job in industry.

More basically, a high HCI presumes an ability to think for one's self, to clarify, to learn, and to understand the world in which the person lives. It is interesting that most stable aboriginal cultures possessed these traits.

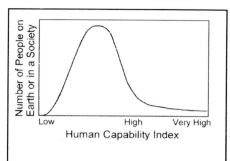

Figure 2. Hypothetical plot showing the prevalence of different levels of human capability.

Let us suppose that a comprehensive and scientific study provides a way to measure and provide a numerical value for the HCI of an individual. Let us also assume that another study is conducted to measure the HCI of a large number of people from all countries, and to determine the number of people at each HCI across the wide scale from 0 capability (for persons totally dependent on others for care, feeding, and upkeep) to a very high capability (for persons scoring very high on all the measures listed above).

Now let us suppose that the number of people is plotted versus HCI values for the entire human population. The plot might look something like the drawing in Figure 2.

Fortunately, there are very few people worldwide with near-zero HCI. Unfortunately, there are also few with very high HCI levels.

The need for humans with high HCI's becomes evident as we examine the forces producing the overpopulation of the planet, and those leading the population toward ever-increasing environmental destruction (despite a few localized reversals of this destruction). We have a global need for better citizens everywhere. We need more intelligent, more capable, more resourceful people, in general, if we are to solve the global problems facing us. As more countries move toward democracy, or democratic-like systems, where masses of people can affect their governance, the abilities of these people to understand their situations and act with good judgment and some degree of wisdom to deal with problems is becoming critical.

We might like to think that the average HCI is increasing. However, David Briscoe reported to the Associated Press in 1998[16] that

Population experts now believe that several African countries may achieve zero population growth in just a few years. But family planners are not cheering. The reasons are gruesome and worrisome: populations devastated by AIDS and further threatened with food shortages, water depletion, ecological collapse and social chaos.

Fueling the concern are the first detailed global figures on AIDS infection percentages released at an international AIDS conference in June. In addition to the impact on Zimbabwe, the U.N. data show Botswana with 25 percent

AIDS infection, Namibia with 20 percent, Zambia with 19 percent, Swaziland with 18.5 percent and several other African countries with 10 percent or more.

Groups working to control rapid population growth around the world are concerned the new projections will be viewed as support for the cynical view that the world's problems will take care of themselves no matter what humans do.

"We must not let people think that an epidemic is going to solve problems. It's going to worsen them," said Amy Coen, president of Population Action International, which conducts research and supports efforts to slow population growth worldwide.

Coen, in an interview, noted that AIDS usually hits people in the prime of life, in their most productive years. In some countries, the number of AIDS orphans — children who have lost both parents to AIDS — is in the hundreds of thousands.

Clearly our HCI index increases as we grow and develop from childhood to adulthood, declining only slightly as we enter old age. The last thing we need is something killing people in or before their years of peak HCI. This is not the best way to stabilize world population either, even though it may be Nature's way of correcting a local imbalance.

Everywhere we turn, forces are working to take us down, pushing the competencies of masses of people downward not upward. All over the world, young girls are born in what we would call very difficult situations. Girls who have very limited self-preservation skills at looking after themselves and getting along in life, are having babies, lots of babies, and are not able to care for them properly nor provide them with necessary life-coping skills.

Boys in some industrialized societies are losing their abilities to father, by not learning the skills of appropriate fatherhood developed by working next to their fathers while growing up. Most child development theorists suggest one needs a balance between "mothering" (supportive) and "fathering" (challenging). Overall we're doing better at mothering than fathering.[17]

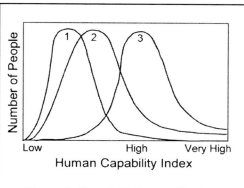

Figure 3. Hypothetical curves for three different populations.

If this trend continues, one can envision that the HCI curve plotted in Fig. 2 will shift to the left, from Curve 2 to Curve 1 in Figure 3. We would rather see an overall *increase* in the HCI world wide, toward a curve like number 3.

One peculiar human trait inhibits action to reverse the destructive trends. Psychologists have shown that people will go against clear fact if everyone around them professes belief in the incorrect information. This has terrible implications for the future — and for future movements in the HCI curve.

What will happen to us, I ask, if the kind of bright, knowledgeable, capable, and well-educated people we need to operate Spaceship Earth safely are fewer in number ... even as the total number of humans swells to unmanageable sizes? Surely we will reach a point of no return, where the number of incapable humans increases rapidly while the number of capable ones decreases — a prescription for demise.

This and other evidence about the capability of the human species to save itself worries many people. Our HCI curve is shifting to the left. We are unable to accept the clear facts of our danger because few people of influence and media access speak about it. The forces of consumerism, materialism, and global corporatism control governments and the media. Because of this, many feel we have already passed the point of no return. Humans will not only produce the sixth mass extinction event, but will participate in it and dwindle to near extinction. Such a crash of human population will be unplanned and it will be filled with pain and anguish.

The good news is that the needed paradigm shift to avoid a terrible fate *has* started, and is slowly, quietly, spreading through human culture. This book is but one of its emissaries. Of course, the forces of overpopulation and growth and development are spreading, too, but it is not yet too late. In another decade or two it probably will be. We will have passed the point of no return and our lives will be more like that of some futuristic science fiction story.

Our goal is to internalize our new understandings, making them not only part of everyday life but part of our spiritual being. This takes us beyond traditional environmentalism into an area of devout respect for Earth and listening to its teachings as we restructure society to survive indefinitely, sustainably. If that happens, fathers will join mothers. Sons and daughters will join grandparents. The world will be changed forever, for the better... protecting the world for the future children, of all cultures, and all species.

References

1. Paul B. MacCready, "Unleashing Creativity," in *Symposium on The Inventor and Society*, Jerome and Dorothy Lamelson Center for the Study of Invention and Innovation, Smithsonian National Museum of American History, 1995.
2. Daniel Quinn. *Ishmael*. 1st ed. Bantam/Turner: New York, 1992.
3. Thomas Berry. *The Dream of the Earth*. 1st ed. Sierra Club Books: San Francisco, 1988, 247 pp.
4. Thomas Berry. *The Great Work — Our Way Into the Future*. Bell Tower: New York, 1999, 241 pp.
5. Brian Swimme and Thomas Berry. *The Universe Story*. HarperSanFrancisco, div. of HarperCollins: San Francisco, 1992, 305 pp.
6. Paul Hawken. *The Ecology of Commerce — A Declaration of Sustainability*. HarperBusiness, div. HarperCollins: New York, 1993, 250 pp.
7. John E. Pfeiffer. *The Emergence of Society — A prehistory of the Establishment*. © 1977 McGraw-Hill: New York, 512 pp.
8. Jean Liedloff. *The Continuum Concept: In Search of Happiness Lost*. Reprint, 1986 ed. Perseus Books: Cambridge, MA, 1985, 172 pp.
9. Paul Tillich. *Dynamics of Faith*. Harperperennial Library: New York, 2001, 176 pp.
10. William Ross McCluney, ed. *The Environmental Destruction of South Florida*, Seventh Printing, 1990 ed. The University of Miami Press: Coral Gables, FL, 1971, pp. 134.
11. Richard E. Leakey and Roger Lewin (Contributor). *The Sixth Extinction : Patterns of Life and the Future of Humankind*. Anchor edition (November, 1996) ed. Anchor Books.
12. Reg Morrison and Lynn Margulis. *The Spirit in the Gene: Humanity's Proud Illusion and the Laws of Nature*. Cornell University Press Comstock Pub Assoc.: 1999, 286 pp.
13. Storrs L. Olson. "Extinction on Islands: man as a catastrophe." In *Conservation for the Twenty-First Century*, edited by David Western and Mary Pearl. Oxford University Press: New York, 1989.
14. Reg Morrison. *The Spirit in the Gene: Humanity's Proud Illusion and the Laws of Nature*. Cornell University Press: Ithaca, NY, 1999, 286 pp.
15. Luke O'Neill, Michael Murphy, and Richard B. Gallagher. "What Are We? Where Did We Come From? Where Are We Going?" *Science* Vol. 263, (1994): 14 January 1994, 181-183.
16. David Briscoe, "African Population Projection Falls," *Associated Press wire service*, Saturday, 26 September 1998.
17. Personal communication, Dianne Benjamin, "Parenting," 2002 to R. McCluney.

11
Problems in Paradise
Life seems good to many of us.
What could be the difficulty?

The flight was smooth. As the plane approached the airport, it swooped low over rolling hills with their gracefully curving streets lined with houses and trees rich with green leaves. The light blue of an occasional backyard swimming pool contrasted nicely with the dark color of the foliage. Off in the near distance was a small shopping center and over to the left an attractive neighborhood school. In all, a very pleasant-seeming place to live, one of the many such suburbs that exist in Middle America.

"How could anything be wrong with what I'm seeing?" I asked myself. Comfortable modern houses with beautiful furniture and well-equipped kitchens. Supplies of gas and electricity flowing through the house, energizing it, making life convenient and comfortable. Well kept lawns and inviting backyards. The kids walk home from school and the grocery is just down the street. In their protective garages are automobiles with their plush interiors, powerful engines, and ample storage spaces. All the accouterments of the affluent lifestyle our wonderful country has made possible.

Life *is* materially good for those who can afford it. If you work hard, save and invest, you can look forward to living this gentle (though possibly a bit boring) lifestyle. House and automobile would epitomize comfort and aesthetic charm. From the viewpoint of your grandparents, you would be *living in the lap of luxury*. You can drive to nearby stores for nearly everything you might want, and you can afford whatever you really need in the way of food, clothing, shelter, and play-toys.

Educational opportunities abound, for all stages of life. You have at your disposal an advanced medical system (at least based on increasing life-expectancy and relative freedom from health-related pain and discomfort). If you take care of your body and your mind (now easier than ever to do), you can expect to be free of pain and crippling or disabling disease most of your life. Fitness centers are everywhere, even in most major hotels and motels, almost nonexistent thirty years ago. The one exception is genetic diseases that cannot be avoided, at least for the time being. With modern genetic research and engineering, prevention of some diseases is now possible through gene therapy; by other careful strategies, you can avoid passing your worst genes to your offspring.

Life's necessities are available to you with relative reliability and comfort. So are an amazing variety of entertainment outlets, from movies and videos to hundreds of satellite and cable TV channels. Dining out has never been easier. Even in cities of modest size, concerts, plays, and other theatrical and artistic performances are available, with skilled and experienced artists in live performances at modest cost. If reading books is your thing, with your new computer you can order any book on the market with a few keystrokes and the book is delivered to your mailbox or front door in a few days.

In short, life seems grand in affluent America.

What's Wrong with this Picture?

Life does seem rather grand, in this community. Isn't the material affluence a reward for hard work, good job training, and doing things right? Isn't this what our society — our culture — pushes us toward, from birth to adulthood? What could be wrong with this picture?

Well, a lot of things. For one, not everyone lives the affluent lifestyle. Are those less "well off" happy? I know some who are. How do they derive their enjoyment and satisfaction in life? Most focus on the social and psychological rewards of a good life rather than on material possessions as trophies of success in the game of business. But isn't it the belief (if not the action) of government and businessmen everywhere that all humans deserve and should have increased affluence? Does it matter that in some cases this is not for altruistic, but selfish motives — to create more consumers for industrial engines?

Is the pursuit of material affluence built into our genes? Don't all animals have the same interests — survival of the fittest and all that? Aren't we programmed toward making better lives for ourselves, and competing with other species (even members of our own species) for it?

If you accept the premise of this question, the conclusion is obvious: we have very successfully out-competed all other living things on Earth. We force many to work for us, and give up their lives, often in terrible conditions, so we can eat. We have subjugated Nature around the globe. We've won the competition. But can we celebrate?

Just because life may *seem* good in some areas and may be exciting, thrilling, and have other desirable features, does not mean it *is* really good for the long run. Experience has shown we need to take a more encompassing, longer-term view of developments that have great potential for good or ill.

Most of us are in no position to see the big picture clearly. Our lives seem too good to worry about hidden problems. We have only limited power and influence, as we struggle to make good lives for ourselves. Few of us have time to study, think, and decide about the larger issues raised here.

Even if we do, we are stymied by the juggernaut of our ambient culture, Mother Culture. She thrusts a certain world view at us everywhere we look. In the past, Nature's signals — the built-in feedback systems — would intrude on our consciousness and loudly warn us of our erroneous actions. Nature told us what didn't work or couldn't be sustained, forcing us to take corrective action or suffer the consequences.

Restoring Lost Feedback

The feedback mechanisms which once existed in our world are now largely broken. This is not being true to our species. We must find ways of restoring *natural* feedback to our daily lives, providing us with the correct signals for both environmentally beneficial and injurious actions. Or we must consciously restructure our society through a better model. This test, of our ability to intelligently overcome very basic tendencies and very powerful societal forces is perhaps the greatest challenge ever to face humanity.

I fear that humans may not be up to the challenge. We are not yet sufficiently advanced to take actions now on perceived threats that are more than a few years away. Can we see beyond the immediate comfort our affluent lifestyle promises? Can we change our ways of thinking and living to protect the future for our children and their children and grandchildren?

Tale of Two Cultures

The magnitude of the task is seen by a somewhat artificial but illustrative comparison of our two cultures: how we once lived as hunter-gatherers with some early agricultural skills and how we live as industrialists (or what I previously called "Separatists"). Our loss of the natural feedback mechanisms is illustrated by a comparison between an aboriginal village on the shore of a meandering river and the modern-day version of that settlement.

The first is illustrated in Figure 1. The village diagramed is on the shore of a free-flowing stream. It symbolizes the way early society operated.

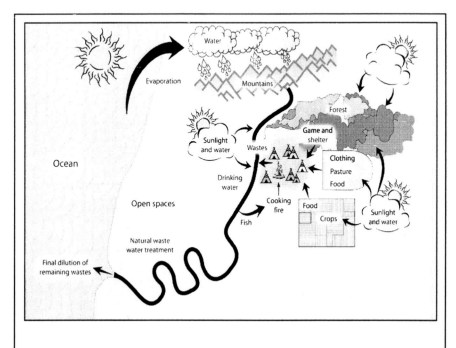

Figure 1. Schematic illustration of energy and material flows in an aboriginal

We can see that all the food, shelter, water, and waste processing systems employed by the village's inhabitants are powered by solar energy. Water from the salty ocean evaporates by natural solar energy, is condensed by the atmosphere and deposited on the land as clean, fresh, desalinated water. Solar-powered photosynthesis (in trees, grasses, and freshwater microorganisms), converts natural minerals through life processes into many and varied complex organic molecules. These molecules are filled with solar energy, available as food for all kinds of animals.

Humans learned to utilize this stored-up solar energy in many ways. Crops were harvested, processed (by human power), and used as food. Natural forest products were used for shelter, clothing, food, and various tools and other necessities.

The stream running down from the mountains was a good source of clean drinking water and aquatic food species. It was also used for washing, bathing, and the dispersal of wastes. The downward meanderings of the stream through grassy marshes provided a valuable filtering and purification system. The few wastes remaining after this process were greatly diluted and organically decomposed in the stream by filtering when it overflowed its banks and transited through marsh and soil. What might have been left was finally diluted in the ocean.

This small human ecosystem was operated entirely by solar energy. The village lived completely within its daily budget of energy from the sun. If valuable materials in the soil on which the crops were grown were depleted, a relatively simple relocation of the village sufficed.

Notice that the quantity and toxicity of the wastes produced by this society were low and easily assimilated by the land, air, and water. Toxicity wielded occasional and minor adverse impacts upon either the environment in general or the inhabitants of the village. (It took the village in Fig. 1 a few years and many illnesses to realize that it should deposit its wastes downstream from where it took its drinking water ... an example of a direct feedback mechanism resulting in altered behavior.)

Next we examine this area several hundred years later, after the growing human population developed a myriad of powerful technological tools (shown schematically in Figure 2).

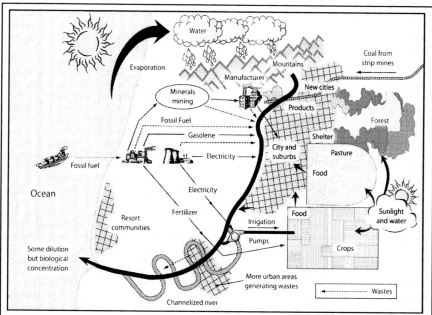

Figure 2. Schematic illustration of the extent to which modern industrialized societies have transformed the land and altered material and energy flows.

The size of the forest is greatly reduced; the area that is cultivated by humans is increased. Urban areas have expanded significantly and become permanent fixtures. The quantity of wastes dumped into the river has increased dramatically, taxing its ability to assimilate them by natural means. The toxicity of these wastes has also increased substantially, with adverse consequences for organisms living in and near the river.

If this were not enough, the river is channelized, its meandering and natural filtration systems removed to promote drainage and make possible more land under cultivation and more urban areas. In consequence, water-borne wastes are carried in relatively high concentrations along the full length of the river. They travel more swiftly than before but are still greatly diluted upon entering the ocean. Biological magnification of these dilute chemicals, in the tissues of various organisms up the food chain, reconcentrates the wastes, in some case as much as a million times. Mercury contamination of tuna has become a serious health problem.

This may seem an unlikely scenario for some readers. We in Central and Southern Florida know it well. The Kissimmee River flows from near Orlando southward to Lake Okeechobee. That water historically continued southward in a sheet flow across the Everglades. The Army Corps of Engineers channelized the Kissimmee River above Lake Okeechobee at some expense, just as illustrated in Fig. 2. The adverse consequences for Lake Okeechobee and the Everglades became so severe that they are now plugging up the channel at much greater expense, in an attempt to restore the meanders which used to be a defining characteristic of the river.

The villages and crops illustrated in Fig. 1 are no longer mobile in Fig. 2. The urban areas now contain greater population with greatly increased demands for food and supplemental energy. This new society has exceeded the carrying capacity of its immediate area and has exceeded its daily budget of energy from the sun. How does it continue to function?

It requires massive infusions of stored-up non-renewable energy from coal, oil, natural gas, and uranium nuclei. River channelization and drainage projects have reduced the amount of available fresh water at a time when the human population and its agriculture require more water. Extra energy must be used for pumping water onto croplands and over great distances to population centers. Often the magnitude of this pumping depletes ancient subterranean water reservoirs, exceeds replenishment rates for near-to-surface aquifers, and causes cities and states to compete for dwindling supplies. As the water table is lowered beneath the ground in areas near the ocean, salt water intrudes into fresh water areas, eventually making the water undrinkable.

Much extra energy in the form of chemical fertilizer, pesticides, and herbicides is also required to support the greatly increased demand for food energy. Adding the fossil fuel costs of food transportation and processing, most of the energy associated with the food we eat comes from fossil fuel. Little known is the fact that the solar energy for growing crops plays only a minor role in the U.S. food production system today. This is illustrated in Fig. 3 [1]. The ratio of (fossil) energy subsidy to the (solar) energy content of the U.S. average food system passed 1:1 around 1911, and in 1980 was approximately 10:1. When the price of energy increases, the price of U.S. food will also rise.

We don't eat solar energy; we eat petroleum.

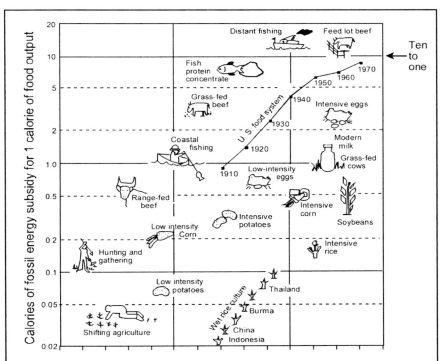

Figure 3. Schematic illustration of the extent to which modern industrialized societies have transformed the land and altered material and energy flows. (After Steinhart and Steinhart.)

Looking again at Figure 2, we see why. Massive inputs of non-solar energy are required for the irrigation, fertilization, growing, processing, and delivery of crops and animal flesh for consumption. This is true as well for myriad other human activities, including the manufacture of building products, clothing, tools and the operation of transportation systems. Huge amounts of energy are also required to process our solid, liquid, and gaseous wastes before we can release them to the environment with some limited degree of safety.

Two crucially important results of this massive use of supplemental, stored up energy are: (1) We are using it up (spending our capital) at an alarming rate. We seem to become more and more dependent on it as it becomes in shorter and shorter supply. (2) In the process of using it, we are poisoning our air, land, and water with highly toxic chemicals...some that kill us now and others that kill us twenty-five years from now.

As *technologicalization* of our society progressed and as population densities increased, society became more complex, fast-paced, and rapidly changing.

The extent of our separation from Nature (our displacing of the consequences of our actions from immediate experience) is made evident by the comparison in Figs. 1 and 2. In our industrialized societies, we are separated from the environmental consequences of our actions by complex and elaborate systems of manufacture, distribution, and waste disposal.

Without direct feedback on our actions, we cannot motivate the concern and outrage to reverse the damaging practices. As we isolate ourselves, we structure an artificial cocoon of materialism and deceive ourselves into thinking we are in control of our lives. But when we look more broadly, outside our lives to those in poverty in the U.S. and outside our borders, we can only conclude that all is not well in Graceland.

The concept of ecological footprint was described earlier. Figures 1 and 2 show that in creating the assumed good life, (in our cities, neighborhoods, and offices), we are requiring greater and greater areas outside our communities to supply the materials and energy we need to support modern, consumerism. We are increasing the area of our ecological footprint. And we are disposing of our wastes in the air, rivers, streams, and soil, placing these adverse consequences away from immediate experience.

Energy's role in our highly consuming lifestyles is critical. Many scientists, scholars, and other thinkers believe a relatively precipitous collapse of civilization will occur as we pass the peak in fossil fuels production and rapidly approach the slope of depletion. In his essay, "Energy and Human Evolution," Price describes the mechanisms of collapse; he discounts the ability of energy conservation and renewable energy sources to postpone the inevitable, if world population growth is not stopped:

Operative mechanisms in the collapse of the human population will be starvation, social strife, and disease. These major disasters were recognized long before Malthus and have been represented in western culture as horsemen of the apocalypse. They are all consequences of scarce resources and dense population.

Starvation will be a direct outcome of the depletion of energy resources. Today's dense population is dependent for its food supply on mechanized agriculture and efficient transportation. Energy is used to manufacture and operate farm equipment, and energy is used to take food to market. As less efficient energy resources come to be used, food will grow more expensive and the circle of privileged consumers to whom an adequate supply is available will continue to shrink.

Social strife is another consequence of the rising cost of commercial energy. Everything people want takes energy to produce, and as energy becomes more expensive, fewer people have access to goods they desire. When goods are plentiful, and particularly when per-capita access to goods is increasing, social tensions are muted: Ethnically diverse populations often find it expedient to live harmoniously, governments may be ineffective and slow to respond, and little force is needed to maintain domestic tranquility. But when goods become scarce, and especially when per-capita access to goods is decreasing, ethnic tensions surface, governments become authoritarian, and goods are acquired, increasingly, by criminal means.

A shortage of resources also cripples public health systems, while a dense population encourages the spread of contagious diseases. Throughout human history, the development of large, dense populations has led to the appearance of contagious diseases that evolved to exploit them. Smallpox and measles were apparently unknown until the second and third centuries AD, when they devastated the population of the Mediterranean basin. In the fourteenth century, a yet larger and denser population in both Europe and China provided a hospitable niche for the Black Death. Today, with extremely dense population and all parts of the world linked by air travel, new diseases such as AIDS spread rapidly — and a virus as deadly as AIDS but more easily transmissible could appear at any time.

Starvation, social strife, and disease interact in complex ways. If famine were the sole mechanism of collapse, the species might become extinct quite suddenly. A population that grows in response to abundant but finite resources, like the reindeer of St. Matthew Island, tends to exhaust these resources completely. By the time individuals discover that remaining resources will not be adequate for the next generation, the next generation has already been born. And in its struggle to survive, the last generation uses up every scrap, so that nothing remains that would sustain even a small population. But famine seldom acts alone. It is exacerbated by social strife, which interferes with the production and delivery of food. And it weakens the natural defenses by which organisms fight off disease.

> Paradoxically, disease can act to spare resources. If, for example, a new epidemic should reduce the human population to a small number of people who happen to be resistant to it before all the world's resources are severely depleted, the species might be able to survive a while longer.[2]

Price's discounting of energy conservation and solar energy is a significant stipulation. He may be right. But we can hope this aspect of his prediction is in error ... and that will give us just enough time for population to level off (and perhaps decline somewhat) by the end of this century, all without the massive societal disruption predicted. On the other hand, we would be well advised not to discount the Price scenario. Elements of it will certainly be experienced as we attempt crash programs to convert to energy conservation and renewable energy use before it is too late. We could say that the current slow pace of conversion is like fiddling while Rome burns.

Looks are Deceiving

In conclusion, life may look grand to some of us right now. But, as the title of this chapter suggests, looks can be deceiving. We must probe deeper and examine how grand life really is. We must ask the hard questions: Can we continue this way? Can the affluent life be brought to all others desiring it? If not, how do we justify the inequities? Should we even *try* to continue this way? What alternatives do we have? Can at least one of them make life meaningful again?

As we found in Chapter 5, the true concern is about what kind of world we want. What values, morals, concerns for other humans, and concerns for other animals do we want to have or preserve?

As we have seen, population levels compatible with numerous possible answers are variable, over a wide range. Once we decide, if we are able to decide, we can begin to limit population to a sustainable level within the values choice we have made. This is a very basic, very important decision.

The question is not yet being asked publicly, much less discussed widely. The single recommendation for individual and group action is to begin the discussion, and make an attempt at some global consensus. Even a majority agreement, much less a consensus worldwide, may be impossible to reach. But we might expect the most consuming, most polluting, and wealthiest nation on Earth to at least make a serious attempt.

References

1. Carol Steinhart and John Steinhart. *The Fires of Culture: Energy Yesterday and Tomorrow*. Wadsworth Publishing, Duxbury Press, Belmont, CA 94002: Belmont, CA, 1974.
2. David Price, "Energy and Human Evolution." *Population and Environment.* Vol 16, No. 4, March 1995, pp. 301-319. Also in: William Ross McCluney, ed. *Getting to the Source: Readings on Sustainable Values*. SunPine Press: Cape Canaveral, Florida, 2004.

12

Misplaced Values

Beliefs and human behavior.
Appropriate and inappropriate values.

W hy do good people do bad things? You know it happens. Sometimes you do it yourself. With the best of intentions, something you do results in a mistake.

These usually happen because of either bad information or just plain bad luck. Most of us either learn from these experiences or try to get better information the next time around.

Bad *thinking* is more difficult to avoid and correct. How we think about things, the world about us and the people we meet, comes from our upbringing and its social context. For example, people from a deeply religious community in some Mid-Eastern country or those in an aboriginal culture in Australia tend to think about things differently than a typical middle class American (especially if the latter lives in a big, bustling city like New York, Atlanta, or Los Angeles.)

How we think and the resulting actions are important to our lives individually, and can be important to society as a whole. They can be harmful on a very large scale. This is about more than just how we think. Fundamental beliefs underlie most of our actions. Addressing these beliefs is critical to developing a sustainable culture.

Values Guide Behavior

Values and beliefs lie at the core of human behavior. Dictionary definitions of these concepts explicitly make the connection between beliefs and behavior patterns. When our value systems become inappropriate for the situations in which we find ourselves, inappropriate behavior patterns can be expected to result. Thus, to change our environmentally destructive behaviors, we must deal with the inappropriate value systems that produce those behaviors. This leads to a study of ethics and philosophy, and more particularly the portions of those fields dealing with the human relationship to the rest of the natural world.

To those engineers, scientists, government planners, and others working to reduce the adverse impact of humans on the Earth by mostly political and technological means, this emphasis on subjects as vague as belief systems and philosophy may appear to be idealistic and impractical. However, most of the changes proposed are doubtful without some massive shift in belief systems. Our Earth cannot remain a viable platform for human life without fundamental changes in our values, however reluctant we may be to make them.

At the heart of this reluctance, I think, is a natural fear of the unknown, the unfamiliar. Expectedly, people wish to work within their accustomed systems of social interaction and commerce, retaining their inherited and developed systems of values and lifestyles. To confront too great or too rapid a change in beliefs and patterns of living and behavior can be frightening[1]. In spite of this, we must begin the process of clarifying our values and goals as a species.

A major purpose of the reform movement should be to identify and codify an ethical framework to support the societal and individual behaviors needed for environmental preservation. This could minimize the perceived and actual sacrifices involved and lead to maximum public enthusiasm for the needed changes. I fear that these may not be compatible goals; for the new ethic to be widely accepted and quickly, it cannot be very effective.

Values and beliefs can be powerful motivators for action. Some can even kill. For example, without strong intervention, economically depressed parts of the world can become dangerous. Small impoverished countries increasingly desire and are approaching, access to nuclear and biological weapons of mass destruction. As their plights become ever more tragic and difficult, they may consider the use of the new weapons to better their situations…especially if they see their wealthy and developed neighboring countries living well while suppressing them (or even ripping-off their natural resources). A possible consequence is nuclear and/or biological conflict, as deprived people attack in a blind search for sustenance. The resulting nuclear or biological releases from various nations may get out of hand.

Belief Scales

Due to all forms of media coverage, we are struck by conflicting beliefs on a variety of environmental subjects. (This was mentioned briefly in Chapter 1.) Miller has pointed out[2] that these beliefs range along a scale between two extremes.

First, there is the viewpoint of the believers in a "full speed ahead, business-as-usual" scenario. As described earlier, these are called the *cornucopians*. They believe that world population, currently just over 6 billion humans, as well as per capita material affluence, can continue growing indefinitely. If any limits to growth are encountered along the way, they will be overcome by science, technology, and business adaptability.

Second is the opposing view of the so-called *neo-Malthusians*. This label comes from their belief in the arguments of 1790s economist Thomas Malthus[3] that population grows rapidly, while subsistence grows slower until disaster strikes: demand exceeds the available supply, and Nature restores a form of balance by devastating the over-populated species or reducing its fertility. Some cornucopians call the neo-Malthusians "tree-huggers," as a term of derision. I'll use that term here, not in derision, but as an easier-to-remember label for neo-Malthusian activists. Most neo-Malthusians are proud to be called "tree-huggers." (The name comes from the *Chipko* Movement (1974), begun in the village of Reni in the foothills of the Himalayas, to protest monoculture tree plantation development.) This linear scale of environmental beliefs is diagramed in Fig. 1.

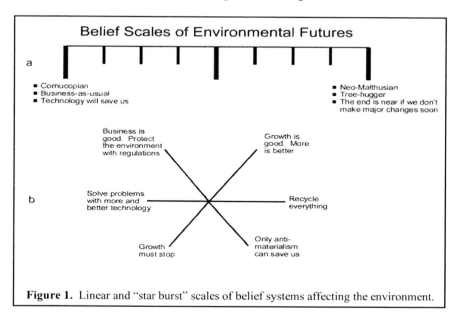

Figure 1. Linear and "star burst" scales of belief systems affecting the environment.

Who is right about where we are headed — the tree-huggers or the cornucopians? These philosophies are discussed in greater depth in later chapters, and conflicts between these two extremes thread through these pages. You, the reader, may form your own judgment about which is the correct perspective...or perhaps develop one in between.

Perhaps you object to the polarizing nature of the linear scale. We could represent the varying beliefs differently, as with the "star-burst" pattern shown in Fig. 1b. This avoids the extremist label, putting all beliefs on an equal footing. But are all beliefs equal in the light of our scientific knowledge of the known past and the expected future consequences of human action?

The two differing viewpoints (at each end of the linear scale) about population growth match extreme beliefs in the more general future of humanity. A wide range of possible outcomes exists: from the tree-hugger belief that world environmental disaster is nearly unavoidable and eminent (without massive change), to the cornucopian belief that catastrophe will be averted through considerable intelligence and technological skills as we encounter and overcome problems — without major changes in our directions, beliefs, and social structures.

Just because a belief is at the extreme end of a linear scale does not mean it is incorrect. But also few things are truly either/or, and few issues are truly black and white. So, it is with the great decision facing us. The optimum path *may* lie somewhere between the two extremes of ecotopia and corporate-sponsored materialistic bliss.

Talking about the extremes, however, has a way of clearing the air, focusing on the core issues. It gives a structure for being interested and curious about the issues, and for examining our educational processes. Once we are informed, maybe then we can look at possible compromises and try to find a safe and sustainable middle ground. On the other hand, we cannot be blind to the possibility that one of the extremes might turn out to be correct.

Indoctrination vs. Advocacy

Indoctrination has been defined as the process of closing minds on open issues. We must keep these issues open and avoid the trap of over-zealous advocacy of any particular view.

Even if neutrality were possible, we would have a big problem with studiously avoiding advocacy. We run a risk of overlooking important possibilities, just because we *will* them to be impossible.

In spite of my desire to remain neutral, I cannot avoid being biased. (Every writer is biased, as a result of having lived, observed, studied, and thought about things.) My bias should be clear from what has been written to this point. I believe the human species to be headed towards a relatively unknown cliff. This puts me mostly in the camp of the tree-huggers, and I'm proud to be there. However, the savvy reader ordinarily dismisses predictions of doom almost before they are stated, and rightfully so. Claims of doom have come and gone over humanity's great history on Earth. Most have proved false.

The predictions found in this book are different. They are buttressed by the conclusions of many scientists, scholars, theologians, and philosophers. We can ignore these concerns, as many are doing, but this will not make the risks go away. I offer a sampling of the evidence to support claims of apparent, impending environmental suicide. The references cited throughout the book provide extensive additional evidence. More can be found on the web site www.futureofhumanity.org.

Whichever perspective you happen to choose, I hope you will agree that misplaced values have resulted in a considerable set of serious problems for humanity.

An Example

Robert F. Kennedy is senior attorney for the Natural Resources Defense Council (NRDC). Kennedy played a leading role in the campaign to save the rainforest home of the Spirit Bear, a nearly extinct white bear living only in British Columbia's Great Bear Rainforest. (Though he is not considered an original thinker and philosopher in the vein of Leopold or Carson, the following brief example of his thought offers its own internal elegance and illustrates the importance of environmental values.)

International Forest Products (Interfor) had renewed destructive clear cutting on Princess Royal Island—the heart of the Spirit Bear habitat. The company was planning to log 18 pristine valleys in the Great Bear rainforest. In addition, Interfor was logging the habitat of endangered species on the border of Pacific Rim National Park on Vancouver Island. They were cutting down extremely rare, 1,000 year old Douglas fir trees in the Stoltmann Wilderness north of Vancouver.

Equally alarming, Interfor's workers had resorted to violently assaulting peaceful environmental protesters. "Interfor is without a doubt the worst destroyer of temperate rainforests on our continent," says Matt Price, an NRDC forestry expert. "It's clear they don't want to be part of the solution. They're intent on liquidating ancient rainforests and flouting public opinion."

From the article "Talking with... Robert F. Kennedy, Jr." In the January/February 2001 issue of *Nature's Voice*, published by NRDC, comes this dialog.

Q: Why are you so passionately committed to saving the Great Bear Rainforest?

Kennedy: Because its destruction will diminish all of humanity. Right now, the last wilderness areas on Earth are being overrun by giant energy, timber, and hydro companies. These remote places are home to the last indigenous cultures on our planet. So when we clear-cut the Great Bear, we're not only destroying one of the largest coastal rainforests left on Earth, we're destroying one of the very last cultures that link us to our own ancestral past. We impoverish ourselves aesthetically, culturally, and spiritually.

Q: How do you answer those who argue that economic growth is paramount?

Kennedy: The choice between environment and economy is a false choice. Interfor would have us treat the planet as if it's a business in liquidation. Sure, we can convert our natural resources to cash as quickly as possible. We can produce instantaneous cash flow and the illusion of a prosperous economy. But our children are going to pay for our joy ride with denuded landscapes and poor health and huge cleanup costs. If you take the long-term view, good environmental policy is always good economic policy.

The heart of this example shows conflict over values and beliefs, between proponents and opponents at opposite ends of the belief scale of environmental values.

Psychological Consequences of Misplaced Values

Our beliefs and the resulting lifestyles can be in conflict with the physical, social, and environmental situations in which we find ourselves. Then quality of life suffers. Joanna Macy writes, "It is hard to participate in social and economic life without feeding, clothing, and transporting ourselves at the expense of the natural world and other people's well-being."[4, p.29] This can lead to emotional difficulties, since our daily behaviors are in conflict with the realities of our world and environmental degradations can affect us deeply and personally.

Called *cognitive dissonance*, this living with actions and/or beliefs that are in conflict can result in mild or acute depressive disorders. The American Psychiatric Association describes a version of the malady as having "...irrational beliefs and distorted attitudes toward the self, the environment, and the future...."[5] and cites A. T. Beck for more information[6].

The society around us is changing faster than many of us can manage. We are called upon to adopt more appropriate value systems faster than we can comfortably do. So we search for rationalizations to deny our need to change. Or we try not to admit that current societal beliefs, such as "maximize short-term gain", are destroying our futures.

Some have difficulty accepting that without major change, we are likely to destroy the very basis of our existence. So these people deny its truth. They prefer to believe, for instance, that technology will somehow advance to allow us to accommodate current and even future population levels. (Such an argument is not something easily proved or disproved. It appears to be a rationalization to prevent us from confronting fundamental changes in our beliefs about what it is to live, prosper, and be fulfilled.)

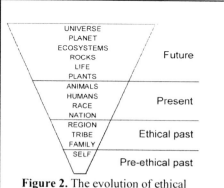

Figure 2. The evolution of ethical rights. (After Nash.)

We need a new system of values and beliefs to guide us. A new set of guiding principles, if generally accepted, could provide rules of behavior supporting our continued survival at an acceptable overall standard of living and with an acceptably high quality of life.

The Right to Rights

As we search for meaning and a viable new system of values, we confront important concepts of worth and rights. In his history of environmental ethics[7], Nash presents two diagrams (somewhat like the ones in Figures 2 and 3), showing his view of how the concept of rights have developed and are advancing. He argues that there has been and will continue to be an expansion of the

Nature	Endangered Species Act	1973
Blacks	Civil Rights Act	1957
Laborers	Fair Labor Standards	1938
Native Americans	Citizenship	1924
Women	Nineteenth Amendment	1920
Slaves	Emancipation Proclamation	1863
American Colonists	Declaration of Independence	1776
English Barons	Magna Carta	1215
Natural Rights		

Figure 3. The expanding concept of rights. (After Nash.)

human acceptance of the rights of others.

Nash sees a trend toward the idea that morality includes the relationship of humans to Nature. He identifies an historical expansion of concern, for the natural rights of a growing number of entities. This starts with limited groups of humans, to the rights of all humans, to those of parts of Nature and, finally, to all of Nature.

At the ultimate end of Nash's evolutionary sequence is a belief, supported by authors in a variety of disciplines that all manifestations of the natural universe derive from the same basic entity[8-16]. This brings us to the idea that all parts of this entity have inherent and equal rights, worthiness, and deserve moral consideration. Thus all aspects of the natural world deserve protection from abuse. It remains to be seen how much farther the human species will progress upward in the chart of Fig. 2.

According to Nash, "Of course, Nature does not demand rights, and some moral philosophers even question whether anything so general as the 'rights of Nature' can exist at all. But...others use the term confidently. At the same time they recognize that wolves and maples and mountains do not petition for their rights. Human beings are the moral agents who have the responsibility to articulate and defend the rights of the other occupants of the planet. Such a conception of rights means that humans have duties or obligations toward Nature. Environmental ethics involves people extending ethics to the environment by the exercise of self-restraint."

John Stuart Mill once claimed that "every great movement must experience three stages: ridicule, discussion, adoption."[17] According to Nash, "What happens in the process, Christopher Stone reminds us, is that the unthinkable becomes conventional — sometimes gradually and peacefully through legislative and legal processes, as Stone proposed, but often, as we know of the events in Fig.2, violently."[18]

Earth Values – Earth Rights

At a workshop on environmental ethics in 1988, Dr. Gary Varner identified four categories of Earth ethics. He felt individuals, business people, and environmentalists are using these to justify various actions by researchers and by governmental agencies dealing with environmental problems[19]. Using his words:

Anthropocentrism is the view that, when it comes to making decisions about the environment, only the interests of human beings matter. An anthropocentric defense of environmental preservation would appeal to or focus on the ways in which environmental preservation benefits human beings while environmental degradation harms humans. So if we argue that an endangered species ought to be preserved because people think it is beautiful, or because people are happy to know that it exists, or because it might someday be useful to people, we would be arguing anthropocentrically.

Sentientism [is the view that] all and only conscious creatures count. [Sentientists] argue that if all human beings have rights (including newborn infants and the severely retarded), then so too do some animals, since intellectual capacities of a normal mammal or bird appear to surpass those of [these humans]. To be sentient is to be conscious of pleasure and pain, [so these people claim] that all creatures who can feel pleasure and pain have interests to be considered. Animals with very rudimentary nervous systems — insects, for instance — may not be conscious at all, and therefore may not deserve moral consideration in this view.

Biocentric Individualism [includes] all living things, including the "lower" animals and all plants [in the group of organisms that] have interests and deserve moral consideration.

Holism [includes] the entire biotic community, taken as a whole system, [in what counts and should be protected]. The most famous example of holism is the "land ethic" espoused by Aldo Leopold in *A Sand County Almanac*[20]. When Leopold writes, "A thing is right when it tends to preserve the integrity, stability, and beauty of the biotic community," he is focusing on the welfare or interest of a system of living things, rather than on the welfare of the individuals who are members of that system. A view like this is called holism because the whole is being taken to be somehow greater than the sum of its parts.

Conflict exists among the proponents of the four different categories of Earth ethics, both within and outside of the environmental movement. Arguments over which of the above Earth ethics is the "correct" one have threatened to dilute and fractionate the reform movement's energy, reducing its effectiveness.

The biggest argument seems to be between the anthropocentrists and the holists. Obviously, if we take anthropocentrism to its logical conclusion, we must accept that humans are totally dependent upon the ecological viability of the entire biotic system and the physical resources upon which this system depends. Thus, the two groups should merge, with unified goals and methods.

Some say we have insufficient scientific evidence in detail to connect minute elements of the biotic community and the survival and quality of human life. To what extent, for example, does human survivability depend upon the survivability of the many species of insects living in Amazonia? Much has been written on this subject[21-23], and the conclusion is clear. Humans depend completely on Nature for survival. Thus, there should be no conflict between the above four points of view, at least as they relate to environmental protection.

Historically (in the West, at least), anthropocentrism has been the prime motivator for interest in humanity's future. The very title of this book is anthropocentric in its direction. The primary motivation for protecting the environment is a selfish one—we wish to save ourselves and that which we value. Now that we see the links between human survival and the survival of our life-support system, we realize that self-preservation must include an equal interest in the preservation of the biosphere.

However, a problem arises. In its purist form, or perhaps only historically, anthropocentrism sets aside the needs of the nonhuman and inherently denies the value of Nature's services. At least in any conflict between humans and the environment, the purely anthropocentric path favors the human against the environment.

This view was specifically espoused by the George W. Bush administration in 2001. The administration would not sacrifice the needs of the citizenry for energy in favor of greater environmental protection. In consequence, the President announced that the U.S. would not sign the Kyoto agreement on the reduction of global warming.

By modifying the definition of anthropocentrism to acknowledge the inextricable link between human welfare and environmental preservation, it will turn into holism. There seems no other choice for the survival of humanity but to embrace the holistic philosophy and strive to incorporate it in every step and in every decision.

A New Kind of Thinking

Albert Einstein once wrote that "...a new type of thinking is essential if mankind is to survive and move toward higher levels."[24] Einstein spoke of the threat of nuclear disaster, but his remarks apply equally well to the current threat of global environmental destruction. He began his statement with, "Our world faces a crisis as yet unperceived by those possessing power to make great decisions for good or evil. The unleashed power of the atom has changed everything save our modes of thinking, and we thus drift toward unparalleled catastrophe."

Let's translate Einstein's cry of alarm to our present situation. If we are to achieve permanent global behavior changes we must develop a new set of values, and a new type of thinking—one more appropriate for our current environmental situation.

We do not need to change all our values. We can retain a belief in the sanctity of human rights, as long as we recognize also the rights of all other living things. We can abhor murder, torture, disrespectfulness, deceit, and slovenliness. We can value love, caring, charity, and playfulness. We cannot, however, continue to see the environment as an "it", as an object to be used and abused without consequences.

We have little choice but to adopt a more respectful attitude toward Nature and incorporate this respect in our laws, customs, beliefs, and educational systems. Only then can we hope to sustain humanity as a viable species on Earth, this third planet from the Sun.

References

1. Robert Theobald. *The Rapids of Change: Social Entrepreneurship in Turbulent Times*. Knowledge Systems: Indianapolis, 1987.
2. G. Tyler Miller. *Environmental Science*. 2nd ed. Wadsworth Publishing: Belmont, CA, 1988. From *Environmental Science: An Introduction*, 2nd edition by Miller. © 1988. Reprinted with permission of Brooks/Cole, a division of Thomson Learning: www.thomsonrights.com. Fax 800 730-2215.
3. Thomas R. Malthus. *An Essay on the Principle of Population*. Prometheus Books: New York, 1999.
4. Joanna Macy and Molly Brown Young. *Coming Back to Life*. New Society: Gabriola Island, BC, Canada, 1998, 221 pp.
5. American Psychiatric Association, "Clinical Resources. Depression. V. Review and Synthesis of Available Evidence B. Acute Phase Psychosocial Interventions 2.a. Cognitive behavioral therapy," World Wide Web, Access date: 21 July 2001. http://www.psych.org/clin_res/Depression2e.book-12.cfm.
6. A.T. Beck, A.J. Rush, B.F. Shaw, and G. Emery. *Cognitive Therapy of Depression*. Guilford: New York, 1979.
7. Roderick Frazier Nash. *The Rights of Nature: A History of Environmental Ethics*. The University of Wisconsin Press: Madison, WI, 1989.
8. Teilhard de Chardin. *The Phenomenon of Man*. Harper: New York, 1959.
9. Thomas Berry. *The Dream of the Earth*. 1st ed. Sierra Club Books: San Francisco, 1988, 247 pp.
10. Thomas Berry. *The Great Work — Our Way Into the Future*. Bell Tower: New York, 1999, 241 pp.
11. Fritjof Capra. *The Tao of Physics*. Bantam, Rev. ed.: 1984.
12. Richard Erdoes and Alfonso Ortiz. *American Indian Myths and Legends*. Pantheon: New York, 1984.

13. David Suzuki. *The Sacred Balance — Rediscovering our Place in Nature.* Promethius Books: Amherst, NY, 1998, 259 pp.

14. Brian Swimme. *The Universe is a Green Dragon.* Bear & Co., Inc.: Santa Fe, NM, 1984, 173 pp.

15. Brian Swimme and Thomas Berry. *The Universe Story.* HarperSanFrancisco, div. of HarperCollins: San Francisco, 1992, 305 pp.

16. Gary Zukav. *The Dancing Wu Li Masters.* Bantam: 1980.

17. Tom Regan. *The Case for Animal Rights.* Berkeley, CA, 1983.

18. C. D. Stone. *Should Trees have Standing? - Toward Legal Rights for Natural Objects.* W. Kaufmann, 1974: Los Altos, CA, 1974. p. 6.

19. Gary Varner "North American Association for Environmental Education, Workshop on Environmental Ethics," 1988, 14-15 October 1988.

20. Aldo Leopold. *A Sand County Almanac.* Oxford University Press: New York, 1949.

21. Yvonne Baskin. *The Work of Nature.* Island Press: Washington, DC, 1997, 263 pp.

22. Gretchen C. Daily, ed. Nature's Services — *Societal Dependence on Natural Ecosystems.* Island Press: Washington, D.C., 1997, 392 pp.

23. Thomas Prugh. *Natural Capital and Human Economic Survival.* 2nd ed. Lewis Publishers: New York, Boca Raton, 1999, 180 pp. From Chapter 3: What Natural Capital is and Does.

24. Albert Einstein, "Telegram sent to several hundred prominent Americans on 24 May 1946," *New York Times*, 25 May 1946.

Part III

Saving Humanity

13
The Big Picture

Taking a longer view.
Avoiding narrow thinking.

S almon off the coast of California are showing signs of infertility. One of the most commercially viable open ocean seafood species is threatened with declining catches and possibly extinction. Scientists were puzzled, seafood lovers chagrined.

The problem was traced to birth control pills. "Birth control pills? Who is dosing the salmon with birth control pills?" The answer turned out to be the women of southern California. Here's the scoop.

Birth control pills are made of hormones. They are not very biodegradable. They are often prescribed in doses much greater than needed for good efficacy. (Doctors do not want to be sued for unwanted pregnancies.) Wastewater treatment plants in Orange County, California, do not adequately deal with these hormones arriving from the urine of California women. Fish living downstream have been tested to have unusually high levels of estrogen.

"These synthetic hormones released into Nature have been the cause of the demise of the salmon and many other species that are no longer fertile. Now Orange County wants to put the discharge into its drinking water!" wrote Monty Campbell in 1999[1]. So a generally good thing — reducing human pregnancies and thereby limiting population growth — results in a bad thing, loss of a valuable fish species.

Unintended Consequences

Problems such as this often result from failures to look at the big picture, to anticipate all the possible consequences of an action. This failure is so common, often humorous, that Representative Dick Armey (R-TX) was inspired to put a name on it. His "Law of Unintended Consequences" (LUC) can be stated as follows:

Large programs designed to accomplish social objectives often go wrong because of failures in conception, vision, or detail, producing unforeseen consequences which in some cases are worse than the problem addressed by the program in the first place.

Examples are easy to find. A topical search on the Internet yielded 4,400 hits; most provide examples of the law in full humor or tragedy. The law reminds us of Murphy's Law (Anything that can go wrong will) and Flanagan's Law (Murphy was an optimist). Creating "solutions" to "problems" that just produce more problems reminds us of Eric Severeid's Law (The chief cause of problems is solutions).

John Pfeiffer gave other examples in his 1977 book, *The Emergence of Society*.

Planners are continually launching grand projects without foreseeing the consequences. More than a decade ago, for example, the World Health Organization sprayed the thatched-roof huts of Borneo villages with DDT. It was part of a major drive to wipe out malaria and one result, the desired result, was the eradication of malaria-carrying mosquitoes and a sharp drop in the frequency and severity of the disease. Spraying also produced some unexpected and unwelcome results. Cockroaches in the huts ate DDT-containing foods and were in turn eaten by lizards. The lizards concentrated the powerful drug in their bodies to such a level that lizard-eating cats were poisoned and died off. In the absence of cats, rat populations soared and so did populations of lice, fleas, and other rat-infesting organisms, thus increasing the risks of such conditions as typhus and plague.

Health authorities moved to combat the new threat. Planes of Britain's Royal Air Force parachuted fresh supplies of cats into isolated villages, and doctors prepared for possible epidemics by stockpiling quantities of antibiotics and vaccines. There were other effects, such as increased numbers of caterpillars that destroyed thatched roofs. Strategies for avoiding similar complications in the future have yet to be devised.

In Egypt, a host of troubles has followed completion of the billion-dollar Aswan Dam, one of the greatest construction feats of the twentieth century — and one of the saddest examples of ecological mismanagement. The dam is doing many of the things it was built to do: it is generating electricity, preventing severe floods along the Nile, and providing irrigation waters for about a million acres of land that once was desert and now yields up to three crop harvests per year.

But it has created new problems, among them a serious health emergency. In pre-dam days irrigation canals had contained snails carrying bilharzia, a lingering and weakening parasitic disease, but the canals dried up periodically and the snails died. Now that the canals are full all the time, snails are flourishing, and the disease has increased tenfold. Meanwhile crop yields have been declining in certain areas. Salts which reduce soil fertility are accumulating, and the only countermeasure is to build a network of special canals to drain irrigated lands. More than a hundred scientists are engaged in an effort to deal with these and other difficulties.[2]

In 2001 Seth Dunn offered another example. "Scientists from France and Italy have found remote regions of Greenland to be contaminated by heavy metals, many of which are likely to have originated from automobile catalytic converters. The finding, published in the March 1 issue of the journal *Environmental Science and Technology*, suggests that efforts to reduce automobile emissions are having unintended global consequences, with potential human health implications."

When the catalytic converters were first installed, some scientists raised concerns that the metals on which the converter technology is based — platinum, palladium, and rhodium — could become widely dispersed in the environment. In writing their journal articles, the authors obtained data from several sources. The finding was that the "levels of these metals in snow from the mid-1990s were between 40 and 120 times higher than their levels in ice 7,000 years ago."[3]

Many people take the threat of unforeseen consequences seriously and then say it is something we just have to accept, cannot avoid, and must not fear, for this would stifle innovation and experimentation. Of course, a degree of reasonableness is required. We can't just stop trying all new things for fear of bad outcomes. But we can be more careful when launching new projects or programs.

Big Picture Thinking

To reduce the likelihood of falling into the LUC trap, we must see the big picture, look more encompassingly at important issues, and avoid narrow, tunnel-vision thinking. The U. S. government requires environmental impact statements (EISs) for many proposed new programs, based on the hope of avoiding unintended consequences that are environmentally damaging. The idea is that if a company or governmental body wishes to pursue a major new project, time and effort should be set aside for a relaxed and thorough study of all the consequences of the proposal — or at least of the environmental ones. This is an excellent policy, but it is often subverted by inadequate preparation and limited public scrutiny.

Perhaps we can avoid projects with unacceptable environmental consequences or restructure them to reduce the damage. In spite of the strict rules governing the preparation of EISs, the proponents of a new development are often those who prepare the

> In 1922, in his book *Public Opinion*, Walter Lippman suggested that 'the primary defect of popular government' is the inability of individuals to garner a reasonably precise picture of the world in which they live. —Richard E. Sclove [4]

environmental impact statement. This encourages bending the truth or interpreting uncertain scientific results selfishly. Just because an environmental impact statement has been written does not mean its recommendations have to be followed in every detail. Though the information is obtained and published, this is insufficient. Government agencies charged with enforcement, starved of funds and staff, are often unable and/or unwilling to enforce pollution laws or even require impact statements.

Background Knowledge

From the environmental perspective, whole systems thinking requires knowledge of natural systems — an environmental literacy. In his book on the subject, David Orr encourages ecological big-picture thinking. He explains the problem:

> There are, I think, several reasons why ecological literacy has been so difficult for Western culture. First, it implies the ability to think broadly, to know something of what is hitched to what. This ability is being lost in an age of specialization. Scientists of the quality of Rachel Carson or Aldo Leopold are rarities who must buck the pressures toward narrowness and also endure a great deal of professional rejection and hostility. By inquiring into the relationship between chlorinated hydrocarbon pesticides and bird populations, Rachel Carson was asking an [encompassing] question. Many others failed to ask, not because they did not like birds, but because they had not, for whatever reasons, thought beyond the conventional categories. To do so would have required that they relate their food system to the decline in the number of birds in their neighborhood. This means that they would have had some direct knowledge of farms and farming practices, as well as a comprehension of ornithology.[5, p.87]

Thinking more comprehensively means not only seeing the forest and the trees, but also seeing *above* the trees. Michio Kaku's interesting little book *Beyond Einstein*[6] explains the process well.

A Law of Everything

Kaku's approach shows that this kind of insightful thinking by very bright physicists was used for major breakthroughs in his field, the development of what is called a unified field theory. One hope for such a theory is that it would tie together so many parts of physics that it would become, in essence, a "Law of Everything." Page after page in Kaku's book shows the benefits and fruits of "thinking outside of the envelope" or "getting out of the box."

Paul MacCready, winner of awards for human-powered aircraft and the creator of a radio-controlled, flying pterodactyl, has made a small study of creativity and seeing encompassingly. In many examples in physics and technology, this kind of thinking has yielded major breakthroughs. (Such examples abound in literature, art, and music. Bill Moyers did a TV series on the subject from 1982 to 1991[7].)

Consider the process of seeing more encompassingly. First you gather as many facts as you can about the area of interest ... and everything else that might be the slightest bit relevant. Then you think about it, sleep on it, and think about it some more, taking notes along the way. You work to see the big picture — the larger issues surrounding your topic. Then you go off and have some fun and try *not* to think about it, allowing subconscious processing of what you have learned. Insight and discovery often follow. Sometimes a team working together this way has valuable insights and breakthroughs in thinking.

The process can work wonders helping achieve new understandings which were not at first evident from the facts alone. This is much like Sherlock Holmes's amazing ability to piece together small bits of forensic evidence, missed by others, into a larger theory of what happened, finding— in most cases — the theory to be correct. The process is continued until insight and clarity is achieved. Then diligent work to predict the unintended consequences must follow. Only when an exhaustive search has been completed can we develop confidence in a proposed new strategy or idea.

We need more whole systems thinking, if we are to understand our place on Earth, what we are doing to it, how this happens, what current trends are, and what might be done to protect our future as a species.

To paraphrase Kaku: Since the 1930s environmental thinkers have been consumed with the frustrating task of solving the environmental crisis. They have searched for meaning in the chaos of environmental destruction, seeking the key to its genesis and how we might avoid the worst consequences. Only in the past thirty years or so, however, have these thinkers realized that the tantalizing clues found in scientific reports, newspaper accounts, and personal experiences form a systematic pattern and stem from some remarkable events in human history. They have discovered the new truths, the realities of our seeming path toward self-annihilation, by looking at the problem differently, by thinking outside the envelope, and by avoiding traps of old thinking.

For mankind to develop the "new manner of thinking" recommended by Albert Einstein, we need our best and brightest to think at even higher levels. They must look at the bigger picture, putting the puzzle together better than in the past. They must also moderate the process with heavy doses of wisdom and humanity.

Of course, this will not be enough. Having a modest small fraction of our population with important insights and understandings about future directions does not mean the whole of humanity can make much progress. The insights and understandings must expand throughout society, over the world, and most especially to those leaders in government and industry who, to a great extent, are calling the shots on a global basis.

We must see the really big picture and properly assess the possible future options with some degree of scientific validity — rather than appeals to an "X-Files" mentality of fantasy and unrealistic optimism. Otherwise, we cannot hope to find a viable path to real sustainability.

Some tell us that the problem really is quite simple. Special insights and understanding are unnecessary. It's simply a matter of overpopulation. Stop population growth, reduce it for a while, and the problems we see will be less pronounced, less severe. Then we will have more time to find solutions. Unfortunately, the huge public reluctance to follow this path, coupled with its diversion to other issues, leads to a need for new ideas for dealing with the problem.

We must find a way to convince people of the severity of overpopulation, get their support for population reduction programs, and inform them better about the population drivers underlying nearly every environmental problem.

Is there hope for this strategy? That is difficult to say. Many current trends lead us to be pessimistic. In much of the world the mind-numbing advertising culture is taking over; our schools are increasingly less capable of teaching kids to think and reason and do for themselves.

Children often come to school without the parenting support, adequate food, and basic skills and knowledge to benefit fully from the educational experience. Thus the fraction of humanity able to think and reason generally and abstractly (and to act on the conclusions thereby derived) is declining as world population increases. The fraction of total global population looking at the big picture, seeing the connections, and able to do something about it, is minuscule.

Encompassing Thinking

Kaku's Vision — thinking outside of the box. Reading through *Beyond Einstein,* we one discovers the emergence of theory after theory. Some are knocked down, others remain valid, and still others are modified and brought into the larger theory, creating a mesh of understanding. Searching for a "law of everything" has a way of forcing the mind to look at more options, examine more connections, and ultimately find meaning in the jumble of facts and figures discovered. The process offers useful application in dealing with the many threats to humanity.

Lapham's Vision—The Donor Party. Working behind the scenes to influence public policy, a group of elite movers and shakers assesses trends and movements. Author and longtime editor of *Harper's,* Lewis Lapham calls these people the "Donor Party" for their proclivity and ability to purchase politicians by massive donations to parties and individual campaigns.

Following Michael Lind's lead[8], Lapham claims the Donor Party consists of those wealthy individuals who contribute large sums to all candidates. Then after the election, no matter who wins, they'll be able to exert strong control over the actions of the winner.[9] In his 1993 book *The Wish for Kings*[10], Lapham touches on this theme when he refers to "the American ruling and possessing classes (i.e. the people who pay for the hiring of presidents)."

Lapham described the Donor Party at greater length in a 1996 speech at the Overseas Press Club in New York:

> No country can exist without a ruling class. That was true in Rome in the first century and that was true in the United States in 1787, and that was true in Britain at the zenith of its empire, and it is true now. So the only question in my mind is what *kind* of a ruling class, what's the nature of it, what's the character of it, what's its worth, made to what specifications and with what passions and objectives in mind.... My favorite term for it is 'equestrian class' because that is an old Roman term. The rank was for sale for 400,000 sesturcies in Rome in the first century AD and the governing class in the U.S. is a rank that is for sale. That's also always been true in the United States but something has happened to that class over the last fifty

years, I think. I think it is no longer a specifically American class. I think it's lost its interest in politics and I don't think it has much use for an intelligent press.

You will now ask me who are we talking about. The figures vary. Numbers of other writers have written on this subject. Bill Greider has written about it, [as have] Kevin Phillips, Christopher Lash, [and] Michael Lind. Essentially we are talking about the one or two percent of the American population that owns ninety percent of the nation's wealth and seventy five percent of its capital assets. It's an oligarchy. It's not a large percentage but it's a fairly large absolute number. Maybe we're talking about two million people, perhaps. Essentially [the equestrian class is] the people who write the laws, who write the news, who run the schools, direct the corporations, own the media, and own the banks. They are the rich and the servants of the rich.

Michael Lind, in a book published last summer, called *The American Nation*, refers to what he calls the *donor party*[8]. The donor party is the group of no more than 200,000 people in the United States that give political campaign gifts in excess of $5,000. To become a candidate you must be first elected by the donor party. That is the beginning and end of the American democracy. If you don't have money — if you're not Steve Forbes or Ross Perot — you don't even appear on television.

Another way of describing the oligarchy or the equestrian class would be to just think of the shoppers on Madison Ave., or Rodeo Drive, or the residents of the zip code section of New York, 10021, that is this narrow golden rectangle in the city of Manhattan, where the annual income is something like two billion dollars a year, income within that one zip code section.[9]

According to Lapham, the change in the elite class in the last fifty years is its sense of responsibility. Fifty years ago this class felt some degree of responsibility for the "lower orders."

The people in the fifties identified themselves with an American commonwealth. There was an American ideal. There was an American idea. There was a sense of obligation. I don't think that the current kids, the ones that I know at [Yale University in] New Haven, or our current oligarchy have the same feeling at all. I think that the members of the American equestrian class today are inclined to think of themselves as aligning themselves with international economic order rather than the American commonwealth. There is very little patriotism among the people I'm talking about. They have more in common with their economic peers in England, Japan, or Germany than they do with the run-of-the-mill Americans in Omaha or Sioux City....

I don't think this is a matter of opinion, it's a matter of sheer statistics.

You can see it in NAFTA... I saw it most clearly the year that the Challenger exploded. Six months after the explosion, AT&T and GE were called to testify before the Senate Foreign Relations Committee, because the cold war was still going on and AT&T and GE had decided to send up their newest satellite on a Soviet rocket. It was the only rocket going and the Foreign Relations Committee took this very seriously and said "You can't do this. This is trading with the enemy. This is our most sophisticated technology," and so forth and so on and the two corporations said we really don't care what you think, Senator, it's not important, because this is about money. If we don't send it up on the Russian rocket, we'll lose to the French. We can't afford to lose to the French and you could make the speech to your friends at the Council on Foreign Relations, but... No and Goodbye.

Of the changed role, Lapham told the media, "To go back to the Roman example, at the zenith of Rome's military power, the returning general would have a tramp through the streets of Rome, standing in the chariot, and behind him would come the train of captured slaves, elephants, trophies, and so forth, but there would stand behind his shoulder in the chariot a man who would whisper in his ear. The man would say, 'Remember, you are mortal.'

"Today, we are at the zenith of our economic power, the wonder of an admiring world in many different ways, and we ride in triumph through the streets of New York or Washington or London and our media stands behinds us in the chariot and says, 'Know that you are a God.'"

This media power is failing its responsibility. It is not seeing more encompassingly... or at least it is not telling us about it. A consequence of this media failure and of the changed ethics and beliefs of the new American ruling class is that populaces around the globe are increasingly losing their freedoms and democracies in subtle ways. The people can vote, but their candidates are limited to whom the Donor Party puts up for consideration. This makes it difficult for the "grassroots" to have the voice it once had in open democracies. This also places a still higher burden on our leaders, both in and outside of the ruling class.

Ferreting out the concept of the Donor Party was an exercise in "big picture thinking."

Pfeiffer's Vision—The Elite. In the introduction on "The Uses of Society" to *The Emergence of Society*,[2] John Pfeiffer acknowledges the power of the elite. First he mentions our rapidly changing society, and its threats to future human survival. Then he asserts the necessity of achieving zero population growth, writing, "the greatest problems remain to be solved. Man, the postponer supreme, has delayed the task of limiting his numbers...for the better part of ten thousand years, primarily from a succession of agricultural advances. He is now realizing that this delaying action must come to an end. Taking the pressure off, achieving zero population growth, will demand changes at the top of the social pyramid.

"The function, the existence, of elites hangs in the balance. They probably ceased serving evolutionary purposes a millennium or two ago. People who have not been admitted into elites have greater expectations than ever. Leisure, prestige, and authority will have to be shared more widely, and that calls for new kinds of hierarchy, *or perhaps for something better than hierarchies*. We have so far managed to muddle through despite the corruption of power and scorn for commoners, strangers, and other excluded majorities so deep that they are treated as inferior species. The question is whether such abuses can be eliminated without eliminating centralized control itself, whether the disease can be cured without killing the patient. Control, however efficient, is never enough for survival." [Emphasis added.]

Quinn's Vision—Eliminate Hierarchies. In *Beyond Civilization*, Daniel Quinn suggests that hierarchies be eliminated completely. "Wherever civilization emerges, tribalism withers and is replaced by hierarchalism. Hierarchalism works very well for the rulers but much less well for the ruled, who make up the mass of society. For this reason the few at the top like it very well and the masses at the bottom like it very much less well."[11, p. 82]

Quinn begins *Beyond Civilization* with a fable, a version of the Donor Party story:

> Once upon a time life evolved on a certain planet, bringing forth many different social organizations—packs, flocks, troops, herds, and so on. One species whose members were unusually intelligent developed a unique social organization called a tribe. Tribalism worked well for them for millions of years, but there came a time when they decided to experiment with a new social organization (called civilization) that was hierarchical rather than tribal. Before long, those at the top of the hierarchy were living in great luxury, enjoying perfect leisure and having the best of everything. A larger class of people below them lived very well and had nothing to complain about. But the masses living at the bottom of the hierarchy didn't like it at all. They worked and lived like pack animals, struggling just to stay alive.
>
> "This isn't working," the masses said. "The tribal way was better. We

should return to that way." But the ruler of the hierarchy told them, "We've put that primitive life behind us forever. We can't go back to it."

"If we can't go back," the masses said, "then let's go forward—on to something different."

"That can't be done," the ruler said, "because nothing different is possible. Nothing can be *beyond civilization*. Civilization is a final, unsurpassable invention."

Quinn's process of seeing through the fog of the "ambient culture" of our civilization[12] is another powerful example of encompassing thinking.

What is the Answer?

Part of my original motivation for studying environmental values has been a desire to find a fundamental new principle. I seek something to form the backbone of a new global consensus — not only on the depth of our difficulties but also on the best strategies for avoiding them. It would be something that could suddenly clarify our environmental dilemma, giving the crisis meaning in a larger context and showing directions toward a viable future. It would be a new "Environmental Law of Everything."

Upon occasion I've found masterful written works which closely approach this new principle or vision. One was *The Dream of the Earth* by Thomas Berry[13] (and the follow-on books *The Universe Story*[14] and *The Great Work*[15]). Another was the amazing novel *Ishmael* by Daniel Quinn[12] (and his follow-on books *My Ishmael, Providence*, and *Beyond Civilization*). Still another was Paul Hawken's *The Ecology of Commerce*[16].

Of course, overpopulation is a significant underlying force, and we could explain nearly all our environmental problems through understanding the nature and consequences of exponential growth. This is why so much space was devoted to the subject in Chapter 5. With remarkable insight, Albert Bartlett (quoted extensively in that chapter) has written and lectured widely on this subject[17-19]. We really could solve many global problems with just a program to reduce global population levels over a period of years.

The major breakthroughs in understanding, described by these and other authors, are very much like the physicists' search for understanding of Nature and quest for unifying theories. None of these environmental writings has yet yielded an all-encompassing theory that can work in all cases, in all cultures. They each address only a portion of the problem, and each addresses the problem in different ways. Their one common thread is success at following Einstein's suggestion: thinking at higher levels of understanding. Clearly, the major works of these new environmental masters are important stepping stones toward achieving a better understanding of the human place on Earth. Several of them are profiled in Chapter 18.

Probably not one hidden truth explains everything. Short of this, I believe the goal should be to provide access to tools for discussing, thinking about, and understanding the problems facing us. Then people can work to actively improve behaviors whatever these turn out to be. We *can* hope for a breakthrough in understanding, in seeing where we are and how we got here, and some of the things we should consider doing to change our patterns of behavior. I suspect it is more a matter of access to tools and strategies than to providing immutable answers to how we solve our earthly problems. I believe that a global discussion about the humanity's future must begin very soon.

Quinn points out that "Mother Culture says it's possible to have *certain* knowledge about things like atoms and space travel and genes, but there's no such thing as certain knowledge about how people should live. It's just not available, and that's why we don't have it."

> Considering the fact that this is by far the most important problem mankind has to solve — has ever had to solve — you'd think there would be a whole branch of science devoted to it. Instead, we find that not a single one of you has ever wondered whether any such knowledge is out there to be obtained.

Such larger issues must be discussed in the mainstream media — on radio, television, newspapers, and magazines. And they must be discussed in political counsels at high levels in the United Nations and other venues. Very serious topics must be addressed and considered if we are to structure a viable future for all of mankind, and for all other creatures with which we share this place. We need a global discourse on the subject. Important works of fact and fiction, such as those mentioned previously, should be held up for public scrutiny, debated and discussed in large-scale forums. Hopefully enlightened public, private, individual, and corporate policy and new behavior will result.

References

1. Monty A. Campbell. "Lawyers and Water." *Photonics Spectra*. (1999): December, 1999.
2. John E. Pfeiffer. *The Emergence of Society—A prehistory of the Establishment.* McGraw-Hill: New York, 1977, 512 pp.
3. Seth Dunn. "Heavy Metals From Cars Reach Greenland." *World Watch* Vol. 14, no. 3 (2001): May/June 2001, 11.
4. Richard Sclove. *Democracy and Technology*. Guilford Press: New York, 1995, 338 pp.
5. David W. Orr. "Ecological Literacy." In *Ecological Literacy: Education and the Transition to a Postmodern World*, edited by David. W. Orr. Sate University of New York Press: Albany, NY, 1992, 210 pp.
6. Michio Kaku and Jennifer Thompson. *Beyond Einstein—The Cosmic Quest for the Theory of the Universe*. Anchor Books, Doubleday: New York, 1995, 1987.
7. Bill Moyers, "Creativity with Bill Moyers," Producer: Corporation for Entertainment and Learning, New York, 1982-1991.
8. Michael Lind. *The Next American Nation: The New Nationalism and the Fourth American Revolution*. Reprint ed. Free Press: New York, 1996, 436 pp.
9. Lewis H. Lapham, "New American Ruling Class," C-SPAN cable network: New York, 1/26/96, Video tape of the event, also broadcast on C-SPAN, Speech to the Overseas Press Club in New York City, 1/26/96, recorded by C-SPAN. Performers: Lewis Lapham www.c-span.org. Transcribed by W. Ross McCluney.
10. Lewis H. Lapham. *The Wish for Kings—Democracy at Bay*. Grove Press: New York, 1993.
11. Daniel Quinn. *Beyond Civilization—Humanity's Next Great Adventure*. Harmony Books: New York, 1999.
12. Daniel Quinn. *Ishmael*. 1st ed. Bantam/Turner: New York, 1992.
13. Thomas Berry. *The Dream of the Earth*. 1st ed. Sierra Club Books: San Francisco, 1988, 247 pp.
14. Brian Swimme and Thomas Berry. *The Universe Story*. HarperSanFrancisco, div. of HarperCollins: San Francisco, 1992, 305 pp.
15. Thomas Berry. *The Great Work—Our Way Into the Future*. Bell Tower: New York, 1999, 241 pp.
16. Paul Hawken. *The Ecology of Commerce—A Declaration of Sustainability*. HarperBusiness, div. HarperCollins: New York, 1993, 250 pp.
17. Albert A. Bartlett. "Reflections on Sustainability, Population Growth, And the Environment - Revisited." *Renewable Resources Journal*, Natural Resources Foundation, 5430 Grosvenor Lane, Bethesda, MD, 20814 Vol. 15, no. 4 (1998): Winter 1997 - 98, 6-23. Note: Also published in Focus, Vol. 9, No. 1, 1999, Pgs. 49 - 68. Carrying Capacity Network, 2000 P Street, NW, Washington D.C. 20036-5915.

18. Albert A. Bartlett. "The Massive Movement to Marginalize the Modern Malthusian Message." *The Social Contract*, 316.5 East Mitchell St., Petoskey, MI, 49770 Vol. 8, no. 3 (1998): Spring 1998, 239-251. soccon@freeway.net

19. A. A. Bartlett. "Forgotten Fundamentals of the Energy Crisis." Am. J. Phys. Vol. 46, no. 9 (1978): November, 876-888. Note: *Jour. Geol. Ed.*, Vol. 28, 1980, pp. 4-35, Proceedings, Nat. Regulatory Conf. on Renewable Energy, Savannah, GA 3-6 Oct. 1993, NARUC, Room 1102, ICC Bldg., Washington, DC 20044. A later version of his writing on this subject "Reflections on Sustainability, Population Growth, and the Environment - Revisited" *Population & Environment*, Vol. 16, No. 1, September 1994, pp. 5-35. Revised version: *Renewable Resources Journal*, Vol. 15, No. 4, Winter 1997-98, Pgs. 6-23, Renewable Natural Resources Foundation, 5430 Grosvenor Lane, Bethesda, MD, 20814. Also in *Focus*, Vol. 9, No. 1, 1999, Pgs. 49 - 68, Carrying Capacity Network, 2000 P Street, NW, Washington D.C. 20036-5915.

14
Visions of Ecotopia
Sustainable futures envisioned.

Why should we have to go back living like cave men? I don't want to live in a tribe in the jungle. Why should I have to? I like the way I'm living; why should I change?

These are common questions following claims that humanity must find new ways to live to keep from destroying itself. All are valid. Not only do we *not* have to "go backwards" and live in less desirable ways, but we simply cannot do so...at least not all of us. Our population has far outgrown the capacity of the land to allow all humans to live the way of either ancient hunter-gatherers or current industrial societies. We need to see the new ways of living as improvements in our lifestyles while greatly reducing our impacts on the environment. Slowing and then stopping population growth is an essential starting point.

Little choice may exist besides living in high population density communities, surrounded by more open space, wilderness, and agricultural lands. Whether these involve high rises or low rises or no rises, concentrated, technologically intensive living tends to separate us from the environmental consequences of our lifestyles. Possibly, small populations can (and probably will) try clinging to the old Earth-depleting way as society changes. They will increasingly be marginalized and outnumbered.

People on the lower rungs of the economic ladder in both industrialized and less-developed countries generally look forward to improving their situations. Those in depressing misery and poverty in the third world do, too. All are highly motivated to change. The model that most desire, however, is often the defective one we affluent societies already are living.

A different model is needed. But what should it be? How should it look? Will it be like one somebody is already living somewhere or a totally new one?

As we search for viable alternative lifestyles, the first challenge is to find a *variety* of environmentally appropriate ways to think, live, breathe, and obtain sustenance. The second is to make them desirable, compelling us to switch to the best of them. Once a significant fraction of our populace makes the change, others will easily follow. But without viable, working models of alternate ways of living, few people will be motivated to try something different.

The first few experiments are critical, however flawed they may be. Without them, we may have to wait until Mother Nature provides powerful negative incentives for change, as she already is doing in some starving and disease-ridden parts of the world.

Sustainable Visions

Daniel Quinn amplifies this need for a vision — not just stopping things, but having a vision of something positive to pursue: "...people need more than to be scolded, more than to be made to feel stupid and guilty. They need more than a vision of doom. They need a vision of the world and of themselves that inspires them. Stopping pollution is not inspiring. Sorting your trash is not inspiring. Cutting down on fluorocarbons is not inspiring. But this . . . thinking of ourselves in a new way, thinking of the world in a new way. . . ." This can be inspiring.[1]

Sustainable visions — the development of living models that can be continued indefinitely into the foreseeable future — are what we seek. With most current industrial-oriented thinking on this subject, the approach toward sustainability is crippled by efforts to embed it in a decidedly unsustainable economic system. Thus new patterns of thinking, seeing more encompassingly, and thinking outside of the box, are important. We need our sustainable visions to be desirable, attractive, and a clear improvement over what we have now. Otherwise, who would want to make the change?

If we can find such a new lifestyle — one we can see ourselves following, and which we know will be better for us and our families — then we will be *compelled* to move to it.

Many people have thought about, written and lectured on this topic, and some are even attempting to live the new visions. These efforts are few and suffer from unavoidable connections with the larger dysfunctional economic system. Thus they can only be considered experiments. This is not to denigrate them. We need much experimentation if we are to find a spectrum of alternative ways of living, each appropriate for its geographic region and ethnic and social group.

Need for Experimentation

Pfeiffer amplifies the need for experimentation and broadens it. He points to the value of "useless" activities:

> doing silly things and things not so silly as long as they have never been
> done before — walking tightropes between skyscrapers, trying to do
> backward double somersaults on skis, training fourteen hours per day to
> break Olympic records, flying to the moon, searching for subatomic
> particles, theorizing about the origins of life and the universe (and the
> origins of society), wrapping buildings and mountains in cellophane, avant-
> garde movements in all the arts.
>
> Play, exploration, and daredeviltry are preparations for evolution yet
> to come. The spirit of experiment and challenge contributes to the creation
> of an enormous repertoire of possibilities, possible inventions and actions
> and concepts, possible worlds. Only a tiny fraction of all man's adventures
> will ever pay off, but there is no way of telling beforehand which fraction.
> Sooner or later we will face emergencies many times more critical and
> complex than those we face now. If we survive them, as we probably will,
> it will be because our ability to control and organize is stimulated by the
> innovations of those who cannot help driving themselves to the limit and
> beyond.[2, p. 25.]

Paul MacCready, leader of the group that won the Kremer Prize for human
powered aircraft, explained the need for creative thinking toward sustainable
visions.

> Working in relatively unexplored areas stimulates innovation, and the
> results broaden perspectives of everyone who learns about them. When
> the developments involve "doing more with less", and emphasize the
> interface between Nature and technology, one even finds oneself
> developing insights about the serious issues of civilization's possible
> global survival.[3]

Coherent Visions

What are the effective new visions of the better way of life we seek? What
will they look like? Will they really compel us to adopt them? An excellent
example comes to us in the novel by Ernest Callenbach, *Ecotopia*: The first
journalist allowed into the relatively new country of that name enters from
the United States. He follows Ecotopia's secession on environmental, social,
and economic grounds twenty years earlier. This account of the withdrawal
of two and a half states from the U.S. is a remarkable example of Quinn's
suggestion that those motivated for change simply walk away from the
currently failing hierarchical society.

The reader follows the journalist's private notes and his official dispatches
back to the U.S. of what it is like to live in Ecotopia (formerly the states of
Washington, Oregon, and Northern California). By the end of the novel,
sensitive, receptive readers often want to live there and are disappointed to
accept that it is only a story, not yet a real place.

Here are excerpts from the journalist's filings back to the States.[4]

ECOTOPIA: CHALLENGE OR ILLUSION?

San Francisco, June 19. Where is Ecotopia going in the future? After more
than six weeks intensive study of the country, I find it still hazardous to
guess. There is no doubt, I have been forced to conclude, that the risky
social experiments undertaken here have worked on a biological level.
Ecotopian air and water are everywhere crystal clear. The land is well cared
for and productive. Food is plentiful, wholesome, and recognizable. All
life systems are operating on a stable-state basis, and can go on doing so
indefinitely. The health and general well being of the people are undeniable.
While the extreme decentralization and emotional openness of the society
seem alien to an American at first, they too have much to be said in their
favor. In these respects, I believe, Ecotopia offers us a difficult challenge,
and we have far to go to even approach their achievements.

On the other hand, these benefits have been bought at a heavy cost.
Not only is the Ecotopian industrial capacity and standard of consumption
markedly below ours, to a degree that would never be tolerated by
Americans generally, but also the Ecotopian political system rests on
assumptions that I can only conclude are dangerous in the extreme. In my
earlier columns I described the city-states that have already, in effect,
themselves seceded within Ecotopia. There is talk currently of formalizing
the Spanish-speaking and Japanese communities of San Francisco — the
latter, of course, an economically sinister development because of the
threat of Japanese capital taking over. Jewish, American Indian, and other
minorities all contain militants who desire a greater autonomy for their
peoples.

It is, admittedly, difficult for an American to criticize such trends when
our own society, after the failure of the integrationist campaign of the
sixties, has grown ever more segregated—though somewhat less unequal.
However, it is still the American ideal that all men and women should
obtain equal protection from the law and have equal status as citizens of
one great and powerful nation. The Ecotopian principle of secession denies
this hope and this faith. While seemingly idealistic, it is in fact profoundly
pessimistic. And the consequences seem clear. The way propounded by
Ecotopian ideologues leads away from the former greatness of America,
unified in spirit "from sea to shining sea," toward a balkanized continent
— a welter of small, second-class nations, each with its own petty cultural

differentiations. Instead of continuing the long march toward one world of peace and freedom, to which America has dedicated itself on the battlefields of Korea, Vietnam, and Brazil (not to mention our own Civil War), the Ecotopians propose only separatism, quietism, a reversion toward the two-bit principalities of medieval Europe, or perhaps even the tribalism of the jungle.

Under Ecotopian ideas, the era of the great nation-states, with their promise of one ultimate world-state, would fade away. Despite our achievements of a worldwide communications network and jet travel, mankind would fly apart into small, culturally homogenous groupings. In the words of Yeats (an early 20th-century poet from Ireland— a very small and secessionist country) "The center cannot hold.".…

WORK AND PLAY AMONG THE ECOTOPIANS

Gilroy Hot Springs, June 22. The more I have discovered about Ecotopian work habits, the more amazed I am that their system functions at all. It is not only that they have adopted a 20-hour week; you can't even tell when an Ecotopian is working, and when he is at leisure. During an important discussion in a government office, suddenly everybody will decide to go to the sauna bath. It is true they have worked out informal arrangements whereby, as their phrase has it, they "cover" for each other — somebody stays behind to answer phones and handle visitors. And it is also true that even in the sauna our discussion continued, on a more personal level, which turned out to be quite delightful. But Ecotopian society offers so many opportunities for pleasures and distractions that it is hard to see how people maintain even their present levels of efficiency.

Things happen in their factories, warehouses, and stores that would be quite incredible to our managers and supervisors. I have seen a whole section close down without notice; somebody will bring out beer or marijuana, and a party will ensue, right there amid the crates and machines. Workers in Ecotopian enterprises do not have a normal worker's attitude at all. Perhaps because of their part ownership of them, they seem to regard the plants as home, or at least as their own terrain. They must be intolerable to supervise: the slightest change in work plans is the occasion for a group discussion in which the supervisors (who are elected and thus in a weak position anyway) are given a good deal of sarcastic questioning, and in which their original plans are seldom accepted without change. The supervisors try to take this with good grace, of course, even claiming that the workers often come up with better ideas than they do; and they believe that Ecotopian output per person hour is remarkably high…

Ecotopians are adept at turning practically any situation toward pleasure, amusement, and often intimacy. At first I was surprised by the ease with which they strike up very personal conversations with casual strangers. I have now gotten used to this, indeed I usually enjoy it, especially where the lovely Ecotopian women are concerned. But I am still disconcerted when, after speaking with someone on the street in a loose and utterly unpressured way for perhaps ten minutes, he mentions that he is working and trots off. The distinction between work and non-work seems to be eroding away in Ecotopia, along with our whole concept of jobs as something separate from "real life." Ecotopians, incredibly enough, *enjoy* their work.

Unemployment does not seem to worry Ecotopians in the slightest. There were many unemployed just before Independence, but the switch to a 20-hour week almost doubled the number of jobs — although some were eliminated because of ecological shutdowns and simplifications, and of course the average real income of most families dropped somewhat. Apparently in the transition period when an entirely new concept of living standards was evolving, the country's money policy had to be managed with great flexibility to balance sudden inflationary or deflationary tendencies. But the result now seems to be that, while enterprises are not seriously short of member-workers, there is also no significant number of people involuntarily unemployed. In any case, because of the minimal-guaranteed income system and the core stores, individuals do not consider periods of unemployment disasters or threats; they are usually put to use, and sometimes deliberately extended, for some kind of creative, educational or recreational purposes. Thus in Ecotopia friends who are unemployed (usually through the collapse of their previous enterprise) often band together and undertake studies that lead them into another enterprise of their own.

If it is sometimes hard to tell whether Ecotopians are working or playing, they are surprisingly generous with their time. I was told, for instance, that many workers in factories put in extra hours to fix machines that have broken down. They evidently regard the 20-hour week quota as applying to productive time only, and take the repair of machinery almost as a sideline responsibility. Or perhaps it is just that they enjoy tinkering: despite the de-emphasis of goods in Ecotopia, people seem to love fixing things. If a bicycle loses a chain or has a flat tire, its rider is soon surrounded by five people volunteering to help fix it...

Seeing the Sustainable Society

Milbrath addresses the need for positive visions, such as this, in his comprehensive, more scholarly, book, *Envisioning a Sustainable Society*[5]. Part I begins with an extensive discourse on the nature and importance of values and beliefs and the critical role of social learning.

In Part II he elaborates on the importance of positive alternative visions.

He emphasizes the new ways of functioning, which the various components society need: making work fulfilling, enjoying life without material indulgence, the role of science and technology, and the critical role of governance. He proposes a learning governance structure and, more specifically, the institutionalization of a new "Council for Long-Range Societal Guidance."

Part III describes scenarios for transitioning from the current industrialized society to a sustainable one.

In an earlier section, Milbrath writes of two different approaches to the organization of society. The competitive order (Society A) is the model that the industrialized nations seem to follow at present. The compassionate order (Society B), he believes, would come closest to setting protection of the ecosystem as its core value while maintaining important human values, as well. He claims that Society B is more sustainable than Society A, because it is more balanced, less likely to go to extremes. There would be built-in value constraints on efforts of some to dominate others:

> In public discourse, we often hear that we must continue to grow economically and exploit natural resources vigorously (particularly to produce more energy) in order to maintain a high standard of wealth — or else we will go back to the horse and buggy days and freeze in our homes. People who pose such a choice assume the selfish, aggressive, competitive value structure of Society A. Within the value structure of Society B, it is unlikely that such a choice would be posed. Ways can be found to limit population, husband resources, protect the ecosystem and yet find richness and quality in living that is not dependent upon high consumption. Life in Society B really is attractive, making it easier for us to abandon the beliefs, values, and social structure of Society A.

This, of course, is the key to a successful vision for a more sustainable society. Learning to live better with less lies at the core of any successful transition. "Less" here means less fossil fueled energy and resource-intensive products and services. "Living better" means addressing the real physical and psychological needs of people, but in ways that are more environmentally benign.

For example, consider two alternatives. The first is jumping into a large, gas-guzzling Sport Utility Vehicle and rushing off to the Daytona 500, sitting out in the hot sun while souped-up and noisy automobiles race at top speed around a track, burning rubber and fuel all the way. The other is to consider less impactful recreational activities, perhaps participation in a competitive sport—like water polo in the swimming pool. Participants would have a lot of fun, get some exercise, and interact more with friends and family.

Building the Sustainable Society

Research and study should produce better examples and create improved understandings of the processes. If we examine, for example, the psychological pleasures of driving down the highway in a large and expensive luxury car, we might find better ways of providing increased psychological benefits. Working together as a family on a challenging jigsaw puzzle or building a new backyard toy can be fun, constructive, and yield a powerful sense of satisfaction and accomplishment, feelings that can last for days. If speed is what we want, there are less-impactful ways of experiencing it.

Music, theater, dance, and low-technology sports offer terrific outlets for spectator as well as participatory fun. These can be as much or more enjoyable and longer lasting than cheap thrills at an energy-consuming car race.

Other visions of alternative social structures and lifestyles can be found, but they are few and sketchy at best. Most authors only give general outlines of what a sustainable future society might look like. Perhaps we need a systematic examination of every component of the industrialized society to see how each might be made more sustainable. There are two levels to this.

Technological change. First is what might be attained through technology alone. This is where recycling can shine. As Ray Anderson is doing with his Interface Corporation[6], one looks at every waste stream in the enterprise and searches for ways of eliminating that stream or rendering it totally harmless. Recycling, to make it not a waste stream but an input to some other process, is a good first step. But if this just displaces the ultimate disposal of the material from company A to company B, only modest improvement will be attained. The limited experimentation with radical resource recovery and recycling must be expanded to all industries and all enterprises.

An example is the vaunted "hypercar" proposal of the Rocky Mountain Institute. We must find out if it is truly viable, and an improvement in the experience of human transport. The vehicle, and a larger freight-carrier version, needs to be designed, manufactured, and tested. Additional reduced-impact technological innovations show promise for a sustainable future.

Values change. The second level of societal examination would look not at technological-only conversions of impacts but to values-and-beliefs-driven behavior changes. Changes in the customs and mores can be postulated and tried out from time to time and place to place.

A few "intentional communities," more environmentally friendly subdivisions, and "new towns" have been conceived and built, and are currently in operation. These, too, need to be studied and their histories followed. Some small communities battle their present connection to the larger industrialized economy, blunting their effectiveness.

The problem of overpopulation cannot be overlooked in all of this. The very best hypercar possible won't solve the problem of congestion on the highways.

A Working Example — Gaviotas

When solar energy was the rage in the 1970s, the government funded a number of solar demonstration projects around the country. The program didn't do so well, however, all because of a single word. That word was "experimental."

Experiments often fail and the experimenters learn from the failures. Most, if not all, of the so-called "demonstration" projects failed because the technology was not mature yet. They either failed technically or economically, "demonstrating" that the technologies were not yet ready for prime time. If the government had properly labeled them as experiments, perhaps they would have received less bad press.

The town of Gaviotas deserves special mention. It is described in a book of the same name by Alan Weisman[7]. It began as an experiment around 1971, just before the 1972 publication of *The Limits to Growth*. It was the idea of one man, Paolo Lugari. The village was established, almost out of nothing, in the Llanos savannah of Colombia, east of the capital city Bogotá, and between the Rio Meta and the Rio Vichada. The soil was poor; the rivers and streams, not swift flowing. So the primary source of energy was solar, along with the few crops they grew. In the beginning the small outpost survived mainly on grants from the United Nations Development Programme and other sources, most importantly a UNDP grant in 1976, which designated Gaviotas as a model community.

Over the years the small village subsisted on an idea and the toils of its clever engineers and other specialists from Bagotá's prestigious Universidad de los Andes. The experiment suffered from, among other things, national violent political unrest during most of the intervening years and a chronic shortage of money.

What saved Gaviotas from early demise was something E. F. Shumaker wrote about in 1989. His book *Small is Beautiful* [8, 9] introduced the world to the concept of "appropriate technology." A giant aerospace industry could invent and build a machine to do just about anything except make it dirt cheap and fabricated from simple, readily available materials.

This is exactly what's needed in the third world, the early Gaviotans concluded. Fortunately they had this asset in abundant supply, thanks to the inventive students, professors, and other talented people residing, doing research papers, and teaching there.

Dr. Gustavo Yepes was director of the faculty of music at Universidad de los Andes. He had been introduced to Paolo Lugari after a choral performance of Bach's sacred music and was invited to visit Gaviotas at his earliest opportunity. That day arrived in October 1995. Here is what Weisman wrote of Yepes' experience.

> What he saw — and heard — belied Lugari's protestations; to Yepes, Gaviotas seemed not only proof that utopia on Earth was possible, but that it was arguably more practical than what currently passed for conventional society. Five hundred kilometers away from his increasingly frightening city, Yepes had found himself in a tranquil village, shaded by the gallery forest of a tributary of the Rio Orinoco and filled with flowers and dazzling, melodious birds. The people of Gaviotas collectively exuded a quality so novel that Yepes wasn't sure he'd seen it before — but once encountered, it was unmistakable: They were happy. They rose before dawn, worked hard and productively, ate simply but well, and were peaceful. The machinery they used dominated neither them nor their landscape: it was mostly of their own design or adaptation, and mostly quiet. "May I retire here?" Yepes had asked Lugari, after watching children playing on a see-saw that was also a water pump, which tapped kid power to replenish a reservoir for the Gaviotas school. "Don't wait to retire. Come sooner. You are exactly what we need." They were walking down a red dirt path that led past a grove of mango trees, an outdoor basketball court, polygonal modular living quarters, and a community meeting hall with a parabolic swoosh of roof, contoured from shining metal to deflect the equatorial heat. Just south of town, the path widened into a road, with a tall pine forest rising on either side. They exchanged waves with six men and a woman dressed in caps, colored neckerchiefs, tee shirts and tool belts, who rode past on thick-tired bicycles. Lugari steered Yepes into the forest as he began to explain. "For the past quarter-century — ever since Gaviotas began," he said, "I've been studying the history and literature of utopic communities."
>
> "I thought you said this wasn't utopia."
>
> "Neither were any of those other places. They were attempts."
>
> Lately, Lugari had been reading about the famed experiment of 11th century Paraguay, when Jesuit priests arrived to evangelize the New World. Until then, colonizers throughout most of the Americas had considered indigenous peoples either expendable savages or exploitable slaves. But the Jesuits who ended up far from the trade routes, in the distant region

where the borders of Brazil, Argentina, and Paraguay now converge, saw the resident Guarani Indians as a kind of *tabula rasa*: untainted *Homo sapiens* in their natural state, potentially perfectable. Being missionaries, of course, meant having certain preconceptions about perfection, and these Jesuits soon set about replacing the natives' language, god, and means of sustenance. Their missions, aptly named "reductions," were consummately paternalistic but nevertheless benevolent, self-sustaining communities that prospered for more than a century, until the Jesuits fell into disfavor with Spain and Portugal and were expelled from colonial Latin America.

Paolo Lugari was not interested in evangelism — Gaviotas didn't even have a church. What enthralled him about that historic Paraguayan experiment was the music. "Everyone," he told Yepes, "was taught to sing or to play a musical instrument. Music was the loom that wove the community together. Music was in school, at meals, even at work: Musicians accompanied laborers right into the corn and *yerba mate* fields. They'd take turns, some playing, some harvesting. It was a society that lived in constant harmony — literally. It's what we intend to do, right here in this forest. That's why I asked you to come."[7, p. 8-10]

Weisman quoted Jorge Zapp, describing the social organization at Gaviotas in the late 1970s, when the community was just transitioning from a field laboratory to a new kind of community: "We're still designing what we are. And really, not much has changed. Our houses, our school, and this dining room all belong to Gaviotas. We all live off grant money we've received, plus the food we raise. We don't have job descriptions — everyone just sort of falls in where needed, or creates something original to do. But its not anarchy. Social rules here are unwritten, but everyone respects and observes them." Later Zapp expanded. "...without even trying, we've become another kind of world here. It's based on solidarity, one in which no one knows when he'll be paid for what he does, let alone get rich. It may just be survival, but it's survival in the best sense of the word: People surviving as considerate, sharing beings. No one demands anything of anybody except to get along with each other and work hard, in cooperation. We do this simply because we love to. In Gaviotas we're driven by something different than competition or pecking orders. And we're content here. Whatever this is, it can't be underestimated."[7, p. 83]

Is Gaviotas a proper model for the rest of the world? That has been one of its intentions. However, it is not a model that can or should work everywhere. Each region must develop its own sustainable ways, appropriate to its own motivations, resources, and desires.

Gaviotas had one special advantage. It started away from cities and large populations. It is important to discover if this model, or some version of it, can work in a more urban setting or even in an inner city.

Whether all its methods and techniques are appropriate for large population centers, one thing is certain. Gaviotas offers us at least one real example of what it might be like to live in a desirable sustainable society.

True Sustainability

I have searched over the last several years for thoughtful accounts of alternative systems. They might be new social structures or new philosophies of life. Often I have been rewarded. Many of the good systems seem to have come into being spontaneously, embodying their remarkably original ideas, with little reference to previous work. Others do cite, here or there, an important book or idea that provided some early influence and/or motivation. All have been remarkable in their overarching, big picture thinking.

But some seem to completely miss one issue. That is the matter of reversing overpopulation. Some accounts fail to identify it as an important component of the total picture. For one who believes overpopulation lies at the core of our problems, this is very disconcerting, and surprising.

We can easily get swept into the exciting and breakthrough thinking exhibited by many contributions to our search for new ways of life. However, after evaluating most of the account, we find that population is not a central issue. Or it may be mentioned in passing as important but is not incorporated in the plan or design of the vision.

Worse still are those breakthrough explorations into sustainable enterprise living which actually *encourage* further overpopulation. We might call this "not seeing over the mountain." They represent a partial failure to see the really big picture. They fail to understand the crucial role of overpopulation in human history and its importance in exacerbating the problems. Or they do not incorporate this issue in whatever solution strategies are being explored. Often this failure nearly negates the whole idea.

Daniel Quinn and Dr. Alan Thornhill, a conservation biologist at Rice University, identify this error clearly in their video on "Food Production and Population Growth"[10].

"We found a way to let human population exceed the natural food supply, by growing more food. By stepping up food production, and the inevitable numbers of people in the process, is how we got here. If we didn't continue chasing population growth with more food there would not be the massive famines we see, but people don't believe this. They think it would be catastrophic for humans not to continue increasing the food supply, indefinitely. This is not true of every other species on Earth. People think that not providing food would lead to a collapse, through famine."

A similar argument applies to energy conservation and renewable energy. All the world's energy efficiency does no good when dwarfed by increasing population consuming that more efficient and new (though renewable) energy. Opening new areas for human habitation, however efficient and however benign with respect to waste products, will not help the long-range human problem, if not coupled with plans to reduce population.

Clearing vast areas for windmills and solar collector arrays will not help the long-range problem, if not coupled with population reduction. Moving people from the terrible shanty towns which extend miles outward from many third world cities can hardly benefit the larger problems of humanity, even if the individuals moved are temporarily benefited...unless this development is coupled with population reduction.

> "Nothing threatens the future of the world more than the uncontrolled growth of our species.... I consider these videotapes [Food Production and Population Growth] equal in importance to all my books combined."
> — Daniel Quinn, author of Ishmael

Gaviotas and Population

Weisman recognized the overarching problem of runaway population growth, and described the visit of Aurelio Peccei to Gaviotas ten days before his death in 1992. Peccei was one of the Club of Rome sponsors of the landmark study resulting in the publication in 1972 of *The Limits to Growth*[11]. Weisman writes about that report:

> ...the report's authors acknowledged in their book *Beyond the Limits*[12] that they had erred — but not as detractors had claimed. Their subsequent calculations and computer projections indicated that, during the two intervening decades, civilization had already surged beyond sustainable limits. Especially in the tropics there was evidence that warnings of impending scarcity had actually stimulated a rush to grab the goods while they still existed. During the final decade of the twentieth century, consequences of this heedlessness were already apparent worldwide, as entire agrarian societies forsook exhausted lands and converged on cities that had begun to spread like stains across the continents.
>
> At mid-century in Colombia — that tormented nation where, improbably, Peccei found such promise — two-thirds of the population had been rural, a third urban. By the 1990s, as in much of the world, those percentages had reversed. The once-grateful capital of Bogotá now heaved against the Andes like surf pounding a cliff, grinding the very bedrock as

new arrivals carved footholds on the mountainsides. As the population of Ciudad Bolivar — a colonization on Bogotá's southern flank, optimistically named for the liberator of South America — approached two million, it was declared the world's biggest squatters settlement.

The fact that similar cauldrons around São Paolo, Lima, Mexico City, Manila, Lagos, *et. al.*, claimed the same bleak distinction didn't diminish the implications for Bogotá. The onslaught was even inching up Guadalupe and Montserrat, two guardian peaks that hover above the city. The alabaster Virgin atop Guadalupe now appeared to lift her palms in despair over the rising menace below — violence was fast becoming Bogotá's leading cause of death — and the funicular that ferried pilgrims down from Montserrat's chapel shrine was often greeted by gangs of muggers. After repeated assaults on their nearby Bogotá office, the Gaviotans regretfully bolted the gate and posted armed guards (albeit carrying blank ammunition).[7, p. 21-22]

This reference to overpopulation and its effects in cities is not matched by discussions of how the Gaviotas experiment will relieve the population pressure (other than by encouraging migration from urban shanty towns into the countryside). We could argue that by providing more food for more people, the Gaviotas experiment encourages overpopulation.

This doesn't negate the wonderful things that have been done at Gaviotas. It merely reminds us how hard really big picture thinking is, and how hard we must work to insure that our visions of sustainable futures are truly sustainable — both comprehensive and exhaustive in their coverage of the issues.

A Failure of Policy

The Gaviotas story offers more. For many years, the small community invented a variety of important technologies, appropriate to Colombia's poorer regions, and received funding from a variety of sources to install this technology in villages and cities over a large area. At its height, it had a solar factory in Gaviotas and another one manned by street urchins in Bogotá. It was exporting this technology to other regions of the country, both urban and rural.

Then two developments greatly reduced funding to Gaviotas and curtailed many of its experiments. The first of these was political. In 1990 a new president was elected who did not believe in government-subsidized assistance, such as the *Plan National de Rehabilitacion* that had funded much of the Gaviotas work around the country, but in economic open market pressures, opening Colombia's markets to the world. This followed President George H. W. Bush's Enterprise for the Americas, outlined in the president's "New World Order" initiative.[13]

Government projects intended to develop rural areas were sharply reduced. These were replaced by increased military presence in the zones controlled by the guerillas. In consequence, Gaviotas shrank in size and in appropriate technology projects. The energy fears of the late 1970s were being replaced by abundant energy and stable energy prices. "Overwhelmed by complex, mounting pressures to save so many plants, animals, and people, the world had backslid, lurching off on a slick, new, self-indulgent technological binge and getting promptly hooked on computerized, jet-fueled supply lines capable of keeping a global marketplace well stocked."

Weisman commented, "There were two possible outcomes of this trend. One was corporate feudalism, based on an entire Third World full of serfs hacking resources from the land until supplies were exhausted. Or, there were visions like that of Gaviotas, suggesting how technology might free people more than subjugate them, and how humanity might restore to the Earth what it borrows."

Unfortunately, the new political order required that governments "purge more and more social commitments from their budgets, in the process yanking many nonprofit organizations off their life-support systems." In consequence, Gaviotas could no longer count on government or UN funding to help translate lofty goals into tools and action. Left to go it alone, out in the eastern *Llanos* wilderness, remote from supply lines for materials and money, the small community fell on hard times. This did not prevent the remaining Gaviotans from enjoying their oasis of natural charm and closeness to the land.

The second unfortunate outside influence came from overpopulation and bad government planning. The vice mayor of *Chingalé*, a village along the *Rio Magdalena*, described the consequences of these circumstances for the river: "It's a different river now. It used to give life. Now it's taking it away."

Most of the wells Gaviotans had dug and furnished with its new pump designs, and which ten years earlier had consistently provided good fresh drinking water, had gone bad. This was a consequence of deforestation and a rigid government policy that forced improper placement of wells along the river, giving the wells a limited life and susceptibility to salt-water intrusion.

According to Weisman, quoting Eusebio, a Magdalena boatman, "For more than a decade, Magdalena Medio had lost about a hundred thousand hectares of forest per year. 'In the entire country, they're saying about six hundred thousand,' he added. Clearing land for cattle grazing was a big reason. Another was that *narcotraficantes*, who, by the 1990s, owned more than one-third of Colombia's arable land, kept buying up choice Magdalena bottomland to launder their relentless supply of drug dollars.... The tremendous erosion due to clear-cutting was now blamed for the collapse of fish harvests."[7. p. 191]

The river had become turbid and much shallower in many places. Fish catches, formerly eighty-four thousand tons per year, had dropped to only thirteen thousand. The fresh water wells were no longer viable.

All the work of the Gaviotans aimed at bringing fresh water to the region had come to naught. Not because of anything wrong with the small community's vision or organization or cleverness, but a result of failed leadership at the top, in the Colombian government and at the international level. To make matters worse, solar ultraviolet levels being recorded at Gaviotas for the World Meteorological Organization were increasing, due to stratospheric ozone depletion. And readings from the four Colombian sites indicated ozone layer thinning over that country was the greatest in the Americas.

Reflecting on these changes, Weisman concludes, "At least, when the land and waters themselves began to die, politics and ideological battles would become irrelevant. Is this what it took to cleanse the Earth again? Or was the future just draining to the sea, finally to drown?"[7. p.196]

A cynic would claim that this is but the failure of "programs." It *was* the programs that failed. Not the vision, not the people, not the inherent success of Gaviotas and those living in and around the community. The problem arose when attempting to venture out and spread Gaviotan technology to other regions. On the other hand, without the initial funding from UN and governmental programs, many of the accomplishments of Gaviotas probably would not have been possible.

The Silver Lining

Gaviotas finally found a way to flourish without handouts. The rescue came in the form of pine saplings planted years earlier. After twenty years of growth, they were mature enough to yield a substantial quantity of resin.

A low-impact, totally renewable resin and turpentine production system was established. This facility employed hundreds of workers and returned the community to economic viability — proving the original vision of Paolo Lugari. In between the surging pines, native tropical forest vegetation started growing, someday destined to take over the pine forest. The pines themselves failed to reproduce in this soil and climate, thereby posing no risk of uncontrolled spreading of this introduced species. In the meantime, millions more pines were being planted for future resin production. And Gaviotas was again being asked to use its remarkable technology for solar and renewable projects elsewhere in Colombia.

The value of the many medicinal substances found, often with the help of the *indigenas* — the Guahibo and other Orinocan Indians with centuries of ethnobiological experience in the region — was recognized. The establishment of a medicinal plants field laboratory was proposed. Medicinal plants proved of much greater value per gram than previous products, making the costs of transporting them to market much less an impediment.

Quoting Oscar Gutiérrez, Weisman writes, "This is the one thing in the world that can compete with illegal drugs. We can save the Indians and tropical forests and stay healthy in the process."

The Gaviotas experience featured the complete absence of hierarchy in its simple system of governance. Describing one of the occasional meetings to discuss problems and make decisions, Weisman related that, during the meeting, "Paolo Lugari listened in frank admiration at how the Gaviotans arrived at decisions by discussing calmly, always looking each other in the eye. No one was intimidated; everyone was respectful. Eventually, they reached a solution and moved on. This was a characteristic, he realized, of a community where everyone had a real stake. Two years earlier, he'd watched how they handled the commissary storekeeper who admitted overcharging to finance his honeymoon: He and his wife were quietly ostracized until their debt was repaid. He kept his post, but no further socializing occurred until the matter was resolved. It was an effective, peaceful, fair, and instructive solution, one that rarely needed to be repeated.

"And their work, as Paolo told everyone he met, was just as impressive as their society. Men and women without university credentials were running the country's most innovative forest industry, annually planting more trees than the Colombian government's entire forestry program — and running a modern processing factory as well. He [compared them proudly to] an empowered work force, one with ownership and pride in the quality of their products, with information generated and shared collectively, not just stuck at the top in some isolated managerial priesthood.

"They'd remained flexible enough to respond quickly to change and to reorganize in a world that was spinning faster than the old structures could withstand. 'Gaviotas is not a model. It's a path.'"[7, p. 214]

Many more such visions of alternate ways of living and of organizing society are needed. Not just one that appears to be working in one place, but a variety of visions for a variety of places in a variety of cultures around the world, including urban settings.

The question remains open as to whether these alternate visions can succeed completely within existing western industrial societies. Can we transform an existing system? Or must we start afresh, as Gaviotas did?

The most likely answer is both. Certainly on an experimental basis, we must try both approaches. We will learn a lot from every attempt.

A Work in Progress—The Hydrogen Economy

The restructuring approach is already being attempted and discussed, at least on a very limited basis. For example, the proponents of another sustainable vision believe that much good can come from replacing the traditional fossil fuels with hydrogen gas. When hydrogen "burns", it couples with atmospheric oxygen to produce pure water vapor, a totally benign substance. Condensed water vapor is distilled water. Adding in a few minerals for health and taste reasons makes it the purest drinking water one can find, and one in short supply in much of the world.

The fuel itself, hydrogen, is available everywhere — in water. If you have a source of electricity, you can use the *electrolysis* process to separate the hydrogen and oxygen in water from each other. Electrical energy is required to split them apart in this way.

How can you get energy from taking hydrogen out of water, and then recombining it with oxygen to end back up with water again? Isn't this the description of a perpetual motion machine?

Yes, this would be a perpetual motion machine if it could be used to generate *net* energy. Unfortunately, energy is needed to split hydrogen and oxygen apart, but it produces about this same energy when you put them back together again. The net result? No new energy is created.

Since the process is not perfectly efficient (and can never be), some energy is lost along the way. The result is less useful energy than originally. The laws of thermodynamics, therefore, are not broken.

Hydrogen itself is no amazing new infinite supply of energy; it is merely a storage and transport medium. Then, how can hydrogen be useful?

In one version of the hydrogen economy, solar energy is converted into electrical energy (through photovoltaic cells or other means, with about a 10 to 20 percent efficiency). The electrical energy so generated is then used to split the hydrogen and oxygen in water apart. The hydrogen is then piped and/or compressed into tanks and transported to where it is needed. (The oxygen can be kept for other uses or exhausted into the air.)

Heat is produced when hydrogen is burned, taking oxygen from the air and yielding water vapor. This heat can provide power for vehicle engines, for water pumping, or for other uses. The water vapor can be condensed and used as drinking water.

Hydrogen can also be used to make electricity simply and quietly in fuel cells. These are small packages in which oxygen and hydrogen are combined to produce electricity, a kind of reverse to the electrolysis process. Fuel cells have been used for many years in spacecraft, and terrestrial versions are now entering the market for a variety of applications.

Having a hydrogen economy is an important component of one vision for a new society. People are already working hard to determine how to convert from the current fossil fuel one to a hydrogen-based economy.

One way is to convert automobiles and other vehicles to run on hydrogen using a number of ingenious methods. Most automobile manufacturers are experimenting with some of them. The U.S. government can play an important role in providing incentives.

Several possible and plausible pathways switch from gasoline to hydrogen-fueled automobiles. However, serious infrastructure problems exist within all of them. Some approaches involve partial conversion, where existing gas stations are only slightly modified to stock and sell hydrogen in liquid form. Hydrogen is also found combined with other atoms in some complex molecules. Hybrid vehicles can use these by pulling the hydrogen off prior to use or converting it directly in the fuel cell.

Conversion to such a system could proceed gradually. From gasoline, to alcohol from biomass, and then to other hydrogen-rich liquid fuels the world could proceed toward hydrogen production by renewable means.

The "cold turkey" approach involves rapid switching to gaseous hydrogen as soon as possible.

All the proposals have pros and cons. Each contains a financial risk. Seth Dunn writes, "the energy business is beginning to hedge its bets on continued hydrocarbon [fossil fuel] dominance, by pouring billions of dollars into research related to hydrogen and its enabling technology, the fuel cell. Fuel companies like Shell, BP and Texaco are forming hydrogen and fuel cell technology divisions. Electric power companies like ABB and PG&E are investing in, and forming numerous partnerships with, fuel cell manufacturers. Automotive firms like DaimlerChrysler, Ford, GM, Honda, and Toyota are racing to put the first fuel cell vehicles on the market by 2004. And the [concept] has moved from GM engineers to GM executives: Executive Director Robert Purcell announced to the National Petrochemical and Refiners Association last year that 'our long-term vision is of a hydrogen economy'..."[14]

People are already exploring a variety of visions for what a hydrogen-based society might look like. These are not just theoretical studies. As the above quote indicates, they involve investments of billions of dollars and many tests of the different concepts. Fuel for vehicles is an important part of any vision for a future economy.

Finding and Living a New Vision

Much more is needed to connect all the important components into a larger vision that is doable and desirable.

The key steps in this process are conception, visualization, design, experimentation, and evaluation. *Ecotopia* provides us with sample visualization. Milbrath offers some scholarly advice on the nature and creation of these visions. *Gaviotas* takes us through the design step to the experimentation process. All successful enterprises incorporate continual evaluation and redesign, as was done so well at Gaviotas. But these steps are not necessarily sequential or in the order listed.

We may not have thirty more years to pursue other concepts through all these steps. Even if we have only the conceptualizations, however, they will serve an extremely useful purpose — showing us what it means to find new ways of living as humans on a stressed-out planet. They offer desirable visions of a sustainable future for humanity. Many will be needed if humans are to realize their full potential and make the needed changes intentionally, rather than waiting for declining resources, spreading poverty, lost habitats and species, extreme political unrest, and armed conflicts to force the changes unintentionally.

This is being true to our species, using our special gift of intelligence to protect not only humanity, but to save the world for all the other species inhabiting it.

I believe we are up to the task. The time to begin is now.

References

1. Daniel Quinn. *Ishmael*. 1st ed. Bantam/Turner: New York, 1992.
2. John E. Pfeiffer. *The Emergence of Society — A prehistory of the Establishment.* Copyright © 1977 McGraw-Hill Education: New York, 1977, 512 pp. Used by permission of McGraw Hill Education.
3. Paul B. MacCready, "Gossamer Aircraft and Where they Lead," Manuscript, Undated. P. 6 dates the writing as 1990. Received from the author by R. McCluney September 2001. Used with the author's permission.
4. Ernest Callenbach. Ecotopia. Reissue ed. Bantam Books: 1990, 181 pp. Copyright © 1975, 2003 by Ernest Callenbach. Used with permission of the author.
5. Lester W. Milbrath. *Envisioning a Sustainable Society*. State University of New York Press: Albany, NY, 1989, 403 pp.
6. Ray C. Anderson. *Mid-Course Correction — Toward A Sustainable Enterprise: The Interface Model.* Chelsea Green: White River Junction, VT, 1998, 207 pp.
7. Alan Weisman. *Gaviotas — A Village to Reinvent the World.* Chelsea Green Publishing: White River Junction, VT, 1998, 227 pp. Used by permission of Chelsea Green Publishing Co.
8. E. F. Schumacher. *Small Is Beautiful : Economics As If People Mattered.* 1989 ed. HarperCollins (paper): New York, 1973, 352 pp.
9. E. F. Schumacher. *Small is Beautiful: Economics as If People Mattered — 25 years later ... with commentaries.* 1999 ed. Hartley & Marks Publishers: New York, 1999, 286 pp. Note: New Preface by James Robertson and Introduction by Paul Hawken.
10. Daniel Quinn and Alan Thornhill, "Food Production and Population Growth video tape." New Tribal Ventures: Houston, TX, Video tape, VHS,
11. Donella Meadows, Dennis Meadows, Jorgen Rangers, and William Behrens. *The Limits to Growth*. Earth Island: London, 1972.
12. Donella H. Meadows, Dennis L. Meadows, and Jorgen Randers. *Beyond the Limits*. Chelsea Green: White River Junction, VT, 1992, 300 pp.
13. Eric A. Miller and Steve A. Yetiv. "The New World Order in Theory and Practice: The Bush Administration's Worldview in Transition." *Presidential Studies Quarterly* 31, no. 1 (2001): March 2001, 56-68.
14. Seth Dunn. "Routes to a hydrogen economy." *Renewable Energy World* Vol. 4, no. 4 (2001): July-August 2001, 18-29. http://www.jxj.com/rew.

15
Creativity
Insights.
Creative problem solving.

D
r. Paul MacCready has a Ph.D. in aeronautics from Caltech. After many years of hard work, he, his wife, and their three sons decided to take a cross-country trip in a recreational vehicle. They needed to escape the rigors of tight schedules, deadlines, and pressures from the world of work.

MacCready had read accounts of a £5,000 prize, originally offered in 1959 by British industrialist Henry Kremer, to the first group to design and build a human-powered aircraft. Applicants had to fly a figure eight around two markers four fifths of a kilometer apart, matching the performance of the early Wright brothers' aircraft.

As he wrote about it later, "I had guaranteed a loan for my friend to start a company, but the company didn't succeed and now I was stuck with a $100,000 obligation. While daydreaming, mining the subconscious, on a vacation trip in 1976, I mused about a possible connection between this debt and the 1959 Kremer Prize for human-powered flight that I knew had reached £50,000. When I noted in a newspaper that £1 was now worth exactly $2, the light bulb of invention turned on! The prize equals the debt!"

This first moment of inspiration made the connection, but failed to produce the final motivation needed to begin such a difficult project.

One day while he was driving along, he watched some hawks and vultures glide overhead. Their movement was remarkably effortless. They hardly flapped their wings. He knew their bodies were very light. The bones of birds are hollow, a marvel of design, providing good strength with minimal weight. He had just written a paper on the similarity between hang gliders and birds in flight and was writing another on the speeds and lift coefficients of birds. After a little mental arithmetic, on the time the birds spent completing a circle, estimating the bank angle, and some other details, he had the idea for some simple solutions to the problem of human-powered flight. "Another 'Aha!' moment," he wrote in 1996[1].

As he told an audience at the Florida Solar Energy Center some years later², after the initial insight Dr. MacCready had one of those quick moments of understanding. These often follow days of study, reflection, pondering, puzzlement, and then forgetting the issue for a while, allowing the unconscious mind to work its magic.

Previously MacReady had little intention of going for the prize. It was just a curious problem that he enjoyed mulling over.

But on this day he had the spark of another idea, a very creative one, startling in its simplicity and logic. He knew it would lead him to win the prize. This second "Aha!" moment was more technical than the first, dealing with "Insights from building indoor model airplanes in the 1930s and hang gliders in the 1970s...." The result was a design involving "exterior wire bracing (0.030-inch piano wire) supporting thin-wall aluminum tubes loaded in compression."

Following his vacation MacCready returned to California, started assembling a team, and searched for a strong, lean pilot. Many months of designing, building, and testing ensued, without funding, but with a team of family and friends.

The prize was finally won, as MacCready had promised himself. He claimed it on 23rd August 1977, eighteen years after it was first offered.

Other attempts to win the prize — and there had been many — aimed not so much at winning the prize but at building a human-powered aircraft. The resulting designs were too heavy and clumsy. As MacCready described it later, "all my early design concepts were like those of some British teams that had logically started with the most efficient airplanes, sailplanes, and made streamlined versions lighter and larger. These elegant, complex machines got off the ground on the initial high power of the pilot, but could not stay aloft long, could not turn effectively, and took forever to repair after a crash."

Paul's first departure was to aim *his* project at just winning the prize, not necessarily making a practical human-powered aircraft. With this different goal in mind, he didn't care if the contraption collapsed into a million pieces three seconds after crossing the finishing line.

So the team built a model. They knew at the outset that difficult tasks such as these require many failures; learning from mistakes is a critical component in any successful project.

MacCready wrote in 1996, "During development we made 400 flights that included four major, and innumerable minor, crashes. Each crash was informative, and helped us toward material design changes. (This is not the way to develop airliners.) We focused doggedly on winning the prize, not even making complete drawings of the plane until after the prize was won."[1]

In order to keep the machine's weight as low as possible, every structural component could be no heavier than the minimum needed to carry the craft through the course. Every time the plane crashed, they looked very carefully at the pieces. They reinforced all the broken places.

But they also did one thing more. They weakened every place that was never broken to reduce the weight of the craft. The goal was that the entire plane could fall apart, upon failure, all at once. Once they discovered that design, they could make the airplane just a little bit stronger, but only strong enough to complete the course on a windless day. This would minimize weight, enabling the pilot/athlete to stay aloft long enough to finish the course.

The rest, as they say, is history. The creativity employed on that first project was used in a variety of succeeding projects. MacReady won a $100,000 prize for the flight of a human-powered airplane (the Gossamer Albatross) across the English Channel in 1979. He created a radio-controlled, flying pterodactyl in 1985. His solar-powered car, Sunraycer, won a race from Darwin to Adelaide in 1987.

The original aircraft, the Gossamer Condor, now hangs in the Smithsonian's National Air and Space Museum, alongside the Wright Brothers' plane.

MacReady's story illustrates the importance of being both smart and creative, of finding important insights and using them productively.

Needing Creativity

The human intellect has brought us to the brink of self-annihilation as a species, and only that intellect can extricate us from impending doom. *Considerable creative thought is needed to overcome the nearly insurmountable problems facing humanity.*

Creativity was not directly listed as one of the contributors to the Human Capability Index, introduced in Chapter 8. However, it is included, at least indirectly, as "... an ability to think for one's self, to clarify, to learn, and to understand the world in which the person lives." Creativity may turn out to be the most important human attribute needed to stop the seemingly inevitable slide toward extinction.

To be successful, any effort at environmental and societal reform should utilize creativity and insightful thinking to the maximum, coupled with efforts to improve both. Many resources are available to aid this quest. Several references will be cited in the remainder of this chapter and listed at its end. These can be consulted for further reading.

Everyday Creativity

Sternberg and Lubart[3, p. vii] point out that not just the superstars of art and music demonstrate creativity. "Creativity, like intelligence, is something that everyone possesses in some amount. Moreover, creativity is not a fixed attribute: A person's level of creativity is not carved in stone at birth, and like any talent, it is something virtually anyone can develop in varying degrees."

Creativity occurs every day when people see new ways to accomplish different tasks, try daring new ways of relating to one another, or find new insight about their lives, loves, and pursuits of happiness. "As we approach the turn of the century, intelligence is not enough. There are plenty of 'smart' people around, and many of them are failing to realize their life goals because they can't keep up with a rapidly changing world. Thus we cannot emphasize enough the importance of creativity. In such a world it may be the key to both survival and success."[3, p. viii]

Creativity takes many forms. Creative artistry is different from creative mathematical problem solving; these are different from creative management and administration. Creativity can be learned and stimulated in the young, or it can be stifled.

MacCready has written about the importance of promoting creative thought in our educational systems:

> Curiosity and creativity are genetic characteristics of humans, well demonstrated in pre-school youngsters. Later, the characteristics often atrophy as people adapt to the pressures of structures, inertias, reward systems, and responsibilities associated with schooling and employment.... In other words, the spark of creativity can be smothered or fanned into flame. The potential is genetic and we all have it; its nurturing determines its strength.... Motivation, preparation, opportunities, positive attitude, teamwork, fun, daydreaming, perseverance, and luck are among the key factors.... Fortunately these characteristics can be unleashed by various means mingling motivation, opportunity, and example with an understanding of how wonderful humans minds are, how they work, and that creativity skills are inherent in us all ...[4]

Sternberg and Lubart also emphasize the importance of creativity in education, describing how easily it can be stifled: "One of the worst things a teacher can do is close off all possible solutions to a problem other than his or her own, and assume that if a student disagrees the student must be wrong. In our experience this kind of closed-mindedness occurs much more often than any of us would like."[3, p. 125]

According to MacReady, to solve the many problems we face in the future, we need creativity, innovation, and invention.

> Civilization is in the midst of unprecedented growth. This presents unprecedented opportunity and responsibility. Creativity and the associated invention/innovation and entrepreneurship, benefiting both individuals and society, are essential elements if civilization is to move to a desirable, sustainable condition. Pioneering schools are changing educational methodologies so as to give creativity the high priority it deserves.[4]

He amplified this theme in a 1990 paper on the Gossamer Condor and its larger meaning in today's society.

> By his large prize, Kremer assured that man's oldest aviation dream would be achieved—a dream that everyone understood to be of no direct practical value once we began flying with engines. It is tempting to use the technique of offering a substantial prize to foster various technological developments. However, when you try to concoct prize rules you quickly realize how special Kremer's challenge was: technologically just barely achievable, and with winning based solely on easily-quantified performance, for a development that would not have high priority were it not for the prize.
>
> Kremer's challenge was far different than that which ordinarily confronts vehicle designers in the U.S. Conventionally, to make a new vehicle we incorporate an existing fossil fuel engine or develop a new one, and operate [it] with hundreds of horsepower. However, Kremer asked, in effect, for us to fly on 1/3 horsepower. His prize was far more important than is usually appreciated. I consider civilization's primary challenge now is "to reach a comfortable accommodation with the flora and fauna and resources of this limited Earth". Kremer inspired us to pay attention to getting by with the puny power of a human, as had been the case when our ancestors co-existed with the natural world instead of taking it over...[5]

The current great challenge for humanity (hopefully, not its last) is to win a very different sort of prize. We are challenged to use our brains and imaginative powers to stop "taking over" the natural world and determine how to run our human systems following the natural model. To achieve this will require some extraordinarily, as well as a lot of ordinarily, creative people.

Characteristics of the Creative Person

Within each of us lies a number of resources that can be tapped to increase creative performance. Following Sternberg and Lubart, some are listed and described below.[3]

Intelligence. Intelligence falls into three categories. First is the *synthetic* kind where we see and form a problem in a new way or redefine it altogether. (An example might be the employee who loved his job, wanted advancement, but did not wish to relocate. Instead, he found his boss a position with another company, and then he took the boss's place in the management of the company.)

The second kind of intelligence is *analytic*. This involves recognizing good new ideas, then structuring a solution around these ideas, and finally allocating resources toward the solution. (An emergency room surgeon cuts into a shooting victim's abdomen. After determining the extent of the damage, he has several surgical intervention choices, and not much time to decide between them. The creative choice will be the one most likely to preserve the patient's life with the least long-term disabilities. There are ethical considerations that have to be weighed as well, so the problem is not always a simple one.)

Finally, we have *practical* intelligence. This is the ability to present one's work effectively to an audience and convince them it is valuable and worth having. All the great ideas in the world are of little value if not used, and this requires others to recognize their merits and follow through with action.

Knowledge. Before creativity on a subject is possible, its background must be known — to avoid reinventing the obvious and to make sure the solution fits within the problem's inevitable constraints. The creative musician first must learn to play a musical instrument, the composer must learn how to write music, the lawyer must study law, the engineer must master a variety of mathematical and scientific subjects, and the statesperson must know a lot of history. The world's greatest creative musicians perform their crafts within the strict limitations of their instruments, the chord structure of the music they perform, and — in the case of most classical musicians — by playing only the notes provided by the composer. An ability to escape the box of constraints like these without producing random gibberish distinguishes the most creative performers.

Thinking Styles. Different people use their intelligence differently, and learn new things by different routes. Within reason, making up rules as you go rather than accepting established ones can be a successful thinking style.

Personality. Creativity is not just a cognitive or mental trait. Having a good sense of humor can be very effective, as can an ability to present oneself and one's ideas to an audience. Willingness to take a stand, to ignore the pressure to conform (and doing so with verve and enthusiasm) is what personality contributes to the creative process.

Motivation. Going beyond mere potential and actually doing something creative requires a degree of motivation. Creative people are usually high-energy, task-focused and generally more productive than others.

A supportive environment. An environment that nurtures creativity is important. Often creativity is squelched by teachers, friends, parents, and co-workers. To counter this in special cases, child prodigies are often sent to special schools or to special teachers; here they have access to specialized instruction and are placed in an environment that encourages and rewards creative pursuits. We must all recognize when the environment is not conducive to creativity and then seek ways of overcoming this disincentive.

Several other important elements occur in the works of creative people. An important one is the practicality of the result.

Practicality here is seen in its broadest context. For example, a creative painting is practical if it is painted with durable paints that retain their color and shape for many years—on lasting canvas. That painting is practical if people find it worth viewing. (This doesn't mean a creative painting can't repulse lots of people. Many great paintings were not recognized at first. However, someone has to be interested in it at some time.)

"We describe a product as creative when it is (a) novel and (b) appropriate." [3, p. 11] *Novel* means statistically unusual, evocative of surprise. *Appropriate* means it serves some function or fits within important constraints. Otherwise, it may be novel but bizarre and irrelevant. Quality and importance are also needed. "A high quality product is one that is judged to show a high level of technical skill and to be well executed in one or more ways." [3, p. 12] To be creative, a person must regularly produce creative products.

Creative scientists deal with large and important problems rather than small and trivial ones, but this is seldom recognized in the way science is taught. Creative scientists commonly question authority; this trait often estranges them from authorities and/or the public.

Questioning is built into the way science works, so the culture of working scientists encourages this in a generally respectful manner. In theoretical physics, creative (even initially bizarre) ideas are encouraged, including right and wrong ones. Experimentalists and other theorists attempt to prove an idea wrong. This gives a certain freedom to push creative envelopes and challenge previous theories.

Books by Richard Feynman, one of the most creative geniuses and astounding physicists to have lived, illustrate this freedom of thought and personality in abundance. [6-9] An Amazon.com reviewer said of *Surely You're Joking, Mr. Feynman:*

> A series of anecdotes shouldn't by rights add up to an autobiography, but that's just one of the many pieces of received wisdom that Nobel Prize-winning physicist Richard Feynman (1918-88) cheerfully ignores in his engagingly eccentric book, a bestseller ever since its initial publication in 1985. Fiercely independent (read the chapter entitled "Judging Books by Their Covers"), intolerant of stupidity even when it comes packaged as high intellectualism (check out "Is Electricity Fire?"), unafraid to offend (see "You Just *Ask* Them?"), Feynman informs by entertaining. It's possible to enjoy *Surely You're Joking, Mr. Feynman* simply as a bunch of hilarious yarns with the smart-alecky author as know-it-all hero. At some point, however, attentive readers realize that underneath all the merriment simmers a running commentary on what constitutes authentic knowledge: learning by understanding, not by rote; refusal to give up on seemingly insoluble problems; and total disrespect for fancy ideas that have no grounding in the real world. Feynman himself had all these qualities in spades, and they come through with vigor and verve in his no-bull prose. No wonder his students — and readers around the world — adored him. – *Wendy Smith*

Fear of Change and Other Inhibitors

The fear of change can be a terrible disincentive for the creative person. "Despite the fact that many people claim to value novel ideas, there is solid evidence that they don't much like exactly what they supposedly value...people like what is most familiar."[3]

The more of something new we hear and see, the more we like it. This is called the "mere-exposure effect." [10, p.20] When presenting a new idea to a politician, for example, repeating the presentation over a period of time may prove beneficial ... supported by independent discussions of the idea, magazine articles about it, and constituent letters in favor of it. After a time, the politician's initial rejection of the idea will melt and it can start to be taken seriously. You know you have succeeded when the politician takes the idea as his or her own.[11, p. 104] Selective use of the mere-exposure effect can be a valuable tool in the arsenal of the creative individual.

Research indicates that people value creativity, expecting it to bring progress or be entertaining. Yet, they are often uncomfortable with it, and may initially react negatively to creative work. (Some of the most flagrant examples of undervaluing creativity are found in the schools. What the teacher says about valuing creative ability and what is done to support it often are not the same.)

"What is creative is new and often brings about positive change. But what is new is also strange, and what is strange can be scary, even threatening — which is why 'they' don't want to hear it. But they are unwise not to listen, for the creative person with original ideas is the one who, with support, will advance and improve the milieu to the benefit of all." [3. p. 2]

Sternberg and Lubart claim that going against the grain, defying "conventional wisdom," and running off on a tangent are important characteristics of the creative person. The new idea, direction, or creative work is often not what others want to hear or see. This departure from the norm is a distinguishing feature of creativity.

Good new ideas are often undervalued and under-appreciated. "Many people who have worked in or consulted with businesses are more impressed by how slowly things change than by how rapidly. Organizational cultures and ways of doing things have a life that seems to extend beyond the particular people who inhabit the organization, just as the culture of a country is passed on even when all members of a generation die. Creativity is as hard to find in the business world as anywhere else, perhaps because — much as executives recognize the need for it — at some level they may be afraid of it." [3]

Creative Problem Solving

The process of solving problems has been studied and analyzed. The findings show a strong correlation between creativity and success. "We have a notion — false, as it turns out — that problem solving is a linear process. There is a problem, we solve it, and the problem is over. Problems thus have a clear beginning, middle, and end. In life this image of an arrow pointing from one direction to another is almost never correct. Rather, the solutions to today's problems soon become tomorrow's problems. In other words the seeds of the next problem are planted in the solutions of the last." [3. p.99]

This reminds us of Sevareid's Law, quoted earlier, that "The chief cause of problems is solutions." We might rephrase it, in the context of creativity, as, "The chief source of solutions is problems."

Placing the creative spark into an established framework of necessary constraints is, unfortunately, too rare. Such people have an almost inhuman ability to bridge and synthesize and create new out of old. "In other words, creative people are well able to transit between conventional and unconventional thinking. They find the transition relatively comfortable and make it with ease. Less creative people, by contrast, even though they may have the facility to use with ease (and even speed) an array of more routine mental processes, find it difficult to transit between conventional and unconventional thinking. Many people who are 'smart' in the sense of doing well in school or on conventional tests are in their element as long as they are reading the words of a problem or making simple comparisons; it is when they must think in terms of concepts that are truly novel to them that they have difficulty. In other words they are fine with conventional problems based on conventional assumptions, but have more trouble with problems requiring unconventional assumptions and inferences." [3, p. 104]

Unfortunately, thinking conventionally and going with the flow, in a global environmental sense, can be disastrous for humans in a world where carrying capacities are widely exceeded, fossil fuels will eventually run out, and habitats are being destroyed.

In the study of problem-solving creativity, some useful themes emerge. The ability to recognize the relevance of information not immediately obvious is called *selective encoding*. In this process, one sorts out the critical pieces of information needed to deal with the problem at hand. (An employee at Eastman Chemical worked to create a new material for use with glass lenses. The experiment seemed to have failed when two lenses became rapidly stuck together following one of the experiments. He thought the test was a failure, but his supervisor, Henry Coover, recognized that a new kind of glue had been born. They named it "Super Glue.")

The ability to use past information for current problems is called *selective comparison*. The process uses what is called "analogical thinking," the art of seeing analogies and using them for problem solving or in creative expression. Aristotle said that "Metaphor, the perception of likeness in dissimilars, is the sign of genius."

Information concerning similarities and differences amongst Earth's species of organisms was available to most scientists of Charles Darwin's era. However, he was the one able to compare and combine these into a theory on the origin of the species. Darwin connected seemingly disconnected pieces of the puzzle into a coherent whole. Darwin's ability to combine nuggets of information whose connections were not obvious is called *selective combination*.

Selective comparison and combination are important for everyday life. To varying degrees, these skills are learned by every child. Taking a limited set of available materials and making something with them fits this category.

A painter has run out of all but three of her many paints. Combining these into a new work of drama and style is selective combination. Educators know that students are more receptive to learning in areas that interest them. The creative teacher can use this to mold a curriculum around student interests, teaching them a variety of essential skills in the process. Sherlock Holmes excelled at selective comparison and combination, using limited evidence to construct elaborate and often correct theories of crime and its perpetrators.

This ability is required when society is presented with conflicting opinions from scientists and other experts who must render judgments and predictions, based on incomplete information. The experts offer their best guess as to what is going on, or what might happen if a course of action is taken or continued. The natural desire is to delay a decision until more facts are in evidence and the best path is more clearly shown.

In some cases, we cannot wait for the solution to become obvious; a decision must be made immediately. In such cases, we rely upon our values and beliefs. We also join a synthesis of the facts with our own personal experiences. With skill, the best path then is discovered and followed.

Creative Change

As we search for ways to preserve humanity and a healthy environment for the indefinite future, we cannot arbitrarily eliminate possibly viable options just because they seem too radical or too far from the established norm.

The world is constantly changing. To stay successful, institutions must redefine themselves. "In their everyday lives, too, people need to keep redefining themselves. There was a time when people would start in one job at the beginning of their work life and change jobs perhaps once or twice for the rest of their career. These days people change more frequently, in part because companies come and go so quickly. But even people who stay in the same nominal job often change what they actually do in the job in just a few years."[3, p. 125]

This is not to say that change itself is an absolute good. After all, change put us into this mess in the first place. But if circumstances lead to a dangerous place, changing may be the only escape.

Fortunately, creative and insightful thinking can be improved through instruction, even for very young children. "Creativity requires not only coming up with ideas but knowing when a problem exists to start with, how to define the problem, how to allocate resources to solve the problem, and how to evaluate the value of potential solutions — knowing which ideas are your good ones. Renzulli and many others have proposed that to be creative, you need some minimum threshold of analytic ability. But most scholars, including Renzulli, believe that the threshold is not terribly high. You don't have to be an IQ star to be creative."[3, p 134]

Saving the World Through Creative Thought

The challenges facing humanity in the next several decades are serious and possibly terminal. Without creative action their solutions may be beyond our grasp.

The problems are not just environmental in Nature, or just with the structure of business. They extend to the need to reform systems of governance all over the world. Some ingrained and powerfully motivated — almost addicting — behaviors must be revised. And our belief systems must be restructured as well. To even *begin* working on these problems, we need a global discourse on the subjects involved. Without access to relevant information, the discussion is unlikely to be well founded or yield correct results.

However, the primary channels for education and communication seem to have a forbidden zone in areas most critical to humanity's survival. The major news media hardly even mention these matters; so-called media "experts" or pundits skirt the issues without ever getting to the core topics, glossing them over or not mentioning them at all.

For example, on 6 August 2001, CNN's discussion web site revealed many topics being explored, posting thousands of messages from all over the world. Only a couple were remotely connected to the survival of humanity.

One category, environmental policies, posted 2,898 messages. Some of the more recent messages revealed interest in specific topics in current news, such as drilling in the Arctic National Wildlife Refuge. However, there was little discussion of the larger issues and longer-range concerns expressed in this book.

A few correspondents raised larger issues, but only briefly and without much substance. This is an area where people are seemingly concerned about longer-range issues. Yet, they do not have a well-informed forum in which to discuss them.

With the explosive growth of the Internet, open and unfettered discussion is now possible everywhere. Even in countries with restrictive policies on communication exchange (such as China), access to the Internet opens a world of ideas, much as Radio Free Europe and Radio Liberty have been attempting for a long time. These offer at least one encouraging sign, and explorations of Internet information will provide much discussion and debate on topics relevant to the subjects discussed here.

A problem arises. This discussion and debate is not mirrored in the professional, trained, and full-time media. We expect our press to evaluate and interpret complex issues for us. Otherwise, why bother with a free press?

The marvelous freedom of the Internet comes with an important price. There are no controls on the accuracy, logic, or comprehensiveness of the information being transferred. Just because someone says something does not make it so. The proper role of journalism is to explore, gather information, evaluate and filter it, and present us not only the facts but also considered opinions on the issues. Little of this can be found today, where many "journalists" seem more intent on being media superstars with huge salaries rather than pursuing their traditional role with vigor and clarity.

Giant corporations are growing larger. Many are acquiring the media companies formerly available for free public expression. In consequence, the largest single vehicle for mass public education is now held captive by a hostile power. Some truly creative thought and action is needed to either wrest power from the multinationals and re-vest it with the people or to find and develop better alternatives.

The media reveals one remarkable contradiction. Right wing politicos are abandoning their traditionally conservative positions, pursuing radically *liberal* goals concerning the environment. The physician's dictum to "do no harm" is ignored as supposedly conservative businesspeople plunge ahead pursuing growth, development, and more powerful technology, without end in sight.

Supposedly "liberal" environmentalists are urging the engine to stop, or at least slow down. These people are asking that we take no action unless it can be demonstratively proven to have little impact on a sustainable future. With roles so reversed, the challenge of waking the people to the threats, informing them of the solid scientific support for the alarmist position, is one of the greatest to face humanity.

Meeting this challenge will require tremendous insight and creativity...by our leaders in academia, business, industry, media, and government — and by *we* the people. Creative insights and innovative problem solving must become a mantra of the new environmentalist.

References

1. Paul MacCready. "Thank Goodness I Owed $100,000." *R&D Innovator* Vol. 5, no. 6 (1996): June 1996, 1-3.
2. Paul B. MacCready, "Creativity," *The Solar Collector*, Florida Solar Energy Center, spring and summer, 1988: Speech at the Florida Solar Energy Center, Cape Canaveral, Florida, 1 May 1988.
3. Reprinted with the permission of the Free Press, a division of Simon and Shuster Adult Publishing Group, from *DEFYING THE CROWD: Cultivating Creativity in a Culture of Conformity* by Robert J. Sternberg and Todd I. Lubart. copyright (c) 1995 by Robert J. Sternberg and Todd I. Lubart. All rights reserved.
4. Paul B. MacCready, Unleashing Creativity, in *Symposium on The Inventor and Society*, Jerome and Dorothy Lamelson Center for the Study of Invention and Innovation, Smithsonian National Museum of American History, 1995.
5. Paul B. MacCready, "Gossamer Aircraft and Where they Lead," Manuscript, Undated. P. 6 dates the writing as 1990. Received from the author by R. McCluney September 2001.
6. *Richard P. Feynman. Meaning of It All: Thoughts of a Citizen Scientist.* October 1999 ed. Helix Books, Perseus Press: New York, 1999, 133 pp.
7. Richard P. Feynman, Edward Hutchings (Editor), Ralph Leighton, and Albert Hibbs (Introduction). *'Surely You're Joking Mr. Feynman' — Adventures of a Curious Character.* Reprint, (April 1997) ed. W.W. Norton & Company: New York, 1997, 350 pp.
8. Richard P. Feynman and Ralph Leighton. *What Do You Care What Other People Think?: Further Adventures of a Curious Character.* Paperback (January 2001) ed. W.W. Norton & Company: New York, 2001, 256 pp.
9. Laurie M. Brown and John S. Rigden, ed. *"Most of the Good Stuff" Memories of Richard Feynman.* American Institute of Physics: New York, 1993, pp. 181.
10. R. B. Zajonc. "Attitudinal Effects of Mere Exposure." *Journal of Personality and Social Psychology Monograph Supplement* Vol. 9, (1968), 1-27.
11. James Redford. "Political Ecotactics in South Florida." In *The Environmental Destruction of South Florida*, 7th printing, 1990 ed, edited by Ross McCluney. University of Miami Press: Coral Gables, FL, 1971, 100-105 pp.

16
Changing Minds, Changing Behaviors
Motivations to change.
Key ingredients of effective change.

Self love forsook the path it first pursued
and found the private in the public good.
— Alexander Pope, *Essay on Man* (1734)

Beliefs guide behavior. We cannot change our destructive actions without changing our hearts, and this can only be accomplished by changes in the ways we think about things. For these to happen in the appropriate direction we will need a new cosmology. For our beliefs to become more appropriate to our situations here on Earth in the new millennium, they must be firmly grounded on an understanding of our past and the future possibilities — a new story.

Here we focus on the next step, living in accord with the new story. We emphasize the practical—what it takes to make lasting behavior changes.

Behaviors and Values

Roberta Miller points out that scientific research on the alterations we see in the Earth's surface and atmosphere has not adequately accounted for human action[1]: "Physical scientists are beginning to recognize that their knowledge of the physical processes of terrestrial or atmospheric change is incomplete without some understanding of the ways human action sets those processes in motion or modifies them. Similarly, biologists and ecologists have begun to realize that the critical element in their study of ecological systems is human action. Social scientists argue that the research task is broader than natural scientists know; we must understand patterns of behavior and interactions far more complex than the relatively straightforward nexus between individual and environment."

Shrader-Frechette links behaviors to values[2]: "If environmental degradation were purely, or even primarily, a problem demanding scientific or technological solutions, then its resolution would probably have been accomplished by now. As it is, however, our crises of pollution and resource depletion reflect profound difficulties with some of the most basic principles in our accepted systems of values. They challenge us to assess the adequacy of those principles and, if need be, to discover a new framework for describing what it means to behave ethically or to be a moral person."

Behaviors and Thought Processes

To change directions, we must alter ingrained behavior patterns and thought processes. The AIDS crisis has stimulated research on behavior and what it takes to change the behavior patterns leading to infection. The AIDS epidemic is altering the human population in regions where it is widespread and growing rapidly.

Evidence supports that overpopulation of the planet, coupled with an increasingly mobile society, promotes the spread of viral infections faster than we can develop effective defenses.

Anne and Paul Ehrlich pointed this out in their 1971 textbook *Population, Resources, Environment.* Their predictions seem to be coming true as the AIDS epidemic spreads rapidly and scientists have trouble finding effective defense mechanisms.

The news from Africa is very frightening. In Zimbabwe AIDS is killing alarming numbers of people. In some parts of Africa, thirty percent of the population is infected.

AIDS in Africa

Approximately 3.5 million Africans became infected in 2001, bringing the total number of adults and children living with HIV/AIDS in this region to 28.5 million. The estimated number of children orphaned by AIDS living in the region is 11 million.

Some 2.2 million Africans died of AIDS in 2001. It is projected that, between 2000 and 2020, 55 million Africans will die earlier than they would have in the absence of AIDS....

The epidemic's toll continues to mount, even in countries already experiencing very high HIV prevalence rates. The number of AIDS-related deaths among young adults in South Africa, for example, is expected to peak in 2010-2015, when it is estimated that there will be more than 17 times as many deaths among persons aged 15-34 as there would have been without AIDS.

At least 10% of those aged 15-49 are infected in 12 African countries. Seven countries, all in southern Africa, now have prevalence rates higher than 20%: Botswana (38.8%), Lesotho (31%), Namibia (22.5%), South Africa (20.1%), Swaziland (33.4%), Zambia (21.5%) and Zimbabwe (33.7%).

—*UNAIDS fact sheet on sub-Saharan Africa, July 2002 http://www.unaids.org/en/media/fact+sheets.asp*

Some see the AIDS epidemic as Nature's way of correcting population excesses. People on the edge of existence have few resources to make changes, to protect themselves from serious threats such as these. Most must rely on outside help and financial and technical assistance.

AIDS is a clear and immediate threat to humanity. Amelioration of its consequences depends on radical changes in the compulsive behavior patterns (sexual promiscuity without condoms, intravenous drug abuse, and even normal sexual intercourse between lifetime partners) of many people. Because of the magnitude of the threat, the United Nations and other organizations are spending millions of dollars each year to educate the public and prevent the spread of the virus.

Scientists and social engineers have embarked upon a grand experiment to get large numbers of people to change unhealthy behaviors. Their methods and the successes of them are important, especially as we attempt to change other destructive, almost equally addictive, behaviors.

We might say that the current growth-is-good, more-growth-is-better, Earth-depleting economic system is as addictive as drugs and as compulsive as sex.

Changing Earth-depleting behavior patterns may be as challenging as changing AIDS-spreading behaviors. Examining the nature of human behavior change could be our most important pursuit at the beginning of the twenty first century.

Factors Contributing to Effective Personal Change

According to a 1988 article on AIDS-related social engineering in *Science*:

> "It seems that altering deeply ingrained behaviors is not like flipping a switch. Some individuals are recalcitrant, a few will never change, many do not even believe that they are at risk, and others need a lot of help," says Thomas Coates of the University of California at San Francisco. Researchers know that humans are capable of dramatic behavior modifications. But the scientists are not really sure why. Nor are they in agreement about how to speed up the process.... In order to change a behavior, the experts say, people must first recognize the fact that they are at risk; then they must be told how best to navigate around the danger.... They must then believe in their own ability to change and in the value of the new and improved conduct.... Finally, the new behaviors must become the "normative" ones in the community, so that they are constantly

reinforced.... In the business of behavior change, researchers say that these community norms are the most important thing of all.

"One of the biggest problems is that information doesn't do much," says Nathan Maccoby of the Stanford Center for Research in Disease Prevention. "In order for the information...to begin working, the threat...must be perceived as real, immediate, close to home. The problem is that people deny risk." "People are very creative when it comes to reasons why their own risk is not high," says Neil Weinstein of Rutgers University.... "Unfortunately, something must break into a person's own life before he'll do anything about it," says Howard Leventhal of Rutgers. The real trick, say public health workers, is to get people's attention focused on behavior modification before rates of [personal disaster] become such that [the problem] is nearly impossible to ignore. But there is a great deal of debate about exactly how to do this.[3]

If information doesn't do much, then neither the Internet, nor reforming the media will save us. This pressures leaders to become better informed and to initiate change, from the top down and from the bottom up.

Fen Rhodes of California State University at Long Beach, studying the role fear plays in individual change, found the highest fear messages to be the most effective. However, for fear to be an effective motivation, experts agree it must be coupled with a solution—viable alternative behavior patterns with no loss in the enjoyment of life (even better when the new lifestyle is perceived as an *increase* in the quality of life.) Environmentalists have this in their favor, and it is the focus of messages by prominent writers and speakers in the burgeoning Earth ethics movement. A sustainable society is a better society.

According to the *Science* article, AIDS researchers are finding that the most effective factor in achieving behavior change lies not with working on relatively few individuals. "If we think about changing behavior one by one, the epidemic will be over before we're through. You've got to change community norms and standards," says Larry Bye, founder of a Stop AIDS project in San Francisco.

"In the beginning a certain amount of brainwashing may have to take place," says Bye. He believes that if a certain percentage of a population — say 10% to 20% — adopts an innovation, the behavior will become the norm throughout the community. Elizabeth Moss Cantor confirms, saying the number is about 20%.

Accurate information is a necessary first step to environmental reform. But it is, in itself, insufficient to stimulate required changes. Clearly, for real and lasting behavior change to take place:

1. A person must know that the current behavior is destructive.

2. A person must know there is another, alternate behavior that avoids the destruction.

3. The alternate behavior should be seen as something he or she can do.

4. It is helpful if the alternative behavior is seen as an improvement, as something desired.

5. The new behavior must become the established norm in the community.

Telling the Truth

Truth has a way of pushing aside certain obstacles. Giving people the truth about our environmental crisis can go a long way toward initiating the steps listed above.

Leaders in government, business, and the media have a special responsibility—to spread the word about good paths to the future.

However, humanity generally resists change. As Zajonc points out, "Despite the fact that many people claim to value novel ideas, there is solid evidence that they don't much like exactly what they supposedly value... people like what is most familiar."[4]

The previously mentioned "mere-exposure effect"[4, p.20] can be a powerful tool for change. The more people are exposed to the new ideas the more comfortable they will be with them and the easier it will be to initiate change.

"What is considered true is often disputed." So just "telling the truth" will be insufficient. It must be coupled with good evidence that the crisis is real and requires serious behavior modification.

The fifth requirement for real and lasting change is probably the most important and the most difficult. Who wants to be the first to establish a new trend? Mankind likes to follow practices that are already up and running. However, if the first four components are in place, Bye and Cantor suggest that even a few community members can establish the new pattern as the norm.

Environmentally, most people realize we are facing serious environmental problems. They are already predisposed to make changes, but need good information and a viable alternative. They need friends, acquaintances, family, and neighbors to help them make the steps toward a better way of living. Even if only a few of these associates get the ball rolling, the others will find it easier to follow suit.

Many individuals amongst us see the threats, heed the warnings of our best scientists, and are taking action to reverse the trend. Even some of our young people (those with the most to lose if we fail) are attempting to take the historical role of the elders, and many feel they are succeeding.

In one sense they *are* succeeding. Environmental awareness is up; energy conservation and recycling programs are growing. But will these efforts be sufficient? This is a real case where the law of averages will prevail. It is not what the few *can* do but what the many really do that will count in the long run.

Human Change History

Throughout history, humanity has been very reluctant to change. We can argue that such reluctance is built into our makeup.

The long-time stability of early humans perhaps imprinted this human reluctance to change. Pfeiffer explains: "Hunting-gathering had far more than habit to recommend it. It persisted not simply by the sheer power of inertia, the resistance to change of any kind, but for a number of positive reasons. The human species was in harmony with nature, one among many wild species living together as parasites of sunlight in cycles of birth and decay. Prey as well as predator, consumed as well as consumer, humans were part of the chain of being as they have never been since. Settling down and congregating in larger and larger groups had serious disadvantages."[5]

The advanced brains which early humans eventually developed gave them (and us) a special, ability to see things in new ways — future things and things in other places.

Change in the lives of early hominids and humans took place very slowly. Almost imperceptible to the life of any one individual, it never really stopped its relentless progression.

"Hominids had to change," says Pfeiffer. "They arose at the margins of things, in transition zones where diverse landscapes merged imperceptibly with one another." "The first hominid was a creature in transition, moving in and out of transition zones, then as now a breed on the make, in the process of becoming something radically different." Slow change was part of us initially. Only later did it accelerate.

"The increasing complexity of life on African savanna favored an increasingly complex nervous system, a larger memory and a greater capacity for weighing and choosing among an increasing number of alternative actions. This process had major repercussions."[5, p. 52] For one thing, it led to an increasing need for language, further expansion of the brain, and increasing migration, eventually taking humans all over the globe. Thus began the inexorable march toward ever more complex societies and economic systems. The ever-increasing pace of change has brought us now to this new turning point in the structure of our society. It is the first major turning point that humans have a chance to consciously direct.

Is this a case of natural evolution, of humans adapting to their surroundings? I doubt it. The coming change must take place very quickly, in too short a time to alter our genetic makeup, our species identity — unless genetic engineering becomes widespread and popular, quickly. How likely is the latter technique to become widely available?

In 1998, Ralph Nader quoted Prof. Lee Silver, microbiologist at Princeton University, as saying there will be, "within a few hundred years, two classes of human beings, which he describes as the 'gen-rich' class, [the] genetically enriched class, and the 'naturals' who never had the money to continually genetically enrich their physical and mental capabilities. And, with full seriousness, he said the time would come when they will not even be able to procreate across each other's lines. They'll be as attractive to one another, as he put it, as a human being is today with a chimpanzee. This is not science fiction. The onset of humanoids produced by commercial establishments is only a few decades away."[6,7]

Will this be the way we humans save ourselves? Will we use technology to shortcut natural evolution, seeking to make ourselves better able to achieve sustainability, increasing the average Human Capability Index? Or, is it a shortcut to disaster?

At a September 1993 meeting in Dublin titled "What is Life?" it was claimed that (non-human) natural selection is still occurring on many fronts (found, for example, in studies of genetic resistance and susceptibility to infectious disease). Manfred Eigen (Nobel laureate and director of the Max Planck Institute in Gottingen) identified population growth as the most urgent of the many problems confronting humans. To feed the world's population in 50 years' time will require great ingenuity, according to Eigen, including the use of nuclear power and genetic engineering to increase crop yields. He concluded that we do not have much time left to prove that we are not the products of a lethal mutation.[8]

We find humanity *beginning* to grasp the ominous threats facing it and taking initial steps in the right direction. The problem lies in the many definitions of *right direction*. The cornucopians believe that we are already changing, rapidly, and in ways bound to extricate us from our difficulties — producing a world of such material affluence and prosperity that only science fiction writers can grasp. The tree huggers believe that this is the path toward a seeable cliff; it is folly to continue our present direction, knowing what we now know. But we don't all know it. Many deny its truth. Many others don't seem to care, focusing only on more immediate problems.

Referring to Thomas Kuhn's *The Structure of Scientific Revolutions,* Donella Meadows writes, "What ultimately causes a paradigm to change is the accumulation of anomalies — observations that do not fit into and cannot be explained by the prevailing paradigm. The anomalies have to be presented over and over because there is a social determination not to see them."[9] This is a source of hope for those committed to transforming industrial society. The longer the current paradigm holds sway, the more of these anomalies we'll see, and be unable to *not* see them.

The globe will be warming, so much that we can no longer ignore it. What E. O. Wilson calls "keystone species" will go extinct, and because they are keystones in the foundation of ecosystems, their passing will be very noticed. As the petroleum supply decreases, the prices for all its products will increase, hardly an ignorable event. Other environmental problems will grow worse and will affect us in more noticeable ways.

The Turning Point

Human civilization is at a turning point. Our special power of future perception may become dominant, leading us as a species to make correct choices about living and preparing for the future, or it will fail to do so and we will continue to drift toward the precipice of species annihilation. Which way we will go remains to be seen.

The pessimistic observer might conclude that we are currently driven by our baser, more infantile, instinct for personal gratification. So we will not make sacrifices today needed for survival tomorrow. The optimist sees many signs that we are realizing the danger and acting on those realizations. We cannot yet tell which of these viewpoints is correct. In another decade or two we shall know. Hopefully by that time, we won't be too late.

Our special human developmental trait — the ability to act to protect the future — is the one thing that will decide the survival of the Earth's human species. Either we take this important developmental leap — becoming better humans directly and/or giving resources to our elders with instructions to use them on our behalf. Or we will descend to an even more narcissistic way of life, hoping against all hope that the cliff is not there…that we can somehow successfully "grow our way into the future."

The elements required for successful change are clear. To initiate them will require leadership, personal dedication, and political courage.

References

1. Roberta Balstead Miller. "Global Change Research Challenges Social Science." *The AAAS Observer*, (1989): 7 July 1989, 5.
2. K. S. Shrader-Frechette. *Environmental Ethics*. The Boxwood Press: Pacific Grove, CA, 1981.
3. William Booth. "Social Engineers Confront AIDS." Excerpted with permission from William Booth, SCIENCE 242:1237 (1988). Copyright 1988 American Association for the Advancement of Science.
4. R. B. Zajonc. "Attitudinal Effects of Mere Exposure." *Journal of Personality and Social Psychology Monograph Supplement* Vol. 9, (1968), 1-27.
5. John E. Pfeiffer. *The Emergence of Society — A Prehistory of the Establishment*. McGraw-Hill: New York, 1977, 512 pp.
6. Ralph Nader. "Civil Society and Corporate Responsibility," C-Span Videotape, Number 102676, Washington, DC.
7. Lee M. Silver. *Remaking Eden: How Genetic Engineering and Cloning Will Transform the American Family*. Avon Books: New York, 1998, 385 pp.
8. Luke O'Neill, Michael Murphy, and Richard B. Gallagher. "What Are We? Where Did We Come From? Where Are We Going?" *Science* 263, (1994): 14 January 1994, 181-183.
9. Donella H. Meadows. *The Global Citizen*. Island Press: Washington, DC, 1991, 300 pp.

17
Earth Learning

Education is critical.
Earth from experience, not just from books.

In the end, we will conserve only what we love,
we will love only what we understand, and
we will understand only what we are taught.
— Baba Dioum, Senegalese conservationist

The child wasn't concerned about the alligators most likely surrounding her as she waded hip deep in a tree-canopied Florida swamp with her parents. A tiny inchworm captivated her attention with its antics on the back of her hand.

We adults were nervous about the danger we perceived surrounding us. But, trusting our leader, we followed him to the edge of a large opening in the trees, the water now reaching our waists.

We had reached an active alligator hole but were told not to worry; our noise and movement would scare away anything potentially harmful. We were excited at being in such a special place and slightly apprehensive because of the novelty of the experience.

After some prodding, everyone quieted down and remained still for a few minutes. We relaxed and enjoyed the wait. The beautiful birds we had chased away by our raucous invasion returned. This was the kind of experience remembered for a lifetime, common to many who venture outdoors on a regular basis.

Such experiences are rare in today's world of high rises, shopping malls, crowded streets, and dangerous neighborhoods. Yet experiences such as this may be the essential motivating force for the changes we need to make — to protect wild areas for wild animals and the whole planet for all of us.

Wildness sometimes offers danger, if you are not familiar with the laws of the wild and venture unprepared and clueless of it. Armed with knowledge, and a bit of caution, we can keep the danger to a minimum.

The rewards are worth the effort. Few make that effort, perhaps because they have never experienced the joys of wilderness and the beauties of nature in a close and personal way.

In the 1980s several researchers interviewed environmentalists about the origins of their commitment to activism. The responses generally identified two sources: "many hours spent outdoors in a keenly remembered wild or semi-wild place in childhood or adolescence, and an adult who taught respect for nature,"[1] according to a quote by Louise Chawla, describing the results of papers by Borden (1986), Chawla (1989), Peterson and Hungerford (1981), and Tanner (1980).

Even when we cannot visit wildernesses, most of us still value trees, flowers, and natural vegetation. We fill our yards — and sometimes our houses — with remnants of the forgotten wild. The more isolated we are, however, the less we know and the more we fear the outdoors. (I knew a lady who decorated her house only with plastic flowers, because the real plants "are so icky.... They might have bugs in them." At least she recognized her need for even plastic imitations of nature.)

Learning Nature

There is something inspiring and uplifting about spending quality time in a wilderness. Our great national parks, perhaps the last refuges in the U.S. for a semblance of wilderness, invite those willing to enjoy them. Anyone can visit, explore, and learn. The ecosystems you see are living, breathing, dynamic entities, revealing the face of Nature in its unadulterated genuineness. (There are exceptions, of course. Many — if not all — of our national parks are facing human pressures that threaten their core naturalness. The law establishing them does make it clear that the primary role of the National Park Service is to protect their wildness.)

This is learning Earth — a natural and automatic process among aboriginal/indigenous peoples. But the rest of us (save for a fortunate few) have isolated ourselves from such immersive Earth experiences, and we are the poorer for it.

If lost thrills and excitement were the only consequences, I guess we could live with them. But an additional result is a certain audacity that comes from thinking you are superior to and in control of something you do not really understand. Earth, in its wildness can be dangerous, but we humans can manage the danger. Can we also manage the whole Earth in a sustainable way?

In the last several decades we have learned that to save ourselves, we must save the Earth. To save the Earth, we must learn again to love it. This is, perhaps, the most important part of an environmental education for the industrial world. Learning Earth from books is useful if the child is developmentally adequate to the task, but there is no substitute for direct observation, personal experience, and guidance from an informed adult.

Loving Earth is not enough, either. We must also know a lot about it. In the last century or two, we have taken it upon ourselves to become planetary spacemen—the operators of Spaceship Earth. In order to operate it properly, we must know how it functions. It once got along just fine, on its own, without human intervention.

As we take over much of its operation, tweaking ecosystems here and atmospheric ones there, we risk doing something seriously wrong. To have any hope of avoiding a resulting calamity, we need a thorough grounding in the basics of planetary operation.

This cannot be left just to our scientists, engineers, and politicians. If they are mistaken, the rest of us face tragedy.

The issue is too important to leave in the hands of a chosen few. This knowledge must become universal. All of us must become Earth-literate again.

Earth Literacy

Education takes place informally, both at home for preschoolers and more generally in adulthood. Formal education in school and college, generally thought to be more efficient, is more structured and intentional. All are important places for introducing environmental education.

An article in the spring, 2000, issue of *Clearing* focused on interdependence as a cornerstone. "In its fullest sense, environmental education concerns the individual's relationship to his or her total environment, including the built environment as well as the natural. Every course taught has something to do with how people relate to each other and to their world.

"From every corner of the curriculum, there can emerge the skills, attitudes and information students need for a creative approach to their environment. The major goal of environmental education is helping students learn to use all their senses to 'connect' them with their natural and human-made surroundings. Each of us shapes and is shaped by the environment. The challenge to educators is to provide an education that will enable people to recognize areas of individual and group responsibility for their surroundings. They can then work intelligently toward structuring a healthy environment, instead of passively accepting whatever they find around them. Such a goal becomes increasingly vital as our world becomes more crowded and more urbanized."[2]

Environmental education, be it formal or informal, must begin by developing a comprehensive understanding of the human place in the long sweep of natural history since Earth was formed.

The Great Forgetting

Essential knowledge of Earth and how it operates was once familiar to nearly every human adult as a matter of survival. Then came that first great transformation of human culture — the invention of what turned out to be industrial agriculture and the formation of civilization. Soon after this tremendous event some 5,000 or so years ago, the growing fraction of humans involved in agriculture, in cities, and in civilization seemed to forget their true origins. They focused on a fairy-tale-like accounting of human prehistory, neglecting the long span of our hunting-gathering past. Quinn calls this "the Great Forgetting." Afterward, "There was, of course, utterly no memory left of humanity's tribal past, extending back hundreds of thousands of years."[3, p. 114]

A relearning of this history can precede basic topics in astronomy, geology, physics, chemistry, and biology — all related to Earth's operation. Basic ecology must be a required subject. If not standing alone, then at least it must be incorporated into other courses. To get it right, we'll have to know how the system worked, sustainably, for billions of years, and how humans lived sustainably on Earth for the million or two of their own years.

Basic features of a variety of subjects (such as population biology, the evolution of the species, weather and climate, and agronomy) must become standard in every thinking adult's knowledge base. This must become the century of environmental education, with every aspect of our lives incorporating what we've learned.

According to St. Louis psychologist Dr. Dianne Benjamin, "The first step in environmental education is exposing youngsters (as well as adults) to the 'magical' wonders of nature. The process of experiencing nature personally can be replicated over and over, as a foundation for motivation to learn new information."

The Glorious Remembering

We must relearn what we have forgotten, accentuated and deepened by the enormous quantity of scientific knowledge we have acquired. Importantly, we must access what we know about the great hunting and gathering societies of the world, over their million-year history.

As Quinn has said, "For hundreds of thousands of years, people as smart as you had a way of life that worked well for them. The descendants of these people can today still be found here and there, and wherever they're found in an untouched state, they give every evidence of being perfectly content with their way of life. They're not at war with each other, generation against generation or class against class. They're not plagued by anguish, anxiety, depression, self-hatred, crime, madness, alcoholism, and drug addiction. They don't complain of oppression and injustice. They don't describe their lives as meaningless and empty. They're not seething with hatred and rage. They don't look into the sky, yearning for contact with gods and angels and prophets and alien spacemen and spirits of the dead. And they don't wish someone would come along and tell him or her how to live. This is because they already know how to live."[3. p.114-115]

We don't need to learn how to live like these people do. That would be impossible. With today's huge population, a dozen more Earths would be needed for everyone to live like hunter-gatherers. But we *can* borrow some useful ideas from them, and from the sustainable Nature within which they did (and do) live. We can determine how best to redesign our own ways of living to be sustainable, rewarding, and fulfilling. To start the process, we must relearn at least some of the old ways. More than this, we need to have more comprehensive knowledge of Earth systems and ecology.

Some of the needed material is already incorporated into traditional K-12 education in the U.S. Much more is needed... more than just "material" or facts and figures. As previously emphasized, experiential observation is essential, as is personal exploration and involvement. The current formal educational system in the U. S. is inadequate to the task.

Short-Circuited Learning

Those who watch children grow from infancy to adolescence know that a young child's mind appears like a giant empty computer just waiting to be filled. They learn at prodigious rates. As Daniel Quinn puts it, "Small children are the most powerful learning engines in the known universe. They effortlessly learn as many languages as are spoken in their households. No one has to sit them down in a classroom and drill them on grammar and vocabulary. They do no homework; they have no tests, no grades. Learning their native languages is no chore at all, because of course it's immensely and immediately useful and gratifying to them."[3. p. 146] Children share a natural curiosity, excitement with the new, and an amazing ability to learn and retain information presented in stimulating and appropriate ways.

In *My Ishmael,* Quinn offered the following dialog between Ishmael and the 12-year-old writer of the account, which capsulates some of the failures of formal education in the U.S. He describes another child's experiences upon first starting school:

> Ishmael: "Like most five-year-olds, she was thrilled to be going off to school at last, and I was thrilled for her, imagining (as she did) that some truly wonderful experience must be awaiting her. It was only after several months that I began to notice that her excitement was fading — and continued to fade month after month and year after year, until, by the time she was in the third grade she was thoroughly bored and glad for any opportunity to miss a day of school. Does this all come as strange news to you?"
>
> Writer: "Yeah," I said with a bitter laugh. "Only about eighty million kids went to bed last night praying for six feet of snow to fall so the schools would have to close."
>
> Ishmael: "What one sees first is how far short real schooling falls from the ideal of 'young minds being awakened.' Teachers for the most part would be delighted to awaken young minds, but the system within which they must work fundamentally frustrates that desire by insisting that all minds must be opened in the same order, using the same tools, and at the same pace, on a certain schedule. The teacher is charged with getting the class as a whole to a certain predetermined point in the curriculum by a certain predetermined time, and the individuals that make up the class soon learn how to help the teacher with this task."[3, p. 131]

According to Quinn, students learn to help the teacher complete the schedule in several ways: 1) Don't tell the teacher you don't understand what's being said, 2) Don't ask seemingly irrelevant questions that pop into your head, 3) Never disagree or point out inconsistencies in what is being presented, especially if they are of a moral or ethical nature, and 4) always try to look like you understand every word spoken.[3]

This approach creates wasted time and energy and missed opportunities for all to learn the exciting things that interest them, and to learn the wonders of our world.

University Education

Students who can continue their educations into college necessarily enter a more formal learning pattern, though not quite so regimented. The students are adults (or are nearing adulthood), so they are given more responsibility for their own educations. Certain content is necessary, to have what is called a "well-rounded education" and to better fit the student for a job in the workforce.

Curriculum developers are given a special responsibility. In the traditional approach, the "faculty" decides what subjects must be taught to achieve educational goals for university graduates. (Today school or university administrators sometimes provide this function.) Some "essential subjects" are identified as requirements for the student to grow, develop, and enter the labor market with job skills and the basic understandings of government. Topics in the humanities and other subjects are also needed to enjoy life fully and be a good citizen. When the student has little curiosity or interest in the curriculum presented, the resulting education suffers.

This "professor knows best" system hopes that the resulting required courses provide the basic knowledge and understanding to meet life objectives. However, many college grads report that what they learned in school is only a small fraction of what is needed in industry. Employers, seldom expecting much from the educations received by their new employees, establish various training or experience-gathering programs within the company. As a consequence, most colleges and universities often attempt to do a better job at training their graduates for employment, further narrowing the curriculum.

As corporations exert increasing influence on higher education, colleges and universities turn away from their historic purpose of providing a good general education, trending toward making these institutions little more than training centers for job skills.[4] They unfortunately decrease emphasis on the larger issues of environmental reform and instead focus more on the details of the technologies causing the problems (and others intended to ameliorate them) rather than fixing the failed system of commerce which created them.

In some respects, the professor-knows-best system is a good one. It provides room in the curriculum for a larger exploration of life in all its forms and nuances — a truly "liberal arts" education. In the current context, however, few colleges and universities require courses on the broader aspects of the environmental crisis or on the thinking and other driving forces that have created it. When such courses are offered, they are generally electives, not required for graduation.

Such could be considered *the* most important course a college student can take. Schools that do require effective courses on these topics are paving the way for more massive and effective future reform. This practice should be expanded to all institutions of higher learning. (Florida Gulf Coast University is an encouraging example. As of this writing, a readings course which includes some material on environmental ethics is required of every student prior to graduation.)

Thomas Jefferson described the university as a place where "the illimitable freedom of the human mind to explore and expose every subject susceptible of its contemplation" would be provided. In *Campus, Inc.*, Ronnie Dugger, founder and co-chair of the Alliance for Democracy, writes that this Jeffersonian ideal is threatened by *gigantilism*, his term for the globalization of corporate capitalism on a gigantic scale. As mergers and acquisitions proceed apace, the current joke is that eventually everyone will work for Mobil. The resulting economic domination by corporate giants is pushing its way into higher education.

According to Rosemary Schofield in her review of *Campus, Inc.*, "University trustees are unelected and unaccountable. In a post-Cold War world ... the gigantilist outlook *is* the status quo, [and] unelected trustees and administrators hold the power to determine curriculum content and who may teach what...." Clearly such a development poses a threat to academic freedom. Schofield says that in *Free Speech on Campus*, its author Martin Golding "reminds us that it is not only ideas that suffer compromise: today's academic climate tends to sideline the very act of thinking objectively and constructively."[5, p. 48]

Universities did once pride themselves on being very open minded, supporting scholarship in numerous areas, allowing professors and students to explore their subjects wherever they might lead. Though they may still profess this ideal in their catalogues, most now are narrower in focus and nearly as regimented as high schools. Noam Chomsky calls them "the reinforcers of the status quo, the endorsers of intellectual and moral stasis." The universities should challenge the system. Instead they tend more and more toward producing "Obedient corporate drones," using Chomsky's words.

The subject is discussed more fully by White and Hauck[6]. In *The Shadow University*, Kors and Silvergate write, "It is vital that citizens understand the deeper crisis of our colleges and universities. Contrary to the expectations of most applicants, colleges and universities are not freer than the society at large. Indeed, they are less free, and that diminution is continuing apace. In a nation whose future depends upon education in freedom, colleges and universities are teaching the values of censorship, self-censorship, and self-righteous abuse of power.... Universities have become the enemy of a free society, and it is time for the citizens of that society to recognize this scandal of enormous proportions and to hold these institutions to account."[7] Restoring academic freedom wherever it might be lost is an important component of the environmental reform our campuses need.

College and university students are at the developmental stage whereby they can easily assimilate abstract ideas and understand remote actions. Colleges and universities should recognize these abilities and offer a rich assortment of information, ideas, and views on issues affecting directly the future of humanity. Exhorting faculties everywhere to decide what is most important for their students to learn, the universities should be in the forefront of requiring a broad education into the facts of human existence (including universe history, human history, and an exhaustive account of the growing human impact on Earth's life-support system).

Instead, they have nearly universally become training grounds for the corporations, largely abrogating their responsibilities to teach students what they most need to learn, about themselves and their futures. The consequence is an extensive environmental illiteracy amongst the most scholastically literate of our citizens.

Perhaps you consider my critique of the modern university education too strong and undeserving. If so, I urge you to speak with students and recent graduates, examine college catalogs, and find out what courses are required for graduation in a variety of subjects. I think you'll find that a curriculum rich in essential environmental topics, well populated by eager students, is the rare exception. Speak with faculty and ask them to what extent their administrations are influenced or even controlled by corporations and/or corporate values. Ask them how much they know of Earth's history and how much of it they teach in their courses.

Learning Models

As mentioned at the beginning of this chapter, too often our educational systems stifle curiosity. Even worse, through regimented book learning, it creates an abhorrence of learning. To regain some semblance of Earth literacy, not only do we need to reform the curriculum, but also the entire approach to education must be reconsidered.

A number of different approaches can be used to implement the needed changes. I classify them as mild, essential, progressive, and radical. The mild approach involves mainly the introduction of more earth-centered material into the curriculum. This one is becoming more widespread in public school systems in many countries and is an encouraging sign to many.

In the essential category, I believe, are systems that better match the educational process to the needs of the child, both developmentally and emotionally. These require a thorough understanding of the physical and biological history of the universe and Earth. A variety of alternative educational systems are found in this category. Ignas and Corsini wrote a book describing some of the models.[8]

My sons had the good fortune to receive some of their elementary education in one of the described systems, called "Individual Education" — later termed the "Corsini 4 R" system for its focus on developing responsibility, respect, resourcefulness, and responsiveness (in addition to offering the traditional "3Rs" of reading, writing, and arithmetic).

More progressive are those approaches which center nearly all the curriculum around Earth awareness, making all disciplines but a part of a total Earth learning process. Perhaps the most important new recognition, one addressed by the Corsini 4R system, is that children are different, have different needs and learning abilities, and tend to learn in different ways and at different paces. The educational system should be tailored to those individual abilities.

The radical category includes educational reform proposals calling for a restructuring of the whole educational process, "from the ground up," often literally. According to Quinn, pre-schooling societies were very open, in the sense that children were allowed to learn everything; they were not shut off from what the rest of the tribe knew or was doing. In *My Ishmael*, he suggests *maieutic* teaching, the sort practiced by Ishmael and Socrates. "The maieutic teacher acts as a midwife, bringing forth ideas from materials that are already in the student."[9]

In some respects, this approach can be more effective than any theoretical system yet devised by scholastic educators. Quinn describes the process as one of taking advantage of and enhancing the natural curiosity of young children, allowing them to imitate adults in a supportive environment.[3, p. 27] Following such an approach, the "curriculum" is postponed until an age where the student can best deal with it. In the interim, learning is made a natural part of life. Knowledge of the developmental abilities of students is essential.

David Sobel criticizes current environmental education when it introduces difficult or abstract concepts at too young an age. "The crux of the issue is the developmental appropriateness of environmental education curriculum. Rainforest curricula may be perfectly appropriate in middle or high school, but I'm not sure it belongs in the primary grades in elementary schools."[1] "Developmental psychology has much to offer to environmental educators who are anxious to avoid falling into the trap of premature abstraction." John Burroughs once said, "Knowledge without love will not stick. But if love comes first, knowledge is sure to follow."

Ecophobia or Ecophilia?

Ecophilia has been defined as the inherent human biological tendency to bond with the natural world. The younger we do this, the easier it is. Instead, modern western civilization, and the manipulating artificial educational system it has fostered, remove people from the natural world. People are put into Nature-isolated classrooms with structured schedules that seem more designed to stifle their natural curiosities and excitements about things new and interesting than to encourage learning for the shear pleasure of it.

If we don't give young children a way to experience environmental issues directly, to learn from Earth itself, they'll have great difficulty understanding the larger environmental, ecological, and sociological issues involved. They may also develop *ecophobia*, a fear of ecology, a fear of both named and unknown consequences of collapsing ecosystems. Once young children see the adult world as speeding us toward ecosystem collapse, such fears and phobias are not surprising.

In teaching about Nature (especially with young children), we must not present depressing abstract ideas about ecosystem losses, without giving them a chance to experience actual ecosystems "up close and personal." In the winter, 1995, issue of *Earth Ethics*, David Sobel described the problem at some length. His thesis is that environmental education, in the context of traditional public and private schools, is more like indoctrination of mostly isolated and abstract concepts than a stimulation of true and open learning and understanding. He says that we are, in effect, "logging our own children." His point is that primary and elementary grades are just too early to introduce, for example, rainforest curricula, and other complex environmental issues.

"For young children, children in kindergarten through third or fourth grade, this technique is counterproductive. Lurking underneath these environmentally correct curricula is the assumption that if children see the horrible things that are happening, then they, too, will be motivated to make a difference. But those images can have an insidious, nightmarish effect on young children whose sense of time, place, and self are still forming. Newspaper photographs of homes destroyed by California wildfires are disturbing to my seven-year-old New Hampshire daughter because she immediately personalizes them. 'Is that fire near here? Will our house burn down? What if we have a forest fire?' she queries, because for her, California is right around a psychic corner. What's important is that children have an opportunity to bond with the natural world, to learn to love it and feel comfortable in it, before being asked to heal its wounds."

Sobel's solution: "No rain forest curriculum, no environmental action, just opportunities to be in the natural world with a modeling responsible adult.... We need a scheme, a big picture, of the relationship between the natural world and the development of the person." Citing Joseph Chilton Pearce's *The Magical Child*, Sobel says that, "Growing up, the individual moves through the mother/family matrix for the first seven years, then moves into the earth matrix for the second seven years." Attempting to achieve an academic Earth sense prematurely can backfire, or worse, produce ecophobia.

Sobel recommends that young children spend more time outdoors, especially in more natural areas. He concludes, "These new homes in the wilds, and the journeys of discovering, are the basis for bonding with the natural world. Children desire immersion, solitude, and interaction in a close, knowable world. We take children away from the landscapes that they draw strength from when we ask them to deal with far away ecosystems and environmental problems."

Instead of trying to teach young children about the problems of rain forest destruction, wouldn't it be better to take them to a real rain forest and show them how it works and what is happening to it? The practical limitations of such an approach are obvious, in which case Sobel suggests the topic be postponed until the student is better able to deal with abstract knowledge.[1]

In the higher grades, where students are more comfortable with abstract thinking and intellectual learning, teaching about environmental problems in far-away places is more acceptable. Even in these grades, however, field trips to natural areas offer inestimable benefit. In the light of the real situations facing children in the U. S. today, sending all to wilderness areas to live for extended periods is fraught with obstacles (not the least of which is the need for permission from parents and fears of educational administrators).

Sobel calls for just spending a little more time outdoors, in the cities and neighborhoods where children live and play. This serves as a more practical way to introduce important environmental values without the difficulties of field trips or foreign travel. Unfortunately, as important social systems break down, increasing threats to child safety are keeping them indoors at a time when outdoor experience is most critical.

The pragmatist in me sympathizes with Sobel and worried parents. I understand the limitations that the current social and economic systems impose on us, making out-of-school experiences difficult. However, if we continue to let pragmatism and fear control our policies and strategies, keeping children from the places they really need to be, we run the risk of losing not only the existing educational system but the life-support system itself.

Most children are born with a natural affinity for nature, their ecophilia. A thorough and effective environmental education will enhance this ecophilia. The traditional way fails to properly educate about the most important things. With good intentions, it can counter the very goal it seeks to provide: happy children who love nature and are comfortable in the outdoors.

To avoid stifling natural curiosity about the world and how it operates, more opportunities should be sought to get children outside. They should explore the region where they live, with a knowledgeable naturalist as a guide, opening up the mysteries and complexities of ecosystems directly, personally. The essential (and "dull") but obligatory subjects would be postponed until later grades.

Experience teaches that children desire to learn interesting new stuff. If it is relevant to their current lives, they have a higher degree of retention of the material. Teaching children about things they really do not want or need at an early age merely stifles their enthusiasm for learning and short-circuits the learning process.

Far better would be if the teacher, and the whole school system, served as facilitators for self-directed inquiry, enablers of experiential learning, and stimulators of young minds. For the first several years of elementary school, teaching children subjects not immediately useful to them would be unnecessary. More structured learning could be introduced at a later age, perhaps in the teen years. Match the curriculum to the child's developmental age, abilities, and needs.

Here's a suggested three-point approach:

1. *Emphasize play and fun outdoors*. Ask questions. Teach children to ask their own questions, about what they see and what you're "teaching" them about the world around them. View teachers as the child's assistant, helping them to ask and answer questions. This is a good time to begin building early skills at directed inquiry. "How do we find out about this, Johnny?" With this skill, children will have confidence in their abilities to find out nearly anything in nearly any subject. Their curiosity about nature and how it came into being and how we know this, can be parlayed into a thorough education about their environment, and about important moral and ethical issues relating to Earth as well.

2. *Guide inquiry* into areas of interest of each individual child. Introduce the concept that sometimes we need to learn tools, such as mathematics, to answer other questions. Give examples where other subjects are needed to

answer exciting questions in the first one. Promote educational research into finding more ways of introducing new environmental subjects in non-threatening, exciting, enticing ways. For example, the teacher might illustrate some math tricks, then ask an interesting math question, and show how simple math skills can solve it. If related to something they are learning about nature, so much the better.

3. *Promote scholastic learning.* As children grow and mature, explain that the mode of education of the early grades, while fun and interesting, can be inefficient in some disciplines where a lot of knowledge is needed in a relatively short time. In such cases there is more to learn and a certain degree of accelerated, more regimented, learning is essential. This can provide motivation for a shift toward more structured learning.

Take your pick

Education is one of the places most in need of change. If you are comfortable only with mild reform, introducing a more Earth-centered curriculum, then work in your local schools toward that goal. If you favor more active change, help teachers get students out on field trips to nature parks and other natural areas. If you desire a deeper change in the system, an inherently political act, then get other people to join you and work together for the desired change.

Though not formally trained in education, I've had a lot of experience as a student. (K-12, 4 years of college, I won't say how many of grad school, and I've taught a few classes myself, at all levels.) I feel sufficiently qualified by this experience, and what I've read, to assert that education first needs to be more fun and adventurous, taking advantage of our natural curiosities. Secondly, whatever learning system you choose, at least four fundamentals need full coverage: 1) the depth of our environmental problem and its origin, 2) an introduction to big picture, whole systems thinking, 3) a good grounding in Earth history, and 4) a full understanding of the arguments favoring fundamental and major societal and economic system reform.

Some environmental material presented in the classroom can be controversial and can result in pressure to change it. Often this diverts discussion from the thoughts propounded, and into a debate over academic freedom and the rights of teachers and students. Of the four fundamentals needing coverage, the first three should not be very susceptible to these distractions. Factual scientific evidence (coupled with informed opinions from many scholars on matters difficult to decide on scientific grounds alone) can hardly be deemed controversial. The fourth one, dealing to some extent with future projections and how best to handle them, is necessarily more debatable and opinionated. Such debate, however, should easily fall within the scope of freedom of speech and its university counterpart, academic freedom.

So let us not be timid. The issue is important and urgent.

I favor the more radical end of the educational reform scale. Perhaps this is a consequence of my own personal difficulties in school. Like the whole of society, however, small reforms in education — patchwork attempts to fix portions of a defective system — are unlikely to succeed in the long run.

To start needed reforms, the process may have to begin with the mild reforms, progressing thereafter to the more substantive ones. The problem, as always, is that one can be deceived when making modest changes into thinking they are sufficient. A large danger looms if we fail to make a significant change now, before it's too late. This is perhaps less important in education reform than in reforming the structure of a culture, but it seems that one goes with the other.

Though there is now much more official environmental education in the schools, that education is weakened by a need for political correctness and a desire to avoid controversy. Since the outside ambient culture only marginally supports what is taught, the lessons learned in school are easily forgotten and considered of little relevance to students' lives. Changing this is the great educational challenge of the new century.

References

1. David Sobel. "Ecophobia." *Earth Ethics* Vol. 6, no. 2 (1995): Winter 1995, p.3.
2. Anonymous. "Interdependence – A concept approach to environmental education." *Clearing*. Vol. 106, Spring 2000, p. 22.
3. Daniel Quinn. *My Ishmael, A Sequel*. Bantam Books: New York, 1997.
4. Martin P. Golding. *Free Speech on Campus*. Rowman and Littlefield: Lanham, MD, 2000, 118 pp.
5. Rosemary J. Schofield. "Campus Politics and Academic Freedom." *Free Inquiry* Vol. 21, no. 4, Fall 2001, pp. 48-49. A review of *Campus, Inc.*, ed. Geoffry D. White, Prometheus: Amherst (2000) and *Free Speech on Campus*, Martin Golding, Rowman and Littlefield: Lanham, MD, (2000).
6. Geoffrey D. White and Flannery C. Hauck, ed. *Campus, Inc.: Corporate Power in the Ivory Tower*. Prometheus Books: Amherst, NY, 2000, pp. 470.
7. Alan Charles Kors and Harvey A. Silvergate. *The Shadow University: The Betrayal*

of Liberty on America's Campuses. HarperPerennial: New York, 1998, 414 pp.

8. Edward Ignas and Raymond J. Corsini. *Alternative Educational Systems.* F. E. Peacock Publishers: Itasca, Illinois, 1979, 423 pp.

9. Daniel Quinn "Comments on education," (e-mail communication), 2001, to William Ross McCluney, 20 December 2001.

18
The Stoppers
Denial, psychological blocks, faulty world views,
problematic political beliefs, misinformation.

The need for change has been amply demonstrated. We might all agree that some change is needed to protect our future. We do not agree, however, on how much change we need, how it should be effected, when it is needed, or who should do the changing.

We have trouble with this for many reasons. Perhaps the most important is lack of knowledge and understanding. Lack of vision and courage on the part of our leaders is another. Even when we start out with good intentions to discover the nature of our problems and structure solutions to them, we often find ourselves being blocked along the way.

I call the reasons we fail to act "the stoppers". They stop us dead in our tracks, inhibiting not only change but also full discussion of the nature of the problems and possible alternatives. In this chapter several stoppers are examined. These are the inhibitors that keep us from doing what needs to be done.

Lack of Information

In Chapter 16 five components were listed as needed for effective long-term behavior change. Failure of any one constitutes a stopper.

The first four are informational in nature. Lack of the needed information in any of those four steps is a serious inhibitor. The fifth one, making the new behavior an established norm in the community, is less informational but more sociological, political, and psychological. (Psychological stoppers are discussed in the next section. Here we focus on the first component of effective behavior change, the need for good information.)

David Orr says, "Literacy is the ability to read. Numeracy is the ability to count." Environmental literacy is the ability to read the Earth, where it has been, where it is, and where it is going. According to Orr:

> The failure to develop ecological literacy is a sin of omission and of commission. Not only are we failing to teach the basics about the Earth

and how it works, but we are in fact teaching a large amount of stuff that is simply wrong. By failing to include ecological perspectives in any number of subjects, students are taught that ecology is unimportant for history, politics, economics, society, and so forth. And through television they learn that the Earth is theirs for the taking. The result is a generation of ecological yahoos without a clue why the color of the water in their rivers is related to their food supply, or why storms are becoming more severe as the planet warms. The same persons as adults will create businesses, vote, have families, and above all, consume. If they come to reflect on the discrepancy between the splendor of their private lives in a hotter, more toxic and violent world, as ecological illiterates they will have roughly the same success as one trying to balance a checkbook without knowing arithmetic.[1, p. 85]

When the populace is environmentally illiterate, it cannot properly understand its problems, cannot be fully motivated to address them, and cannot structure and carry out the changes needed to solve them.

Providing basic environmental literacy should be a priority at all levels of education, from K through 12, in our colleges and universities, and in "nonformal" or adult education. This issue was addressed in the 1979 Club of Rome report *No Limits to Learning: Bridging the Human Gap*[2]. The report called for the establishment of "new literacy learning centers," worldwide. Providing access to the needed information is only the first step, however. Our organizations, clubs, churches, and educational institutions must recognize the importance of this new literacy, incorporate it in their curriculums and operations, and take steps to promote it widely.

Business has a special responsibility to learn essential information about our world and the human place on it. Nattrass and Altomare speak of replacing the outmoded mechanistic model for business organizations with a "learning organization," or using an "organization-as-brain" metaphor.[3, p. 10] "Learning organizations can respond to a rapidly changing environment because they embrace change as the norm. In contrast to the skills required in a context of the rigid mechanistic certainty implied in the organization-as-machine metaphor, the learning organization must develop competencies in

- Creating compelling aspirations and a shared vision that energizes and inspires organizational stakeholders;
- Scanning and anticipating changes in the wider environment;
- Questioning, challenging, and changing operating norms and assumptions; and
- Creating new strategic directions and patterns of organization"[4, p. 91]

Realizing these competencies is compatible with maintaining profitability. Stuart Hart of the University of North Carolina says, "Researchers in the field of strategic management have long understood that competitive advantage depends upon the match between distinctive internal (organizational) capabilities and changing external (environmental) circumstances."[5, p. 987]

"Learning to be a learning organization is no easy task because conventional management thinking and management structures are still strongly influenced by the organization-as-machine image. Becoming a learning organization often requires a fundamental shift in corporate culture, in the way people interact and collaborate, in the way they think and view their internal systems and interrelationships, and in the way they organize work. The real power of the learning organization is the ability to create vision, purpose, and direction as the motivating force for action. For many companies this is not only very new and exciting, but also frightening territory."[3, p. 11]

All organizations must convert to the new learning, new literacy model, to avoid being stoppers on the road toward effective environmental reform.

Psychological Blocks

According to USDA Forest Service psychologist Dr. Patricia L. Winter[6], in spite of our knowing about the seriousness of our environmental problems, we still fail to act. Her description of some psychological stoppers:

• *Competing attitudes and values.* Some energy using products cost more than their energy efficient competitors. Often we buy the least initial cost option even though we know the more efficient one is better for us and saves energy and money in the long run.

• *Lack of awareness.* "Sometimes people are not aware of what they are doing," Winter says. "They may be simply uninformed about what is harmful and what is helpful to the environment, or they could be acting out of habit — a serious driver of human action." To tackle this problem, environmentalists can pair education with alerts that promote more environmentally appropriate behavior — such as using signs and other reminders to do double-sided copying and other incentives for desirable behaviors.

• *It takes too much effort.* Sometimes people want to do the right thing, but the needed action is too complex, says Winter. In research she conducted, she found that some people did not make double-sided copies because the machine was much more likely to malfunction if they did.

• A *"someone-will-do-it-for-me" attitude*. An example of this is waiting for the automobile manufacturers to make the car you want more energy efficient rather than switching brands to one with a high MPG rating.

• *Misperceptions about environmentalism*. Some people consider those who engage in eco-friendly behaviors to be "on the fringe" or overly zealous. "Until positive feelings about the environment translate into true commitment to sustain them ...the gap between where we are and where we need to be is considerably vast," says Winter.[6]

I would add that old, reliable standby, *denial*, to the above list. Denying problems because they are too difficult to consider is a serious psychological block. Once a problem is denied, inaction is easily justified, at least to ourselves. We become amazingly inventive in finding ways to deny the existence and seriousness of problems we do not want to see. We rationalize them away, saying that the science is just too uncertain, or that the scientists don't know what they are talking about. We claim that it will be a long time before the problem becomes critical, so we can just pass the problem to someone else later.

When born, humans are very narcissistic. They want what they want when they want it and are not yet capable of care or concern for the welfare of others. Perhaps this is a result of evolutionary coding, to promote survival and advancement of human populations. As we grow and develop, we begin to socialize and to see other humans as connected to us. We acquire powers of empathy and the ability to care for others, especially family, and other friends and loved ones. Mature humans also can look into the future, see dangers, and act personally to protect themselves and others from perceived future harm. Immaturity can be another serious psychological block to environmental reform.

Various sources for more information on the psychological aspects of human relationships with the Earth are available. The *Journal of Environmental Psychology*[a] occasionally offers relevant articles.

Political Blocks

Having an ability to see possible future threats leads a nation, acting from its

[a]*Journal of Environmental Psychology*, ISSN 0272-4944, Academic Press, apsubs@acad.com, David Canter, editor, Academic Press, Block A2, Westbrook Centre, Milton Road, Cambridge CB4 1YG, U.K.

concern for the future, to dedicate valuable resources for the creation and maintenance of armies and other means of military defense. It also puts money into medical research, and devotes time and effort to education and the general welfare of its children. In these areas we have demonstrated an ability to take action to protect our future, and, to some extent, we have done so environmentally as well. But the actions taken are insufficient. The subtle step toward maturity — from simple socialization to developing concerns for the future and acting on them — must be enhanced in our political bodies and in the populace.

In most human social structures, the elders are given responsibility for long-term thinking, leading to actions to protect the future. In the United States, our form of governance codifies this tenet. The senior members of our Congress are given the responsibility not only for thinking of the future but also for acting on their discoveries about that future. These individuals have a special responsibility to transcend short-term political nuances and take action to help us protect ourselves.

Government by ideology rather than by sound science is another problem. When the ideology leads to errors in judgment about environmental matters, the results can be serious. When government fails in this and other ways, future threats can be misperceived and valuable resources can be diverted to protection from nonexistent dangers. Failed political leadership is a serious stopper.

Misplaced Values

Dogged adherence to outmoded beliefs, excluding ideas and information because they are incompatible with our pre-conceived notions, is one of the most effective stoppers. Numerous examples have been presented already, including 1) beliefs in unrestricted population growths and in consumption, 2) that Earth was created solely for humanity's use and enjoyment and 3) belief in the power of unrestricted free markets to provide environmental balance "naturally." We need to identify misplaced values wherever we can, comment on them, and encourage more appropriate ones.

For example, how do you respond to a news report about an environmental problem — such as saving the Coho salmon in Oregon? Most people, knowing a little about the facts of the issue (as you might hear on NPR), rely on their own core belief systems. If you believe that private property is the owner's right to keep and use as he or she sees fit, you will respond to this report accordingly. The companies are there to make a profit and it is their right to use the land as they see fit. (This argument seems to make good sense, and because it supports your position, you are reluctant to change it. That's a stopper.)

On the other hand, if you've spent quality time in the forests, have experienced directly Nature's beauties, or you particularly enjoy salmon fishing, then your perspective is likely more in touch with Nature. You are likely to side with the environmentalists (and those suspicious and skeptical of any enterprise dedicated to the pursuit of profits at the expense of ecosystems). You'll view the previous argument with great suspicion, and you'll search for places where they've made environmental mistakes: where the salmon habitat is hurt or destroyed, or where there are other environmental difficulties associated with what the timber companies are doing.

Is there any one "right" way to view this (or any other like) issue? That depends on your perspective. If your emphasis is on having jobs now, understanding this might be at your children's expense. You might want to proceed anyway, making an argument in favor of the timber companies. Perhaps your children should be invited to join the discussion.

We could use science and logic to decide. But what if you don't believe in science and logic? What if you don't accept what the scientists say? Again it falls back on your values and beliefs. That is a stopper.

To decide conclusively or to say with assurance that the loss of one single species will have global environmental significance is difficult. Each extinction is a small contribution to the gradual whittling away of ecosystems. With any one loss, we have difficulty showing how bad it is in the long run, with a few exceptions. So you can't easily place a strict scientific test on each of these actions and policies. In such a case, it is our preconceived (and often misplaced) values which prevail, and which can serve as powerful blockers of environmental protection.

The human species must sort through its values and beliefs, rooting out the inappropriate, environmentally destructive ones. If you get the principle wrong, all that follows from it will be wrong as well. If your values are misplaced, the behaviors that follow from them will be flawed.

We need to recognize this simple truth in the environmental context and begin the difficult task of evaluation, revision, and reform of our value systems.

Spiritual Blocks

At least one institution, common to all cultures, sees itself as the primary source of values, beliefs, and ethical teachings. That is religion. As mentioned by Roger S. Gottlieb in his introduction to *This Sacred Earth*, many writers have noted a tendency in most religions — including direct instruction —

for humanity to dominate and master the Earth, seeing in this "an essential source for the havoc wreaked by Western societies upon the Earth."[7]

The anthropocentric orientation of most religious teachings about the human/Earth relationship is well known. Religion has provided support over many centuries for the idea that creation stopped with humanity, that Earth and its many creatures were provided for our use, and, as Gottlieb says, "not with any notion of their inherent value." To the extent this philosophical perspective is still assumed, used, and taught in religious institutions, we must acknowledge the great damage it continues to do in slowing or stopping our struggle toward sustainability.

Fortunately, there *are* environmentally positive messages to be found in religious writings. In spite of this, the number of religious scholars, ministers, priests, rabbis, etc. speaking out against the movement of western civilization toward Earth-damaging actions has been very small until recently. Religions have encouraged values and beliefs inappropriate for our dire environmental situation for a long time. These have been used by industry to justify its often aggressive use and abuse of Earth's bounty.

The growing movement within religious institutions to revise, re-write and amend past teachings should be supported. Religious instruction must shift toward increased understanding of the intimate connection humans have with Earth, and away from the domination paradigm.

The task is not an easy one. Gottlieb writes, "It is too much to expect ancient traditions to be fully adequate to the crisis of today.... We now live in a very different world. To begin with, ancient traditions could not have foreseen the scope of modern technological power. No past empire was able to threaten the Earth's climate or so pollute the air and water that mothers' breast milk may not be fit for their babies to drink."

In spite of the difficulties, the revisioning of religion is in full swing. New ideas and religious practices are being created. This is a most welcome movement. Many people receive their primary values and beliefs about the human place in the universe and about their relationship to nature from religion. To the extent that its more environmentally negative teachings persist, religion will remain a large obstacle blocking true environmental reform.

Momentum

A pervasive stopper is the momentum that keeps societies pointed in the same (albeit wrong) direction, steadfastly dedicated to the group belief that the current course is the correct one. They believe that any problem can be solved within existing social, business, governmental, and economic structures.

Resistance to change is a natural human trait. It has been seen over millennia of slow evolutionary influences. Before industrialization, societies looked basically the same from generation to generation. What worked prospered. What didn't disappeared. Archeologists know of spectacular failures in past cultures resulting from resource depletion. But the vast majority of early human cultures were stable and lasting.

Now we are being asked to do something unnatural — to reverse our "instinct" not to make big changes. Ironically, we got into this mess by *making* big changes but making them slowly, spread over a very long time. Now new big and quicker changes are needed to escape the environmental crisis we've brought upon ourselves.

What else?

More stoppers exist than are listed here. Through self-examination, critical reflection, and studious observation, we can identify them. Identification is but the first step. To eliminate them will take serious work and determination.

Everyone should be steadfast in the critical effort of avoiding change-inhibitors. Until we identify and overcome the things that block us from reform, we will be bound to the current course (like being tied to a runaway train headed for a dead-end tunnel at the heart of a giant mountain). Creative and innovative thinking, new organizational structures, and true leadership are needed to overcome the stoppers, opening us to a new path away from the danger facing us.

References

1. David W. Orr. "Ecological Literacy." In *Ecological Literacy: Education and the Transition to a Postmodern World*, edited by David. W. Orr. Sate University of New York Press: Albany, NY, 1992, 210 pp.
2. James W. Botkin, Mahdi Elmandjra, and Mircea Malitza. *No Limits to Learning: Bridging the Human Gap.* Pergamon Press, Maxwell House: Fairview Park, Elmsford, NY 10523, 1979, 159 pp.
3. Brian Nattrass and Mary Altomare. *The Natural Step for Business — Wealth, Ecology and the Evolutionary Corporation.* New Society Publishers: Gabriola Island, BC, Canada, 1999, 222 pp.
4. G. Morgan. *Images of Organization.* Sage Publications: Thousand Oaks, CA, 1997.
5. S. L. Hart. "A Natural-Resource Based View of the Firm." *Academy of Management Review* Vol. 20, no. 4 (1996), 987.
6. S. Martin. "We all like the idea of being green—so what's the problem?" *Monitor on Psychology* Vol. 32, no. 4 (2001): April 2001, p. 45. Copyright © 2001 by the American Psychological Association. Portions reprinted with permission.
7. Roger S. Gottlieb, ed. *This Sacred Earth: Religion, Nature, Environment*, Second ed. Routledge: New York, 2004.

19
Insightful Writings

Thomas Berry, Paul Hawkin, McGregor Smith,
Rachel Carson, Daniel Quinn, Al Bartlett,
Paul Hawken, John Pfeiffer, Miriam MacGillis.

Our new understanding of humanity's place in the world and how we must change is described in some remarkable writings. Their authors have studied the past, examined the present, and offer a variety of visions for the future. Their written works help guide our way forward.

We can embrace the new understandings with the fervor of a new religion. But we must learn never to be completely dogmatic again. We should build into our new worldview mechanisms for continued adaptation to the realities that surround us.

Understanding the ideas of these insightful writers is but a first step in what may become the greatest transformation in human culture since the planting and cultivation of the first food seeds.

The offerings of these thinkers are, in some cases, small bits of insight. Others offer more encompassing descriptions of what has happened and what is coming. A few offer prescriptions for curing the disease of wrong-headed thinking that inhibits proper action.

No one has the final, perfect, ultimate solution. All have parts of it. Together we must understand the new insights, make some of them our own, and modify some to suit our needs.

The main purpose of this chapter is to focus on the offerings of these new truth-seekers. In the next few sections, I provide glimpses of some of their exciting discoveries. The writings of these individuals give us the beginning of an answer to the riddle described in Chapter 2. It is barely possible, with the few words offered here, to describe (and it is impossible to encapsulate) the total message of each visionary. I have sought to present some of the essence of their writings. The reader is urged to consult the complete works directly. Only this way can you correct any misconceptions that might result from these limited excerpts. Only a few of the many truth-seekers are included, but I have tried for a representative sample.

Aldo Leopold

Leopold authored an early and eloquent statement of environmental ethics. "The Land Ethic" was published posthumously in his book *A Sand County Almanac* in 1949. In it he describes the difficulty of incorporating inherently non-monetary natural assets in a money-based economic system, when the latter is used as the primary principle of a society's operation. His essay began with a discussion of ethics, an explanation of the new land ethic he proposed.[1]

> When god-like Odysseus returned from the wars in Troy, he hanged all on one rope a dozen slave-girls of his household whom he suspected of misbehavior during his absence. This hanging involved no question of propriety. The girls were property. The disposal of property was then, as now, a matter of expediency - not of right and wrong....
>
> There is as yet no ethic dealing with man's relation to land and to the animals and plants that grow upon it. Land, like Odysseus' slave-girls, is still property. The land-relation is still strictly economic, entailing privileges but not obligations....
>
> An ethic may be regarded as a mode of guidance for meeting ecological situations so new or intricate, or involving such deferred reactions, that the path of social expediency is not discernible to the average individual. Animal instincts are modes of guidance for the individual in meeting such situations. Ethics are possibly a kind of community instinct in-the-making....
>
> All ethics so far evolved rest upon a single premise: that the individual is a member of a community of interdependent parts. His instincts prompt him to compete for his place in the community, but his ethics prompt him also to cooperate (perhaps in order that there may be a place to compete for).
>
> The land ethic simply enlarges the boundaries of the community to include soils, waters, plants, and animals, or collectively: the land. This sounds simple: do we not already sing our love for and obligation to the land of the free and the home of the brave? Yes, but just what and who do we love? Certainly not the soil, which we are sending helter-skelter downriver. Certainly not the waters, which we assume have no function except to turn turbines, float barges, and carry off sewage. Certainly not the plants, of which we exterminate whole communities without batting an eye. Certainly not the animals, of which we have already extirpated many of the largest and most beautiful species. A land ethic of course cannot prevent the alteration, management, and use of these 'resources,' but it does affirm their right to continued existence, and, at least in spots, their continued existence in a natural state.
>
> In short, a land ethic changes the role of *Homo sapiens* from conqueror

of the land-community to plain member and citizen of it. It implies respect for his fellow-members, and also respect for the community as such.

In human history, we have learned (I hope) that the conqueror role is eventually self-defeating. Why? Because it is implicit in such a role that the conqueror knows, *ex cathedra,* just what makes the community clock tick, and just what and who is valuable, and what and who is worthless, in community life. It always turns out that he knows neither, and this is why his conquests eventually defeat themselves.

Rachel Carson

Rachel Carson's 1962 book, *Silent Spring,* stunned the world. Revealing the previously hidden consequences of what has been called a "chemical warfare" against Mother Nature, Carson was no alarmist. A trained and meticulously scrupulous scientist, she was herself alarmed about the things she was discovering. Not only did she alert us to her terrible findings, but she also thought long and hard about their implications, and wrote eloquently about them.

This excerpt is taken from the last chapter of *Silent Spring*, "The Other Road."[2]

We stand now where two roads diverge. But unlike the roads in Robert Frost's familiar poem, they are not equally fair. The road we have long been travelling is deceptively easy, a smooth superhighway on which we progress with great speed, but at its end lies disaster. The other fork of the road — the one "less travelled by" — offers our last, our only chance to reach a destination that assures the preservation of our Earth.

The choice, after all, is ours to make. If, having endured much, we have at last asserted our "right to know," and if, knowing, we have concluded that we are being asked to take senseless and frightening risks, then we should no longer accept the counsel of those who tell us that we must fill our world with poisonous chemicals; we should look about and see what other course is open to us....

Through all these new, imaginative, and creative approaches to the problem of sharing our Earth with other creatures there runs a constant theme, the awareness that we are dealing with life — with living populations and all their pressures and counter pressures, their surges and recessions. Only by taking account of such life forces and by cautiously seeking to guide them into channels favorable to ourselves can we hope to achieve a reasonable accommodation between the insect hordes and ourselves.

The current vogue for poisons has failed utterly to take into account these most fundamental considerations. As crude a weapon as the cave man's club, the chemical barrage has been hurled against the fabric of life — a fabric on the one hand delicate and destructible, on the other miraculously tough and resilient, and capable of striking back in unexpected ways. These extraordinary capacities of life have been ignored by the practitioners of chemical control who have brought to their task no "high-minded orientation," no humility before the vast forces with which they tamper.

The "control of nature" is a phrase conceived in arrogance, born of the Neanderthal age of biology and philosophy, when it was supposed that nature exists for the convenience of man. The concepts and practices of applied entomology for the most part date from that Stone Age of science. It is our alarming misfortune that so primitive a science has armed itself with the most modern and terrible weapons, and that in turning them against the insects it has also turned them against the Earth.

John Pfeiffer

John Pfeiffer is a less-known pioneer of environmental thought. In the Introduction to his 1977 book, *The Emergence of Society*, Pfeiffer identifies that point in human history when things started to go bad environmentally (with the people oblivious to the gigantic future consequences of the changes they were making). Here he describes what happened.[3]

Whatever the future, man is moving into it faster and faster, swept up in a revolution which started ten thousand years ago when all the world was a wilderness and he was a wild animal living essentially as his ancestors had lived for millions of years—foraging within his home ranges, exploiting other wild species, moving on when local abundances dwindled.

Stone-age man, the hunter and gatherer, is known by his camping grounds, by sealed deposits excavated in rock shelters, caves and open-air sites. The transformation, the first stage of the revolution, is also clear in the prehistoric record. There are constructions, walls of stone and clay bricks in standard sizes, plaster and windows and niches, neatly fitting joints, prefabricated clay slabs, sockets for doors. The people who built them were no longer nomads. They had come to stay. They had invented a new kind of place, and more significant, a new world view whose impact they could not have foreseen.

Ten thousand years ago man's earliest life-style, his original traditions, and his ethics began to crumble. The rule among foragers, hunter-gatherers, had always been to stay small; they lived in small bands, huddled at night around isolated campfires, rarely saw strangers. The new people stayed small also, at first, their earliest communities clusters of houses sheltering a few related families. When the families became larger, they tended to split into two communities. As the land filled up, however, the process went into reverse. Slowly, then at an accelerating rate, people streamed by the hundreds into a few centers of trade and ceremony and bustling marketplaces. They were creating new environments that in turn attracted others, a new glamour and new opportunities to explore activities beyond hunting and gathering and cultivating the land....

Crowding separated people as they had never been separated before. The hunter-gatherers' world had been a world of equals. Braggarts had been ridiculed until they fell silent. Would-be hoarders had been made to feel so uncomfortable, so resented, that valued possessions quickly became gifts and passed like hot potatoes from person to person and band to band. Now for the first time there were places for big men and elites, pomp and circumstance, arrogance and the accumulation and display of wealth. The emergence of complex society, the most radical development in human evolution since the emergence of the family of man from ancestral apes some 15,000,000 years ago, is one of science's deepest mysteries. It must have been a response to the threat of extinction. Nothing less could have brought about the abandonment of a way of life that had endured for ages....

Perhaps the world could have been made forever safe for hunting-gathering then and there, if man had been able to change his preceding habits, if populations had stopped rising. He multiplied instead and, in the process, changed nature. He settled down, developed farms and irrigation systems, and multiplied even faster. The last ten millenniums have been a struggle to keep in balance, a race between rising population and increasingly sophisticated use of the land, with population always running ahead....

With the coming of large communities, families no longer cultivated the land for themselves and their immediate needs alone, but for strangers and for the future. They worked all day instead of a few hours a day, as hunter-gatherers had done. There were schedules, quotas, overseers, and punishments for slacking off.

People could never justify their efforts merely because of the need to survive. They needed special reasons for working long and hard against their better judgment, reasons over and above necessity. They may have begun accounting for and validating necessity by establishing new beliefs, artificial environments for sustaining those beliefs, and a work ethics sanctioning and glorifying the task of organizing institutions for survival.

Garrett Hardin

Trained as an ecologist and a microbiologist at the University of Chicago and Stanford University, Garrett Hardin is best known for his 1968 essay, "The Tragedy of the Commons."[4] Now reprinted in over 100 anthologies, the composition is widely accepted as a fundamental contribution to ecology, population theory, economics and political science.

Hardin was Professor of Human Ecology at the University of California for more than thirty years. He and his wife of 62 years, both members of the Hemlock Society, took their own lives in September 2003.

Professor Hardin's interest in bioethics was the common thread running through his work. In his view, bioethics is more than ethics applied to biological problems. Rather it is ethics, sometimes called "tough love ethics," built on a biological foundation. Essential elements of such ethics are relative quantities, feedback processes, and the changes that time brings forth as unforeseen consequences of actions taken.

In his 1985 book *Filters Against Folly*[5] he argued that ethical theory, to be useful, must employ three intellectual filters: *literacy* (concerned with the correct use of words, whether written or spoken); *numeracy* (involving the appreciation of quantities) and *ecolacy*, (the study of relationships over time).

Following is a brief excerpt from "The Tragedy of the Commons."

The tragedy of the commons develops in this way. Picture a pasture open to all. It is to be expected that each herdsman will try to keep as many cattle as possible on the commons. Such an arrangement may work reasonably satisfactorily for centuries because tribal wars, poaching, and disease keep the numbers of both man and beast well below the carrying capacity of the land. Finally, however, comes the day of reckoning, that is, the day when the long-desired goal of social stability becomes a reality. At this point, the inherent logic of the commons remorselessly generates tragedy.

As a rational being, each herdsman seeks to maximize his gain. Explicitly or implicitly, more or less consciously, he asks, "What is the utility *to me* of adding one more animal to my herd?" This utility has one negative and one positive component.

1. The positive component is a function of the increment of one animal. Since the herdsman receives all the proceeds from the sale of the additional animal, the positive utility is nearly + 1.

2. The negative component is a function of the additional overgrazing created by one more animal. Since, however, the effects of overgrazing are shared by all the herdsmen, the negative utility for any particular decision-making herdsman is only a fraction of - 1.

Adding together the component partial utilities, the rational herdsman concludes that the only sensible course for him to pursue is to add another animal to his herd. And another.... But this is the conclusion reached by each and every rational herdsman sharing a commons. Therein is the tragedy. Each man is locked into a system that compels him to increase his herd without limit — in a world that is limited. Ruin is the destination toward which all men rush, each pursuing his own best interest in a society that believes in the freedom of the commons. Freedom in a commons brings ruin to all.[4]

Through his many books and articles published since this early seminal work, Hardin gives us crucial insights into human functioning on an Earth with limited resources. His lucid style and penetrating depth, coupled with easy reading, make him another of our valuable "seekers of truth."

Albert Bartlett

"The greatest shortcoming of the human race is our inability to understand the exponential function."

With these words, Prof. Bartlett starts his one-hour talk. First he gives a very elementary introduction to the arithmetic of steady growth, showing the meaning of steady population growth in real terms. Then he examines the situation of steady growth in a finite environment. The results are then applied to fossil fuels, particularly petroleum and coal. Data from the U.S. Department of Energy show that the realistic lifetimes of U.S. coal, U.S. petroleum, and world petroleum are much shorter than the optimistic figures often quoted.

Next the talk examines reassuring statements from experts, the press, scientists, political leaders, and others who are wildly at odds with the facts. Bartlett then addresses the widespread worship of economic growth and population growth throughout the western world. These facts give the listener a better understanding of the real meaning of "sustainability," which Dr. Bartlett explains in terms of his "First Law of Sustainability."

Bartlett is a retired Professor of Physics from the University of Colorado in Boulder. In 1978 he was national president of the American Association of Physics Teachers. He is a Fellow of the American Physical Society and of the American Association for the Advancement of Science.

Since the late 1960s, he has concentrated on public education on problems relating to and originating from population growth. Over a 29-year period he presented his lecture, "Arithmetic, Population, and Energy" 1,280 times to audiences of all levels from coast to coast. More recently he has written on sustainability, pointing out the widespread misuse of the term, and examining the conditions that are both necessary and sufficient for sustainability in any society. (Some of his work was spotlighted in Chapters 5 and 6.)

The following excerpt comes from "Reflections on Sustainability, Population Growth, And the Environment–Revisited", published in

Renewable Resources Journal. Bartlett characterizes the views and values of what he calls the "believers" and the "critics."

Two hundred years ago Thomas Robert Malthus was instrumental in introducing the world to a revolutionary new concept: the quantitative analysis of population problems. The analysis focused mainly on the different arithmetics of the growths of populations and of food supplies. Malthus showed that the use of numbers and simple analysis could yield an improved understanding of contemporary and future population problems, and that steady growth of populations would produce great and grave problems. Two hundred years of debate over the ideas of Malthus have left the debaters divided into two camps: the *believers,* who accept the idea that it is appropriate to use quantitative analysis to gain an improved understanding of the growth of populations and of food supplies, and the *critics* who don't. Here is a graphical representation of the *believers* and the several subgroups of *critics.*

I - Believers
II - Critics
    a) Non-believers
    b) Diverters
        1) Other Causes
        2) Sustainers
        3) Them: not us

THE CRITICS OF MALTHUS

The world today faces enormous problems that the believers hold to be caused largely by population growth.

The *non-believers* say that the world population is much larger today than Malthus could ever have imagined, and thus far starvation seems not to have been a major limiting factor in stopping the growth of world population. Hence, they assert, the Malthusian message of quantitative analysis is wrong. From this they sometimes extrapolate to say that the human population can go on growing "forever."[6]

It is easy to suspect that some of the *non-believers* are innumerate. ("Innumeracy" is the mathematical equivalent of illiteracy.)

The *diverters* do everything they can to divert attention away from the quantitative Malthusian message about population growth, asserting that the numbers are not a central or important aspect of the problem.

The diverters

The *diverters* are divided into three groups:

The *other causes* group would have people believe that the problems of population growth are best addressed, not by looking at the numbers, but by focusing our attention on other important things.

The *sustainers* try to convince people that we need not worry about population growth because "sustainable development" will solve the problems.

The *them-not-us* group seeks to divert attention away from the population problem in the United States and instead to focus people's attention on the growth of populations elsewhere.

In total, the works of the several groups of *critics* constitute a massive effort to marginalize the modern Malthusian message.[7]

The remainder of Bartlett's paper is an extensive compilation of his previous and current analyses of a variety of population- and growth-related topics. These include definitions and uses of the terms "sustainability" and "carrying capacity," the role of denial in overpopulation discussions, a critique of the Environmental Protection Agency's position on population growth, and debunking a number of population myths. He discusses several "pseudo solutions," which are bound to fail or be inadequate from failure to properly handle — or a complete ignoring of — the population issue. Extensive discussions include war and peace, economics, and the relationship between population growth, democracy, injustice, and inequality.

Bartlett's paper, "Reflections on Sustainability," is a classic. It includes sections on "Laws Relating to Sustainability" (included herein as an Appendix to Chapter 5), Garrett Hardin's "Three Laws of Human Ecology," "Boulding's Three Theorems," Virginia "Abernethy's Axiom," and additional issues relating to sustainability.

Bartlett's enthusiasm as a teacher is conveyed in his publications, and in the video of his talk, "Arithmetic, Population, and Energy (Forgotten Fundamentals of the Energy Crisis)," which can be ordered from Information Technology Services, University of Colorado, Boulder, CO 80309. The original paper on which the talk is based appeared in the *American Journal of Physics*, Vol. 46, pp. 876-888, Sept. 1978.

Daniel Quinn

In his book *Providence*, Daniel Quinn describes "The Story of a Fifty-Year Vision Quest" which led to the publication of his best-selling book, *Ishmael*. I first heard of *Ishmael* when close friend Jody Bryan suggested that I read it. I asked her what it was about. She said it contained a dialog between a man and a gorilla. We laughed, but I did at least buy the book. It sat on my shelf for about a year or so. Then one day I finally read it.

I had been on my own vision quest, from 1970, when I helped organize the University of Miami's observance of the first Earth Day Teach In, until the mid 90s when I read *Ishmael*. My quest was a search for meaning in the environmental crisis that first affected me in 1968 when Joe Browder and Judy Wilson of the Miami office of National Audubon Society explained the coordinated nature of human attacks on our life-support system.

Over the intervening years, I occasionally participated in, observed, and studied the environmental movement. In the early 80s I realized that something was wrong with the approach of traditional environmentalism. "Why," I asked myself, "do we have to save the environment by pitting one side against the other in adversarial processes that waste a lot of time and seldom result in much long-term benefit?" The goals sought by the environmentalists should be everyone's goals.

For the first time I realized that most of the environmental issues of the day were mainly disputes over conflicting values. Both sides of most arguments usually believe (or profess they believe) in protecting Nature. Both sides believe in civilization and industrialized societies (or at least live in them and do not fight against their basic structure and form of governance). But one side puts priority on the environmental belief while the other's highest priority is on growth and development. This seemed unfortunate and I realized that the difference was a consequence of conflicting values and beliefs (plus a degree of misinformation).

This was a revelation, but one question remained. How did we come to the place of systematically "closing down of the basic life systems of the Earth" as Thomas Berry puts it?

Then I read *Ishmael*. With this book Quinn found his voice, an author's voice, through fiction revealing and explaining his topic in an engaging way. The more I read, the more revelation it provided. Nearly every page offered some new perspective, factual as well as perceptual, on how it all happened. It became like a "whodunit" thriller. I couldn't wait to see what clue might be uncovered next.

I briefly described a central concept from *Ishmael* in Chapter 3: the separation of humans into two classes, the *Leavers* and the *Takers*. The Leavers had and have an intimate connection with the land, live lightly on it, and leave it no worse off than when they arrived on it.

All humans once were Leavers. Now only a few remnant examples exist, in tribes of aboriginal or indigenous people. Leavers have inhabited the Earth sustainably, since the emergence of humanity, one or two million years ago.

The Takers are mostly industrialized societies whose very lifestyle is predicated on the concept of taking resources, processing them, using them, and spitting out mainly the waste products, most of which are not easily assimilated in a healthy manner back into the ecosystem. This includes altering the landscape on a scale not realized since the last ice age.

Civilization is about 3,500 years old, while industrialized societies have been around only a couple of centuries. Following are some excerpts and summaries of Quinn's writings about all this, taken from *Ishmael*.

> Okay. As I make it out, there are [three] things the Takers do that are never done in the rest of the community, and these are all fundamental to their civilizational system. First, they exterminate their competitors, which is something that never happens in the wild.... Next, the Takers systematically destroy their competitors' food to make room for their own. Nothing like this occurs in the natural community. The rule there is: Take what you need, and leave the rest alone.... Next, the Takers deny their competitors access to food. In the wild, the rule is: You may deny your competitors access to what you're eating, but you may not deny them access to food in general.... [The Taker policy is:] Every square foot of this planet belongs to us, so if we put it all under cultivation, then all our competitors are just plain out of luck and will have to become extinct. Our policy is to deny our competitors access to *all the food in the world*, and that's something no other species does.[7. p. 126-128]
>
> ....
>
> [The laws of Nature promote diversity.] Diversity is a survival factor *for the community itself*. A community of a hundred million species can survive almost anything short of total global catastrophe. Within that hundred million will be thousands that could survive a global temperature drop of twenty degrees—which could be a lot more devastating than it sounds. Within that hundred million will be thousands that could survive a global temperature rise of twenty degrees. But a community of a hundred species or a thousand species has almost no survival value at all.[8. p. 130]

Quinn indicates that the laws of Nature are branches of a single law, the trunk of which is: No one species shall make the life of the world its own. In other words, the world was not made for any one species.

> As you see, one species exempting itself from this law has the same ultimate effect as all species exempting themselves. You end up with a community in which diversity is progressively destroyed in order to support the expansion of a single species.
>
> Yes. You have to end up where the Takers have ended up — constantly eliminating competitors, constantly increasing your food supply, and

constantly wondering what you're going to do about the population explosion.[8, p. 133]

We've discovered that any species that exempts itself from the rules of competition ends up destroying the community in order to support its own expansion.[8, p. 136]

The Taker culture appears to have an unstated belief that the hunting-gathering life is grim and dangerous, fraught with difficulties, a struggle just to stay alive. As Ishmael says,

> But in fact it isn't anything of the kind. I'm sure you know that, in another compartment of your mind. Hunter-gatherers no more live on the knife-edge of survival than wolves or lions or sparrows or rabbits. Man was as well adapted to life on this planet as any other species, and the idea that he lived on the knife-edge of survival is simply biological nonsense. As an omnivore, his dietary range is immense. Thousands of species will go hungry before he does. His intelligence and dexterity enable him to live comfortably in conditions that would utterly defeat any other primate.
>
> Far from scrabbling endlessly and desperately for food, hunter-gatherers are among the best-fed people on Earth, and they manage this with only two or three hours a day of what you would call work—which makes them among the most leisured people on Earth as well. In his book on Stone Age economics, Marshall Sahlins described them as 'the original affluent society.' And incidentally, predation of man is practically nonexistent. He's simply not the first choice on any predator's menu.[8, p. 230]

This can be confirmed by an afternoon at the library.

We cannot all return to the Leaver way of life, because Earth cannot support so many hunters and gatherers. A new transformative model for the Taker culture is needed. This is the central revelation.

Those with leanings toward the environmental movement probably accept Quinn's claim that the Taker Culture is destroying the world. Everyone else (apparently the majority of people on Earth) would probably deny this. They seem to believe that the few small advances in environmental protection, mostly technically based, can be continued indefinitely and will eventually overcome the inherent destructiveness of our industrial society.

At the core of this Taker belief is optimism, a faith in human capacity and their technological advances to overcome every problem without major changes in the ways that we think about ourselves and our place on Earth. As with so many matters of faith, these beliefs are not based on any scientific proof or other rational argument. They posses a sort of blind faith that the starvation and death by warfare which millions in the undeveloped countries experience are but symptoms of inadequate development and lack of training.

The reasoning of committed Takers seems to be: First we send capital expenditures into the underdeveloped countries, putting an industrial base into place, and training the people to work in the new factories. Then life for everyone will be better. And the massive experiences of famine, pestilence, and anarchic warfare will become history.

No one has assessed the ultimate carrying capacity of the planet, at any level of development. We accept through blind faith that more growth and more development can be continued indefinitely. Such "progress" is believed to be good, not only for the poor people but also for the western businessmen seeking new sources of cheap labor and new markets for their products.

Since *Ishmael,* Quinn has graced us with a number of additional books, including *Providence* (1994)[9], *The Story of B* (1996)[10], *My Ishmael* (1997)[11], and *Beyond Civilization* (1999)[12]. The last one is a response to readers of *Ishmael* who felt they were left hanging at the end. At the beginning of *Beyond Civilization,* Quinn writes this.

> My first concept of this book was reflected in its original title: *The Manual of Change.* I thought of this because there's nothing the people of our culture want more than change. They desperately want to change themselves and the world around them. The reason isn't hard to find. They know something's wrong — wrong with themselves and wrong with the world.
>
> In *Ishmael* and my other books, I gave people a new way of understanding what's gone wrong here. I had the rather naive idea this would be enough. Usually it is enough. If you know what's wrong with something — your car or your computer or your refrigerator or your television set — then the rest is relatively easy. I assumed it would be the same here, but of course it isn't. Over and over again, literally thousands of times, people have said to me or written to me, "I understand what you're saying — you've changed the way I see the world and our place in it — but what are we supposed to DO about it?"
>
> I might have said, "Isn't it obvious?" But obviously it *isn't* obvious — or anything remotely like obvious. In this book I hope to *make* it obvious. Humanity's future is what's at stake.

As a central theme of *Beyond Civilization,* Quinn's suggests that a new tribal model seems best for guiding us into a more sustainable society. He introduced this concept in *My Ishmael.* In *Beyond Civilization* he suggests that a good place to begin experimenting with a new tribalism is in our system of commerce. Here is his entire chapter on "Cradle-to-grave security?"

> Undoubtedly the greatest benefit of the ethnic tribal life is that it provides its members cradle-to-grave security. As I must always begin by saying, this isn't the result of the saintliness or unselfishness of tribal peoples. Baboons, gorillas, and chimpanzees enjoy exactly the same sort of security in their social groups. Groups that provide such security are obviously going to hold onto their members much more readily than groups that don't. Once again, it's a matter of natural selection. A group that doesn't take good care of its members is a group that doesn't command much loyalty (and probably won't last long).
>
> But will occupational tribes provide such security to their members? Not instantly, obviously. If you and your brother start a conventional business on Tuesday, he can hardly expect to retire on Wednesday with full salary for the rest of his life — though he may hope to do that in twenty years, if he helps to build the business during that time.
>
> The fact that ethnic tribes can provide their members with cradle-to-grave security is a true measure of their wealth. The people of our culture are rich in gadgets, machines, and entertainment, but we're all too aware of the dreadful consequences of losing a job. For some people — all too many — it seems to spell the end of the world; they go "postal," pick up the nearest automatic weapon, open fire on their former bosses, and finish off with a bullet in their own brains. These are people who are definitely short on feelings of security.

Here is another excerpt from *Beyond Civilization*, "Tribes of the mind."

> People tend to imagine occupational tribes in a sort of postapocalyptic fantasy world. They're startled when I point out that they can have health insurance and retirement plans (if they want them) or that the government is going to be just as interested in collecting their taxes and social security payments as anyone else's. But if that's the case, they then ask, what's the point of what we're doing? If the world is just going to go on as before, why bother? These are questions that can't be answered often enough.
>
> Mother Culture teaches that a savior is what we need–some giant St. Arnold Schwarzenegger who is a sort of combination of Jesus, Jefferson, Dalai Lama, Pope, Gandhi, Gorbachev, Napoleon, Hitler, and Stalin all rolled into one. The other six billion of us, according to Mother Culture, are helpless to do anything. We must simply wait quietly until St. Arnold arrives.
>
> Daniel Quinn teaches that *no* single person is going to save the world. Rather (if it's saved at all), it will be saved by millions (and ultimately billions) of us *living* a *new way*. A thousand living a new way won't cause

the dominant world order to topple. But that thousand will inspire a hundred thousand, who will inspire a million, who will inspire a billion — and *then* that world order will begin to look shaky!

(Next someone will ask, "But if the dominant world order gets shaky, what about my health insurance?")

With some trepidation, I originally thought of titling this chapter "The Speakers of Truth." This could imply that these thinkers have the only, immutable answers to our questions, and that everything they say is correct and certain.

Quinn identified the danger:

> One of the most striking features of Taker culture is its passionate and unwavering dependence on prophets. The influence of people like Moses, Gautama, Buddha, Confucius, Jesus, and Muhammad in Taker history is simply enormous.... What makes it so striking is the fact that there is absolutely nothing like this among the Leavers — unless it occurs as a response to some devastating contact with Taker culture, as in the case of Wovoka and the Ghost Dance or John Frumm and the Cargo Cults of the South Pacific. Aside from these, there is no tradition whatever of prophets rising up among the Leavers to straighten out their lives and give them new sets of laws or principles to live by....
>
> Millions have been willing to back their choice of prophets with their very lives. What makes them so important?[8, p. 85-86]

The prophets were trying to straighten us out and tell us how we ought to live. Quinn asks:

> But why? Why do you need *prophets* to tell you how you ought to live? Why do you need *anyone* to tell you how you ought to live?....
>
> Questions about how people ought to live always end up becoming religious questions among the Takers — always end up being arguments among the prophets.

You are, therefore, encouraged to read with an open but critical mind, and form your own judgments.

Karl-Henrik Robért

Robért's founding of The Natural Step movement was described in Chapter 14, where the four "system conditions" and other principles of the movement were described. Robért offers a vision of how to reform business into a more eco-friendly model. He also offers a structure for gathering knowledgeable people together to seek the truth and find a consensus for changing the world. Robert uses the metaphor of a funnel to visualize our declining life-sustaining resources and increasing demands spelling disaster for humanity. Unfortunately, he barely touches the problem of overpopulation.

The newsletter's editor Peter Montague takes the following from an article in Rachel's Environment & Health Weekly.[13] In this excerpt Montague quotes Robért, from an interview editor Sarah van Gelder conducted with him (appearing in her magazine YES — A Journal of Positive Futures in 1998[14]), and offers some comments of his own.

"Fairness is an efficiency parameter if we look at the whole global civilization. It is not an efficient way of meeting human needs if one billion people starve while another billion have excess. It would be more efficient to distribute resources so that at least vital needs were met everywhere. Otherwise, for example, if kids are starving somewhere, dad goes out to slash and burn the rain forest to feed them — and so would I if my kids were dying. And this kind of destruction is everyone's problem, because we live in the same ecosphere."

Will businesses voluntarily make the transition to sustainability? Robért does not think so. "My belief is that free will of individuals and firms will not be sufficient to make sustainable practices widespread — legislation is a crucial part of the walls of the funnel, particularly if we want to make the transition in time."

Despite the need for legislation, businesses acting voluntarily have a tremendously important role to play. "The more examples we get of businesses entering the transition out of free will, the easier it will be for proactive politicians. In a democracy there must be a 'market' for proactive decisions in politics, and that market can be created by proactive businesses in dialogue with proactive customers. For example, in Sweden, some of these proactive business leaders are lobbying for green taxes. In that triangle of dialogue: business-market-politicians, a new culture may evolve, with an endorsement of the values we share but have forgotten how to pay attention to," says Robért.

How will the transition to sustainable behavior evolve? "A deepening intellectual understanding is a good starting point for change of values." And, he says, "The Natural Step introduces a shared mental model that is intellectually strict, but still simple to understand. These are the rules of sustainability; you can plug them into decision-making about any product."

"The first thing that happens is that this stimulates creativity, because people enter a much smarter dialogue if they have a shared framework for their goals...."

A strict shared mental model can really get people working together," Robért says.

What does the future hold? Will we successfully make the transition to sustainable practices? Robért is not sure. He says the world is probably in for very difficult times in the years ahead, perhaps even collapse. He says, "What worries me the most is the systematic social battering of people all around the world, leading to more and more desperate people who don't feel any partnership with society because of alienation, poverty, dissolving cultural structures, more and more 'molecular' violence (unorganized and self-destructive violence that pops up everywhere without any meaning at all)."

Robért fears that a drop in what I call the Human Capability Index will come so soon and be so extensive that it makes the needed changes impossible.

"The response of the establishment is too superficial, with more and more imprisonment and money spent on defense against those feared, leading to a vicious cycle.

If this goes on long enough, a constructive and new sustainable paradigm in the heads of governments and business leaders will not necessarily help us in time. We will have more and more people who are so hungry to meet their vital human needs that it will be hard to reach them," Robért says.

A few businesses have already begun the process of converting to the new model, with clear success. Robért believes this is a source of optimism in a world frightened of terrorism and suffering from an overload of information about our environmental atrocities.

Paul Hawken

Hawken also has strong influence over the new thinking about restructuring the industrialized world of business. His breakthrough work was *The Ecology of Commerce*, published in 1993. Hawken was instrumental in bringing The Natural Step to the United States. And following the success of his first book, Hawken co-authored (with Amory and Hunter Lovins of the Rocky Mountain Institute in Snowmass, Colorado) *Natural Capitalism*, a more thorough and systematic treatment of their vision for a new corporate paradigm for the future.

Ultimately, Hawken calls for the creation of a new definition of what

America means and stands for: "The creation of a new story for America, ... would insure that once again life is celebrated on Earth. Such conventions are ultimately an endless discussion by people on how to say grace, knowing that we *do* take and harm as we live; that life is always a moral question that lies before us sweetly, dependent on our gratitude and constant struggle to cause as little suffering as possible to all and everything around us."

In the summer, 1995, issue of *In Context* magazine, Hawken answered a question from Sarah van Gelder[15]:

Sarah: *A lot of people are very concerned with recent events, particularly in the US, where we're seeing attacks on environmental legislation at the state and federal levels, and an overall sense that our economic and governmental institutions are failing us. How do you interpret all this?*

Paul: I see these events as masking a more fundamental shift, a shift so powerful that it will occur over the span of one lifetime if not more. We're so accustomed — if not addicted — to rapid change that we are not able to perceive a powerful long-term shift, especially one that is so quiet and pervasive that it is not discernible by the methods we use to gauge change, power, and control.

When you read the papers of Volta, Galvani, Barrows, Shelley, Blake *et al* at the beginning of the industrial revolution, they didn't describe industrialism *per se* — they didn't use the word — but they did describe its benefits, its promise, and its shadow. Nobody knew exactly what it was that they were describing. Nobody at a party could say, "How does it feel to be at the beginning of the industrial age?" And yet that is exactly what was happening. People could sense it.

My guess is that we are in precisely the same situation. People are naming it the Third Wave, the Information Age, etc. but I would say those are basically technological descriptions, and this next shift is not about technology — although obviously it will be influenced and in some cases expressed by technologies.

Industrialism is about the appropriation by a relatively small group of white Europeans of global resources that they mistakenly thought were theirs, that they "discovered." That appropriation of resources and the transformation of them into goods and services through the European production system characterized, and characterize to this day, all industrial systems including the information age. If anything, the technologies used to "produce" the information age are proto-industrial. There is nothing about its underlying principles that are post-industrial.

The next stage, whatever it will be called, is being brought about by powerful and much-delayed feedback loops. Information from destructive activities going back a hundred years right up until today is being incorporated into the system. And as that happens the underlying framework of industrialism is collapsing and causing disintegration. We are losing our living systems, social systems, cultural systems, governing systems, stability, and our constitutional health, and we're surrendering it all at the same time.

Thomas Berry

Thomas Berry entered a monastery in 1934 and earned his doctoral degree in western intellectual history from the Catholic University of America. For ten years he taught the cultural and religious history of India and China at Seton Hall University in New Jersey and at St. John's University in New York. From 1966 until 1979 he served as director of the graduate program in the History of Religions at Fordham University. Founder of the Riverdale Center of Religious Research in New York City, he was its director from its beginning in 1970 until its termination in 1995. He was president of the American Teilhard Association from 1975 until 1987. (Teilhard de Chardin was a visionary French Jesuit, paleontologist, biologist, and philosopher, who spent the bulk of his life trying to integrate religious experience with natural science. He lived in America for part of his life, but died before the full depths of the environmental crisis were known.) During this period Berry lectured widely on the intersection of cultural and ecological issues.

Sierra Club Books published Berry's reflections on ecology, *The Dream of the Earth*, in 1988, winning him in 1995 the Lannan Prize for non-fiction[16]. This book introduced the world to Berry's carefully considered philosophy of the human place in the world, and started (or accelerated) a new movement in environmental ethics.

Physicist Brian Swimme sought to make some of Berry's teachings more accessible, and added his own interpretation to them with his 1988 book *The Universe Is a Green Dragon: A Cosmic Creation Story*[17]. Much of this book is a dialog between "THOMAS" and "YOUTH", referring to Berry and Swimme, respectively.

Berry teamed with Swimme to write *The Universe Story: From the Primordial Flaring Forth to the Ecozoic Era*, published in 1992[18]. This offers the context for an educational program from the earliest years through university and professional training, an education suited to the needs of the emerging twenty-first century. Berry's latest work in this area is *The Great Work–Our Way Into the Future*, published in 1999[19].

Berry extended de Chardin's earlier work, finding meaning in scientific discoveries about the origin and evolution of the universe and Earth. He claims that this historical record has greater meaning than most realize. This "new story" is important because it is "our primary source of intelligibility and value." From it we derive "the psychic energy needed to deal effectively with crisis moments in the lives of individuals and society."[16, p. xi]

Such crisis moments occur when we find our old stories of who we are, where we came from, and where we are going — our cosmology — inadequate. In such moments of crisis, we become confused. Our historical situation becomes profoundly different and our old cosmology is inadequate to the task, keeping us from properly interpreting the changes or benefiting from them.

In *The Dream of the Earth*, Berry summarizes and interprets the many assaults on Nature our current industrial way of life is making. One explanation for this assault is found in the 17th century writings of Sir Francis Bacon, which provided a "vision of a better order in earthly affairs through scientific control over the functioning of the natural world." Berry concludes: "By a supreme irony this closing down of the basic life systems of the Earth has resulted from a commitment to the betterment of the human condition, to 'progress'." In times of such stress new historical visions arise to guide us toward a more creative future.

Berry states that scientific understanding of our history makes new vision possible. Previously we never knew enough. We weren't sufficiently intimate with all our cousins in the great family of Earth. We couldn't listen to the creatures of Earth, each telling its own story. "The time has now come, however, when we will either listen or we will die. The time has come to lower our voices, to cease imposing our mechanistic patterns on the biological processes of the Earth, to resist the impulse to control, to command, to force, to oppress, and to begin quite humbly to follow the guidance of the larger community on which all life depends. Our fulfillment is not in our isolated human grandeur, but in our intimacy with the larger Earth community, for this is also the larger dimension of our being. Our human destiny is integral with the destiny of the Earth."[16, p. xiv]

"If the Earth does grow inhospitable toward human presence, it is primarily because we have lost our sense of courtesy toward the Earth and its inhabitants, our sense of gratitude, our willingness to recognize the sacred character of habitat, our capacity for the awesome, for the numinous quality of every earthly reality. We have even forgotten our primordial capacity for language at the elementary level of song and dance, wherein we share our existence with the animals and with all natural phenomena."[16, p. 2]

We might say that the pre-war Germans were asleep to what Hitler was doing. Berry seems to be saying that we are asleep to the daily tragedies in our destruction of Nature. He says that to wake up to what is happening and to rescue Earth from the impending destruction we are imposing on it, a re-enchantment with Earth as a living reality is required. To do this, we must re-invent the human as a species. "Our sense of reality and value must consciously shift from an anthropocentric to a biocentric norm of reference."[16, p.21]

Some religions have asked us to believe that creation stopped once humankind was created. But we now know that creation is an on-going process, except when we attempt to interrupt it (or alter it by genetic engineering), as we are doing with our high-impact industrial societies.

Another problem, according to Berry, is that western religious traditions have been so occupied with redemptive healing of a flawed world that they tend to ignore creation as it is experienced in our times. This leads to our western division into a secular scientific community and a separate religious one.

We cannot instantly reform our current system of commerce. But we must find a way to achieve what Berry calls "a comprehensive change in the control and direction of the energies available to us. Most of all we must alter our commitment from an industrial wonderworld achieved by plundering processes to an integral Earth community based on a mutually enhancing human-Earth relationship. This move from anthropocentric sense of reality and value to a biocentric norm is essential."[16, p.30]

Berry sees a reason for hope and optimism in the many organized efforts at environmental reform.

> A new energy is beginning to appear. Already a pervasive influence throughout the North America continent, this energy is finding expression in more than ten thousand ecologically oriented action groups on this continent; it is distributed through all the professions and through all the various forms of economic, political, educational, religious, literary, and media enterprise.
>
> If this movement has not yet achieved its full efficacy in confrontation with the industrial vision, it is not primarily because of the mythic power of the industrial vision. Even when its consequences in a desolate planet are totally clear, the industrial order keeps its control over human activities because of the energy generated by the mythic quality of its vision. We could describe our industrial society as a counterproductive, addictive, paralyzing, manifestation of a deep cultural pathology. Mythic addictions function something like alcohol and drug addictions. Even when they are obviously destroying the addicted person, the psychic fixation does not permit any change, in the hope that continued addiction will at least permit

momentary survival. Any effective cure requires passing through the agonies of withdrawal. If such withdrawal is an exceptional achievement in individual lives, we can only guess at the difficulty on the civilizational or even the global scale.[16, p. 31]

As an antidote to our addiction, Berry turns to "the great story of the universe" for meaning and direction. He claims that it "presents the organic unity and creative power of the planet Earth as they are expressed in the symbol of the Great Mother; the evolutionary process through which every living form achieves its identity and its proper role in the universal drama as it is expressed in the symbol of the Great Journey; the relatedness of things in an omniscentered universe as expressed by the mandala; the sequence of moments whereby each reality fulfills its role of sacrificial disintegration in order than new and more highly differentiated forms might appear as expressed by the transformational symbols; and, finally, the symbols of a complex organism with roots, trunk, branches, and leaves, which indicate the coherence and functional efficacy of the entire organism, as expressed by the Cosmic Tree and the Tree of Life."

These seemingly illusory, mythic visions of Nature may initially appear superfluous and of little interest to citizens of the industrialized society (and those aspiring to industrialization). However, to stimulate cultural transformation, we need massive educational reform. Instruction in these emotional, artistic, literary, and other humanities-related subjects will be an important component of the total educational experience. The universe story must be taught, with ample treatment of Earth and all its functioning chemical, biological, and physical systems. Then the historical understandings of these and the religious and artistic interpretations of its functioning can be presented.

According to Berry, what is currently in progress is the ending of the geologic Cenozoic era and the beginning of what he calls the Ecozoic era. This is a period when "the Earth is mandating that the human community assume a responsibility never assigned to any previous generation. We are involved in a process akin to initiation processes that have been known and practiced from earliest times. The human community is passing from its stage of childhood into its adult stage of life. We must assume adult responsibilities. As the maternal bonds are broken on one level to be reestablished on another, so the human community is being separated from the dominance of Nature on one level to establish a new and more mature relationship. In its prior period the Earth acted independently as the complete controlling principle; only limited control over existence was assigned to ourselves. Now the Earth insists that we accept greater responsibility, a responsibility commensurate with the greater knowledge communicated to us."

In his more recent book, *The Great Work*, Berry notes previous overarching moments, major transformational periods in history. The *great works* of the people in those times shepherded these transitions. But they were all limited in their fulfillment, flawed by human imperfections.

The Great Work now, as we move into a new millennium, is to carry out the transition from a period of human devastation of the Earth to a period when humans would be present to the planet in a mutually beneficial manner. This historical change is something more than the transition from the classical Roman period to the medieval period, or from the medieval period to modern times. Such a transition has no historical parallel since the geobiological transition that took place 67 million years ago when the period of the dinosaurs was terminated and a new biological age begun. So now we awaken to a period of extensive disarray in the biological structure and functioning of the planet.

Since we began to live in settled villages with agriculture and domestication of animals some ten thousand years ago, humans have put increased burdens upon the biosystems of the planet. These burdens were to some extent manageable because of the prodigality of nature, the limited number of humans, and their limited ability to disrupt the natural systems. In recent centuries, under the leadership of the Western world, largely with the resources, psychic energy, and inventiveness of the North American peoples, an industrial civilization has come into being with the power to plunder Earth in its deepest foundations, with awesome impact on its geological structure, its chemical constitution, and its living forms throughout the wide expanses of the land and the far reaches of the sea.

Some 25 billion tons of topsoil are now being lost each year with untold consequences to the food supply of future generations. Some of the most abundant species of marine life have become commercially extinct due to overexploitation by factory fishing vessels and the use of drift nets twenty to thirty miles long and twenty feet deep." Berry mentions the high rate of species extinction in the world's rain forests and elsewhere.

This entire disturbance of the planet is leading to the terminal phase of the Cenozoic Era. Natural selection can no longer function as it has functioned in the past. Cultural selection is now a decisive force in determining the future of the biosystems of the Earth.

The deepest cause of the present devastation is found in a mode of consciousness that has established a radical discontinuity between the human and other modes of being and the bestowal of all rights on the humans. The other-than-human modes of being are seen as having no rights. They have reality and value only through their use by the human. In this context the other-than-human becomes totally vulnerable to exploitation by the human, an attitude that is shared by all four of the fundamental establishments that control the human realm: governments, corporations, universities, and religions — the political, economic, intellectual, and religious establishments. All four are committed consciously or unconsciously to a radical discontinuity between the human and the nonhuman.

In reality there is a single integral community of the Earth that includes all its component members whether human or other than human. In this community every being has its own role to fulfill, its own dignity, its inner spontaneity. Every being has its own voice. Every being declares itself to the entire universe. Every being enters into communion with other beings. The capacity for relatedness, for presence to other beings, for spontaneity in action, is a capacity possessed by every mode of being throughout the entire universe.[19, p. 3-4]

Miriam MacGillis

Miriam Terese MacGillis is a Catholic nun and founder of Genesis farm in New Jersey. She has been giving oral presentations for many years. I have heard her speak several times, and am inspired anew at each hearing. The following excerpts are from notes I have taken and tape recordings of her talks, an attempt to paraphrase her remarks (with her permission), and to quote her words verbatim, where possible.

"The fate of the Earth. That is really up for grabs," says MacGillis. We are at a moment that provides no guarantees as to its future. It is a question of our own critical choices, the choices of the human species on the planet. But before we can make those choices, we must have something very special and very important: a transforming vision, a vision deep enough to take us from where we are now to a new place, opening the future to hope and excitement. We must change from being people of despair and desperation to people of hope and confidence. We'll still be frustrated and anxious, but our anxiety and frustration will come not so much from despair as from regret that we cannot implement our new vision fast enough.

Our problems do not stem from a moral and ethical decline. We are really in a crisis of cosmology. Cosmology is the story of our origins and place in the universe. Even the most primitive people have cosmology stories. We have them too. But our western story of the creation of the universe is flawed, and this is at the center of all our problems.

If we can find a new vision, a transforming vision, based on a revised and hopeful cosmology, then we can develop positive images of what can be. Then we can live up to these, rather than see ourselves as an inherently destructive species.

If we have these negative images of ourselves, then they will become self-fulfilling prophecies and we will sink into hopelessness. How can we have hope in the midst of all the terrible things that are happening to our environment? Read this short poem by Wendell Berry[19]:

In the dark of the moon, in flying snow, in the dead of winter,
war spreading, families dying, the world in danger,
I walk the rocky hillside, sowing clover.[20]

We can see the terrible things happening, and be very upset by them. But at the same time we can plant trees, sow clover, and celebrate the joyous things still available in Nature. It is not enough to work hard, all the time, at saving the Earth. We must also enjoy this Earth, celebrate its beauty, and be amazed at its complexity and magnitude. The hope and significance of doing things for life (expressed in that poem) is what we have to be about.

Before Europeans came to North America, the Native Americans had a well-developed cosmology, based not on modern scientific understandings, but on centuries of direct experience. They developed an explaining story that we would do well to understand. This story gave them a sense of the great spirit, the divine creative force in the universe, that lived in the universe that lived in the world. They believed that Earth was made up of this creative spirit.

This basic idea determined their moral and ethical systems and their economic systems. If the spirit was inside all things, then everything that lived was a relative of the spirit and reflected in a concrete way the power of that spirit being transmitted to them through that creature. The water and the trees are relatives and they are living because the spirit that dwelled within them breathed life into them.

Once you grasp this idea, your relationship with all life changes. And your relationship with the land in and on which all things live alters dramatically. This is why it was impossible for the Native Americans to come up with even the *concept* of private property. They lived here for 7 to 10 thousand years and it never dawned on them, once, in that entire period, that they could own, or buy, or sell land. When the Europeans came, the Native Americans learned to converse with them in English and other languages, but their understanding of certain "civilized" concepts was very deficient. So they thought that the settlers who bought Manhattan Island were crazy. How could you own or buy or sell this womb from which you came, this Earth Mother that gave you birth, sustained you, and would take you back? It was incongruous. This was not because of their religion but their cosmology.

The human is the being in whom the Earth has become spiritually aware, has awakened into consciousness, and has become self-aware and self-reflecting. In us the Earth begins to reflect on itself, its meaning, who it is. In our deepest definition and deepest subjectivity, we are Earth's consciousness. Through us, Earth thinks, knows, comprehends, analyzes, rationalizes, judges, remembers, chooses, acts, and decides.

The problem arises because we are unaccustomed to thinking of ourselves in that way at all. This is rather upsetting and we don't know what to do with it. It doesn't fit into our categories. Quoting MacGillis:

> As Teilhard [de Chardin] would say, the human person is the sum total of fifteen billion years of unbroken evolution now thinking about itself. That's who you are. You are irreplaceable and unrepeatable and the way the Earth is thinking at this moment in you is totally unique. Totally. And we will never think the old way again.

This is powerful stuff. We've learned to understand ourselves from the social paradigm given to us by our culture and our educational systems that has remained unchanged for thousands of years. At its very core, our culture is based upon the assumption that Nature is purely material and that we are separate creatures, disconnected from it.

We are living within centuries-old institutions, inflexible and totally rooted in the old cosmology. You can't make a shift within structures as quickly and easily as you can shift understanding. That is one of the remarkable gifts to the human species. But it is also a source of great frustration, for it leaves us with a dichotomy between what we know we need to do and our inability to do it quickly.

> The tension, conflict, and ambiguity we are experiencing now is inherent in what we are trying to do. It is painful. We know things are not working. But we don't have a roadmap. We don't have an ethics that is defined and ready to pass on or to give us the correct new direction for our lives. Struggling with this new cosmology is part of the process that we are going through. We've got to look at it, chew it up, and integrate it. If it doesn't fit, all right, but if there's truth in it then we've got to deal with it, because it changes everything....

What we have done is take the Earth off remote control. The internal guidance system that has brought our Earth to this present state in its development is being set aside and we humans are taking over. We are putting it on manual. That's what is happening. Consciousness is taking over.

In the past, Earth's internal guidance provided the conditions needed for creation to continue toward life, life at every stage. If we screw up through our actions, if this finely-tuned balancing act which sustains our planetary life-support system gets whacked out, if it gets violated, then its own consciousness will be at fault.

It is not so much a question of ethics; we don't have a tradition of ethics to apply to it. It is because our aberrant cosmology created an ethical system that was based upon incorrect assumptions.

Our cosmology created an ethical system that was human-human-God, but not human-universe-process. We don't have it. The Indians do but we don't.

Something's interfering with the process so that at the lowest, the most profound level, we are altering the capacity to do what the universe has mandated it to do and that is to continue to live and heal and nourish and regenerate it. Consciousness is causing the violation of that. That's us. I would maintain not because we're evil, but because we think we have a full deck of cards but we really don't, and we're dealing like mad and we're laughing all through the game, and we keep waiting for that other card to come, based on our projections of the past. The card's going to show up that will get us out of the mess. But we don't have a full deck.

Our consciousness is so young and primitive and we don't understand who we are. We don't have a definition for what we know and can do. We're still unable to understand who we are as humans in this whole community of life. We're still operating out of old assumptions, which is a pattern of behavior that deals with war or conflict in a totally inappropriate and immature way.

So who is doing all this? You and I are doing it. We, who are the collective consciousness of the planet, are destroying it because we are not moving quickly enough to the new cosmology. You and I are important. The way we think is important and totally relevant and totally significant. The Earth thinks as we think. The Earth is in a process of coming out of its adolescent fixation with itself and its powers into a whole new level of maturity. The degree to which you and I can make this jump, the Earth makes the jump, this leap of planetary consciousness from adolescence to maturity. It is as simple and profound as that.

We've got to come home. We've got to own our identification with the Earth and with the spiritual dynamics of the universe. We don't have our life and our nourishment and our learning except as it comes out of the Earth that is our very body. The Earth as a body is a communion and a community. At its deep level it is in communion with itself and in its external manifestation it is a community of all the beings who share existence on this planet, from oxygen to the highest organisms.

If this Earth is sick, we will be sick. We have to come home, we've got to get out of the dualisms of the past and we've got to become members of the community of home and I mean home in terms of the larger sense of where we live on this planet.

Our water is sick. Our air is sick. Our soil is sick. Our vegetation is sick. And they no longer even can become the source of our inspiration or our poetry or our knowledge of God.

How will we baptize children with toxic water and tell them about God? How will we give pills and medication with toxic water and make people well? How will we eat contaminated food and think that we will be nourished? We've got to come home, in a new humility, and become members of the community, or else we're simply going to have to be a bad experiment on the planet and get kicked out.

Earth does not abide by political boundaries, as Chernobyl has taught us. The differences between us are part of the natural evolution of complexity on Earth. They are to be celebrated not denigrated.

In diversity there is strength, both in the natural world and in the uniquely human social context. We now know that only through communion and cooperation and an acceptance of our differences are we going to achieve a unity of purpose on the planet.

A set of six audio cassette tapes by MacGillis is available from Genesis Farm[21].

Critique of Berry, Hawken, and The Natural Step

As insightful as Thomas Berry's works are, they seem to share a problem with the publications of Paul Hawken and Amory and Hunter Lovins reflected (in The Natural Step, as well). They insufficiently emphasize the critical role of overpopulation in driving the bad things they seek to overcome.

In Berry's defense, human overpopulation is but one symptom among many of a species out of balance, out of whack ecologically. According to Berry, Earth is primary; humanity derivative. Earth is considered self-nourishing, through photosynthesis and the complex set of mechanisms producing the web of life in all its manifestations. Earth is also self-healing, in the sense that species exceeding natural limits—species that no longer work in a participatory way with the rest of creation—get kicked out of the system and become extinct.

Earth is also considered self-propagating (in the context of life species coming forth and evolving). Through humanity's new belief that it is separate and distinct from other life forms on the planet, it has broken most of the natural constraints limiting human population to sustainable levels. By our numbers and by our actions, we are overwhelming all other living communities on Earth.

Since we no longer fit within the system, we are racing along a path toward a cliff, becoming another in the long line of extinct species. Tragically, we are in the process of taking out many other species with us.

According to this model, humanity can reverse the trend — overpopulation along with it — only by reconstructing itself. We must change the conceptualization and context of who we are and how we live on Earth, accepting that ecology is not a subject but the context of everything else. Overpopulation is but one of the symptoms of our dysfunctional relationship with Earth and its operations.

The late B. Meredith Burke, Ph.D., a Senior Fellow at both Negative Population Growth and Californians for Population Stabilization, was a prolific writer on environmental issues. She offered the following 22 August 2001 letter to the editor of Grist Magazine, her criticism of *Natural Capitalism*, by Paul Hawken, Amory Lovins, and Hunter Lovins.

Paul Hawken and the two Lovinses pay lip service to the role population growth plays in destroying natural capital:

Misconceived or badly designed business systems, population growth, and wasteful patterns of consumption are the primary causes of the loss of natural capital, and all three must be addressed to achieve a sustainable economy.

However, none of their four strategies for reducing the depredations on natural capital addresses stopping or reversing population growth.

When the last U.S. wetlands have been drained for housing, when Brazil's mangroves have been removed for shrimp farms, when fragile environments the world 'round have been assaulted by global warming and rising sea levels – will we really confront population growth in the U.S. and in the Third World with equanimity? I suspect that the political costs inherent in dealing with U.S. immigration and foreign-aid policies have inhibited these three authors.[22]

The "seekers of truth" profiled here are but a sampling of the thinkers, speakers, and writers on this important subject. The reader is encouraged to study their works more. Educators are encouraged to incorporate relevant ideas into their teachings. The ideas accessed should be widely discussed and evaluated, in our homes, our schools, our offices, and the news media.

References

1. Aldo Leopold. *A Sand County Almanac*. Oxford University Press: New York, 1949.
2. Rachel Carson. *Silent Spring*. Fawcett Crest, Houghton Mifflin: New York, 1962, 304 pp. Copyright © 1962 by Rachel L. Carson, renewed 1990 by Roger Christie. Reprinted by permission of Houghton Mifflin Company. All rights reserved.
3. John E. Pfeiffer. *The Emergence of Society — A prehistory of the Establishment*. Copyright © 1977 McGraw-Hill Education: New York, 512 pp.
4. Garrett Hardin. "The Tragedy of the Commons." *Science* Vol. 162, (1968), 1243-1248. Excerpted from Garrett Hardin, *SCIENCE* 162:1243 (1968). Copyright © 1968 American Association for the Advancement of Science.
5. Garrett Hardin. *Filters Against Folly: How to Survive Despite Economists, Ecologists, and the Merely Eloquent*. May 1986 ed. Viking: New York, 1985.
6. Julian Simon. "The State of Humanity: Steadily Improving." *Cato Policy Report* 17, no. 5 (1995): September/October 1995, 131.
7. Albert A. Bartlett. "Reflections on Sustainability, Population Growth, And the Environment - Revisited." *Renewable Resources Journal, Natural Resources Foundation, 5430 Grosvenor Lane, Bethesda, MD, 20814* Vol. 15, no. 4 (1998): Winter 1997 - 98, 6-23. Note: Also published in Focus, Vol. 9, No. 1, 1999, Pgs. 49 - 68. Carrying Capacity Network, 2000 P Street, NW, Washington D.C. 20036-5915.
8. Daniel Quinn. *Ishmael*. 1st ed. Bantam/Turner: New York, 1992.
9. Daniel Quinn. *Providence — The Story of a Fifty-Year Vision Quest*. Bantam: New York, 1995.
10. Daniel Quinn. *The Story of B*. Bantam Books: New York, 1996, 325 pp.
11. Daniel Quinn. *My Ishmael, A Sequel*. Bantam Books: New York, 1997.
12. Daniel Quinn. *Beyond Civilization: Humanity's Next Great Adventure*. Harmony Books: New York, 1999.
13. Peter Montague, "The Meaning of Sustainability – Part 2," Internet newsletter, Last update: 16 September 1999, erf@rachel.org.
14. Sarah van Gelder and Karl-Henrik Robert. "The Natural Step: The Science of Sustainability." *YES! A JOURNAL OF POSITIVE FUTURES* P.O. Box 10818, Bainbridge Island, Washington 98110, (1998): Fall 1998, 50-54.
15. Sarah van Gelder. "Business On A Small Planet." *In Context*, no. 41 (1995): Summer 1995, p. 17.

16. Thomas Berry. *The Dream of the Earth*. 1st ed. Sierra Club Books: San Francisco, 1988, 247 pp. Copyright © 1988 by Thomas Berry. Reprinted by permission of Sierra Club Books.

17. Brian Swimme. *The Universe is a Green Dragon*. Bear & Co., Inc.: Santa Fe, NM, 1984, 173 pp.

18. Brian Swimme and Thomas Berry. *The Universe Story*. HarperSanFrancisco, div. of HarperCollins: San Francisco, 1992, 305 pp.

19. Thomas Berry. *The Great Work — Our Way Into the Future*. Bell Tower: New York, 1999, 241 pp. Copyright © 1999 by Thomas Berry. Used by permission of Bell Tower, a division of Random House, Inc.

20. "February 2, 1968" from *Collected Poems: 1957-1982* by Wendell Berry. Copyright © 1985 by Wendell Berry. Reprinted by permission of North Point Press, a division of Farrar, Straus and Giroux, LLC.

21. Miriam Terese MacGillis, "To Know the Place for the First Time: Explorations in Thomas Berry's New Cosmology," Global Perspectives,Sonoma, CA. Available from Genesis Farm, 410 Silver Lake Road, Blairstown, NY 07825: six audio cassette tapes.

22. B. Meredith Burke, "Re. A Capital Idea, Books Unbound, by Paul Hawken, Amory Lovins, and L. Hunter Lovins," World Wide Web, Access date: 8/22/01, http://www.gristmagazine.com/grist/letters/letters082201.asp.

Part IV

Taking Action

20
The Puzzle Solved
Answering the riddle posed earlier.

Much of the story of human excesses leads to pessimism. The problems seem large and intractable. Considerable literature shows, in excruciating detail, clearly where humankind has gone wrong. This does not mean optimism is excluded. Hopeful signs abound. We have both visions of sustainable, alternate futures and examples where they are being put into practice. Encouragingly, people experimenting with these alternate futures are reporting that we are not facing a new dark age of austerity. The wonderful things that really matter in life will be available in abundance. All we need is the courage to take the step, to cross the threshold, and enter a new world of stability, health, and fulfillment.

Answering the Riddle

In Chapter 2, I promised to answer the puzzle of how we came to the point of systematically taking apart the life-support system of Planet Earth, why we continue doing it, and how we might stop. The answer is this.

Our problems are natural consequences of the great human transition from being a part of Nature and thoroughly imbedded in it to taking control and directing Nature to serve us. Amazing scientific discoveries have allowed human domination of the natural environment to such an extent that previous limitations on our population growth have been far exceeded. Every step of the way, we have sought to improve our conditions, materially, medically, and in many other ways. We have succeeded beyond our ancestors' wildest dreams. But now we can no longer continue in the same old way. Naturally we want to go on, without substantive change in direction. We have carefully removed most of the damaging consequences of our modern society from view, so finding adequate motivation to change is difficult.

But our huge and growing population and the toxicity of our industrialized economic system now threaten humanity's eons-old participation in the workings of Earth. We think we are no longer a part of Nature. We have become a consumer and discarder of it. The new perspective is disastrous for the ecological, chemical, and physical systems supporting human life on the planet. We are just beginning to see the truth in these statements — and are making modest initial attempts to reverse the destruction. But we are finding our efforts inadequate.

To halt the destruction will require us to reconnect with Nature, and to abandon our terribly damaging practices: overpopulation, toxic injections into the Earth's physical and biological systems, habitat destruction, global warming, extinction of species, and resource depletion and damage.

We need both technological and organizational changes. We need to redirect the human enterprise toward sustainability and then find *ways* to do so (following Bartlett's Laws of Sustainability). Included will be a new formulation of how we use technology to support our desires. Our industry must become cyclic, recycling everything that is not easily re-assimilated into Nature. Everything we do must have less adverse impact—on the Earth, on each other, and on human dignity. "Use less stuff," might be our most important motto.

This task will be impossible without also nearly completely transforming our world-views — our stories of who we are, where we came from, and where we are going. These transformations will be empty without personal reconnections to the natural world. They will be impossible without massive public discussion of them and experimentation with the conclusions we reach.

We must make a conscious shift, not "back" to our hunting-and-gathering way of life, nor a continuance of our growth-worshiping, technologically fixated current path. We will need to find a new way, honoring both of these pasts, seeking to eliminate our destructive impacts on Nature while using our technology in ways that deal gently with Earth and no longer isolate us from it.

We have succeeded in conquering Earth. Before we subdue it, and ourselves with it, we must alter course and see ourselves and our relationship to Earth differently. The civilization we have achieved is truly remarkable, a monument to the capabilities of inventive minds and hard work. But we now find that monument to be exceedingly destructive. It must be taken down, or at least set aside while we explore different visions. This is what we've learned from our Seekers of Truth. This is the answer to the puzzle.

Reasons for Hope

Hopefulness is a uniquely human quality. It permits us to awaken each day, put aside the difficulties of yesterday, and look forward to a bright future. For our hopefulness to be real and reliable, however, it must be based upon an underpinning of fact and knowledge that what we anticipate is possible. The discoveries of our seekers of truth are the enabling nuggets of wisdom which allow hopefulness in a world that seems in many ways to have gone mad.

The remaining chapters focus in greater depth and detail on this needed transformation. They offer a number of ideas and suggestions for individual and group action ... some guidelines for change. We cannot know if the changes we must make are possible unless we act — with the same vigor, determination, and hard work that created our amazing industrial civilization. Now we need a new civilization, founded not so much on industrialization (indeed a degree of de-industrialization is required), but on basic new principles of sustainable thought and action. We need a recovered sense of belonging — to Nature and all its intricate interconnections. The details of the new civilization will escape us for a while, but we cannot be inhibited by this.

Our hope for the future is well grounded in fact and in demonstrated performance. If we take some important conceptual, philosophical, behavioral and organizational steps in the next couple of decades, we will have every reason to continue our hope into the indefinite future. Failure to make the needed changes, however, can only lead to a growing sense of frustration, futility, and despair. The powerful forces of natural reality will correct the imbalance of a species gone wrong — out of balance and reaching limits. (As the world passes its peak of oil production and begins the downward slide, we can take this as one among many signals that we've gone too far and that substantive change is unavoidable.)

Unlike other species before us facing extinction, we have the unique ability to understand what is happening. We also possess the power, if we will assume it, to stop the "extincting" process before it gets out of hand.

The challenge is before us. Let us step forward and meet it with courage, excitement, and vigor.

21
Reconnecting with Nature
Beyond learning Earth—
Physical and spiritual immersion.

To be truly human is to have an abiding love for Earth
in all its motions, intricacies, and varieties.
To be truly human, is to feel a direct connection with Earth,
not just the urbanized part of it.
To be truly human, is to accept that we come from Earth
and will return to it, as do all living things.
To be truly human is to have knowledge of and be in awe for
the connectedness inherent in Earth and its functioning.

Our Earth-senses have been dulled by the ambient culture, by our developed world, and by the media's incessant carping on exceedingly narrow subjects. We are further numbed at work in windowless offices and by living in highly urbanized settings. This is not healthy, either for us as humans or for Earth which birthed us.

Reconnecting with Nature is essential for any transformation to a sustainable society. While we need Nature for its many services, a less identified "service" is the psychological benefit derived from that connection. Evidence is growing that humans need regular intimate contact with the natural world for psychological balance. We live in houses and work in buildings for the comfort, security, and protection they provide from the elements. But we still need a strong and personal connection with the outdoors.

In a special issue on "The Greening of Psychology" of *Monitor on Psychology*, Rebecca Clay describes the positive experiences of psychologist Rachel Kaplan at the University of Michigan in Ann Arbor upon moving into a new office with an improved view of the outdoors. She and her husband Stephen have researched the psychological effects of human connections with nature for decades.[1]

The Kaplans and other researchers have found that spending time in the woods, on the water, in the hills, or nearly anywhere outdoors, has a restorative effect and soothes the psyche. In one of her studies, Rachel Kaplan found that "office workers with a view of nature liked their jobs more, enjoyed better health, and reported greater life satisfaction."[1]

At the Institute for Housing and Urban Research at Uppsala University in Sweden, Terry A. Hartig, performed a series of experiments (in the lab and in the field), examining whether time outdoors helps people recover from the usual psychological stresses of life. In one study Hartig performed, participants did better on a reading task after spending some quiet time outdoors—reading or walking in the woods.

Other studies have found that patients with views of the outdoors generally recover more quickly from surgery. Alert business managers believe that access to natural daylight and views of Nature increase employee job satisfaction and productivity, sometimes substantially.

Clay quotes Joseph B. Juhasz (a professor of architecture and environmental design at the University of Colorado in Boulder) as concluding, "What we desperately need is connection with our blood and soil ... We're estranged from our blood—ourselves as human beings, and our soil, our natural environment—at this moment in our culture."[1]

Psychologist Judith Heerwagen, senior scientist at the Pacific Northwest National Laboratory in Seattle (formerly in the Department of Architecture of the University of Washington), is an expert on the psychological effects associated with the daylighting of building interiors.[2,3] She writes that "In our evolutionary past, information on time of day, seasonal changes in vegetation, weather, and other forms of environmental 'data' were likely to have had a pronounced influence on survival and health. Thus, it made sense to pay attention to changes in daylight that provided time cues, or to assess cloud formations for information about future weather conditions. These events influenced our ancestors' daily decisions, such as where to sleep at night, as well as much more difficult decisions such as where to look for food next week." She adds that it is not surprising, therefore, that loss of natural information on time of day has been implicated in the poor recovery of patients in windowless intensive care units."[4]

Rebeccah Clay quotes Heerwagen on the value of having windows and daylight in buildings: "Once you start thinking about it, this kind of [building] design makes perfect sense," she says. "We didn't evolve in a sea of gray cubicles."[1]

More than just better building design is needed to reconnect us with Nature. We need more parks and playgrounds and more extensive educational programs for school children at nearby nature parks. The need for more nature-immersive experiences within educational systems was discussed in Chapter 17. Many organizations in the U.S. and elsewhere offer field trips to members and guests. The Sierra Club and other environmental organizations have much experience leading outings year around. Other organizations have and can expand existing programs to encourage participation in rewarding Nature experiences, including those targeted to children and young adults.

In the design of our buildings, in our daily activities, and in our educational programs, we can find ways to re-establish the ancient art of enjoying, knowing, and loving Earth that sustains us. Those without this ability might wish to start easily, with modest beginnings and activities which are positive and reinforce our ancient affinity for Nature.

We must find other ways to reconnect with nature, with the life-giving Earth from which we originated. Until we re-establish this direct, personal, and psychological connection, we may not gain the motivation needed for the transition to a more Earth-connected way of life, a sustainable one with hope for humanity's future.

References

1. Rebecca A. Clay. "Green is Good for You." *Monitor on Psychology* Vol. 32 no. 4 (2001): 40-42.
2. Judith H. Heerwagen, "Windowscapes: The Role of Nature in the View from the Window," in 1986 *International Daylighting Conference*, Ross McCluney and M. Stephen Zdepski, eds. Long Beach, CA, 1986.
3. Judith H. Heerwagen. "Affective Functioning, 'Light Hunger,' and Room Brightness Preferences." *Environment and Behavior* Vol. 22 no. 5 (1990): 608-635.
4. Judith H. Heerwagen, "The Psychological Aspects of Windows and Window Design," in *EDRA 21 Symposium*, Richard Wener Environmental Design Research Association, 1990.

22
A New Environmentalism
Failed environmentalism.
The birthing of a new movement.
Polemic on activism.

Our environmental problems...are not, at root, political; they are cultural. ...our country is not being destroyed by bad politics; it is being destroyed by a bad way of life. Bad politics is merely another result. To see that the problem is far more than political is to return to reality.... – Wendell Berry

The U. S. environmental movement was thriving in the 70s. But by the 90s it had become somewhat bogged down pursuing narrow reforms. It lost sight of important fundamentals, the most critical of which is overpopulation — a core problem, in many respects leading to all others — and the central role of misplaced values and beliefs. Most environmental organizations fail to address the need to restructure society in fundamental ways.

In the first decade of the new century, the environmental movement has lost its way in America, and perhaps to a lesser extent in Europe. This movement has hardly even started in many other regions of the world, especially the less developed areas that hope to avoid expensive environmental restrictions as they develop along the western model.

Despite the current narrow goals of many environmental organizations, they still have grown over the years, possibly even faster than general population growth. Most are relatively prosperous, with ample memberships and generally adequate incomes. To maintain their apparent success, they seem driven to stay with what has worked for them in the past.

The movement *has* had many successes. Improvements still continue in many areas. But the environmental destruction produced by the industrialized societies grows faster than environmental organization memberships.

A new approach is clearly needed, but finding it will be difficult. We are being called upon to change the ways we live, think, treat each other, and treat our Earth. We are challenged to examine difficult ideas, especially those that require altering our beliefs. It *is* scary — and threatening — to challenge the society's very structure and organization.

Many large environmental membership organizations have built their numbers on certain hobby aspects (bird-watching, nature outings, and hunting and fishing experiences, for example) as well as a degree of commitment to more general environmental protection. They are most successful when supporting and protecting these hobby interests and the environmental interests flowing directly from them. Going beyond habitat and wilderness protection, beyond general environmental education, beyond pollution laws, seems to require a degree of extra bravery, a willingness to accept resignations from irate members unable to deal with fundamental societal reforms.

It seems safer not to challenge the beliefs of the membership too deeply, safer to focus on the entertainment functions of the organization, safer not to rock the boat too much. Such a strategy certainly keeps dues coming in.

But the current moderate paths most large environmental organizations are following I believe to be inadequate in a more absolute sense. Narrow reforms, I think, will be ineffective for the long run. We must take time to consider more fully the nature of the problem, then select the most effective actions available.

Examining our beliefs, directions, goals, wants, and pursuits as a society, in the context of the universe story, is an important first step. I believe that if we do this, our resolve will be firmer and our efforts will be more efficient, effective, and properly directed.

Failed Environmentalism

The environmental movement — supposedly leading us into a sustainable future — must become stronger, more dedicated to true reform, more thoughtful, and more truthful. Even if no one else does, at least the environmentalists have to get it right.

They started well. The environmental movement of the 70s was successful against great odds because it spoke the truth and seldom compromised. Volunteer organizations, with occasional help from government scientists and pro bono attorneys, slew the giants of industry — with their hired scientists and expensive attorneys — because the cause was right and just. Facts and truth were on the environmentalist side. Society at least *professed* to decide contentious issues on the truth, as best it could be determined, and environmentalists worked hard to tell the truth.

Aldo Leopold told the truth. He recognized that land had become an economic market commodity rather than the nearly sacred entity that requires proper human respect. He called for an Earth-centered restorative land ethic and a new way of seeing ourselves as part of Nature.

Rachel Carson told the truth, as difficult as it was to hear. The chemical industry was regularly cutting costs and increasing profit margins by taking what should have been legitimate operating costs off their books and shifting them to society at large. She blew the whistle, not only on industry, but also on society, for ignoring what was happening. This initiated a massive movement to reverse many of the damaging practices.

Paul Ehrlich told the truth. He studied population biology and concluded that the Earth must have zero human population growth (ZPG) for humanity to survive. His conclusion was widely accepted. After all, growth has limits, and society began to recognize them, and start doing things about it. Many people, myself included, were careful to "stop at two" children per family. The President's Commission on Population and the American Future concluded that stabilization of the nation's population would contribute greatly toward the solving of its problems and recommended that the nation welcome and plan for population stabilization.[1, p. 192] In 1969, President Nixon wrote that population growth is one of the most serious challenges to human destiny.[1, p. i]

Bill McKibben told the truth. In the essay, "A Special Moment in History," he addressed the apparent failing of some past environmental rhetoric.[2, Ch.2, 3, Ch.2] True, some of the predictions of disaster in the 70s either have not yet occurred or were more muted. Many did happen, but in a slightly different way and with only modest media coverage. This should not be surprising. Future-predicting is an uncertain science. But this cannot negate the essential truths Carson and Ehrlich were telling us.

McKibben concluded that we *are* approaching certain physical limits. Though earlier predictions of imminent doom may have failed, at least on the expected time schedule, time has run out. We are not only facing the limits; we are right up against them. The response of the environmental movement has been muted. Rather than considering something might be seriously wrong with the *system* by which humanity operates, it seems content to attack a few specific problems, save a few ecosystems, and stop a few developments.

The promising activist beginning of the 70s was failing by the 90s. The failures resulted from fundamental weaknesses in the scope of environmentalism, in the growing power of those opposed to environmental reform, and a growing indifference of the populace. This occured as materialism ran rampant and led people to believe things were going better than they were.

The early dedication and militancy of the environmental movement has given way to a quieter, political strategy. This plan seeks to work within established frameworks to get what is practical and avoid wasting time and effort on what is not winnable. In consequence, the remarkable free public education that used to result from splashy headlined stories of environmental abuse has largely disappeared. The lack of militancy also has blunted the movement's effectiveness and many are claiming that some organizations have compromised away the whole movement.

Following the end of the cold war, the peace movement lost some of its ability to inspire ire in the public against things military. Many peace groups embraced the environmental movement, and vice versa. No greater environmental impact can be found than global thermonuclear war, save possibly a giant asteroid impact. Following the collapse of the Soviet Union, with somewhat less to protest, most came to the environmental movement with their social justice backgrounds fully intact.

As Beck and Kolankiewicz found, if not properly directed, this can be a diverting influence, because it brings into the movement people with strong, and sometimes exclusively, anthropocentric beliefs.[4] The result is to place human interests above the interests of other organisms, and above the Earth itself. "Yes," these newcomers admit, "the environment is to be saved and protected, but mainly for the use and enjoyment of humans. And social justice and equality must be maintained, no matter what."

I do not disagree. But it is not an either/or proposition, as Carol Mosley, State Coordinator of the Florida Coalition for Peace and Justice for many years proved every day, with effective programs on both peace *and* environmental education.

Chapter 9 pointed out that carrying anthropocentrism to its logical conclusion, it merges with the holist viewpoint, placing the value of Earth ecosystems at its core. But when the goal is too narrowly focused, and when human social justice interests are considered of primary importance, the former primacy of concern for the Earth becomes diluted and diverted. It can become secondary in the plans and goals of the newcomers to the movement.

The most damaging consequence of this shift in environmental thought is a denial amongst many that overpopulation is one of the two most fundamental causes of our environmental problems (the other being increased per capita impact, amplified by technology). Otherwise good and dedicated environmentalists, because of their social justice interests, value people so much that any talk of limiting their "right" to reproduce wantonly, or their "right" to immigrate is considered a terrible plot — or even motivated by racism, or some other red-herring thrown into the argument.

The situation is almost akin to the McCarthyism of the past, when you could cause a lot of trouble for someone you didn't like just by calling them communist or a communist sympathizer. Fortunately we no longer see the worker blacklists experienced in the entertainment industry of the McCarthy era. But now we see a black*out* of serious discussion of population and immigration reform by branding proponents as racists.

Beck and Kolankiewicz studied the population policy components in the recent new directions of the environmental movement.[4] They concluded that "no national environmental group today works for an end to U.S. population growth." They found a number of reasons behind this startling fact, including:

- Many Americans, including environmentalists, apparently confused "replacement level" fertility with ZPG. They mistakenly concluded that the overpopulation problem was solved.
- Environmental groups seeking membership funds and support from a wide spectrum of Americans had good reason to steer clear of population issues altogether, rather than risk offending current and potential members who were also members of America's largest religious denomination, the Catholic Church.
- As environmentalists abandoned population issues in the 1970s, the population groups de-emphasized environmental motives in favor of feminist motives.
- A relatively recent branch of modern environmentalism emerged in the 1960s as an outgrowth of what was called New Left Politics. It focused more on urban and health issues such as air, water, and toxic contamination, especially as they related to race, poverty and the defects of capitalism. The "Environmental Justice" movement and Green political parties grew out of this, and its leaders have downplayed the role of population growth as a cause of environmental problems. This faction grew so strong in many organizations that by the 1990s it forced an end to their population stabilization policies and later defeated efforts by conservationists and preservationists to reinstate them.
- Modifications to immigration law in 1965 inadvertently set in motion an increase in immigration through extended family members. Immigration snowballed during the 1970s. At the same time American fertility declines put population stabilization within reach, immigration was rising rapidly

to three or four times traditional levels. Efforts to lower immigration to historic and manageable levels ran afoul of the environmental justice faction. These have prevented many traditional environmental organizations from accepting a need to stop U.S. population growth from this important component.

"For all these reasons, the environmental establishment has dropped U.S. population stabilization. But the scientific rationale underlying the need for stabilization is as valid as ever."[4]

To those who argue that limiting immigration to replacement level won't do much for world population growth, I point out that the U.S. has, by far, the most per capita environmental impact. The last thing the world needs is more of us. The currently high level of immigration into the U.S. hardly dents overpopulation in the source countries, so it cannot be considered helping those countries.

Much of the environmental impact from increased U.S. population is felt in third world countries, from which the U.S. imports increasing quantities of materials, and with generally more lax environmental protection laws.

The environmental movement is divided by these issues into what I'll call the old guard — the generally older members who still retain some of the militancy of the 70s. They recognize the human as the aberrant species, the Earth destroying organism — and the narrowly-anthropocentric newcomers. If the numbers of humans is too great and growing, the old guard accepts the truth. It pursues policies, programs, and practices to not only stop human population growth but also *reduce* the population level to a more sustainable number. They do not, yet, propose onerous government restrictions on fertility to achieve this goal, but they recognize that drastic situations sometimes call for drastic remedies.

The anthropocentrists, the civil libertarians, legitimately concerned about government intrusion into our private lives, fail to see that loss of freedom and liberty is an inevitable consequence of overpopulation. Thus, they continue supporting policies that are adverse to a sustainable future. This divides the movement and blunts its effectiveness.

Siding with the old guard, I claim the narrow anthropocentric position is one of effectively burying one's head in the sand, wishing that we could have unlimited freedom (both to reproduce and to immigrate at will — open borders) and a truly sustainable future with every human receiving adequate food, clothing, and shelter. This is impossible. The world cannot sustain the current 6 billion human population with everyone having a high material standard of living. (Following fossil fuel depletion, it may eventually be able to support a third of this population with a high quality of life, but only with a greatly lowered material affluence and minuscule technological impact.)

It appears to me that the cutting edge of the 70s environmentalist is gone. The relatively new environmentalists, I believe, yield too easily to the narrow anthropocentric view. The result is a failure to mature intellectually, but instead to take that most human of responses, the easy way out. They accept the simple answers, whether they be right or wrong, whether they are substantiated with clear scientific evidence or just wishful thinking elevated to the status of a belief.

Beyond Environmentalism

To make the transition, we need to approach the problem differently. Conventional notions of reform are insufficient. Over thirty years, the environmental movement has worked hard and has enjoyed many successes, but a permanent solution has yet to be found. Environmentalism in the current model is inadequate to the task of total societal transformation.

To go beyond past environmentalism is to examine the values and beliefs that currently direct the human enterprise, especially in the light of the historical record. We must see where these values and agendas are misleading us. We need to start from the very beginning — pondering what it means to be human and where humanity is going. We can no longer hide our heads in the sand when our most eminent scientists sound the alarm. The economy may be temporarily soaring, and the material affluence of the developed countries is greater than ever and spiraling upward. But this does not mean things will always be this way, or that all other nations can share our abundant wealth.

We must be more informed about the underlying trends and patterns leading toward the unseen cliff. We must test every land development, every major governmental policy decision, every corporate pronouncement and expansion, for its sustainability, in both material and philosophical terms.

Most developments, most governmental policy decisions, and most corporate expansions currently are *not* sustainable. We must examine the hidden assumptions, the unstated beliefs, goals, and directions of every human enterprise, and measure their sustainability by a different standard. We can no longer avoid the truth but must come to terms with it. This will take more than mere rational acceptance of the logic of our scientists. We must include, as well, our hearts and emotions.

The planet's life-support system is just too valuable, in an absolute existential sense and in an anthropocentric one, to leave only in the hands of essentially hobbyists and volunteers — people living their normal lives but spending a little time now and then, doing a little public service on behalf of the environment. These are important and useful activities, but insufficient. We need more professional, full time, active environmentalists, in and out of business, government, religion, and education.

By no means should these remarks be construed as a suggestion that 90s environmentalism should be abandoned. We must continue fighting the tactical holding actions, stopping as best we can the most egregious insults to Mother Earth. If we do not, we could lose the whole shebang before we get to the permanent changes in understanding, attitude and paradigm that are needed.

The environmental movement has done much to protect ecosystems, save species, and reverse our polluting ways. This old great hope, while still active and somewhat effective, is just not realizing its full potential. We need to redefine environmentalism.

The "New" environmentalists

We can learn from the remarkable environmental thinkers profiled in chapter 19. With a better-designed, more Earth-centered society, and a smaller human population, we can have it all — both a viable and sustainable ecosystem and peace and social justice...maybe. The "maybe" is a reference to the speed with which the coming societal transformation takes place. Too slow and population growth will overtake us and peace and freedom will be its victims.

Fortunately, a truly new environmentalism has begun. It is formed from an amalgam of the "truth at any cost" old guard approaches and the new philosophical big-picture thinking that our "truth-seekers" are demonstrating. It is this new environmental movement that gives us hope. This movement guides us toward the new ways of thinking Einstein said would be needed for humankind to progress and move to higher levels. No more important challenge faces us today than to embrace the new environmentalism and incorporate it in all aspects of society, making real, practical changes in the ways we do things, putting the new principles into action.

The new environmental movement should be more multi-faceted. Traditional lobbying cannot stop. Neither can efforts toward environmental education. These must be expanded and additional components incorporated. We must find ways to reach multitudes of people, using all the means outlined in the next chapter.

Starting with your friends and neighbors, you can grow the movement, adding people, voices, and their financial support. Many environmental organizations produce documentary movies, books and pamphlets, and slide shows. They present these to small or large groups, in libraries, schools, and meeting halls. With the advent of powerful but small and compact notebook computers and LCD projectors, presenting a slide show in full color, with sound and video clips interspersed, is a simple matter. With the addition of a DVD player, documentary videos and other video material can be shown nearly anywhere, to nearly any sized group at modest cost. News release packages can be sent out to advertise a showing of a video or slide show and publications can be given or sold to the audience at the event. By massive spreading of the word, the true power of the grassroots can be captured and used to good advantage.

With swelling memberships, the new environmental organizations can lobby news media, pressuring them to cover the new movement and our universal need to find more appropriate world views. Pressure can build toward more educational pieces and more in-depth reporting in the media. With more coverage, the politicians will be better informed and with grass roots pressure can be given the support needed to make some important changes, even if their corporate sponsors are against them.

References

1. Chairman: John D. Rockefeller, "Population and the American Future: The report of the commission on population growth and the American future," Report to the President and the Congress, *Presidential Commission on Population Growth and the American Future*, 27 March 1972, Washington, DC. Note: Published 1972 as a Signet Special in New York by the New American Library.
2. Bill McKibben. *Maybe One: A Case for Smaller Families*. Plume: 1999, 256 pp.
3. William Ross McCluney, ed. *Getting to the Source: Readings on Sustainable Values*. SunPine Press: Cape Canaveral, Florida, 2004.
4. Roy Beck and Leon Kolankiewicz. "Have U.S. environmentalists abandoned population stabilization?" *Journal of Policy History,* Pennsylvania State University Press, Vol 12, No. 1 (2000), pp. 123-156.

23
Taking Action
Proper directions. Action suggestions.

W e come at last to the question of what to do. A general answer is offered: sweeping changes in the most fundamental tenets of the industrialized way of life must be made. We need a new cosmology, a new explaining story. One possible way to find this story is to read the scientific history of the universe and Planet Earth. This "universe story," as Thomas Berry and Brian Swimme call it, contains nearly all the information needed to see our way toward a viable, and sustainable, future for humanity. Of course, "reading" this story may not be that easy for everyone, nor does it tell the whole story. So additional readings will also be required.

This is where we must begin. It's rather simple, but this beginning may seem too abstract and philosophical for many. Those of us committed to reform want to move ahead; we have no time or patience to pause, read, think, learn, and reflect. We don't think we can linger while society searches for consensus. When we hear of environmental problems in the news, we naturally think of actions that might be taken to reverse the destruction.

Perhaps this is right. Perhaps we don't have time for namby-pamby, time wasting, theoretical discourse, seemingly spinning our wheels, while the truly committed move forward to get the job done. Such immediate action might be the solution. Most of us share this sense of urgency and frustration over the difficulties and slow pace of reform.

Look Before You Leap

But whenever we have taken knee-jerk approaches to problem solving, some previously attempted actions turned out to be worse than doing nothing at all. Then we spend so much time dealing with the unforeseen difficulties that we risk forgetting what we initiated in the first place.

In hopes of avoiding this, humanity must spend a little time learning and teaching Earth history and Earth/human history, looking at the bigger picture. Then we can consider the broader issues and find properly directed and lasting steps to a sustainable way of living. Much of what follows is aimed toward this goal. But we cannot abandon immediate action.

We have no choice but to work on two fronts simultaneously. First we must deal with ongoing environmental degradation and its causative agents (if for no other reason than as a holding action). This will provide us with some sense of accomplishment ... confidence that we *are* respecting and protecting Mother Nature. Second, and more important, is the task of transforming society.

The threads of a variety of actions humanity can take on both fronts have wandered through these pages. This chapter is intended to tie these together into a set of suggestions for individual and group actions to initiate intelligent change.

As already mentioned, putting a lot of effort into small or misguided action *not part of a larger societal transformation* can be self-defeating, or at least can deceive us into thinking we are succeeding when we really aren't. When making changes, we must be very careful to properly direct our energies. Misguided activism is doomed to fail in the long run. But how do we know planned actions will accomplish the desired goal?

Getting it Right

David Suzuki once wrote, "In a world of info-glut, we are constantly assaulted by often contradictory claims about many of the items we buy and use." The Union of Concerned Scientists addressed the problem of conflicting recommendations and misdirected actions. *The Consumer's Guide to Effective Environmental Choices*, by Michael Brower and Warren Leon[1] resulted.

The book goes beyond just recommending what products to purchase, which to avoid, and what to do with the trash. It suggests things to ask of government and recommends changes in behavior each of us can make. Reading that book would not be a bad starting place if you are intent on taking immediate action in your personal life.

A word of caution is needed, however. The UCS book does not offer a total answer to our problems and, to some extent, misses the mark in failing to address total system reform. For example, it does not even mention the problem of overpopulation. And it takes the stance that an "across-the-board approach" to reducing the amount of goods and materials we buy, own, use, and discard is unnecessary; its authors favor a more targeted strategy aimed at appealing to a wide segment of the population.

The action suggestions I offer below are of a different nature. They are aimed more at the *whole systems* approach to reform without neglecting the need for stopgap measures now.

On the individual level, different people have different interests and abilities. To enlist the support of everyone, people must be allowed to follow their specialties. Some will be good at telephoning, others at writing letters, still others at meeting with people.

As you look through the list of actions, don't think that everyone has to be involved in all of them. A diverse but coordinated effort has the highest likelihood of success. Choose the most effective combinations of actions in which you would like to participate.

In every case, stopping population growth and addressing issues more encompassingly must be central to the actions taken and reforms pursued.

Specific Suggestions

Below are some suggestions for personal and small group action. You can use these strategies to accelerate the trend toward redesigning our societies. Individuals will want to pick and choose, matching their actions to their personal interests and abilities.

Overpopulation is critical. Place this at the front of your agenda for learning, teaching, lobbying, and activism. Groups are advised to seek a balance of actions in a variety of areas, using the varying talents and propensities of members.

Individual Action

Read. Read books by the authors spotlighted in Chapter 19, taking notes on important points you wish to remember. Read some of the other books mentioned. Encourage your friends and family also to read about this subject. Give gifts of your favorite books and offer to discuss them with anyone willing. Subscribe to magazines such as *YES: A Journal of Positive Futures*, *EarthLight magazine, E: The Environmental Magazine*, the online *Grist* magazine, the magazines published by environmental organizations, such as *Audubon* and *Sierra*, also *Population Press*, published by the Population Coalition, and the newsletters of additional population organizations.

Look elsewhere for information on the values aspects of our problems, and on more encompassing thinking. Many newsletters and other periodicals are available. The United Nations web site offers background information on population growth, as do several organizations focused on population issues. These include the Population Reference Bureau, Negative Population Growth, the Population Coalition, the KZPG Overpopulation News Network,

Sierrans for U.S. Population Stabilization, Diversity Alliance for a Sustainable America, ProjectUSA, NumbersUSA, and Floridians for a Sustainable Population. Point your Internet search engine to the names of these organizations and to "population reform", "environmental reform", "environmental education", and "earth literacy".

Listen. Contact your nearest college, university, or seminary and see if you can find a knowledgeable professor, scientist, philosopher, or historian, willing to offer one or more public lectures and discussions *on subjects of direct relevance*. If there is no faculty member comfortable with presenting sustainability, overpopulation, and societal transformation, suggest some reading materials and push for a public lecture/discussion based on these.

Some environmental organizations offer speakers for a variety of functions. Urge them to get or train speakers on environmental ethics and the restructuring of society for sustainability. Seek lecturers on the overpopulation crisis.

Public libraries usually have free or low-cost meeting rooms where these sessions can be held, as do colleges and universities. Sometimes banks and other businesses have meeting rooms they make available to citizens for public meetings. Publicize a scheduled lecture widely and encourage attendance.

At the meeting, offer a sign-up sheet for people interested in finding out more. Use this list to form a new local group, or a special committee of an existing organization. If you are on the web, provide your Internet address as well as phone number.

Learn. Many resources are available for more formal learning about humanity's natural history, the history of the universe, and the other issues introduced here. The Public Broadcast Service, at www.pbs.org/als has an Adult Learning Service that might be helpful. Another online education access site is www.universalclass.com.

Your local college or university may have courses of relevance. Beware of "training-for-a-job" educational services. Though these can be useful for developing job skills, they are unlikely to offer anything specifically targeted to developing a sustainable society.

If an educational service, college, or university doesn't offer the kinds of courses you want, ask for them. Large universities offer an amazing variety of classes, a few of which might already be on target. Contact departments of philosophy, biology, environmental science, psychology, sociology, astronomy, and anthropology for information on relevant courses, or to promote their formation. The more students (of all ages) requesting, the greater the chance the courses will be offered.

Write. Write letters to the editor to magazines and to other print, radio, and television media; insist that they cover news about the future of humanity, about global environmental decline, and especially about new ideas for dealing with these issues. Call them on any stupid reporting they might make related to this subject — such as any urban sprawl report that doesn't mention the words "population," "population pressures," or "overpopulation."

Insist that they take the long-range, encompassing view in their reporting of environmental issues and of threats to humanity's future. Encourage reporting of interviews with Paul Hawken, Brian Swimme, Miriam MacGillis, David Suzuki, E.O. Wilson, Peter Raven, Colin Campbell, Bill McKibben, Mathis Wackernagel, Joanna Macy, Hazel Henderson, William McDonough, Albert Bartlett, Virginia Abernethy, Jim Motavelli, Amory Lovins, and others demonstrating whole system visions.

Discuss. Invite your friends and neighbors to discussion parties. Talk about the issues raised in this book. Be sure to let your discussants have plenty of time to describe what *they* think of the issues, however misguided you may initially feel their thoughts to be. This will show them that you are open to their thoughts and your group takes their ideas seriously. (Most people will take some time to see the truth and value in new ideas which may be counter to their own.) Give them time, and encourage them to vocalize the arguments they have or have read. Guide the discussion toward truly long-range solutions, societal reform, and the importance of stopping population growth and whole systems thinking.

Organize more formal readings and discussions. Many resources are available to help. For example, the World Wide Web has a program whereby you can create your own discussion group. (As of this writing you could find the appropriate link at www.universalclass.com. Searches on "distance learning," "discussion groups," and "usenet" should prove fruitful as well.)

Many news networks and other media organizations also host Internet discussion groups. You could introduce subjects of population reduction, the need for media reform, changing the paradigm of commerce, and reforming politics. In each case, you absolutely must be armed with substantive information to support your arguments. And you must stay with the discussion for a while; do not just drop in, initiate a discussion thread, and then disappear before it runs its course. Try not, if possible, to let the discussion degenerate into an electronic shouting match unlikely to produce enlightenment.

There are many internet-based opportunities for joining existing discussion groups and bringing up this subject. Or form your own discussion group. An advantage of the Internet is that participants often join from all over the world, providing a variety of different viewpoints and personal experiences. Americans often are too parochial. Hearing diverse viewpoints is critical.

Join. Attend meetings of environmental organizations, such as your local chapters of the National Audubon Society and the Sierra Club, and push for population reform. Join these and other local and national environmental membership organizations (such as the Isaac Walton League, the National Wildlife Federation, the Natural Resources Defense Council, Negative Population Growth, Numbers USA, the Union of Concerned Scientists, and Carrying Capacity Network). Get active in their programs to stop current environmental degradations, bad legislation, and damaging corporate policies. Also encourage them to expand their scopes of interest to include whole system thinking and promoting increased Earth literacy in the schools and in the population at large. Suggest brainstorming sessions to find ways of reforming misdirected systems of commerce, communication, campaign financing, and education.

Teach. Teach your children what you have learned. With young ones do this in short conversations tailored to their attention spans, and spend time with them outdoors, in as natural a setting as you can find. (Longer discussions are appropriate for those old enough to participate actively.)

Take the whole family on outings into Nature, ideally with knowledgeable guides. Volunteer to help schools with field trips to parks and wilderness areas. Encourage schools and colleges to offer expanded curricula on the subject of humanity's future — and the social, commercial, governmental, and environmental problems which threaten that future. Offer to help them get started — with educational materials, curriculum guides, outside speakers, discussion leaders, and with field trips. Encourage your child's teachers to promote environmental teaching appropriate to their age levels.

Vote. Vote with your dollars and with your feet, boycotting products you think most damaging to the Earth and its living creatures. Vote in elections for politicians and issues favorable to major societal change aimed at a more sustainable way of living. These are the real leaders. They have much to say. Their voices must be heard. Find them and help them get elected.

Brian Swimme, speaking for Thomas Berry, says that "We reinvent human society by transforming our codings .... Our fundamental values and programs will be altered, and individuals and character types considered marginal during the past two centuries will find themselves selected by society for political power."[2, p. 160]

By finding these previously marginal voices and electing them to governmental and other positions, you will magnify and amplify the change process. Even if you cannot find such individuals, you can do much to inform and encourage existing political leaders about the larger issues of our predicament.

Lobby. Perhaps the most effective action you can take is to lobby — even picket — the national news media; call attention to their failure to report on declining hopes for humanity's future. Don't just hold up signs reading, "The World is Coming to an End," unless coupled with a humorous slant on the issue or an associated penetrating insight. Everyone loves humor and picketing does not have to be confrontational or attacking.

The fate of humanity is arguably the single most important subject we should be discussing — and hearing and reading about. With letters, e-mails, phone calls, and even picket lines, push the media for more good investigative journalism ... the kind which follows thorough research of the subject, and interviews with the people who know the issues and have offered viable solutions. Extend your lobbying activities to local, state, and national political leaders.

Be relentless. You have the "mere-exposure effect" working for you[a].

Initiate. When you can, initiate action at the state, national, and even the international level. Go to the news editor or editorial page editor of your local paper, telling the paper how it should be covering this story — the new universe story and the place of humanity on Planet Earth. Repeat the process with the business managers or news directors of your regional television stations. Go to State legislators, Boards of Education, and Librarians. Take copies of books by Berry, Hawkin, Estes, Macy, Callenbach, Capra and others. Leave copies at the library and suggest they form the core of a new section on Earth Literacy.

Environmental organizations composed mostly of local volunteers are too often reactive, waiting for some local environmental atrocity to motivate them to action. What is now needed is a more pro-active stance. We can take actions to both head off the atrocities and teach important new paradigm basics.

[a]The "mere-exposure effect" was described in Chapter 15.[3]

For example, some people in my community started an initiative to revise our county's charter to require a unanimous vote of any legislative body in the county (the county commission and the city councils) before a developer can get building density of a zoned area increased. Such an increase would enable the construction of more units on the site and would increase population density. The new initiative doesn't prohibit such density increases. It merely says that before such an increase can be permitted, a very good reason — enough to convince all members of the deciding body — must be presented.

Such a measure was previously passed by the city of Cocoa Beach, Florida, thanks largely to Green Party member Eric Fricker, elected in 2000 to the City Commission. Now we see a statewide referendum action designed to require voter approval of changes in the state's land use master plan. (Florida's Growth Management Act requires all of Florida's 67 counties and 476 municipalities to adopt Local Government Comprehensive Plans to guide future growth and development. Local zoning must be compatible with the local plan.)

Though these measures won't stop population growth in Florida — current zoning allows for considerable growth — at least they are steps in the direction of limiting and eventually reversing growth. And they can get the populace thinking about issues of carrying capacity and the role of land use planning as an instrument of the developer.

The 2000 population in Florida was about 16 million. If the State builds out to the full limits permitted in the master plan, the population would grow to 101 million,[4] making it clear that planned growth is often little more than planned environmental abuse.

Initiatives on a variety of environmental issues, using the pro-active approach rather than always being reactive, are being undertaken elsewhere. Just a couple of people can start a referendum or initiative, a few more can collect the required number of signatures to place them on the ballot.

Beware of efforts of legislators and businesses to make the process more difficult. Make the wording and design of your measure simple, to avoid litigation over the wording, intent, or meaning. Take small steps at first, larger ones later. Offer two or three at the same time. The opposition will spend a lot of money fighting all. Perhaps the one you most want passed will be the one that squeaks by.

Group Action

If you feel small and powerless working alone, find a few (or more) other people sharing your interest in societal transformation. Work to become better informed about the issues outlined in this book. You can have small, short meetings in your home to discuss readings and/or to watch videos. Then expand out from there.

Decide upon useful and effective local actions. Then "take your show on the road." For example, you might decide that the local newspaper needs more coverage of this topic. As a group, if you present news editors with a relevant story idea, they should be more apt to listen. You should also be able to schedule a meeting with the paper's editorial board.

The changes we seek include opening the media to public access and returning it to more professional journalism. Both broadcast and print media should be targeted. Government takeovers of media companies are *not* recommended, except possibly as a last resort (and even in this case there is great risk). However, finding mechanisms for public funding and public control of at least *a few* outlets in each market and in each different media category might be a good idea.

In your workplace you might not feel very confident in making policy suggestions by yourself, or might otherwise fear repercussions from adversarial supervisors. If you can get a small group of fellow employees interested, however, and if you approach management respectfully and make reasonable suggestions, they should listen. Most will appreciate your concern and want to learn more.

Identify values and goals in your employer's literature that support a sustainable vision, at least in principle. Or ask a leader for what he or she values in employees. Besides "hard work," you should be able to elicit values of responsibility, resourcefulness, and responsiveness. These can be connected to the need for environmental responsibility, and your suggestions for ways your employer can provide support in that direction.

Tie your suggestions for organizational reform to already established values. You should be able to show how some of your ideas can make the organization run better, more responsibly, and — in most cases — more profitably too, promoting sustainable practices in the process. Don't give up if your first effort is rejected. The "mere-exposure" effect works. Always try to avoid confrontation.

This same approach can be helpful with your state and federal legislators. They seem genetically disposed toward listening to the electorate. Going as a group should insure that you get past the aides and administrative assistants and directly to the elected official. Suggest that some staff attend the meeting, since they are likely to do the follow-up work after the meeting.

In each case, take with you a limited amount of supporting documentation and publications, or at least references to the literature on the subject. The paper, a local radio or television station, your company, or your legislators will probably want to research the topic further (if for no other reason than to gain confidence that you're not fabricating all this). As difficult as it may be, going as a group is very important. While one of you is talking the others can be observing, listening, and formulating additional comments tailored to the interests of the individual with whom you are meeting.

Perhaps your group would like to create an "Earth Literacy Learning Center" as a service project at one or more local public libraries. If you approach the head librarian with your proposal, there's a good chance that a special collection shelf could be set up to hold the books in relevant subjects you donate to the library. The library might even purchase additional copies with its own budget for its regular collection, if the ones you provide prove popular with patrons. To insure this popularity, you could print and distribute flyers, or send e-mails, announcing the new "center" and inviting the public to take advantage of it. Local schoolteachers could be encouraged to send their students to these book collections for special reading projects. With such interest, librarians can respond with additional relevant materials, lecture series, and video showings.

Earth literacy learning centers can be more than just shelves of books. They can offer lectures and discussions on Earth literacy. They can offer continuing education credits or even full high school or college credit, if meeting the relevant requirements.

Working in a group, an important advantage is that, when one member pursuing his or her favorite strategy needs help, everyone can pitch in.

Leadership Action

Colombia's Paolo Lugari provides the example of a person with an idea whose leadership successfully led to the formation of an experimental new town based on a goal of sustainability. Find and support such leaders and help them fight the courageous battle, "going against the grain". (Ray Anderson of the Interface Corporation is another example of such a leader, who made the effort to learn and change.)

Search out leaders you admire in your community, in your local or state government, or where you work, and start talking with them. Take them to lunch and ask questions about the future as they see it and where they think the real problems will arise. Use their answers to begin a dialog on the issues. "Sustainability" is currently a popular buzz word and they will likely warm to the topic. Ask if they are doing anything to promote sustainability in their domain. Ask them how they define sustainability. Ask them about "real" sustainability. Be prepared to hand out Bartlett's "Laws of Sustainability."

The goal is to create a discussion on this topic, with several follow-up meetings. As time elapses, you can introduce more topics. Both of you are likely to learn much in the process.

These are not projects you can accomplish overnight. You most likely must approach the subject slowly, wary not to step too hard on strongly held beliefs. We all have conflicting values. Environmentalists have long-practiced the art of reinforcing and playing off pre-existing beliefs which support their causes, downplaying the adverse ones. (I once saw an important dredge-and-fill permit application, about to be passed, be defeated because one of the development-prone commissioners was reminded that the area would destroy one of his favorite fishing spots.)

As you encounter resistance, don't be discouraged if the person is negative at first. Concentrate on getting the right information into his or her hands, in a form they are most likely to appreciate (be it a short written article, a video tape, or listening to a speaker in a public forum).

In all your encounters list and describe some of these activities: reduce, re-use, recycle, save energy, work with local government, etc., but then it is crucial to emphasize the insufficiency of these actions alone. Drastic reforming of the campaign finance system, reducing the power of corporations, improving the media, and increasing earth literacy at all educational levels are critical additional goals.

Whenever you find a receptive leader, provide support as best you can. Ask others to do the same. Perhaps friends are elected to your city council or county commission. When they cast a vote for sustainability, praise them and get others to join you. Take advantage of all "teachable moments."

Finally, consider assuming a leadership position yourself. It could be within an environmental organization or some other club to which you belong. It could be the chairmanship of a committee. From this experience you can decide if you like the work and if you feel you are effective at it. If so, consider assuming even more responsible leadership positions, right on up the ladder of increasing power and responsibility, in government, industry, and elsewhere.

Breaking the Circle of Failure

The path we take is filled with barriers. In every sector of society, we seem caught in a circular loop of inhibited possibilities. We are confronted by terrible obstacles, also thought of as "insurmountable opportunities."[b] We are struggling to find ways to break the circle, the chain of impotency. Let's examine the links in the circular chain of frustrated possibilities.

Leadership is a critical part of the loop. Leaders have the responsibility to act and the power to convince and lead. But they often find their hands tied by forces keeping them from taking bold steps, or they simply do not know enough about the relevant issues.

The media have a very important role to play in educating, initiating, and sustaining global discussions. But their corporate masters too often restrict them and they are themselves insufficiently educated about the problems and opportunities to report them accurately and sufficiently.

Our teachers provide hope in educating the next generation, providing accurate knowledge and a motivation to take the torch of environmental reform and speed away with it. Many are pursuing this goal but often are restricted by a variety of forces and serious limitations. Major classroom change will need support from the head office, the school board, and the public at large. This support is unlikely to be provided without strong leadership and an educated public pushing the needed changes in curriculum and instruction. The lack of knowledge and understanding is probably the most difficult inhibitor.

Government, the most natural institution for guiding change in a society, has its own problems, and also seems unwilling or unable to act strongly without widespread and vocal support from the electorate, or the presence of a dramatic and terrible threat. The U.S. government, motivated by the terrorist acts of 11 September 2001, moved boldly against the forces of terrorism worldwide, commanding enormous resources to fight the enemies of its people. It asked other nations to join in the effort and was initially gratified at the support and participation.

The current threat of the extinction of humanity is no less important, no less urgent. Unfortunately, the need for bold action to avoid this threat is shackled by many restraints. The problems are too diffuse, spread amongst

---

[b]The quote is "We are surrounded by insurmountable opportunities." Apparently it was attributed to the Pogo character in Walt Kelly's cartoon strip of the same name. Chuck M of "The Pogo Page" at http://www.nauticom.net/www/chuckm/ responded to a question about the quote, saying that Walt Kelly's relative, Pete Kelly said this: "About the insurmountable opportunities quote. Selby Kelly told me in 1979 that Walter Mondale had used it, crediting Pogo, and I embarked on a search of all Pogo books. I didn't find it either. But it sure sounds plausible, doesn't it?"

a variety of academic disciplines, government departments, economic sectors, and geographical regions. To protect ourselves from the threat we will be unable to marshal armies, ships, planes, rockets, bombs and other powerful This proposal is motivated by a frustration from seeing the selfish and ill-informed actions of certain businesses. Shouldn't some basic level of protection be built in to the way business operates and the way people go about their daily lives? The opposition, profiled in Chapter 8, seems in many cases so sure of itself. The argument here is to give them a section of the country to pursue their philosophies to their ultimate and logical conclusions, and see what happens. My guess is that it would not take long for droves of people to flee the designated area, much like the many environmental refugees we see around the world, persons displaced for environmental reasons. (On October 19, 2001 the Worldwatch Institute reported, "more people worldwide are now displaced by natural disasters than by conflict. But more and more of the devastation wrought by such natural disasters is 'unnatural' in origin, caused by ecologically destructive practices and an increasing number of people living in harm's way."[6])

The inaction strategy suggested by Hanson and others would be very risky. We might not act until it is too late. This could result in such a degraded environment that the quality of human life would be gone, and sickness and other adverse effects would be much more widespread. A consequence would likely be massive political strife and conflict, and the accelerated misery.

The "do-nothing" strategy is appealing to those who are lazy, and frustrated at the lack of immediate response to our small, meager, beginning steps. It can also be used as a rationalization for what we really want to do anyway — ignoring the problem and going about our daily lives in hopes that it will just go away. It is the de facto strategy followed currently by billions of people around the world.

The morality of this approach I leave to the moralists. My problem with it is that waiting for — or even hastening — environmental disaster to energize us to action, will most certainly backfire, degrading the quality of human and most other forms of life on the planet. It could upset very critical ecosystems in such a way as to produce major system collapse and turn nearly *all* of us into "environmental refugees."

Following his presentation on the environmental crisis to a church group a number of years ago, a friend of mine, George Bortnyk, was approached by an older person in the audience who said the problems seemed intractable. George said there is no fundamental reason to believe that the human race cannot become extinct. He was then asked what we can do if human extinction seems inevitable. His response was that we have two choices. Do nothing. Or do whatever we can to prevent the seemingly inevitable. I think most people, however pessimistic about our prospects, would choose the path toward life, toward protection, toward creation. Presuming this to be the case with you, I offer additional support for taking the actions listed previously.

Additional Resources

This section is intended as a bridge to existing organizations, projects, and individual actions available for use as tools to initiate positive change *now* rather than in a decade or so when the situation will become more desperate.

We should be heartened to discover that there are so many organizations already formed and working generally toward the goal of saving humanity — and the total biosystem along with us. The value of these organizations comes from their abilities to amplify and magnify the efforts of their members, spreading the word not just to millions of individuals but to millions of teachers and other groups who magnify the effect by further spreading the word.

The web site http://www.futureofhumanity.org contains a list of organizations that are effective in a variety of holding actions — some going beyond that to explore new structures and methodologies for promoting the global discussion so essential to species level reform. Their addresses, phone numbers, links to their web sites, and their e-mail addresses are not listed in this book because these often change. The directory on the web site will be updated from time to time, to keep the information relatively current. As more organizations are identified, in the U.S. and elsewhere, they will be added to the list.

In addition to the organizations, government agencies and university web sites contain vast amounts of environmental information and links to sites with additional information. Most of this is relatively basic information — a chronicling of the good and bad things happening in conventional environmentalism. Search out sites with a more encompassing focus. If you do not have web access yourself, your local library should be able to provide it. Check with the reference desk for assistance.

A number of Earth Literacy Learning Centers has been created, such as the Environmental Ethics Institute (EEI) at Miami-Dade College in Dade County, Florida. The main web page for the college is http://www..mdc.edu. At time of writing, the EEI web page could be found at http://www.mdc.edu/wolfson/academic/environethics/. A list of Earth Literacy Centers was at http://www.mdc.edu/wolfson/academic/environethics/resources.html.

These resources offer tools. The actions listed previously are steps we can take to get things started.

Education Reform

Success in making profound changes will require an enormous amount of public education at all levels. A fundamental shift in education is critical but seems difficult to get started and sustain. Daniel Quinn addressed this in *Ishmael* with these words.

> "What you do is teach a hundred what I've taught you, and inspire each of them to teach a hundred. That's how it's always done." "Of course it's not enough. But if you begin anywhere else, there's no hope at all. You can't say, 'We're going to change the way people behave toward the world, but we're not going to change the way they think about the world or the way they think about divine intentions in the world or the way they think about the destiny of man.' As long as the people of your culture are convinced that the world belongs to them and that their divinely-appointed destiny is to conquer and rule it, then they are of course going to go on acting the way they've been acting for the past ten thousand years. They're going to go on treating the world as if it were a piece of human property and they're going to go on conquering it as if it were an adversary."
>
> "You can't change these things with *laws*. You must change people's *minds*. And you can't just root out a harmful complex of ideas and leave a void behind; you have to give people something that is as meaningful as what they've lost—something that makes better sense than the old horror of Man Supreme, wiping out everything on this planet that doesn't serve his needs directly or indirectly."[7]

Invited to a symposium on "The Inventor and Society" in 1995, Paul MacCready identified[8] creativity's critical role in solving problems. But creativity is often stifled in educational systems. He offers a way we can help teachers introduce more creative thinking on environmental subjects into their classrooms.

> Creativity is just one element of thinking skills, but an especially valuable element because it is a "buzz word" that helps serve as an attractive "Trojan Horse" to help new concepts of broad thinking and questioning, and seeing all sides of issues, be sneaked past school boards into inertia-ridden school systems. By simple exercises, as enjoyable as recess, in just a few hours students can shed many of their inhibiting habits of thought and become more creative, motivated, and interested in all subjects. Adults can also benefit, although the habits of decades typically make them slower

than youngsters in adapting to new thought patterns. You can use your mind like a Swiss Army knife, consciously selecting the right tool for the task in hand—daydreaming, focusing, exploring alternatives, examining critically, networking, etc. For creativity there is emphasis on looking at things in unconventional ways. Also, there is emphasis on broadening or eliminating the filters. For example, consider the tyranny of the word "the". When a teacher asks for the solution, that seemingly innocuous word "the" is actually pernicious. It signals that there is a single answer, and thereby puts blinders on the minds of both teacher and student who might otherwise look for many solutions. Language certainly is a tool for facilitating broad thinking, but it can also have an inhibiting effect....

Some schools welcome and promote creativity, thinking skills, and questioning, but for most people these skills are advanced by hobbies, or a mentor or parent, or involvement in an extracurricular program such as Odyssey of the Mind or competitions established by various invention organizations. The situation is improving, slightly, as more schools, K-12, colleges, and universities are incorporating inquiry-based learning, hands-on experiments, and team activities. It is surprising how much these techniques are fought by institutions and people with feet firmly planted in the past, but the dynamic new educational innovators are starting to turn the tide.[8]

A suggested curriculum

To begin the change process, we need a basic educational underpinning. Here is a suggested outline for that education.

The basics. The material to be presented can start with the basics, relatively uncontroversial information about our past — the history of the universe, Earth, and humanity's occupation of it, at least in broad outlines, focusing on the critical shifts in values and societal organization which have occurred. A thorough understanding of the way Earth's physical and ecological systems worked before humans is a critical component of such an education. Also needed is background information on humanity's biological and societal evolution, a fairly exhaustive description of the services Nature provides humanity, and an introduction to the destructive things we are doing to Nature. Based on solid science and undisputed facts, this account can hardly be considered controversial. Being so core to what it means to be a human, who could object to it on educational grounds?

Interpretations. Next come *interpretations* by such authors as Bill McKibben, E. O. Wilson, and David Suzuki of what has been learned. With such credentialed and knowledgeable interpreters, little objection to teaching some of their ideas should surface. Interpretation is the essence of good education.

Philosophical underpinnings. Next comes an exploration of possible philosophical and ethical underpinnings for the restructuring of society. These can be represented through the offerings of Aldo Leopold, Thomas Berry, E. O. Wilson, Brian Swimme, J. Baird Callicott, Holmes Ralston III, and Daniel Quinn, for example.

Predicting the future. Potentially controversial are predictions of possible future scenarios, alternate paths humanity might take over the next half-century or so. As we offer a variety of alternate philosophies and futures, most criticism of this educational program should be blunted or easily deflected. Students can be encouraged to make their own choices amongst the alternatives and decide for themselves which path society should pursue.

Other cultures and other societies are likely to make different choices. This is good. There is no one right way for everyone.

We all need to preach and practice tolerance and inclusiveness. The latter is not opposed to diversity. America prides itself on having become at least a "melting pot," bringing together a variety of cultures, nationalities, and ethnicities, and making possible the great diversity of people we see in the U.S. We all can work toward common goals of freedom, liberty, and equal justice.

We should be the nation *most* tolerant of other cultures. We also should work to dispel perceptions of "the ugly American" who pushes our values, beliefs and ways of life on everyone else. Such would meet with resistance, and, as we have seen recently, sometimes violent resistance. Our goal should be to demonstrate what can be achieved when inappropriate values are corrected ... followed by appropriate actions.

By grounding this educational system, this new Earth literacy, on the critical thinking skills used in science, most opposition should be mild and easily converted.

Next comes action. Education alone is not enough. If not followed by appropriate action, the effort will be less effective. Education can open people's minds, allowing them to form their own conclusions.

In matters as significant as this — self-preservation — action cannot easily be stopped. With knowledge and renewed dedication, we can search for that new global consensus, that new vision of what it means to be human on this now very human planet called Earth.

Religious Reform

As mentioned in Chapter 18, many religions struggle to update ancient teachings, revising them to be more compatible with our new understandings of the Earth/human relationship. As Gottlieb wrote, "Religious beliefs provide primary values concerning our place in the universe, our obligations to other people and other life forms, and what makes up a truly 'good' life. All these are part of the religious world-view and part of what must be scrutinized and altered if we are to pull through."[9]

If you are active in a religious organization, or if you think you might like to be, much can be done to aid, assist, and support the new directions being sought within religion. Begin by finding out what is already happening on the local scene in this area, by attending environmental meetings within your church, synagogue, temple, ashram, or congregation. Relevant regional and national meetings might exist. Read, study, participate, and then lead in these activities.

Earth Passion

By reading this book, you have assumed the role of a change agent. By merely knowing what you have read, you already have a different perspective on who you are and where humans are headed. The transformation to a sustainable new society is already unfolding in you, in me, and in the millions of others receiving the message ... whether it comes from us, from their own readings, from their conversations with others, or the powerful signals Earth has started providing.

Once you see the depth and severity of the environmental threats facing us, you will naturally want to step out to fight the demons preventing needed reforms. To have the motivation, strength, and determination to begin the arduous fight, you must develop a passion for Earth. The love of Nature comes to many and drives us to "take up arms" in defense of her virtues and beauty. The deeply committed among us seem to be saying, "If you, society, won't see the light, won't stop destroying what we love so much, then, by God, we'll *make* you see it. We'll force you to stop killing Nature."

The struggle can be biblical in its breadth and severity. It often pits the most powerful corporations against a handful of committed individuals, a truly David against Goliath struggle.

But if there is one thing we've learned in the history of reform movements, it is that violence is self-defeating. It polarizes, divides, and stops true reform. If you have to force people to do something, they'll resist.

You end up struggling over the struggle rather than the important principle on which the struggle was originally based.

This is, indeed, a time for action. But misdirected action is intolerable. We haven't the luxury of going repeatedly down blind alleys as we search for a path from the morass in which we've found ourselves. A few mistakes teach us, but too many could destroy us.

The central issue of our time is whether we can continue toward the future along the lines of the current industrial society's path: using unfettered population growth and narrowly defined economics, spreading this western system to receptive populations around the globe. Or must we transform that society more fundamentally? If the latter, then the changes must involve our core beliefs—our understandings of what it means to be human at this time in Earth's history—the paradigm of our existence. Nothing short of an alteration of our cosmology, and an incorporation of the new worldview into our psyches and our daily lives, will be sufficient.

References

1. Michael Brower and Warren Leon. *The Consumer's Guide to Effective Environmental Choices: Practical Advice from the Union of Concerned Scientists.* Three Rivers Press: New York, 1999.

2. Brian Swimme. *The Universe is a Green Dragon.* Bear & Co., Inc.: Santa Fe, NM, 1984, 173 pp.

3. R. B. Zajonc. "Attitudinal Effects of Mere Exposure." *Journal of Personality and Social Psychology Monograph Supplement* Vol. 9 (1968), 1-27.

4. Bureau of Economic and Business Research at the University of Florida. *Florida Population Forum*, (1999): June 1999.

5. Jay Hanson, "The Immorality of Reducing Energy Consumption," World Wide Web, Access date: 29 August 2002, http://www.oilcrash.com/consumption.htm.

6. Janet Abramovitz, "Unnatural Disasters," *Worldwatch Institute* Report No. 158, 18 OCT 2001, P.O., Box 879, Oxon Hill, MD 20797.

7. Daniel Quinn. *Ishmael.* 1st ed. Bantam/Turner: New York, 1992.

8. Paul B. MacCready, Unleashing Creativity, in *Symposium on The Inventor and Society*, Jerome and Dorothy Lamelson Center for the Study of Invention and Innovation, Smithsonian National Museum of American History, 1995.

9. Roger S. Gottlieb, ed. *This Sacred Earth: Religion, Nature, Environment*, 2nd ed., Routledge: New York (2004).

24
A Better Future

Western industrialized business and the modified free enterprise system under which it supposedly operates today largely are responsible for past advances in technology, health care improvements, and economic growth. They have created a society with art, music, space travel, laborsaving technology, and amazing new understandings of our world.

They also lie at the core of the problems faced by industrialized nations at this crucial point in history. Clearly, rapid growth and industrialization have served us well. But they have run their course. As the saying goes, too much of a good thing is a bad thing. We have concluded that the very structure of business — indeed our entire society — is contributing to the environmental declines we read and hear about daily. Understanding these facts and how they came about is the first step. Next comes a search for viable alternatives, for new worldviews and value systems.

People who know and have the power to make big changes are thriving, feeling good, and doing well. The economy is generally progressing (even through the occasional recession) and democracy is spreading around the world. The general human condition seems to be improving, though in some areas conditions are worsening for hundreds of millions. Those with money are also producing great environmental impact, the greatest per capita impact coming from the U.S. People with money and power generally lack the direct personal motivation for making sweeping changes in society, leaving it to others to initiate them when necessary. But they are the ones most capable of doing so.

On the national level, wealthy countries may continue their current path for several more years, possibly another decade or two, but probably at the expense of less fortunate societies and certainly at the expense of general species viability. The question is whether the powerful elite, and the rest of us, must wait until the direct evidence is overwhelmingly bad and immediate, leaving no choice but to change or lose the benefits we feel so blessed to possess.

I think it is clear we must start now making the needed transformation. The future of humanity, and of many other species, hangs in the balance.

Many say we have already started making the necessary changes, and, to some extent, this is true. A modest number of people *are* aware of the problem, thinking about it, discussing it with others, and trying experiments at alternate, less-impacting lifestyles. Others are experimenting with alternate systems of commerce. In both cases, these efforts suffer considerably from being imbedded in the larger society which doesn't really get it, which marches on its merry way, spreading huge impacts throughout the global fabric of life.

The societal and business alterations currently being made are too small. They suffer from insufficient resources, failing governmental structures, inadequate laws, and failed visions. Some say the methods of change, and even the environmental organizations promoting change, are becoming increasingly irrelevant, cannot be reformed, and should be discarded. They suggest that we just walk away from the current system and forge a new path, going off in a new direction. Others say this will be too disruptive — reform of the current system is the only way we can go. The reader is left to decide which path is possible and best.

To make the choice, viable alternative ways of living must be available and known. Otherwise, we may lack the motivation to change. Current experiments in alternate lifestyles must be expanded and their successes and failures documented.

Our scientists warn that forces are at play in the world today; these forces, if left to continue growing, can destroy nearly everything you and I hold dear. Much has already been lost and much more could be on the way out, unless we find and follow a better path.

Since humanity has caused the problem, only humanity can solve it. We are learning to dig deep inside ourselves, hoping to find the energy, meaning, and motivation for taking the needed steps. If only humans can save humanity, we must take full advantage of our special gifts to do so.

Picturing a Better Future

How might a sustainable future look? How would it feel to live in a radically different world? That depends upon the culture within which you live. Change will not be needed for some of these, and only slight change in others. The industrial world, however, must make huge changes. The culture producing the most impacts is the one that must produce the greatest reform. It is also the one with the greatest financial, human, and educational resources to support reform.

Less industrialized countries may not need as many changes, at least currently. But if they aspire to the affluent model of the U.S. and the other fully developed countries, they must ultimately join us in seeking sustainable alternatives — great departures from the affluent model. Perhaps it would be better for them to find a more sustainable way now, instead of waiting until the whole industrial world model starts to collapse.

The less-developed societies have much to teach the fully developed ones. Most retain a greater connectedness with Earth. We in the industrialized societies can become their students; together we can search for more sustainable directions for both our cultures. Hopefully, this will end feelings of alienation and economic domination. Attempts at such cooperative dialogue might even defuse some of the pressures leading to war and terrorism.

As we ponder the future, we want to know how our lives will be changed. What will it really be like each day? The short answer is that we cannot now know all of it for sure. Much work is needed to see what changes will be both effective at reducing impact and desirable to us, providing sufficient incentives that we'll make them. On the other hand, we *can* look at the most impacting activities and postulate alternative scenarios. Two phases of the coming change can be hypothesized.

The first wave of change will most likely deal with the transport of people and goods, where and how we live, and where and how we grow our food. These are currently petroleum-based, energy-intensive activities, and are generally very polluting. As worldwide petroleum production declines faster than renewables can replace them, oil-dependent transportation, home heating and cooling, and energy intensive agriculture are likely to be the first affected. Included will be changes in the ways we design, build, and operate our buildings, how far we drive to work and to purchase goods and food, and what kinds of food we eat — all operated on or subsidized by fossil fuel energy.

A new model for human habitation is expected to emerge. Most likely we will need to live in denser clusters of homes, with our places of work nearby. This will enable walking, bike-riding, and riding on frequent, convenient, energy-efficient, and non-polluting mass-transit systems. All are healthier, physically and mentally. We'll be better connected to each other and to the natural world.

As to the purchase and consumption of goods, the question arises whether it is best to ship material to the person or "ship" the person to the material. Which is least impacting? That depends on the nature of the products purchased. In many cases, shipping small goods to the purchaser will be better. Warehouses and factories can be made smaller and more distributed, closer to customers, to reduce energy, dollar, and pollution costs. A result could be quicker delivery, since most purchases will come from nearby factories and warehouses.

As resource depletion inflates energy prices, people will likely move from climatic regions requiring twenty-four hour air heating or cooling to areas where the buildings can be left open to nature most of the time, receiving nature's, sights, sounds, and smells in abundance. (With air pollution eliminated, the smells should be good ones.)

Areas with exceedingly long cold winters and very long hot summers will have less favor, and milder climates will become the popular norms. This does not mean areas of extreme climate will be avoided. They will contain exquisite wildernesses we'll want to visit whenever we can and when weather permits. They'll have environmental monitoring stations and research centers. The few who work there will also live there, but with energy and food subsidies from the outside (since these will be very expensive, beyond the incomes of the workers involved).

Most crops will be grown in the flood plains, but with fewer dikes, levies, and sea-walls. This will allow nature to replenish soils during floods, lessening the need for chemical fertilizers, just as 2000 years ago along the Nile River in northern Africa. Residential areas will be safely located in hills above the flood plains. Agriculture will be further transformed by reduced dependence on chemical pesticides and herbicides, and there will be less energy- and resource-intensive factory growing of meat. Reduced population and its slightly negative growth for a time, as well as more-expensive energy during the transition period, will reduce economic justifications for expensive means of food production.

Because of our reduced use of polluting transportation systems, the food we eat will be more locally grown. There will be greater variety over the course of the year. We'll mostly eat what is seasonal for our region, with canned goods making up for any serious deficiencies. Cities and towns will be relocated, piecemeal at first, possibly en masse later. Areas where food is not easily grown without massive irrigation and pumping operations, or without massive infusions of fossil-fuel-based chemicals, will become very expensive or will lack viability. Thus, they will be less populated (just the opposite of what has happened and is happening today, most notably in the arid regions of the U.S. west).

The second wave of change can be expected to reach deeper into our patterns of living and behavior and can now only be surmised. Major shifts in values, beliefs, and living patterns can be expected. As we make the changes required in the first wave, many repercussions, politically and culturally will occur. Interest in the arts is likely to increase, as a low-impact form of recreation. Increased communication is another likely outcome.

We'll transport ourselves virtually (electronically) instead of physically, for many of our meetings and other visits intended primarily for information exchange. The use of computers in every aspect of our lives is likely to increase, but they will become trivially easy to use. We will talk to them and they'll generally talk back (unless we command them otherwise). We are likely to find different ways of managing our system of commerce, and our financial institutions are likely to be substantially transformed.

We will see other impacts of the coming transition on our food, home furnishings, clothing, housing, and the ways we make a living. We cannot possibly describe in detail the needed changes in all these areas. Dreaming about this and/or discussing it with friends and neighbors could make for a lively form of recreation, in homes and community centers. We must have these dreams, and create desirable visions for the alternate lifestyles into which we'll be moving. Otherwise, we'll feel continued discouragement as we read, hear about, or see, Earth in continued decline; we will not be able to contribute anything significant toward stopping the downward trend.

What is the real challenge facing us? It is to achieve some degree of consensus on a desired future direction, hopefully knowing — by the nature of the proposed transition — that it will with some certainty lead to true sustainability and improved quality of life. We must have reasonable hope for a desirable future, with an appropriately-sized population moving onward with vision and a love for creation unmatched in human history.

The Extrication Question

Many know what's basically wrong. But no one knows the one right way to extricate us from it. Many good ideas are available for those who want to make a change and be reasonably sure of going in the right direction. We don't have to start from scratch to figure it out. But we must begin the learning, discussing, and debating immediately.

From a variety of thinkers and writers, we have already learned some helpful ideas and suggestions. We have found a lot of questions, too.

- "Programs" are how we historically have addressed goals, often with some success. But our history with programs is not a particularly positive one. Will this approach be workable today?
- "Walking away" might be a good beginning, but do we have enough time? If we abandon the defective system, can we grow the new

approach fast enough, promoting its deep penetration into the world economic system, and even our psyches?

- Political reform seems essential. Through politics — in communications media, public institutions, and governing bodies — we get things done, be they democracies or dictatorships. Must we abandon political reform as hopeless?

- Media reform is an "of-course" suggestion, but it is a chicken-and-egg problem, depending upon major political and economic reform. Is it possible without these? Even with major political reform, can our media be returned to us and be made to provide the necessary re-education?

- Corporate/commerce reform is another "of-course". Will we need a massive political act to initiate and sustain this reform?

- Individual action is the first and most direct tool available to us. To be effective, it needs to be based on our best evidence, and be well coordinated, powerfully motivated, and seen as successful. How can we assure these attributes?

- Education is essential. How can we begin if we do not know the nature of the problems, the need to overcome them, and how things work? Can we devise effective reform without mass public education? Will massive changes in public education be necessary, or even possible?

- Starting a new environmental movement might appear to have promise. Traditional environmentalism already exists, however limited it might have become. Do we have to abandon that, or can we manage with mere reform of current environmental organizations?

- Is the change required so fundamental that we do not have it in us genetically, or culturally, to make the needed changes? In other words, have we evolved far enough to make major societal change consciously, or must we wait for Mother Nature to force change upon us?

- Is a new form of government necessary? Some have suggested that the U.S. needs a revised constitution. Drafting one would be a useful exercise for both students and environmental attorneys. Other countries might like to revise their tenets of operation.

Each scholar offers his or her own pet idea for solving humanity's fundamental problem. To explain it thoroughly and convincingly, each has to focus on one approach, usually to the exclusion of many others.

It is *our* job as educated readers and world citizens to sort through the possibilities, pull from each one what is most likely to work, and then test for viability wherever we can. (This is using our species intelligence.) Then we must synthesize the extracted components into something meaningful, doable, and successful. The synthesis step is the most important, but has, to date, barely started.

I think we must look at our goals and then address the means. Here is a brief and somewhat over-simplified description of the goals envisioned by several prominent writers:

- Stephen R. Palumbi suggests that because humanity has wrested control of evolution away from Mother Nature, we can make a sustainable future through genetic engineering and other means of directing the future history of our biosphere. "By admitting the speed and pervasiveness of evolution, predicting evolutionary trajectories where possible, and planning mechanisms in advance to slow evolutionary change, we can greatly reduce our evolutionary impact on species around us and ameliorate the economic and social costs of [altered] evolution.... Because our impact on the biosphere is not likely to decline, we must use our knowledge about the process of evolution to mitigate the evolutionary changes we impose on species around us."[1]

- David Pimentel directs us to take a variety of steps needed to stop species extinction. If we can do this, perhaps we'll stop human extinction as well.

- Paul Hawken proposes a major reform of our system of commerce.

- Al Bartlett and many others focus on world population reduction. With fewer people, their overall environmental impacts would be less, giving us time to reduce the remaining ones to near zero.

- Riane Eisler suggests that the struggle for our future is not between capitalism and communism, or any other "ism", but rather toward a social and ideological organization oriented toward either a partnership or dominator model of society. Eisler believes the partnership approach will be most beneficial.

- Daniel Quinn calls us to walk away from a failed system, and instead to follow a new tribal model he thinks will be more likely to produce the qualities we would like in our culture, while protecting our futures.
- Thomas Berry calls for a new cosmology based on the universe story. From a thorough understanding of the history and nature of our universe, we can devise a better template for living sustainably in our world.

Looking at these suggestions from an individual's perspective, each person should pursue whatever combination of goals and means is appealing. At the societal level, I don't believe we have the time or luxury of debating which one would be *the* best. We have to pursue several "best ones" simultaneously. Through our experiments with different approaches, perhaps we'll find a few which are both popular and effective.

The Voice of the Earth

You may disagree with the direst of predictions presented in this book. But the threat is real. We must start discussing the issues openly, seriously, at the lowest and highest levels, both within and without our governments.

The greatest challenge to education now faces us. We all must become better informed experts on the operating principles of Spaceship Earth. We have to understand the history that brought us to this crisis. We have to listen to the thinkers who have spent their lives pondering the questions and devising answers. And we must begin formulating answers for ourselves.

This book can *tell* you what's wrong, but it cannot give you the solution in the form of your own new, more appropriate cosmology. You are offered some ideas and suggestions for exploring new ways of thinking, believing, and acting — ways that should work, that are Earth-respecting and Earth-integrated.

Perhaps we can all agree on a few essential truths about ourselves and our places in the universe. If so, then we can organize our society like never before. Our primary goal can be a reversal of our most destructive tendencies, replacing them with goals toward life and a new kind of prosperity, for Earth and for humanity.

With appropriate new stories that are embraced by the world's peoples, we should be able to accomplish this. Through massive global education and extensive discussion of the issues — and by experiments at living the new cosmologies — we can explore what works and what doesn't. If we can think of coordinated world programs to fight giant imaginary asteroids, certainly we can create one to avoid the real "asteroid" of environmental self-annihilation, devising new approaches to society that both work and respect cultural and other differences.

Then we'll finally be free to use humanity's powerful and special gift of intelligence to find our sustainable future. I hope the needed discussion begins soon, and that it will be centered and meaningful. It will be a multi-decades multi-generational process. Such a shift in world view is unprecedented in human history, save for the original shift to a cosmology of control over and separation from Nature.

In the end, what is suggested here may seem hopelessly idealistic, impractical, and unpragmatic. This may be true, but what other ways do we have? To protect the future of humanity, something of incredible magnitude is required. A global discussion, following by some degree of consensus, will be needed if humanity is to consciously and purposefully make the sweeping changes required in the organization of society. This *is* a very idealistic vision. It may seem impractical.

An alternative would be to have very strong, enlightened leadership action. For this to be possible on a massive scale, the leaders need extensive education. Strong political support for their actions must be provided. In either case — leadership action or grass roots mobilization — the people must generally become more informed. The action suggestions provided in the previous chapter are aimed toward meeting these dual needs.

It is astonishing that we can be alive today and see ourselves as part of this transformation of what it means to be human. We are all being challenged and compelled to search for a larger context in answering age-old questions about life's meaning and purpose. Our ancestors tried to answer these questions with only their unaided senses, without the benefit of modern science and technology. Now we have amazing tools for understanding our world and its history. By taking advantage of the new knowledge, let us revise and update our origin stories, our cosmologies, our world views.

Humans have the gift of distinguishing what we know from what we believe. With modern science we have a new context for learning and understanding. The universe is what exists; it is our reality. We know it better now than ever before. But we have to realize that evolution cannot go backwards. We cannot undo the extinctions we have caused. [a]

We have already altered natural evolution and have begun directing it in ways we think are beneficial to us. To see it in the largest context, our goal must be to seek what is most beneficial for the whole system. Understanding this is critical — perhaps the most important area of knowledge we can have. Next comes what to do about it, how we should behave with our new understanding.

As Miriam MacGillis says, "The universe has waited fifteen billion years to hear your voice. It is not available anywhere else. We are the voice of Earth asking the questions of who we are, where we are, and why we are here. This is the great revelation that is starting to dawn on us — after

---

[a]On March 12, 2000 the Associated Press reported that scientists analyzing fossils calculated it takes about 10 million years after a plant or animal becomes extinct before anything resembling it reappears.

fifteen billion years of documented changes in the Earth, ending with me."
We have before us the most exciting opportunity ever presented to the
human species: redefining ourselves in the light of new knowledge about
the universe and the Earth.

Let us join together with open minds and open hearts. Let us develop
new and better visions of a sustainable future, for a truly better world,
honoring Mother Earth. Let us face this monumental challenge with the
best of our humanity — our intellect, our love, and our hope — and look
forward to a better life for all.

Only then can Earth's history be our history, celebrating together the
wonders of existence.

Reference

1. Stephen R. Palumbi. "Humans as the World's Greatest Evolutionary Force."
   Science Vol. 293 (2001): 1786-1790.

Index

William Ross McCluney, Principal Research Scientist at the Florida Solar Energy Center, has enjoyed a career spanning several disciplines. For his B. A. degree (Rhodes College in Memphis) he studied physics, mathematics, economics, philosophy, English literature, and religion. His M.S. thesis research (University of Tennessee in Knoxville) dealt with the diffraction of laser light by high frequency sound waves in water.

While working as an optical engineer at Eastman Kodak Company in Rochester, McCluney studied the new field of holography at the University of Rochester's Institute of Optics, then pioneered at Kodak the use of holographic interferometry for diagnostic tests of optical systems. This work continued while he pursued his Ph.D. degree on a National Science Foundation fellowship at the University of Miami, where he developed a complex holographic interferometer for detecting minute changes in the density of a gaseous medium inside a test cell made of optically imperfect clear acrylic plastic.

During his studies in Miami, McCluney became concerned about humanity's destruction of Earth's ecosystems and contacted the Miami regional office of National Audubon Society for more information. This led to founding of the University's first student environmental organization, Environment!, and his service as organizer of the University's observance of the first national Earth Day Teach-In, on 22 April 1970. While at UM, he taught a semester-long adult education class on South Florida's environmental problems. An outcome of these experiences was the suspension of his physics studies for a year to work on a graduate assistantship at the University's new Center for Urban and Environmental Studies, then headed by Carl McHenry. Working at CUES for the renowned ecologist, Art Marshall, McCluney edited a series of essays about the environmental problems of South Florida. The University's Graduate Research Council agreed to underwrite the project, and the manuscript was published by the University of Miami Press in 1971 as *The Environmental Destruction of South Florida*. This book went out of print in 1992.

Upon returning to his physics work, McCluney switched research topics to optical oceanography, studying the light scattering properties of marine phytoplankton. Following receipt of his Ph.D. degree in physics, he worked three years as an optical oceanographer at NASA's Goddard Space Flight Center in Greenbelt, MD.

Dr. McCluney was appointed in 1976 to the Florida Solar Energy Center, a research institute of the University of Central Florida. Drawing on experiences while working at Kodak, he wrote the textbook, *Introduction to Radiometry and Photometry*, published by Artech House (Boston) in 1992.

Dr. McCluney has studied, written, and lectured widely on environmental topics, concentrating on the ethical and philosophical aspects of the subject. He currently teaches a course at UCF's Cocoa campus on Philosophy, Religion, and Environment while pursuing research on advanced systems for the daylight illumination of building interiors.